T0369050

COWBOY CRUNCHER

THE UNFORGIVABLE SCIENTIFIC LEGACY OF
BUCKY LAROO

LANE BRISTOW

authorHOUSE®

AuthorHouse™
1663 Liberty Drive
Bloomington, IN 47403
www.authorhouse.com
Phone: 1-800-839-8640

First published by AuthorHouse 12/19/2011

ISBN: 978-1-4567-1964-7 (e)
ISBN: 978-1-4567-1965-4 (sc)

Library of Congress Control Number: 2010919542

Printed in the United States of America

OTHER BOOKS BY LANE BRISTOW

Slice of Heaven
The Mercy of Wolves
The Doorstop (with Corinthia Purdy)
Last Stand at Coyote Yelp Pass
Kelly's World-Fixing Machine
Earthworm Wink

FOR HOLLIE,
who believed in dragons
when I only believed in monsters.

SPECIAL THANKS TO JOHN MCTIERNAN,
for all the lessons Michael Bay never learned.

*"Evolution has been observed.
It's just that it hasn't been observed
while it's happening."*

–Richard Dawkins, 2004

SCIENTIFIC DISCLAIMER

◇◇

THE SCIENTIFIC ESTABLISHMENT HAS conclusively determined that this book contains pseudo-scientific religious propaganda of the most horrific western fundamentalist variety. Worst of all, this book is presented from a Canadian cowboy's perspective, widely considered to be the most infectiously unstable viewpoint of all.

If you read this book, you will lose your job, suffer complete left-brain death, and be shunned from all rational society. If you allow your children to read this book, they will forever after believe that you hate them and are attempting to murder them, and no amount of desperate reassurances of your undying love will persuade them otherwise. In addition, your marriage will be ruined, and your former spouse's unemployed cousins will move into your basement and never leave.

All proceeds from the purchase of this book go directly toward the establishment and continued funding of terrorist training camps across Western Canada, wherein the terrorist initiates subsist on an exclusive diet of insanely cute little puppy dogs who are first cooked alive in vats of boiling peanut oil.

Trust us. It's science.

Sincerely,
The Scientific Establishment

INTRODUCTION

◇◇◇◇◇◇◇◇◇◇◇◇◇◇◇◇◇◇◇◇◇◇◇

A LOT OF PEOPLE TOLD me that I was insane to write my cowboy memoirs before I was thirty years old, and the rest of them just told me that I was insane. Fortunately, I don't actually know that many people, so I can remain cautiously optimistic as to my current mental state, frazzled though it may be.

In retrospect, I suppose it is an odd move to write a memoir that only tells the story of the first twenty-seven years of your life. However, considering the amount of people who had already tried to kill me, I figured that I'd better put my life on paper before someone got a bit more serious about disliking me. And, wouldn't you know it, my life blew up all over again a couple of years after the publication of my first book, *Last Stand at Coyote Yelp Pass: The Tragic Cowboy Memoirs of Bucky Laroo*. Once again, I have survived all of the various disgruntled interest groups, assassins, and beautiful celebrities who wanted to kill me, so I'm now chronicling the recent series of events as fast as I can, because, as my older sister, country-western recording artist Sassy Laroo, assured me, "Third time's the charm, Bucky. And, in this case, 'charm' means the inevitability of somebody getting around to icing you properly."

"Yeah, I got that," I assured her. "Any requests this time around?"

"Yes, actually," Sassy agreed. "Can you plug the band somewhere in the introduction? *Lost Cause Kin*'s Grand Ol' Opry debut is next Saturday, nine central on CMT."

"I'll see what I can do," I said. "I'm not sure if I can get the whole thing written and published inside of a week, but stranger things have happened. Heck, last year I would have told you that the Ogopogo didn't exist."

"The Ogopogo doesn't exist," our brother Corky coldly reminded me. "And I think we all remember whose fault that is, buddy-boy."

"Hey, I only killed one," I protested. "I'm sure the lake's still full of them. It's a big lake."

"You tell yourself that, butcher block," Sassy growled. "You just keep on telling yourself that...."

I will, thank you very much. In these trying times, we've all gotta believe in something, whether that something be mythical Canadian sea dragons or prehistoric aquatic reptiles that reportedly died out with the dinosaurs sixty-five million years ago. Sometimes the lines get really blurry once you actually find one. And, contrary to popular belief, that's not my fault.

> Buy my first book. Please.
> Bucky Laroo.

THE BALLAD OF BUCKY™
(PART ONE)

Music and Lyrics by Sassy Laroo.
©2010, *Potpourri and Lentil Records*.
All rights reserved. Reprinted with permission.
Special Guest Balladeer: Ian Tyson,
Featured courtesy of
Grooviest Canadian Ever Records.
(Single release delayed pending artist cooperation.)

Ian Tyson:

> *"Our parents raised us noble,*
> *But every clan's got one bad seed.*
> *He lived his life on thorny paths,*
> *And relished evil deeds.*

> *"A drinking, gambling polygamist,*
> *That was our baby brother.*
> *So many sins can be forgiven,*
> *But this one trumped all the others.*

> *"He rode on down to Kelowna town,*
> *In the spring, two thousand ten.*
> *In a murky cave where no man had trod*
> *Was where he crossed the line ag'in.*

> *"So many have searched for the Ogopogo,*
> *As a gift to all mankind.*
> *But when Bucky decided to join the hunt...*
> *Char-grilled steaks was on his mind!"*

Corky and Sassy:

> *"With his steed and shining blade,*
> *He bumbles 'cross the plains!*
> *A hero for our time,*
> *Except he's clinically insane!*
> *Don't cry out for the Air Force!*
> *Don't call the Armada!*
> *Just call on out for Buckyyyyyyyy...!*
> *Dragon Butcher of Canada!"*

JELLIED SALAD OF DOOM

◇◇

T HE *COMPOUND FRACTURE* SERIES, starring
world-renowned Hollywood action hunk Sting
Ripblood, has been called the greatest action movie
franchise of this or any preceding decade. Most action series
begin to stagnate sometime around the second or third
sequel, but *Compound Fracture* has thus far lived up to its
star's confident boast that "Each successive installment is
going to pulverize the one before it!" With its heartrending
drama, daring plot twists, and even more daring stunt-work,
it is hard to think of a more entertaining way to spend an
evening than watching Sting Ripblood dole out justice in
his career-making role of mercenary Frank C. Pound, a man
haunted by his past as he fights for our future. Displaying
a mind-bogglingly natural combination of empathy and
brutality, it is easy to see why this role sent Sting Ripblood
to the top of the Hollywood A-List.

Given the amount of anticipation that surrounds each
sequel, I suppose it is understandable that moviegoers
were a bit peeved at me for allegedly delaying the release
of *Compound Fracture IV: Greenstick Pinch* by almost a
full year. The summer blockbuster of 2011 was forced to
become the spring blockbuster of 2012 as Sting Ripblood
waited for his own various compound fractures to heal, and

various anti-Bucky websites were clearly less than happy with that turn of events. (Even the official Bucky Laroo Wikipedia page seemed to be leaning in the direction of partial judgement, much to my shock and disillusionment. If we can't even trust our free and unregulated online resources anymore, then what's left?) However, I think I can safely say that Sting brought this misfortune on himself with little or no help from me. The superstitious elders of my hometown of Coyote Yelp Pass will back me all the way on this one. They know that what happened to Sting was clearly the result of his lack of reverence for the hostile mountain spirits which haunt the misty bogs encompassing the base of Banshee Screech Peak, and he should just be thankful to still be alive. Even my moderately unsuperstitious grandfather agreed with that.

Gramps Laroo was a God-fearing man who believed in angels and the devil and Noah's ark and the virgin Mary, but he didn't hold much with any supernatural aspect that he couldn't find in his big King James Bible. He scoffed at notions of vampires, werewolves, anything from Greek mythology, hobgoblins, and even the more animal-based monsters such as Sasquatch and the Loch Ness Monster. But the old cowboy would swear to his dying day that the hostile mountain spirits of Banshee Screech Peak were real. "We keep to our side of the mountain," he would say. "The Spirit Realm ain't our business, no sir, boy."

My parents had abandoned me and my siblings with Gramps in the summer of 1985, but it wasn't until 1995, when I was fifteen, that Gramps finally revealed the source of his belief to us, figuring that we were old enough to handle the horrifying tale by then.

"It was the fall of '78," he told me, Corky, and Sassy from the comfort of his old wicker rocker on the front porch of the cabin, gazing uneasily toward the distant blue slopes of Banshee Screech Peak, which was barely visible to the west of our remote ranch valley. "Awful dry year. So dry the marshes started to dry up, all crispy-like, and that made me awful antsy, cuz those marshes are the defining line. They're what keeps the wolfs at bay, metaphorically speaking anyhow, since no wolf or pack of wolfs would ever be caught dead in them marshes. But once that dividing line was wiped clean, there goes ninety percent of the spirits' preferred pond slime and moss muskeg diet. And that's when they started venturing further from their mother tree, looking for something else warm and stringy and mushy to cram between their teeth.

"'Twas 3 a.m. that night, the unholiest of all unholy hours. I don't know what waked me first, the panting or the reek, but then I heard your Grams' good china fallin' off the mantle, so I goes out to the sittin' room, and all I sees is this putrid shadow in the pitch black, 'bout the size of a man. Must've been a young one."

"There's young hostile mountain spirits now?" I ventured, sipping my glass of Old Bessie's milk.

"Button it, boy," Gramps growled.

"You shut up!" Sassy whined her agreement, glancing nervously at the gathering shadows of twilight and clutching her double-barrelled 10-gauge shotgun (affectionately dubbed "Bucky-Blaster") to her chest. Even at age eighteen, Sassy never was very good with monster stories.

"Sorry," I said. "Please continue."

"Well, I grabbed a chunk of firewood and clubbed him across the head with it," Gramps dutifully reported. "He went down like a lamb, but he came up sorta like a lion, and then he flat-out wouldn't leave until I got him in a headlock and bit off his right ear. After that, he kind of lost the initiative and ... left."

We all sat in the evening silence, pondering the preceding evidence of the paranormal for a few moments.

"Okay, that might answer at least one question that's haunted me for the last ten years," I conceded. "As long as I've lived here, I've been too terrified to ask why you keep a human ear pickled in alcohol in a mason jar over your headboard."

"That ain't human," Gramps grumbled. "That ear is pure spirit."

"No kidding," I agreed. "It's gotta be around ninety-seven proof by now. For the record, it really looks human."

Gramps shrugged. "I understand most apparitions do."

"So, you can't tell us what it looked like?" I clarified. "All you saw was a shadow in the pitch black, which might need a bit of clarification in and of itself, and a human ear?"

"Don't get snotty with me, boy," Gramps snarled. "I know what I saw, and it weren't no man. If you must know, they are great shadows with people's ears. Their fangs are like Bowie knives, and their tails are great winding serpents with which they wreak great mischief."

"Please don't ever use the term 'with which they wreak' again," I requested, shuddering involuntarily. "It sounds oddly ... creepy and paganistic."

Even after hearing of Gramps' close encounter of the fourth kind, I didn't consider myself to be superstitious, but, fourteen years later, I had to admit that the year 2010 seemed to have put a curse on Coyote Yelp Pass before 2009 was even over. Given the history of my life up to that point, the unpleasantness that followed really shouldn't have surprised me as much as it did. Sometimes, I guess we all just get lulled into thinking that things are actually looking up for a change, and I unfortunately cannot claim to be the exception, although I think I've got a heck of a lot more right to be by now.

Things really were starting to look up on that summer morning at the end of August, only a few hours before old Mrs Quivercake brought a jellied salad to our community potluck and almost killed the whole dang town. No, it wasn't poisoned. It was just a very bad salad to be in proximity to when you live in the ominous shadow of Banshee Screech Peak, reverently referred to by our local populace as The Spirit Realm. But I'll get back to that in a minute.

I had striven to live my life as just an average, unobtrusive cowboy in the remote northeastern Rockies of British Columbia, Canada. Unfortunately, this goal was hard to maintain, as I was also a cowboy who inexplicably kept having unpleasant run-ins with various famous people who initially hated me, and then tried to kill me, and then end up sort of liking me, but I had kind of gotten used to that. Then, just when I thought that my life was smoothing out enough for me to hold on for the full eight seconds, I discovered a monster and everybody tried to kill me all over again. It can be a wild ride when your life is shaping up to be perpetually tragic, and you've just gotta hang on tight, cowboy, and pray that somebody less tragic finds the next monster.

Relax, it'll all make sense eventually. I hope.

My publishers at *Snazzy Spiffy Perfect Literary House* have informed me that a good sequel must seamlessly incorporate essential details of the previous work into a new and original story in such a way as to pique the curiosity of unfamiliar readers, without necessitating prerequisite reading of the prequel, but also without boring or "*deja vu*-ing" your preexisting fanbase. In other words, don't make fans of the first book skim over several pages of "catch-up" narrative only to find that they are reading the exact same story all over again, and don't make potential fans feel lost without the first book. I tried to argue that leaving first-time readers of my work feeling lost would inspire them to purchase and read my first book, thereby boosting my year-end sales tally, but, historically, that's never been a very commercially successful strategy. Perhaps my brother Corky said it best: "Seriously, what was the deal with *Alien 3*? Did the producers even watch the first two?" (Okay, somebody else probably said it better than that, but I've always preferred to get my inspiration from close to home. Otherwise, it tends to fall into the category of tiresome literary due diligence.)

Anyway, my publishers' notes suggest subtly incorporating the relevant details from the prequel into the dialogue, narrative, and scenic descriptions of the first chapter, so that you're more or less caught up to speed on the sequence of life events that brought me to this point by the time we get to chapter two. However, that sounds suspiciously like something that would require a lot of literary finesse, outlining, rough drafting, and proofing, whereas I prefer to just sit here at my kitchen table and fill in the lines until I get hungry or attacked by a Charlie horse. Good grief, how much time do you think I want to spend on this? I already know what happens in this chapter, and, trust me, this isn't even one of the interesting ones. So suck it up and cinch it up, because you're getting the most pertinent details from the first book in a bullet list, as follows:

Okay, I wrote that last sentence five hours ago, and I still can't figure out how to set up bullet lists on this dang computer, so suck it up and cinch it up, because you're now getting the most pertinent details from the first book in a series of rundown paragraphs, as follows: (My apologies to the "skimmers" who already read the first book.)

Hi. I'm Bucky Laroo. Born August 2, 1980, the Year of the Monkey according to the Chinese Zodiac. Red hair and freckles, 5'11", 99 lbs soaking wet. I have two beautiful (physically, anyway) older siblings, a dark-haired brother named Corky who fits at least nine out of ten of the basic cowboy hero stereotypes, and his eight-minute-junior twin sister Sassy, a feisty, shotgun-toting brunette firecracker who scares me more than the average Chlorine gas leak in an unventilated area.

After being abandoned by our hippie parents, Wisp and Flower Laroo, we were raised as cowboys and cowgirl by Gramps on Cattle Poke Ranch near the tiny northern British Columbia town of Coyote Yelp Pass. It was a good life, even during the detrimental times, such as when I found myself being trampled by cows on a regular basis, and later being targeted for annihilation by assassins and beautiful celebrities.

Perhaps I should expound on that last bit.

When I was six years old, and Corky and Sassy were nine, we had a chance encounter in Coyote Yelp Pass with another Year of the Monkey lad by the name of Morton Lincoln von Justin, who was in the process of being abandoned by his hippie parents. (Hippies did that a lot in the 80s, claiming to model their parenting skills after lions following wildebeest across the desert. I suppose this is a good example of natural selection in action, as the thinning of the herds keeps the hippie population in check, and the world can only benefit from that.) After a simple matter of losing a coin toss for a deep-fried prawn to me, Mort quickly decided that he hated me, and managed to maintain that hatred for the next twenty-plus years, which was really amazing as he would not even see me again for nearly twenty years.

A few months after I met Mort, I met a three-year-old neighbouring farmgirl named Betty-Sue Perkins. Following an unsettling trend which I was beginning to detect, she also decided to hate me for the next twenty-plus years. Then she apparently got over it, because she fell in love with me and eventually married me in February of 2008.

Meanwhile, Mort had moved down to Los Angeles, California, disowned his parents, and changed his name to Max-Ram Target, quickly becoming the leading juvenile Hollywood action hunk of the 80s and 90s. Over the course of his stellar career, he appeared in fifty action movies, all of which inexplicably featured at least one appearance by a whiny and severely ill-fated cowboy villain, his grimy clothing frequently patterned with red maple leafs.

My siblings, who also routinely claimed to hate me, channelled their loathing into lyrical therapy, eventually forming a successful country-western band with Sassy's long-suffering fiancé, Junior Van Der Snoot. Called *Lost Cause Kin*, the band gained a great deal of international publicity for their inspirational hit single *The Old Pickle Barrel Song*.

As the 21st century dawned, the fame of both Mort and *Lost Cause Kin* began to slump a bit, mostly because the general public began to realize that my siblings' band was formulaic, and that Max-Ram Target was the worst actor on the planet. Everyone adapts to career hiccups in different ways. Corky and Sassy adapted by grudgingly admitting that they had acclimatised to me, and thenceforth writing songs about love and heartbreak and fast horses and pickup trucks. Mort adapted a bit more creatively by faking a reconciliation with me, while simultaneously staging his own kidnapping and framing me for it in the hopes of living out a highly-publicized action drama which would get him back in the limelight.

Long story short, on one fateful night in June of 2007, I somehow survived the combined wrath of the RCMP, the LAPD, the FBI, a former East German assassin named Klaus Klotzern, and a seriously cheesed-off pop star named Minnie Marshmallow. (Look, folks, make it easy on yourselves. Just read the first book.)

After having a last-minute change of heart and saving my life, more or less, Mort briefly returned to Coyote Yelp Pass the following February to attend the wedding of myself and Betty-Sue, at which point he stated publicly that I was now his best friend. He then went back to Hollywood, and I hadn't seen him since. Apparently, no one else had either, because they were all too busy watching the movies of the millennium's hottest new action star, Sting Ripblood. How quickly we forget....

It was the last day of August, 2009, and the lingering remnants of the infamous night that Max-Ram Target saved my life had been all but carried away by the endlessly-shifting sands of time, reminiscent of a cat sneezing in a litter box, to borrow an expression from one of the people who tries to kill me later in this book. It had been a great year for Coyote Yelp Pass, with all of the surrounding farms and ranches producing bumper crops of wheat, barley, oats, and calves. As if that wasn't cause enough to celebrate, the town itself was booming, as the population jumped from 48 to 53, the largest census explosion since the Great Maple Rush of 1854. It was an exciting time, and, when the annual community Harvest Potluck rolled around, my life truly felt like it was approaching something close to normalcy. In fact, the morning before the anticipated event was the very last time that bounty hunters showed up at the ranch, seeking the twenty-seven billion dollar dead-or-immolated-alive bounty offer which, unbeknownst to most of the world, had been removed from my head more than two years earlier. (Yeah, you read it right. Twenty-seven billion dollars. I just record the history. Heck, I considered turning in some non-essential part of my anatomy for a 3-5% cut. Nobody really needs two ears, right?) Take my advice. Go out of your way to keep Hollywood happy, because you do not want to find yourself on the wrong side of their combined wrath. Maybe you can still avoid it, even if I can't. Apparently, it's an inherent aspect of being tragic and Canadian.

It seems that most of the world's media outlets, who had been so quick to put the story of Mort's so-called kidnapping on the front page of every periodical on the planet, were more concerned about the potential publicity fallout resulting from "killing the buzz" than they were with actually getting the truth out to the masses. Blinded by the sensationalist demands of a drama-starved populace, the global media settled on what they considered to be a fair compromise. A full retraction of the Max-Ram Target kidnapping story was printed, comprehensively declaring my complete innocence in the matter, and also assuring any homicidal money-grubbers that the twenty-seven billion dollar bounty was no longer an option. However, this retraction was only printed in a single issue of one periodical, *The Gorilla Growl Gulch Gazette*, a quarterly Mozambique farmer's almanac written primarily in Franco-Swahili, a hybrid language whose existence I had previously been unaware of. The completed article formed a square 1.5" block of text on page four of the classified ads, inserted neatly between the sections advertising *Jobs for Juniors* and *Used Kitchen Appliances*. Well, it was better than a kick in the head, I guess, and, as a career cowboy, I have more than enough firsthand experience to back up that statement.

My saving grace over the years had been the fact that no one on the planet knew where Coyote Yelp Pass was, as it does not exist on any known map, government voter registry, or GPS search engine. Therefore, I only ever had to worry about the bounty hunters who stumbled across my tiny town by chance, and that had only happened half a dozen times in the past year. Life was good.

Anyway, it was 6:30 a.m. on Monday, August 31, 2009, and I was just getting back to the ranch after an early morning run into town to pick up the mail from the Coyote Yelp Communal Mail Bin, something I like to do at least once a month, but had forgotten about entirely since mid June. Somehow, supermarket flyers and fast food coupons lose a lot of their significance when you live nearly eighty kilometres from the nearest supermarket or fast food chain. However, Betty-Sue had been nagging me about the mail ever since she had started sending mail-in stuff to her favourite reality television show in the hopes of winning seats to one of their live airings. I suppose after watching *Canada's Next Top Best Dance Crew* religiously for the past four seasons on a 12" black and white rabbit-eared TV-VCR combo with really grainy reception, Betty-Sue was justified in wanting to see her beloved talent competition in hi-res 3-D technicolour for once.

It was a foggy morning, and the ranch was still and quiet. Gramps had recently stated that his reward for making it to the age of eighty-five was to begin sleeping in for an extra three hours every morning, which meant that sometimes I wouldn't see him until a quarter to seven, or even later. Corky, Sassy, and Junior were on the road, finishing up their very successful *Burn, Bucky, Burn Eastern Canada Summer Tour*. They still liked to keep the ranch as a home-base, but an upsurge in public demand for *Lost Cause Kin* concerts had recently inspired them to trade in their battered old tour van for a luxurious tour bus with a tow-behind Hummer H2 so that they could spend as much time wreaking havoc on the road as possible. The summer tour had officially ended on August 29, and they had been driving back from Winnipeg for the past couple of days, hoping to be back in Coyote Yelp Pass in time for the Harvest Potluck that night. No matter how much the fame and fortune may have gone to their deranged heads, Corky and Sassy never forgot where they came from, mostly because they loved seeing the sheepish looks on the faces of any poverty-stricken locals who may have wronged them at some point during their wild childhood.

"To see the worms squirm, Bucky," Sassy had wistfully said to me a year or so earlier, while lovingly stroking a fistful of hundred dollar bills. "There's nothing like it."

And this mature attitude was coming from a woman who was on the shady side of thirty-two years old at the time. Of course, I never really blamed my twin siblings for having reached their developmental pinnacle at age fifteen. Our hippie parents were living a fully indulgent lifestyle during Flower's first pregnancy, ingesting and inhaling whatever struck their fancy at the moment. Heck, the only reason I was born as the voice of reason in my family was probably because Flower attacked an undercover RCMP Narcotics Officer with a garden rake for selling her a plastic bag of coriander two days after I was conceived. During her subsequent eight and a half months of incarceration in a "post-modern women's facility," my mother was forced to eat and breathe such things as fresh fruit, whole grains, Omega-3, and pure oxygen via therapy mask while listening to the masterworks of Beethoven, Mozart, and Waylon Jennings. I don't usually wish prison on anyone, but sometimes it's the only hope for a prenatal hippie kid like me. Add Flower's lifelong irrational fear of breastfeeding into the mix, and I suddenly had a better than average shot at being normal. (Trust me, the chemical composition of "hippie milk" is scary.)

The lights were still off in Gramps' cabin, but the bedroom light in my partially-constructed cabin across the road was on, so I guessed that my blushing bride was awake. We had been working on the cabin for most of the summer, and it was pretty much finished, except for the log-sanding that Betty-Sue was insisting on. Well, whatever it took to keep her happy was fine with me. I still had a hard time believing that somebody as tragic as me had managed to find a wife like her, considering that the fierce competition for her petite hand had once included a dashingly-musclebound suitor named Max-Ram Target. Just read the first book.

Betty-Sue Laroo.... How to describe my lovely bride? I once heard our local restaurateur, Mr Hayashi, describe the girl of his dreams by saying, "Her entrance into the room was as welcome as the windshield of a big-rig on a day with lots of mosquitos." It made perfect sense to me, but it's also possible that such expressions of devotion were part of the reason that Mr Hayashi was paying child support on his first-born child before she was even born. Some women just can't appreciate the warrior poet type.

Maybe the fact that I'm not a poet has actually kept me married. I've just kept my complimentary descriptions of my wife to the tried and true basics: "Gorgeous," "Breath-taking," "Jaw-dropping," "Stunning," and any other phrases that I habitually glean from the DVD jacket blurbs of movies that get cinematography award nominations. Yes, I have a beautiful, full-figured, tawny-haired wife with emerald-green eyes and the complexion of room-temperature peach yogurt. What more could a humble, stick-figured, redheaded cowboy with freckles and the complexion of biscuit dough ask for?

"Good morning, my little jar of mint jelly," I said gallantly, kissing her undeniably luscious mouth as I kicked off my boots in the doorway.

"Morning, lover," she yawned, rubbing the blear out of her sparkling emeralds.

"And how's little Rusty Laroo doing?" I queried, playfully poking my wife's stomach through her red bathrobe.

"As well as your delusion wants him to be," Betty-Sue sighed. "I told you, I'm not pregnant."

"The toilet bowl begged to differ yesterday morning," I chided her, placing a hand over her midriff and eagerly awaiting the first kick. "Morning, baby Rusty. Daddy can't wait to meet you!"

"And Mommy can't wait for Daddy to stop trying to make stir-fry for supper," Betty-Sue said dryly. "You feed me butter-drenched lettuce for supper, and then you wonder why I'm hugging the toilet bowl in the morning?"

"You know, he can hear every hurtful denunciation you spew forth," I admonished her, then leaned down to assure my son, "She's joking, my li'l buckaroo. She's just not good at it."

"Can I just have the mail, please?" Betty-Sue groaned, rolling her eyes.

"This is as much as I could find," I replied, handing her the small stack of envelopes I had managed to recover. "That family of porcupines knocked the bin over again and moved in. I found what was left of the invitation to Flat Ed's wedding lining an eagle's nest."

"Don't forget to toast them tonight," Betty-Sue reminded me. "This is our first time hosting the Harvest Potluck, and we don't wanna leave anyone out."

"Got it," I agreed. "And don't you forget to congratulate Sassy and Junior on the twelfth anniversary of their engagement. It's quite a feat these days. I can only imagine how long they're actually going to be married once they finally agree on a date."

"Yeah, I'm working on a poem for them," Betty-Sue acknowledged. "I'm just stumped on finding a word that rhymes with twelve. Shelve? Delve? I'm just not sure how to incorporate them in. Hey, did you mail that reply to the Hawkins Cheezies people?"

"Nope," I said, pouring myself a mug of coffee. "Still haven't made up my mind on that one."

"Why not?" Betty-Sue demanded. "It's a rare honour. How many ribbons are you going to get to cut in your lifetime?"

She made a good point. On the one hand, I was thrilled that the makers of my favourite cheese-flavoured, corn-based snack food had asked me to be a ribbon-cutter at the gala opening of their new Hawkins Cheezies factory in Kelowna the following summer. On the other hand, I wasn't sure if my invitation was a real honour, or just good business sense on the part of W.T. Hawkins Ltd. Their Cheezies sales had reportedly more than doubled in the months following the publication of my autobiography, *Last Stand at Coyote Yelp Pass: The Tragic Cowboy Memoirs of Bucky Laroo*, which apparently referenced Cheezies twenty-five times. After briefly considering the possibility of suing me, the Hawkins company instead chose to accept the offered free promotion and run wild with it. I was named an honorary spokesperson of Hawkins Cheezies, as was Max-Ram Target, whose own autobiographical account of the night that he saved my life frequently mentioned his sinister misuse of the delectable cheddar corn twists as incriminating evidence with which to frame me. Both of us were also awarded lifetime supplies of Cheezies, and Mort was further honoured by being prominently featured in Hawkins next major ad campaign. The slogan *The Canadian Treat That Nearly Killed Max-Ram Target* was added to all 210 gram Cheezies snack bags between February and September of 2008. Amazingly, and somewhat ironically, this promotion sent Cheezies' sales even further through the roof, while simultaneously creating an unprecedented American demand for the exclusively-Canadian marketed snacks. This demand would only relent after a notable 2008 increase in northbound tourism, and the eventual creation of an extensive black-market pipeline operation behind the mists of Niagra Falls. (Somehow, even that one got blamed on me.)

The upsurge in sales, particularly in western Canada, led the Ontario-based Hawkins company to fulfill its long-overdue dream of opening a second snack production factory in the west. The city of Kelowna in southern British Columbia was determined to be the ideal location, although I honestly have no idea why. (If you have already read the back cover and feel the sudden urge to scream, *"Plot contrivance!"* I really can't blame you. Sometimes history feels contrived, okay? Seriously, if I didn't know better, I would have said that *The Texas Chainsaw Massacre* was complete fiction.) But the Hawkins Cheezies company wanted me to cut the ribbon when the new factory opened.

Betty-Sue had been ecstatic when we were first notified of the invitation more than a month earlier, but a lifetime of backfires obligated me to be cautious and dig a bit deeper. The first rather obvious discovery was that Hawkins had originally wanted Max-Ram Target to wield the golden scissors, but the former-action-hunk-turned-bestselling-non-fiction-author could not make room in his schedule, as he was tied up in the publication of his eagerly-anticipated second book. So they called me.

"It's not til June," I reminded Betty-Sue, pouring myself a cup of coffee. "I'll decide, I just haven't yet."

"Next month's supply arrived while you were out yesterday," she reminded me in turn, sitting at the table and flipping through the mail. "That's thirty-one 210 gram snack bags of Hawkins Cheezies in the deep freeze right now. I think we owe them a thank-you for that. If nothing else, we owe them a thank-you for being the only delivery people in the world who can find Cattle Poke Ranch. The grain guy still needs smoke signals to get here. You're doing the ribbon-cutting."

"I did say thank you," I said defensively. "I sent a copy of my autobiography, *Last Stand at Coyote Yelp Pass: The Tragic Cowboy Memoirs of Bucky Laroo*, to the address on the back of the snack bag. With a note."

At the sound of my full book title, Betty-Sue paused to glance irritably at me over the West-Can Hydro mailing she was reading.

"Bucky ... you know I hate it when you do that."

"Sorry," I chuckled. "No shameless plugging in the kitchen. Got it. What's in the mail?"

"Okay, we've got a request from the power company," Betty-Sue announced, scanning the unfolded paper in her hand. "They're wondering if we would be interested in running the ranch on something besides electricity, because they don't want to, and I quote, 'be associated in any capacity, direct or alternating, with the man who tried to murder Hollywood Titan Max-Ram Target. While we readily admit to having supplied electrical power and utilities to the most deviant of criminals in the Canadian penal system for over one hundred years, we strongly feel that the line of morality must be drawn somewhere, so we would like to start at the very bottom and work our way up toward the light.'"

"Have you ever noticed how the more people loathe me, the more mixed their metaphors become?" I commented. "Why is disdain equated with justifiable grammatical blunders?"

"Beats me," Betty-Sue shrugged. "Oh, and this is interesting. They're offering us a lifetime supply of plutonium radioisotope power cells and a micro-reactor so that we can transition from electricity to nuclear ionization."

"I'm not sure about the long-term effects on our beef quality," I grimaced. "Or our ability to have kids. What else is there?"

"Let's see," Betty-Sue murmured, shuffling the envelopes.

"Big winner ... big winner ... bank statement ... big winner. This one's weird. Did somebody nominate you for reality television?"

"Not again," I groaned. "Reality TV is Corky's thing, not mine."

"'Dear Mr Bucky Laroo,'" Betty-Sue read aloud. "'Congratulations on your precedent-setting unnominated offer to appear in season three of TLC's hit reality series, *Canada's Worst Canadian.* Join our charming host Svend Robinson as he continues his seemingly vain search to find even one of our fellow citizens who is more deserving of the title than himsel–'"

"Intriguing," I interrupted dryly, sipping my coffee, "but somehow I think I'll probably end up passing. How's it looking outside? I thought I heard someone creeping into the yard in low gear a minute ago."

Betty-Sue carefully leaned across the table and pulled the window blind back half an inch, scanning the barnyard and driveway with one eye.

"Nothing major," she reported dismissively. "Just one truckload of hillbillies with guns. And they look stupid."

"What are they packing?" I sighed, standing and pulling on the denim jacket which I had barely finished taking off.

"Two dudes with bolt-action .308s and a lady with a chainsaw."

"Huh, they're going easy on us today," I grunted, flipping on the power to the public address system that I had been obligated to install on the cabin roof. I unclipped the transmitter from the wall-bracket and depressed the PTT with my thumb.

"You want pancakes?" Betty-Sue inquired, pushing the rest of the mail aside and standing from the table.

"Yeah, that sounds great," I assured her, turning my

attention to the squelching radio in my fist. "Attention, all bounty hunters. Hi. I'm Bucky Laroo."

There was a moment of silence as my amplified words were carried across the rooftop by the megaphone lashed alongside the chimney stack, and then the apparent Alpha-male of the intruders shouted back their reply.

"Come on out with yer hands up and yer pants down, or we'll blast ya! We didn't drive all the way up from Hudson's Hope for a parlay!"

"There's no bounty, people," I said patiently. "Please return to your vehicle, get it off my crabgrass, and get off my ranch. You're trespassing." I released the button and asked Betty-Sue, "Are they leaving?"

The sound of a chainsaw being fired up answered the question before Betty-Sue could reach for the blind again.

"Nope," she said. "Want the guns?"

"Naw, don't worry about it," I remarked with a shrug. "Bacon?"

"Bacon would be really nice, actually," I agreed, keying the mike and addressing the greedy mob again. "Seriously, there's no money, people. The twenty-seven billion dollar bounty was rescinded two years ago."

"Prove it!" the second hillbilly male bellowed back.

"Babe?" I said, holding out an expectant hand. Betty-Sue obligingly slapped our worn copy of *The Gorilla Growl Gulch Gazette* into my palm. I cracked the front door open and tossed the almanac out onto the porch.

"Git it, Cledus," I heard the first hillbilly whine. "We'll cover ya."

A moment later, a pair of clodhoppers pattered frantically up the front steps and onto the porch, and then made a hasty retreat.

"What in the blazes is this, Earl?" Cledus' voice

demanded, once he was behind the bullet-stopping pickup once more.

"The printed retraction," I supplied generously. "Page four of the classified ads."

"It's Chinese!" the woman's voice said in disgust.

"Franco-Swahili," I corrected her via megaphone. "Can you put it back on the porch when you're done? It's our only copy."

"Lemme see that, Bobbi-Jo," Earl requested. "I studied eight different Swahili dialects when I was doing that junior oil executive stint with Africanada-Co in Kenya.... Aw crap, he ain't lying. There ain't no reward."

"Kin we blast'im anyway?" Bobbi-Jo simpered. "It was an awful long drive."

"We need to get a dog," I advised my wife, putting on my battered brown cowboy hat. "Big dog."

"Put it on the list," she mused, sifting flour in a stainless steel mixing bowl. "You want the blueberries in or on?"

"On, please," I replied, tugging on my cowboy boots. "I'm going to feed Sassy's chickens. I think they're leaving."

"Goodbye, I love and appreciate you!" Betty-Sue blurted as I stepped outside, just in case I was wrong about the withdrawing horde. I wasn't, but her thoughtfulness was appreciated.

The hillbillies were long gone and breakfast was ready by the time I returned from feeding my sister's prize-winning pullets. (Celebrity-branded products are always a reliable money-maker, and much of Sassy's recent wealth was attributable not only to *Lost Cause Kin*'s sold-out summer tour, but also to her highly-successful marketing of *Sassy Laroo's "Great, eh?" Canadian Farm-Fresh Eggs.*®) Betty-Sue was setting a platter of pancakes and bacon on the table and listening to her favourite classic radio station, Affluenceville FM 302.7, *The Trump.*

"Pancakes smell awesome, pudding puff," I applauded her, sitting down and heaping three of the golden cakes onto my plate. "This'll give us energy to spare for the day."

Betty-Sue patiently waited until I had thanked Jesus for the meal before assuring me, "I can't work today. I told you."

"You can't?" I said through a mouthful of syrup and flapjack.

"No, silly-banilly," Betty-Sue giggled. "The season finale of *Canada's Next Top Best Dance Crew* is tomorrow in Affluenceville, and FM 302.7 is giving out two front-row tickets and backstage passes to meet the winning dance crew *and* Britt 2.0! Not to mention the fact that Britt 2.0 is dating Sting Ripblood, and he just happens to be in Affluenceville as well, filming *Compound Fracture III: Spiral Torque*. There's no way he's not going to be there! All I have to do is be the 3027th caller after they play Britt 2.0's hit single *Sandpaper Me Softly*. I'm going to be on the phone all day. If you want to go, you know this is our only shot."

"I don't want to go," I reminded her for the fourth time that week. "I have unresolved issues with beautiful pop stars and the Hollywood action hunks who date them."

"Bucky, seriously," Betty-Sue scoffed. "What are the odds of us meeting two pure evil Hollywood dream couples in one lifetime? You're being paranoid. It's almost like you want your life story to be formulaic."

"I could live with that," I admitted.

"C'mon, lover," she said in that teasing tone that she knew darn well I was incapable of resisting. "It'll be fun."

"Well, whatever's most important to you, sweet bean," I conceded. "Putting up a new two-mile stretch of five-rung barbwire fence is really more of a one-man job anyway."

Betty-Sue was not a reality television fanatic, unlike Corky who had used his fledgling celebrity status to make a handful of appearances in said shows, but we all have our vices. Betty-Sue's was the annual search for *Canada's Next Top Best Dance Crew*. (Call me a hopeless romantic, but I was always more of a fan of the cowboy drama, *Heartland*. The assistant art direction of Dale Marushy is really incomparable.) Every summer, the national talent search would begin on behalf of a hot new musical act in need of backup dancers, the quality of which is apparently more important than the vocal quality of lead singers in the modern pop music scene. The first three seasons of the show had been modest successes, while developing a significant cult following, but season four had promised to be the biggest season yet. Rather than focussing on finding a dance crew for a fledgling Canadian pop act, as in previous seasons, CTV spokespersons had shocked the western world with the announcement that the gorgeous and globally-idolized American pop-music diva known only as Britt 2.0 had turned down her highly-publicized offer to be featured in NBC's highest-rated reality show of the fall lineup, *America's Next Top Best Dance Crew*, choosing instead to star in the Canadian spin-off the following summer. The USA was devastated, but most Canadians, including my wife, were ecstatic, and *Canada's Next Top Best Dance Crew, Season Four: The Search For Britt 2.0's Backup* had quickly become the most-watched show in the nation. Millions voted for their favourite dance crew every Monday, and then millions more tuned in to see the results every Tuesday. With the season finale less than two days away, and only two barely-literate dance crews left in the running, it was anyone's guess as to which one would win the honour of dancing in Britt 2.0's voluptuous shadow for the rest of their careers. The more conservative voters that I had spoken to showed a preference for *Free Movement, Free Minds*, but the liberal-dominated media seemed to be giving an unbalanced amount of ad time to the opposing *Sweet Conformity*. It was going to be a potboiler. (The media stories of American devastation were legendary and, quite likely, sensationalised. Apparently, twenty-four-year-old Britt 2.0 had made the controversial decision because she was already planning to spend the summer in British Columbia with her boyfriend, Sting Ripblood, who was, as Betty-Sue rightfully mentioned, filming the action-drama *Compound Fracture III: Spiral Torque*. The movie was being shot on location in Affluenceville, which, coincidentally, was the same city that *CNTBDC* was airing out of that year. The aptly-named modern gold-rush city was located only an hour or so to the east of Coyote Yelp Pass, close enough that I could almost smell the wafting snoot from my front porch on a muggy day. According to rumour and urban legend, Hollywood magnate Nigel Wexworth, creator of *America's Next Top Best Dance Crew*, had personally stormed the Beverly Hills offices of Sting Ripblood's film producers and beaten several of them into pulpy messes with a left-handed 9-iron in response to their economically-based decision to substitute Affluenceville for *Spiral Torque*'s Los Angeles setting, thereby costing his show the biggest pop star on the planet. "Do you really think people can't tell the difference?!" he reportedly screamed as he was being dragged away by studio security. "Nothing in Canada works as a stand-in for the urban jungle of Los Angeles! *Nothing!* They've got like six Hispanic people in the whole country, and none of them have tattoos!" His generalization was not only offensive, but inaccurate as well, as was made readily evident when one of the final two Canadian dance crews, *Sweet Conformity*, turned out to be made up of twelve young men of Puerto Rican descent, several of whom had really scary tattoos.)

After breakfast, I found Gramps down in the winter feeding grounds, up to his grizzled white beard in an excavated pipe shaft, as he worked his way through a maze of plumbing with a crescent wrench in each hand. That hole may not have looked like much more than a hole at the time, but it was supposed to become a new cattle waterer before the first snowfall. We had run the water piping earlier that month, so now it was just a matter of connecting the waterworks, pouring the concrete base, and capping it all off with the prefabricated plastic reservoir and floating covers. Not a terribly complex job, but Gramps knew that it was one which he would be forced to complete on his own, which was why I had been assigned to fencing duty for most of the week. (My overconfident attempt at installing the new bathtub in Gramps' cabin as a surprise for his eightieth birthday five years earlier could have been made into a fairly decent half-hour television sitcom.)

"These new watering rigs are supposed to be amazing," Gramps mumbled, holding a pipe in place with his teeth as he tightened the elbow joint with both monkey wrenches. "It uses flat plastic floats instead of floating ball covers. Apparently, they don't freeze up like the round ones."

"Wow," I said, impressed by the outlandish claim. "You're suggesting that we go through a northern Rockies winter without digging ice out of a frozen cattle waterer in minus forty weather with our bare hands and a crowbar?"

"I know," Gramps said a bit glumly. "I'll miss it, too, but we put our cows ahead of ourselves, even if that means we have to put up with a disturbing lack of environmental exposure. It's like the 1984 upgrade from horse-drawn bale wagon to the front-end loader all over again."

"Gramps, what is all this?" I had to ask, looking around at our unusually spit-polished barnyard. "New waterer, new post pounder, hot water in the bathrooms.... What's with all the improvements this year? Seriously, Cattle Poke Ranch is starting to feel ... comfortable. It's weird."

"Well," Gramps grunted, still wrenching on the stubborn pipes, "this whole place is gonna be yours and Betty-Sue's sometime soon. Figured I'd better leave it better than I found it for ya."

It was surprising to hear Gramps say such a simple couple of sentences. He had never mentioned retirement or inheritances before, although it had always been obvious that I was the only one of his grandchildren who had any interest in carrying on the day-to-day running of the ranch after he was gone. I wondered if age was finally catching up with him, and this was the only way he knew of to admit it. But I had my own tasks to attend to at the moment.

I worked hard on the fence all day, continuing right through lunch as I had promised Betty-Sue that I would be back at the cabin by five o'clock to help her finish cooking multiple moose casseroles and transport them out to the Coyote Yelp Community Lean-to for the potluck. I wasn't much of a cook, as evidenced by my infamous stir-fry attempt, but Betty-Sue needed the extra set of hands so that she could keep one of her own on the telephone at all times. The lack of a speed-dial option on our old rotary phone didn't even slow her down. Nobody could redial that wheel of numbers faster than my wife. It was a gift.

She didn't win. A guy named Floyd Shorthorn did.

The triumphant honking of the tour bus's horn signalled the return of my celebrity siblings and Junior Van Der Snoot at around five-thirty. The tour bus had never looked better as it eased down the driveway, sporting a spiffy new coat of glossy black paint with flame detailing and the proud christening "Bucky-Paver" running down the length of the vehicle in lightning-bolt lettering. It was always nice to know that they were thinking of me, even on the road.

Corky and Sassy were exchanging high-fives and whooping with the delight of being home as they disembarked from the bus, followed closely by Sassy's fiancé, squeezing his massive frame through the narrow doorway with some difficulty. Junior Van Der Snoot is as bald as a turkey vulture, but anyone who has ever laid eyes on his largely fat-free 300 lb frame thinks twice about teasing him about that premature fact. However, I am happy to report that he is the very definition of a gentle giant, and I looked forward to the day when I could actually call him my brother-in-law, although that was starting to feel like wishful thinking. Sassy had been over-thinking the ceremonial specifics and floral arrangements for well over a decade, and I think the delay was beginning to take a toll on Junior. It was subtle, but his ever-genial smile looked just a little bit tighter with each passing month. I worried about the long-term effects of being such an understanding guy.

"How was the tour?" I obligingly asked, setting a five-gallon bucket of homemade potato salad in the box of my old red-and-black Chevy Sierra truck, next to the seven foil pans of moose casserole.

"Bucky, you should have been there," Sassy said nostalgically, a look of lingering rapture shining from her pretty face. "Don't get me wrong, I continually thank all that is holy that you weren't there, but still.... It was indescribable. Terri Clark asked for *my* autograph!"

"Wow, that is genuinely impressive," I admitted. "Congrats."

"Thank you," Sassy said appreciatively. "And, man alive, you should have seen the look on her face when I said 'no.' Epic."

"And there's the other foot," I sighed. "I pray for you every night, big sister. I pray that you manage to be a celebrity without actually being a celebrity, but I don't think I'm using the right words."

"Oh, but that's not even the biggest news," Corky

assured me, rubbing his hands gleefully. "But I'm not telling you yet. The whole town needs to hear this one, so make sure you build it up properly before you introduce me tonight. You are still hosting, right?"

"Yeah, me and Betty-Sue both are," I acknowledged, slamming the tailgate.

"Who?" Corky asked blankly.

"My wife," I said tiredly.

"Is she still hanging around?" Corky said, looking legitimately surprised.

"Yes, and she even seems happy," I said dryly. "Okay, right now she's a bit despondent over not winning backstage passes to *Canada's Next Top Best Dance Crew*, but she'll get over it. Get in the truck box. I need you on potato-salad balancing duty."

"In good time, baby bro," he soothed me. "Priorities first. Are you taking her to that thing in Kelowna next summer?"

"How is an event ten months from now a priority?" I asked.

"I'll give you this much, Bucky. Nobody can sugar-foot around a question like you. Are you going or not?"

"I haven't decided. Why are you so interested in a trip that has nothing to do with you, anyway?"

"I'm not," Corky quipped. "*Heh heh!*"

"Corky, last month you called me from Toronto at two o'clock in the morning to ask if I was going to Kelowna or not. I said I didn't know, and you said, 'You're killing me, Bucky,' and hung up. I was fine, by the way. The grain shed had caught fire earlier that day, and I nearly died from the smoke inhalation, but what really matters is that you were up to date on my indecisiveness about whether or not to go to Kelowna next year. Yeah, I'm the one who's killing you."

Corky shrugged. "Well, I could have meant any number of things by that, literal or metaphorical. So are you going or not?"

"Yes," I said.

"*Hot dang!*" Corky whooped, punching the air. "History books, here I come!"

"That was a bluff," I countered flatly. "I haven't decided."

"Dude, you're killin' me," Corky groaned, wearily resting his forehead on the edge of the truck box.

"Just hold the potato salad," I requested.

We piled my entire extended family into my truck, and the six of us made it to the Coyote Yelp Community Lean-to on the western outskirts of town just before six o'clock. Several long tables had been set up around the raised stage, and many of the locals had already arrived, including Betty-Sue's father, Bob Perkins, and Mr Hayashi, setting out a selection of rural delicacies from his restaurant. Even Betty-Sue seemed to be enjoying herself as we began unloading the truck, much to my relief. I knew how much she had wanted to go to that meet-and-greet, and I did not want her to be sad, no matter how thoroughly the prospect of attending the event with her had repulsed me. You'll have to forgive me if my general attitude toward celebrities isn't as sunny as it was in the innocent days of my youth.

More than half of Coyote Yelp Pass's populace had arrived by the time we had our casserole dishes and potato salad bucket set out. The traditional bonfire was raging nearby to the delight of the local children, and it was my turn to welcome everybody. Sassy took the opportunity to introduce me.

"Ladies and gentlemen, meet the man behind the pickle barrel!" she called out with her hands cupped around her mouth, climbing up and standing on top of the head-table that our family had been honoured with for the first time. "To you, he may just be the man who tried to kill Max-Ram Target, but, to me, he will always be my primary source of both lyrical inspiration and revenue. And I even kind of like the dead-eyed lummox now. My dear Coyote Yelp Passians, please give it up for my baby brother, Bucky Laroo!"

I couldn't help shaking my head as I took the stage, although the polite applause and cheers were appreciated.

"Thanks, big sister," I acknowledged. "Well, folks, it's been quite a year, ain't it? I want to start by throwing a big shout-out to Flat Ed on his engagement to his second-cousin Rita, which I'm pretty sure is legal in most western nations, so ... fourth time's the charm, I guess. When's the big day?"

"Friday!" the feisty young Rita cheered. "Never could stand the thought of a long engagement."

"Yeah, they're sickening, aren't they?" I said without thinking. "Congrats."

I led the following round of applause as Flat Ed and Rita raised their joined hands victoriously, wearing the widest pair of matching gap-toothed grins I had seen in a long time. It was heartwarming, even if the family resemblance itself was unnerving. Junior looked like he had food poisoning.

"And let's hear it for my beloved brother and sister and Junior Van Der Snoot," I continued grandly, feeling that I was starting to get the hang of this whole event MC thing. "I think we all owe them a big hand for devotedly mentioning Coyote Yelp Pass at every one of their more than fifty *Lost Cause Kin* concerts over the summer. Thanks to them, hundreds of thousands of people across Canada are aware that Coyote Yelp Pass exists! They don't know where it is yet, but, as the old saying goes, beggars can be losers ... or something like that. Let's hear it for them."

The crowd responded more enthusiastically than before,

although that also may have been an attempt to get on my recently-affluent siblings' good side. Coyote Yelp Passians may be the salt of the earth, but the dream of being the cream of the crop is universal.

"Thank you all for coming out on this beautiful summer evening," I said sincerely. "You people have always been there for me, ever since my hippie parents ditched me here nearly twenty-five years ago. Every one of you is like family, even though I know full well that you all plotted to offer me as a placation sacrifice to the hostile mountain spirits on more than one occasion."

The entire seated crowd, including my wife, ducked their heads and looked a bit sheepish, their scuffing toes clearly audible on the grass beneath the tables. Only Corky and Sassy were able to laugh uproariously at the not-too-long-ago memory.

"Yeah, that's what I thought," I said. "Whatever. I love you all, and I'm proud to call Coyote Yelp Pass my home. Now, if you'll all please rise, I'll ask our resident really old person, Donald Budgekins, to lead us in recitation of the Coyote Yelp Pass pledge of allegiance. I would ask our resident really, really old person to do it, but I don't see Mrs Quivercake here yet, and I'm hungry. Donald?"

The white-headed World War II veteran and local airstrip traffic controller stood solemnly, and we all stood with him, placing our hands over our hearts as he began the traditional town blessing.

"With the yelp of the coyote, tears spring to our eyes. Coyote Yelp Pass, we salute you each day."

The rest of us then joined him in the dramatic completion.

"*When they enforce it ... we will stop.*"

"Thank you," I said, forced to wipe away an emotional tear as Budgekins took his seat once more. "Let's eat."

The meal was excellent, as was the company, and, once again, I could not shake the feeling that this was one of those significant turning points in my life, a shining indication that things were on their way to getting better for me. This feeling was only solidified further when Gramps stood from his seat as dessert was being served, and tapped a fork against his tin mug. Silence fell over the chattering assembly as my rural neighbours gave their undivided attention to my grandfather.

"You all know me," Gramps said gruffly, his disdain of public speaking quite evident. "You know what I do, or rather what I did. It's been a real pleasure working with you salts of the earth all these decades, since I was just a pup myself.... But, dang it, I'm *old*. Been sleepin' in to all kinds of hours lately, and that ain't no way to run an enterprise of no sorts. So I figures this is as good a time as any to let y'all know that your MC ain't a cowboy no more. Well, he is, but he's more. Bucky, Cattle Poke Ranch is yours now. You and your pretty bride can do whatcha like with it. Build it or burn it, it's up to you. Love ya. Thanks."

He sat down and turned his attention to the saskatoon cobbler in front of him.

A moment later, the crowd was cheering and clapping again, and Betty-Sue was gleefully hugging me, but I could only sit in shock, unable to believe what had just happened. One of the first things that had been apparent to me from my earliest years of acceptantly blue-collar existence was that life without rent payments was not even worth thinking about. I was just a cowboy and a farmhand. Marrying the farmgirl down the road and buying Gramps' 1990 Chevy Sierra extended cab pickup truck were the closest things to property ownership that I had ever attempted. But, with a few dismissive words from Gramps, I was at the helm of six hundred cows on a five-thousand-acre ranch and seventeen-thousand-acre federal grazing lease. It was mind-boggling.

"Thanks, Gramps," I managed to crack after a few moments.

Gramps shrugged and gave a dark chuckle. "Don't mention it, Bucky. Could've waited until I was dead, but I figured I'd rather see you sweating the gallons of blood to maintain your inheritance, rather than just imagining what it'd look like after I'm gone."

And only Gramps could say those exact words with both sincerity and love. Or maybe it was just sincerity, but I dare to dream.

The celebration continued for a few more minutes as most of the Coyote Yelp Passians came over to the head-table to shake my hands and congratulate me. Even Corky and Sassy seemed overjoyed by the knowledge that they would never again feel any sort of obligation to do work at the ranch. Gramps may have been able to guilt them into pulling their weight in between tours, but they were quite confident that they would never have that problem with me.

I thought the evening had hit its high point, but then Corky and Sassy smugly made their big announcement that really blew the lid off the gathering. It turned out that *Lost Cause Kin* had been named as one of the honoured Canadian acts chosen to perform at the 2010 Winter Olympic Closing Ceremonies in Vancouver's prestigious BC Place the following February! I had never been so proud of my siblings, and even they had rarely been prouder of themselves. Betty-Sue and I led the crowd in three "Hip-hip-huzza!"s, and then we all gave a standing ovation.

It was in the midst of this congratulatory occasion that a strange and haunting voice first spoke, with a chilling power that made everyone's mouths snap shut in one single bloodcurdling moment.

"Horseman of the northern sun...." the voice rasped by way of introduction.

The instantly-silenced crowd turned toward the sound, while those closest to it took a few involuntarily steps back, parting the gathering just enough for me to glimpse the source of the voice.

He was an unfamiliar, painfully-thin old man, standing about fifty feet away from the nearest table, having emerged from the wild forests to the north without being seen by anyone. He wore a hairy black-and-white Holstein robe and dark sandals, and his snowy white hair and beard hung past his waist. His bony left hand clutched a twisted walking staff, and his right hand held a scroll of weathered brown paper. Strangest of all were his eyes, which were blocked from view by a pair of small round sunglasses. And he was pointing that creepy-looking staff in my direction.

No one dared move or speak. One by one, the marshmallows being roasted in the bonfire by small children burst into silent flames, but none of the short people dared to so much as withdraw their sharpened willows from the inferno.

"Horseman!" the old stranger snapped again, stepping closer in short, shuffling paces. It was obvious by then that he was speaking to me.

"Me?" I said, pointing a questioning finger at my chest.

"Yes," he growled. "Many a hundred of mile have I trod, guided by the sound of my staff and the smells of the air. Listen now to the message delivered to me on your behalf, a message of what is to come at a time ... TBD."

"A blind prophet, huh?" Corky commented to Sassy. "I can't remember. Is that a classical homage, or has it been

33

re-created in popular culture enough times to be considered a cliché?"

Sassy shrugged apathetically. "It's a grey area."

"Silence, Bucky!" the blind prophet growled, showing an uncanny knowledge of how to formally address me for a perfect stranger. "Great and dark times are coming, and are perhaps already here. Be warned, all who dwell in these hills and in all the nations! Heed the words of what must be, but is not yet ... is."

He took a moment to dramatically clear his throat as he unrolled the brown scroll and proceeded to read aloud the Braille words that his right forefinger was gliding over, while my neighbours and I listened in understandably creeped-out silence.

> *"Now Chil the Kite brings home the night*
> *That Mang the Bat sets free.*
> *The herds are shut in byre and hut—*
> *For loosed til dawn are we.*
> *This is the hour of pride and power,*
> *Talon and tush and claw.*
> *O hear the call! Good hunting all*
> *That keep the jungle law!"*

"Whoa, baby," Sassy remarked, impressed. "I've got goose-egg goosebumps."

"Yeah, me too," I admitted. "I mean, I know for a fact that he just recited Rudyard Kipling's *Night-Song in the Jungle* rather than an actual prophecy, but it still gets me every time."

"What?" the blind prophet demanded, hurriedly running his reading finger over the scroll once more. "Oh, shoot. You're right, this is the wrong prophecy. I must have left yours on the kitchen table. This is the prophecy I was supposed to deliver to BC Premier Gordon Campbell before the next full moon because of that whole wolf-bite incident at the petting zoo. You get a different one."

"That whole what incident?" I asked, not sure that I had heard him correctly.

"*Silence!*" the blind prophet roared, his thunderous voice causing a couple of crystal drinking vessels to sing with resonance. "Hearken unto the conveniently-rhymed words of your destiny."

He had to kill a few more agonizing seconds with dramatic throat-clearing, which was actually kind of nauseating to listen to, before beginning his recitation from memory.

> *"Beloved and yet loathed,*
> *By all and by none,*
> *A horseman arises*
> *From the far northern sun.*

> *"So blessed with—"*

"Crap, that's not right," the blind prophet interrupted himself, scratching his snowy head in frustration. "The great ignorance verse was later. Shoot, it's official. I can't remember. I know the last line was something about 'the way of the cow.' I really need to get a tape recorder."

"How far did you say you walked to get here?" Corky had to ask.

"Wait a second," I interjected. "Did you just say 'the way of the cow?'"

"Yeah, that much I do remember," the blind prophet asserted confidently. "Why?"

"Because it was the title of chapter one of my autobiography, *Last Stand at Coyote Yelp Pass: The Tragic*

Cowboy Memoirs of Bucky Laroo," I said. "Did you read it? I have some copies in the truck if you haven't. Unbeatable prices, too."

"Bucky...." Betty-Sue said ominously. "Let the creepy man speak. Sir, are you saying that you received that prophecy about Bucky? What does it mean?"

"Beats me," the blind prophet readily confessed. "If I had clarification, I would have deciphered it at home and just brought you the rundown. Do you think I like being cryptic?"

"Well, we really don't know you that well, Matt Murdock," Sassy remarked. "You could like a lot of things that would shock a lot of people, as do most of us. For example, I happen to know that Flat Ed over there secretly enjoys watching his knuckle acne develop from whitehead to blackhead. Isn't that sick?"

"You get knuckle acne?" Rita cringed, tossing a quick look of revulsion at her fiancé.

"Only if I eat sharp cheddar," Flat Ed weakly admitted, glowering at my sister. Sassy only cackled.

Before I could ask for further details on who the blind prophet was, or where specifically his messages were handed down from, the sound of a cheerfully-honking car horn pierced the uneasy silence. We all looked to the south to see old Mrs Quivercake's ancient yellow sedan pulling into the grassy parking area. Our local centenarian proudly stepped out of the car, balancing a large jellied fruit salad in her surprisingly steady hands.

"I brought jellied fruit salad!" she triumphantly stated the obvious, which seemed to be her most reliable resource in her recent war against senility. "Everybody come and get some. Sorry I'm late, but I'm just starting to lose track of so much time lately."

"It looks great, Mrs Quivercake," I said cordially. "But

there's a guy here who was just saying something kind of importa–"

"Pish-posh," the ever-smiling old lady chided, shoving past the indignant blind prophet and setting the wobbling rainbow tower on the table, directly in front of me, Betty-Sue, and Sassy. "I remember a time when you would cry for hours when I ran out of my famous homemade jellied salad, Bucky. You would cry, and scream, and curse like an Irish sailor, and throw your toys, and threaten people with carving knives.... Oh, where does infancy go?"

After obligingly giving the potential memory a few moments to upsurge, without any success whatsoever, I had to state for the record, "I honestly don't think I ever did that."

"I remember it," Sassy quipped, digging a finger into the jelly and gouging out a sample. "Like it was yesterday. Ooh, this looks like one of your best yet, Mrs Quivercake. Mmmm, I'm seeing pineapple in there, and split maraschino cherries, and is that.... Is that...?"

I couldn't understand why my sister suddenly froze and turned as white as a sheet, her eyes bulging and wild. And I really couldn't understand why she then sprang out of her seat, and tackled Mrs Quivercake to the ground with a sickening *Crunch!* However, my confusion was immediately turned to horror when Sassy put two fingers in her mouth and let out an eardrum-piercing whistle that echoed across the western mountain ranges. Every man, woman, child, and dog who had lived in Coyote Yelp Pass for the past two hundred years knew what that whistle meant. The only thoroughly confused person was Mrs Quivercake, whose mental-lapse susceptibility had obviously progressed to dangerous levels without our knowledge in the past months. No fully-cognitive person within fifty kilometres would have ever made that particular jellied salad, or even been in possession of the ingredients therein.

"Code Death! I repeat, Code Death!" Sassy bellowed, still holding the futilely-wriggling Mrs Quivercake against the sod. "Bucky and Betty-Sue, stay where you are! Everyone else, evacuate to the cold zone with holds at one hundred fifty metres. This is not a drill! The jellied salad's been compromised! *The hostile mountain spirits are en route!* They'll be here any minute!"

"This is the real deal, people!" Gramps shouted, lunging out of his chair and following the sudden stampede of Coyote Yelp citizenry to the perimeter positions, leaving myself, Betty-Sue, Sassy, and Mrs Quivercake alone in the small meadow in front of the lean-to stage. "This is why we have drills! Mr Hayashi, you're leading Team Alpha. Set up Decon Station One. Corky, take Team Bravo and establish a secure buffer zone at one hundred metres from the hot zone. No one gets in or out, and report any changes in wind direction immediately. Bucky and Betty-Sue, you and Sassy and Mrs Quivercake all know what's expected of you."

Although frightened, Betty-Sue and I obligingly remained in our seats as we recited the hot zone quarantine procedure in well-disciplined unison:

"Do not attempt to egress the hot zone until instructed to enter the perimeter decontamination unit by a designated decon team member. All those failing to comply with quarantine protocol will be summarily shot in the interests of preserving the remainder of the unaffected population from contamination."

"Dang right you'll be shot," Corky snapped, grabbing Sassy's Bucky-Blaster shotgun from the back of my truck and tossing it to her. "Sassy, that's you."

"Gladly," Sassy complied with unnerving sincerity, breaking open the twin barrels and making sure the weapon was fully loaded, even as she continued to shout out directions to the frantically scrambling townsfolk. "Team Delta, that hole needs to be at least seven feet deep, and you're going to need at least twenty pounds of lye, or five sticks of dynamite. Everybody not yet assigned a position, link up with Charlie Team for the cross-contamination containment mop-up. Mrs Quivercake's car is priority one, and then you'll need to set her house on fire as well."

"My house?" Mrs Quivercake gasped with unmasked horror. "You're going to burn it down?"

"Darn-tootin,'" Sassy said cheerfully. "You have arson insurance, right?"

"No, I'm far too poor and debt-ridden," Mrs Quivercake whimpered, trembling with grief. "Ever since Leroy passed, all I've had in this world is that house. The wolf is at the door, Sassy! I have nothing else."

"I wouldn't worry about it, Edna," Sassy soothed her. "You are really, really old. I'm sure that as your senility gets a bit more advanced you won't even remember all of the cherished items you had in there. *Spark it up, boys!*"

A couple of local teenagers on Delta Team had already fashioned Molotov cocktails and were gleefully lobbing them at the yellow sedan from a safe distance upwind.

"Is it possible that we're overreacting?" I ventured. "After all, me and Corky are pretty sure that we've figured out what the mountain spirits really are. Jeepers, Sassy, you were there, too! They're just a bunch of—"

"Silence, Bucky," Corky snapped, not wanting to spoil the drama of the moment with unnecessary reality. "It doesn't change the threat to our lives."

"True," I admitted. "Carry on."

"I'm going to need a couple more buckets of pemmican and suet and a dash of nutmeg to fully decontaminate four people!" Mr Hayashi called out from the makeshift Decon Station One, stirring what ingredients were readily available to him in a large black cauldron, which I didn't even know existed in Canada. Of course, Mr Hayashi also has a hooded cloak in his closet at home for similarly urgent occasions.

I'm not even going to tell you what the decontamination

process involved. Suffice it to say, by the time it was over the offending salad was buried under seven feet of earth and corrosive materials, the perimeter was still clear, and Mrs Quivercake was accepting pamphlets for extended care facilities. And the mysterious blind prophet who had never been seen before, and has never been seen since, was nowhere to be found, vanishing in the midst of the chaos as if he had never existed at all, although it was quite obvious that he had taken Mr Hayashi's last tray of bacon-wrapped prawns with him.

So that's what happens in a small Rocky Mountain town when people allow superstitious beliefs in hostile mountain spirits and forbidden fruit to roam unchecked amongst the populace. Maybe it never hurts to be too careful, but it sure can put a damper on outdoor community events. My first hour as a real-estate owner was not off to a great start.

(By the way, at my publishers' insistence, there are a whole lot of relevant details that I deliberately left out of the preceding paragraphs, which probably would have greatly illuminated the situation for you had they been included. However, my publishers are probably right about me not being a good enough writer to bait you along like I'm supposed to, with skilful titillation admittedly being my greatest literary adversary. So I'm just going to leave you dangling in the interests of effectively delivering a surprise ending later on. Sorry about that, but let's face it. Anytime a first-person narration successfully culminates in a shocking, last-frame twist, you've just been manipulated by a deceitful narrator who obviously knew more than he cared to reveal at any given time. I fully admit that it is my intention to give you a surprise ending of sorts, but the least I can do is be upfront with you about it. Unlike a lot of narrators, I was raised honest. Alex Cross, you should be ashamed of yourself.)

REALITY TV, AND ITS
GLORIOUS RELEVANCE
◇◇◇◇◇◇◇◇◇◇◇◇◇◇◇◇◇◇◇◇◇◇◇◇◇◇◇◇◇◇◇◇◇◇

I NEVER COULD TELL IF old Donald Budgekins was a wise man or not. Our local war hero freely, and proudly, claimed to have been shell-shocked since June 5, 1944. I once told him that the condition was actually called PTSD, and he retorted that French prostitutes were the vice of the inconsequential man. However, like ninety percent of all legally crazy people, he had extended periods of lucidity. It was during one of these periods, when I was nine years old, that Donald stopped his unnerving habit of sharpening table forks with a flint rock long enough to give me his monthly dose of morbidly-depressing wisdom.

"My mammie saw a lot of rough stuff in her day, Bucky," he grumbled to me, lounging in the lawn chair that served as our local airstrip's control tower. "But she said the things that made it worst of all was what was going on behind your own eyes. She used to say that if we had three lives to live, we'd live the first one the way we is right now, spend the entirety of the second one rewatching the home video of every second of the first one, and then spend the third one crying over just about everything we'd seen ourselves do the first time in the second time."

I had to give that one a few moments of thought before blankly replying, "Uh ... what?"

"Forks...." Budgekins rasped, which was generally my cue to head for home. The man got very intense when he reverted back into fork mode, as was readily testified to by many of the servicemen from his old unit, a disturbing number of whom had eyepatches in addition to their other war wounds.

Gramps, on the other hand, was a man of extremely practical wisdom, albeit somewhat eccentrically presented. He didn't appreciate questions that he believed to have obvious answers, although he tended to have poor judgement on what was obvious to the rest of the world. I was eleven years old when I first noticed that he only ever wore one spur while we were out horseback riding, but, much like the mystery of the pickled ear above his headboard, it took several years for curiosity to get the best of me.

"Ain't seen a blue jay in the past few years," Gramps was rambling during a cattle drive to the grazing lease during my sixteenth summer, that lone spur on his left boot glittering in the sunlight and burning into my eyes and psyche. "That's a shame. Always did like seein' blue jays. All we gots is these blamed robin redbreasts, and, man, do I hate them. But blue jays is something else. You look at a blue jay, and you can tell, that there is a buzzard with character. Not as smart as ravens, but a lot classier. One time, I seen this blue jay getting in a scuffle with a bunch of finchy birds, and he was—"

"*Why do you only wear one spur?*" I blurted, unable to hold the question in for another second. Also, I had heard the finch/blue jay smackdown story several times before.

Gramps took about fourteen seconds out of his precious life to stare at me as though I was an imbecile before stating,

"One side of the horse moves, Bucky, the other side won't be far behind."

Of course, once I actually got the answers to the obvious questions, I always ended up feeling like an imbecile anyway. Furthermore, I have had this strange sense of lingering stupidity and needless self-indulgence every time I've buckled on that pointless second spur in the years since.

The weird wisdom of many old people was swirling in my mind as I awoke in the predawn hours on the morning after the bizarre Harvest Potluck of 2009. For some reason, Budgekins' words were at the forefront, pushing past even the enigmatic words of the blind prophet. I finally decided that old Donald had been trying to tell me about living a life worth living, without regrets. As I looked down at Betty-Sue, still slumbering peacefully on the straw tick mattress, I realized that a life worth living for me had to be about doing for others, and most of all for my wife.

That's probably why I immediately got the 411 on a man named Floyd Shorthorn, got him on the phone, and asked him how much he wanted for his front-row tickets and backstage passes to the *Canada's Next Top Best Dance Crew* finale that night. (Having picked up a few haggling techniques from Sassy, I shrewdly figured that a man stupid enough to announce his full name on air upon winning a coveted radio prize wouldn't be that hard to haggle with. As it turned out, all I had to do was promise him $75.00 and a date with my celebrity sister.)

I left Betty-Sue an ambiguous kitchen-table note about making a quick run into Affluenceville for "supplies," and then hurried over to Gramps' cabin, following the sound of raucous snoring to my old room, where the ancient bunk bed was now shared by Corky and Junior when they weren't living out of the tour bus or Junior's Affluenceville condo. (Yeah, we were raised Christian, with Gramps strictly enforcing the "No rings, no bedsprings" policy with Sassy and Junior.)

"Corky, wake up," I whispered, shaking him as tentatively as I could, not wanting to venture too far under Junior's top bunk, which had begun to bear an unsettling resemblance to a threadbare hammock sagging under his massive surface-area-to-volume ratio.

"Mmph," Corky replied. "Get lost, you rooster. It's not even five o'clock yet."

"I need you to make a celebrity appearance to convince a guy in Affluenceville that I'm legit," I explained quietly. "And I need you to help me sell our engaged sister to him. Just for one date."

"Okay, I'm all over it," Corky yawned as he quickly sat up, always easy to rouse when his celebrity side was required. "Get my guitar. One bar of *The Old Pickle Barrel Song* should make a believer out of him. But you're buying the coffee."

Betty-Sue responded with an anticipated level of berserker-esque behaviour when I returned home with the tickets three hours later. As refreshing as her joy was, I immediately thereafter had to suffer through my inevitable daily backfire. In this specific incidence, it took on the form of Betty-Sue assuring me that she would love me forever but, once again, she couldn't possibly help me with the new fence construction for the day, as she was now obligated to spend it in a vain search for an outfit worthy of wearing in the presence of her favourite singer, Britt 2.0. I tried to remind her that Britt 2.0's devotion to her sex-kitten image meant that she probably had little appreciation of any outfit quality, to say nothing of quantity, but my reasoning fell on star-struck deaf ears. (Personally, I consider the pop-diva's personal fashion lineup, sold under the highly-lucrative brand name *Gravity-Defiant Glitter and Lace by Britt 2.0*

Inc, to be the single leading cause of demoralization amongst fourteen-year-old girls in North America, but I'll belay that rant until old-age permits me to get away with being so curmudgeonly. I actually caught myself starting a sentence with "Back in my day...." a few weeks ago. And I liked it.)

Although her clothing choices had occasionally made me wonder whether or not Britt 2.0 had ever known her birth parents, I did have to credit her with actually having a lovely singing voice, which was considerably more than could be expected from most pop stars in the new century, male or female. Add her stunning beauty and natural showmanship into the mix, and it was small wonder that she was an international superstar, although her lyrical quality had a tendency to be cringingly-commercial fodder. (Her lyricists apparently thought that rhyming a breathy "oh baby" with a whispered "just maybe" was the song-writing breakthrough of the new millennium, as this exact lyrical pairing appeared in at least seven of her chart-topper singles. Of course, my own siblings once rhymed "redhead Bucky" with "dead-dead ducky" in a song that topped the Canadian country music billboards for a month and a half, so I'm probably not justified in nitpicking.)

It may seem odd that someone as famous as Britt 2.0 would even be looking for backup dancers in foreign talent competitions, as most pop acts have label-assigned dancers, cookie-cutter varieties of which are prolifically spawned each year in urban subway stations. In fact, Britt 2.0 was one of the few pop acts who didn't fire her dancers every five minutes for giving her "a look," but her hand had been forced by the tragic events of the previous December. Her entire previous crew of hard-partying backup dancers, known appropriately enough as *The High Five,* had overdosed on inert bodily gases previously dissolved under high pressure, after a split-vote decision on whether to go scuba-diving or sky-diving to celebrate the beginning of Kwanzaa had resulted in what seemed to be a fair compromise at the time. ("the time" actually being five minutes after their all-night San Diego beach party finally ran out of booze and aerosol whipping cream containers. Don't do drugs, kids. And don't go to Hollywood.) To her credit, Britt 2.0 still lights a memorial kinara to her fallen employees every December 26th.

Anyway, after another fatiguing day of fencing by myself, I staggered back into the cabin with barely enough time to grab a quick shower before we had to leave. I was still buttoning my blue Sunday shirt as I hurried out of the cabin, while Betty-Sue leaned across the front seat of my old Chevy, honking the horn like an impatient child in a supermarket parking lot. Corky and Sassy were watching in blank confusion from the porch of Gramps' cabin across the dirt road.

"Let's go, lover," Betty-Sue cheered, looking stunning in her favourite little green sun-dress. "Reality television waits for no man!"

"Hey Bucky, where're ya going?" Sassy asked casually, moseying over with her hands in her pockets to see what all the fuss was about. She had traded in her expensive and glamourous "country star duds" for her preferred attire of denim bib overalls, a *Credence Clearwater Revival* T-shirt, and grungy cowboy boots, her tussled muddy-brown hair twisted into her signature twin pigtails.

"Didn't Corky tell you?" I said. "We got tickets to the *Canada's Next Top Best Dance Crew* finale."

"Wow, that's interesting," Sassy said with forced graciousness. "Where're ya going?"

"I just told you."

"No, you didn't," she corrected me. "You ambiguously told me about some tickets you have acquired to attend

Canada's Next Top Best Dance Crew at an unspecified time. That tells me nothing about your current heading and destination."

"Good point," I acknowledged. "We're going to the *Canada's Next Top Best Dance Crew* finale."

"That's tonight?" Sassy said incredulously. "I thought it was eight weeks from now!"

"Why would you possibly think that?" I had to ask.

"*Corky, they're leaving!*" Sassy hollered back at her twin. "They're torpedoing family country fun time!"

"Unspeakable!" Corky blurted, dashing across the road to join in the highly-necessary conversation.

"Can't we just do that tomorrow night?" Betty-Sue groaned.

"On a *Wednesday?*" Sassy said disgustedly, then whispered to me, "Bucky, who is this woman?"

"My wife," I growled. "You were her maid of honour last year!"

"I have no memory of that," Sassy stated, turning her attention back to Betty-Sue. "Lady, you may be new to the Laroo family, but you've got a thing or two to learn about the sacred Tuesday night bonding ritual of family country fun time. We were going to take the H2 up the old long-haul skid trail and watch the odometer roll over to one hundred thousand. It's only seventy-six kilometres away! You can't miss that."

"Hmm," I mused, pondering the admittedly-tempting offer. "Does it promise to be more mind-blowing than when we all watched it roll over to fifty-five thousand, five hundred fifty-five?"

"Exponentially!" Sassy exclaimed. "Jeepers, Bucky, we're actually making a concerted effort at including you in our lives for the first time in thirty years, and you're getting all distant and aloof, as if we're somehow below your attention level."

"Can you tell me how that makes you feel?" I asked, genuinely curious. "Please go into some detail."

My sister's eyes were glossing over with the dawning horror of realization as she admitted, "It makes me feel all ... diminished and unworthy. Wow, it's horrible. Can you imagine someone living their entire life like that?"

"I couldn't even fathom it," I sighed, getting into the truck and cranking the engine into a squealing, puttering life.

"No kidding," Sassy muttered, still looking rattled. "I think I need to go write a song based on this unfamiliar sense of pain and neglect. Junior! Get me a pen and a napkin! Junior? Dang it, where is he? I haven't seen him all day."

"We'll have family country fun time tomorrow night," I called out my promise as Sassy numbly plodded back to her tour bus/writing den. "Sorry, Sassy, but wife trumps sister. I didn't make the rules."

"Nice going, Bucky-brain-of-bean," Corky commented, watching our sister depart. "I've never seen her so shaken up. You and your stupid empathy. Can I come with you? Britt 2.0 is seriously *shmokin'* hot."

"No," I said cruelly. "Now get off the hood of my truck. We're going to be late. And don't try throwing a pitchfork across the road again. You've met enough celebrities."

After previously airing out of Regina, Edmonton, and Toronto, the fourth season of *Canada's Next Top Best Dance Crew* was being hosted for the first time in British Columbia. It was naturally assumed that Vancouver would be the host city, but the eventually-unanimous decision was that there was no more lavish location in all the province than the city of Affluenceville. After that, it was a no-brainer to air the competition live from the world-famous

Tommy Haze's Days of Solomon Party Palace and Casino-Hotel, the shining jewel of Affluenceville decadence. As the name suggests, the seven-star establishment was founded by former Affluenceville tycoon, and Corky's childhood nemesis, Tommy Haze. (Coincidentally, Tommy Haze was one of the many people who tried to kill me during the night that Max-Ram Target saved my life. Just read the first book.) Although his name was still attached to the centre out of "sentimental business reasons," the Days of Solomon was currently owned by various renowned shareholders, including Corky's current nemeses, the other great Canadian brother and sister country-western duo from British Columbia, Ronnie and Cherie Mackenzie, better known by their label-assigned name *The Fighting Mackenzies*. (After failing to kill me, Tommy Haze had been banished for all eternity from Affluenceville and all of his previous forms of affluence, as the city's mayor and council had deemed him to be "a business liability of the highest degree. How are we supposed to trust our investments to a man who can't even murder a cowboy?" Disgraced and outcast, Tommy Haze had migrated to the deep burning south of Chetwynd, British Columbia, where he now operates a really lousy pizza parlour and inline-skate repair shop called Tommy Knows Pizza.)

Apart from the rarely-used Coyote Yelp International Airstrip, there is only one way in and out of my hometown, and it is to the east, requiring one to pass through the luxury resort city of Affluenceville before linking up with Highway 97 which grants you access to the rest of the world. The drive from Coyote Yelp Pass to Affluenceville is anywhere between one and two hours, depending on factors such as weather, road conditions or, more often, road existence. Fortunately, recent local upgrades had renovated the route to a point where it consisted of nearly 35% road,

18% passable goat trail, 28% level rock or packed earth, and only 19% mind-bending terror. As a result, 2009 had been an exceptionally good year for Coyote Yelp Pass commuters, with only a handful of unheeding tourists from down south disappearing en route to our fair town, never to be seen again. Life was good.

Motivated as I was to keep my wife giddy at all times, thereby never allowing her time to ponder why she had married someone like me, I successfully completed the drive into the city in one hour, thirteen minutes, with less screaming than usual. We still had nearly an hour before the finale kicked off, but I knew that, after fighting our way through the inevitable lineup of hyperventilating teenage girls outside the building, we would probably make it to our front-row seats with only minutes to spare.

Teenagers in Affluenceville, as in most urban centres, are a lot like cows. They like to travel aimlessly in herd formations, and they make a lot of superfluous noise while doing so. However, this familiarity makes them quite easy for people like me and Betty-Sue to handle and navigate through. After leaving the underground parking structure, we were able to make our way into the glistening Days of Solomon building in under five minutes with a few tried-and-true cattle sorting techniques. In the process, we only had to deliver a couple of discreet jolts from Sassy's homemade palm-sized cattle prods, aka "Shocking Sillies," into the flanks of a couple of the more ornery adolescent critters. (Need the perfect pocket tool for managing irate cattle or getting your teenager out of bed? Order yours now from the new Cattle Poke Ranch user-friendly online store, at www.lostcauseloot.ca. Just type "The Shocking Silly, Ver. II" into our easy-to-use search engine. Patents pending, must possess valid FAC.)

After being admitted to the building and passing

through a front lobby that looked like the Queen's summer home, we were directed to the massive florescent auditorium at the building's core, which was already packed to capacity with hundreds of hyperventilating teenage girls and their belligerent teenage boyfriends. I was twenty-nine years old at the time, and I had the unshakeable impression that I may have been the oldest person in the room. I guess finding old people in the live audiences of pop-themed reality dance competition airings is about as common as spotting fat women on *CSI: Miami*.

Betty-Sue didn't seem to mind. Her only concern was shouted into my ear as we walked down the aisle to the semicircular front row, the only way to be heard over the incessant screaming and blubbering. (Have you ever noticed that urban teenagers sound exactly the same when they are overjoyed as they do when they are terrified? Seriously, watch the movie *Sleepover Slaughter 3: Burnt Popcorn Aftermath*, and then watch the DVD release of *Britt 2.0: Live at Sing Sing Juvie-Hall*. The first forty-five minutes of both videos sound exactly the same.)

"Shoot, they all have banners and signs!" she shouted. "We should have brought banners and signs!"

"I loathe the fact that I am in this building," I replied. "Please kill me."

"What?" Betty-Sue yelled back, cupping a hand behind her cute left ear. "Can't hear ya, lover!"

We had scarcely taken our seats before the houselights dimmed, and the distinctive first notes of the *Next Top Best Dance Crew* franchise's theme music began pounding out of the ceiling, walls, and floor, although not quite deafeningly enough to drown out the ever-amplifying crowd. Security personnel had already begun forcibly removing the most off-the-wall adoring fans, several of whom had been driven by their delirious revelry to literally start biting the people around them. When blood is spilled before the idolized pop star even takes the stage, it's a safe bet that there's a storm coming, although the full magnitude of that storm would not be revealed to me until several months later. (Britt 2.0 turns out to be secretly evil in the final third of this book. Hey, I told you I was going to be honest. I should also tell you that my secondary motivation for writing this book is because I like money more than I generally care to admit. And I'm not wearing pants right now.)

"Ladies and gentlemen!" an unseen male announcer's voice roared across the auditorium. "Tonight is the night, and the finale starts now! We're down to two spectacular acts, but only one can win the title! The votes are tallied! The wait is over! The results are in hand! Literally, the results are written down on a piece of paper that is in my hand right now. I'm not supposed to have it, but I downloaded it off the tallying mainframe last night, just so that I could make a point to you all. I could tell you who Canada's Next Top Best Dance Crew is right now, and then we could plug the network into live coverage of the genocide going on in various parts of central Africa, and you, along with millions of viewers across the nation, would all go home with information that has shamefully-overlooked relevance to you as human beings. Perhaps you would even be inspired to take a stand and make a difference in a suffering world, giving of our national bounty to help those who have none. But the network producers and advertisers are counting on at least nine commercial breaks in the next ninety minutes, and they write my paychecks, and I have no other life skills, so I'm going to stick with the over-dramatized pointlessness that is this program! That's right, ladies and gentlemen. Get ready for an hour and a half of unabashed celebrity screen-mugging, because this ... is *Canada's Next Top Best Dance Crew*!"

"Forget Britt 2.0," I remarked as the crowd went wild all over again. "I kind of want to meet the announcer."

"*Shh!*" Betty-Sue hissed excitedly. "It's starting!"

Indeed it was. The dimmed houselights had erupted into a psychedelic explosion of multicoloured strobes, spinning spotlights, and various flames and sparklers blasting out of the stage, resulting in an overall lighting effect that would have put a Japanese cartoon to shame. Paramedics were on standby to aid anyone who happened to experience a drama-induced seizure, and the fire marshal was standing near the end of our seat row, with one hand on the nearest exit door and terrified tears in his eyes. It made me proud to be North American.

For a moment I thought that an earthquake was splitting open the wide floor space directly ahead of the front row, but it turned out to just be more pointless drama. Apparently, the panel of celebrity judges had been elevated to a status that made the use of stairs or even their own feet below them. Instead, they needed to emerge from the circular hole in the floor on a raised platform, already seated in their throne-like chairs behind the long white judgement table. Taking contractually-obligated sips of a sponsored soft drink that I do not feel like endorsing right now, the three of them rose into view simultaneously with all the speed of a lineup at the lottery ticket counter with an indecisive senior citizen at the front. The elevating platform added to its own goosebump-raising pointlessness by slowly rotating, thereby allowing the screaming audience to get a glorious three hundred sixty degree view of the British guy, the black guy, and the really loud white lady before reaching floor level and locking into place with a hydraulic hiss that sent a cloud of hot steam shooting up my Wrangler jean legs.

"Yeah, drink it up, Canada," the announcer's voice said dryly. "Whoop it up for your judges, none of whom have actually had to do anything to earn their six-figure weekly salary since you started voting two months ago. Think about it. Two months? For what? To be mean, loud, and street-smart, respectively? I can't take two weeks vacation without eating tuna out of the can for three months in advance, and I still manage to contribute to Amnesty International every month. Seriously, why are they even here? Are we going to die without their input at this stage of the game? And I'm not even going to tell you which one of them never finished high school!"

"Do you think maybe his contract didn't get renewed for next season?" Betty-Sue couldn't help shouting at me, as the crowd responded in their usual delighted manner and the judges glared up at the overhead speaker.

"And now the reason we're all here," the announcer droned on. "Literally, the only reason I've stuck around until this point. Ladies and gentlemen, make even more noise for the richest woman in show-business, and my only reason for getting out of my ex-wife's rented basement suite every morning ... your host, *Britt 2.0!*"

"I have got to meet this guy," I remarked, not even able to hear my own words.

The seizure lighting abruptly cut to a single spotlight locked onto the stage, and Britt 2.0 appeared a moment later, impressing me with her ability to still use her own feet in spite of her celebrity. The blonde beauty was as stunning as ever from head to toe, a fact made all the more evident by her sequined red-and-gold cheesecloth outfit that didn't contain enough woven material to make a decent lampshade. (Did I mention that she turns out to be evil in the final third of this book?)

"I love you, Canada!" she shouted triumphantly into her wireless headset, which was probably the most concealing piece of clothing she had on. "And I love Affluenceville! Moose and maple syrup, baby!"

We all appreciated the effort, anyway. Betty-Sue was on her feet, cheering and attempting to clap, which wasn't easy to do with one hand clamped over my eyes.

"Welcome to the season finale of *Canada's Next Top Best Dance Crew, Season Four: The Search for Britt 2.0's Backup!*" Britt 2.0 cheered, raising her arms over her head like a presidential candidate. "It's down to your final two choices, *Free Movement, Free Minds* versus *Sweet Conformity*. As our enthusiastic announcer has made clear, the results are tallied, but we've got plenty of superfluous dance numbers and celebrity cameos to fill in the next ninety minutes, starting with a live re-enactment of the infamous 'kickback-blowback' scene from last summer's number one Hollywood blockbuster, *Compound Fracture II: Comminuted Shard!* Reprising their award-winning roles are none other than Alexander Godunov as Senator Gore Longfang and, of course, the love of my life ... *Sting Ripblood as Franklin Conagher Pound!*"

Even I couldn't help getting a shiver in my spine as the stage went dark, followed closely by a second shiver when the crowd fell into reverent silence, and Frank C. Pound's trademark one-liner gurgled ominously across the auditorium.

"*Let me reset that for you!*"

Okay, this is probably another example of bad narration, but you've probably already figured out that Sting Ripblood plays a larger role later on in this book, so I'm going to gloss over his first appearance in my life for now. Sure, it was a great, exciting re-enactment, but, according to official polls, ninety-one percent of the world's population has already seen *Comminuted Shard*, so I won't bore the majority of you with a written replay that can't do justice to the theatrical spectacle anyway.

Eighty-five minutes later, the superfluous dance numbers and celebrity cameos had been exhausted, and Britt 2.0 welcomed the final two dance crews to the stage for the winner's unveiling. Opening the solid gold envelope, she dramatically announced, "And the winner is...!"

After four and a half minutes of bated breath, she concluded, "...*Sweet Conformity!*"

The crowd was allowed to cheer for all of ten seconds, and then the credits rolled over the final twenty seconds of the winners' teary-eyed embraces and the runner-ups' silent stares of good-natured venomous rage.

"Okay, it's a wrap!" one of the producers snarled from the base of the stage, never slowing his incessant iPhone texting. "Get this auditorium cleared before I start caving some skulls."

It's a tough business, TV. Even from behind the safety of the yellow backstage pass that was hung around my neck, I felt a little wary remaining in my seat as burly security guards began advancing up the aisles, forcing the hoarse multitudes toward the nearest exits. However, they ignored me and Betty-Sue altogether, and we were soon shocked to realize that we were the only audience members left in the vast theatre.

"These are *exclusive* backstage passes?" Betty-Sue blurted. "How stupid was that Floyd Shorthorn guy? I thought we'd be getting a guided tour with fifty other people!"

A small young man with large spectacles and a premature comb-over appeared at the stage door before I could answer, his thin hands holding a plastic clipboard.

"Pooky Laroo and Betty-Sue Laroo?" he called out, scanning the auditorium, even though we were obviously the only ones remaining in it.

"Yeah, I'm Pooky," I sighed, taking Betty-Sue's hand as we stood from our seats.

"I'm Jerry Fleahop," he whined, beckoning for us to follow him backstage. "Britt 2.0 is expecting you. You will have exactly thirty seconds with her, bearing in mind that a minimum of four of those seconds will be required to access and egress the room, so use the remainder wisely. Please refrain from touching her unless invited to do so, and even then only the areas specified. If she graces you with a direct address, don't raise your eyes above her ankles unless given permission to. Should you have any amount of saliva in your mouth, please expectorate it into these complimentary Dixie cups before speaking to Britt 2.0 to avoid unnecessarily humidifying her. All questions must be screened by myself or another member of her personal staff, unless they are subtly praising statements. For example, you may query, 'Have you always been the most beautiful person in the western hemisphere?' or other questions of that nature. You don't have any lint in your pockets, do you?"

I wondered if it would be appropriate to reply that I had occasionally lost my castrating knife in the midst of all my pocket lint, but decided that this was not the sort of man who would appreciate knowing that his client was in the same building with a man who habitually carried a pocketknife. As we approached the dressing rooms backstage, more and more aides, costumers, makeup artists and security personnel came into view, all of them staring suspiciously at my pockets, which can get really unnerving really fast. I can understand the need to take security precautions around celebrities, but this was getting ridiculous.

Apparently, Britt 2.0 thought so as well. Before Fleahop could even knock on the dressing room door labelled *Britt 2.0: Update last will and testament before attempting entrance*, the lovely starlet had swung the door open and enveloped Betty-Sue and I in a crushing bear hug.

"Wow, I'm so thrilled to meet you!" she whooped, kissing both of us on the cheeks. "Meeting fans is such a hoot, and when I heard you were cowboy and cowgirl.... Even better!"

"Your eminence, please...!" Fleahop whimpered, attempting the pin my arms to my sides, lest I be tempted to return the embrace. He needn't have worried. There was something oddly terrifying about my wife seeing my hands anywhere near the body of a beautiful female celebrity whose outfit looked as though it had been woven from a single spider-web with a few oak leaves patched on for the sake of modesty. It is such oddly terrifying things that are the foundation of any solid marriage. Paranoia kept the spark alive, and my hands deep in my pockets.

"Your M&Ms is busy, Hoppy," Britt 2.0 retorted, dragging me and Betty-Sue into the lavish dressing room, and slamming the door in her manager's face, amid the frantic protests of her equally-neurotic entourage. She locked the door, then turned to hug us again.

"Sorry about Hoppy," she chuckled, guiding us to the world's smallest sofa and pushing us onto it, plopping herself contentedly down between us with her arms around our shoulders. "He's my stepbrother, so I had to give him the job. Trust me, that dude is unemployable. Just forget everything he said. You're with your new friend Britt 2.0, so look anywhere above my ankles that you like."

"Um...." my wife and I said in discomfited unison. As much as I may complain about the aloof nature of most celebrities, it at least gives you space for the traditional boundary testing when you're in their hallowed presences. There is nothing more unsettling than a celebrity who refuses to allow for such periods of adjustment.

"By the way, I'm sorry Sting couldn't stick around to meet you," Britt 2.0 added, playfully twirling Betty-Sue's ponytail in her fingers. "You know how it is being the biggest action star on the planet. He's got to hone his craft every night, so that means about nine hours of working out, combat training, and method acting before he can get to bed tonight, and then he's got to be on set three hours later. But he's so cute when he's devoted. Not like that poser, Max-Ram Target. Sorry if you're fans, but that guy is such a cretin."

"Um," Betty-Sue replied, still trying to untangle her tongue in the presence of her favourite singer.

"C'mon, don't be sheepish," Britt 2.0 chided us, giving me a playful cuff on the back of the head. "You two are normal, I can tell just by looking at you. Do you have any idea how rare it is to meet normal people in my life? I cherish the experience. So tell me all about yourselves. Are you real cowboys?"

"Um," I replied, still trying to get past the fact that I felt like a sardine packed into a can. When you grow up in the open valley, you get used to the sanctity of elbowroom.

"Bucky's been on the ranch since he was five," Betty-Sue finally answered for me, apparently warming more rapidly to our host's invasive, touchy-feely nature than I was.

"Bucky?" Britt 2.0 blurted, nearly giving herself whiplash as she spun around to face me. "Bucky Laroo?"

"Yeah, that's me," I agreed, realizing that both of my arms were falling asleep due to their tight confines between Britt 2.0 and the sofa's armrest.

"No way!" Britt 2.0 exclaimed. "They told me your name was Pooky! You're *the* Bucky Laroo? The Creepy Canadian who tried to kill Max-Ram Target?"

"More or less," I sighed.

I had been expecting a horrified stare, or possibly a

punch to the face, but the pop star was suddenly laughing with glee.

"I have got to shake your hand, Buck," she giggled, pumping my hand vigorously with both of hers. "Anybody who tries to rid the world of that idiot is alright in my books."

"I honestly didn't try that hard," I commented.

"But you tried, Buck, and that's all that matters," she assured me.

"Do you know Max-Ram?" Betty-Sue asked.

"Who doesn't?" Britt 2.0 scoffed. "There isn't a party in Hollywood that he hasn't crashed in the past five years. It's kind of sad, actually."

"How's he doing?" I couldn't help asking.

"Who knows?" Britt 2.0 said dismissively. "His autobiography about the night he saved your life sold like hot cakes, so he's got to be doing okay. *Heh heh!* As long as he's got some kind of spotlight, right?"

"Why did you cackle just now?" I asked.

"I didn't," Britt 2.0 said too quickly. "*Heh heh!* Anyway, he's a best-selling author now. He should be content with that."

"But he wrote that book two years ago," Betty-Sue pointed out. "Have you heard from him recently? I haven't seen him in any of my celebrity gossip magazines in a long time. Actually, I don't think I've heard anything about him except his books since you burst onto the scene two years ago. Awesome debut album, by the way."

"Poo on Max-Ram Target!" Britt 2.0 guffawed, with a suspicious amount of personal disdain. "Forget about him, and let's move on to more pleasant topics. Do you think Canada made the right decision tonight?"

"You mean about *Sweet Conformity*?" I clarified. "They are a heck of a good dance crew. I've never seen such complex synchronized routines. They make most boy bands look like a bunch of arthritic slipper-scuffers."

"Well, you should thank their choreographer for that," Britt 2.0 said, giving credit where it was due. "MC Morlock is amazing."

"MC what?" I asked.

"Amazing?" Betty-Sue cringed. "I saw all his confessional segments before the performances. Isn't he a bit ... you know ... insane?"

"Well, the most wonderful thing about Hollywood is that the ends are always judged above and beyond the means," Britt 2.0 said with a shrug. "Insanity and Hollywood are like water and duck backs. Do you guys want to meet him? Hoppy was supposed to take you to him after you met me, but I'm not going to make you suffer through any more time with that mopemiester. Heck, you know what? *I'm* not spending any more time with him, or any of those other smotherers! Hang on, I'll be right back!"

With the unbridled energy of all spontaneous-natured celebrities, she lunged off the sofa like a startled cat and bolted to the door, yanking it open to reveal more than a dozen sweaty left ears that had been pressed against it, desperately trying to determine whether or not their owners' employer was in any form of peril.

"Attention all staff!" Britt 2.0 barked, as they sheepishly stepped back from the doorway. "Does the term 'breathing room' mean anything to any of you? *I didn't think so!* You're all fired. Get out of my sight, and see Hoppy for your severance checks. Hoppy, can you be a dear and get me something to eat? Hey, Laroos! Are you hungry? I'm old school when it comes to down-home hospitality, like all former-farmgirl pop stars."

"I'm starving," I admitted without thinking, trying to

sound casual while ignoring the horrified expressions and brimming tears of Britt 2.0's former employees.

"Bucky, we can't impose," Betty-Sue whispered. "And somehow it seems even ruder while she's in the process of, uh, firing her entire staff."

"I didn't get supper," I said defensively.

"Ha!" Britt 2.0 laughed. "You two are adorable. Shellfish allergies?"

"No," Betty-Sue sighed, oddly reluctant to accept the generosity of a celebrity host.

"Excellent," Britt 2.0 chuckled. "Hoppy, we need three lobsters, nothing under ten ounces, nine jumbo prawns, and something with tentacles. And I want the lemon butter *clarified* this time! Clarified, I say!"

"Yes, Britt 2.0," Fleahop whimpered, scribbling the order onto his clipboard amidst the wailing and teeth-gnashing of the rest of the recently unemployed entourage.

"Oh yeah, and, once you're finished getting the lobsters and severance checks, you're fired, too," Britt 2.0 added as an afterthought. "You can have my old apartment in Vegas until you get another job ... by which I mean until you get night-schooled enough to be employable at *any* level."

"I'll tell Mom!" Fleahop protested belligerently.

"And I'll tell her what I found under your bed in high school," Britt 2.0 countered shrewdly.

"You want the sweet-chili-garlic rub on the prawns?" Fleahop asked acceptantly.

"That would be lovely," Britt 2.0 said sweetly, slamming the door. "Whew, what a load off my butt that is!"

She turned back toward Betty-Sue and I, leaning contentedly against the door. We smiled awkwardly back at her.

"Not to be rude," Betty-Sue queried, raising an inquisitive hand, "but don't you ... need staff of some sort? I mean, Bucky's family gets by on low-overheads and Junior Van Der Snoot's accounting skills, but you're a bit bigger-time than that, right?"

"Don't you worry your cute tawny head about it, Betty-babe," Britt 2.0 assured her. "This is long overdue. All I was waiting for was tonight's results. My old dance crew were some of the best minio– ...uh, *staffers* that I could ever ask for. But now that I've got *Sweet Conformity* and MC Morlock, I'm ready to take over the world again ... metaphorically, of course. *Heh heh!*"

"Congratulations?" I ventured.

"Yes, it's a great day to be Britt 2.0," the singer laughed, prancing triumphantly back toward the sofa. "It's regrettable, sure, to put thirty-plus people out on the streets, but nobody ever said the music industry was a cakewa–"

She was rather rudely interrupted by a sharp crash and a shower of splinters from the door, as one of her well-dressed, but emotionally-dishevelled, male makeup artists shoulder-slammed the door open with a deranged cry of, *"Nobody's gonna save you now, Britt 2.0!"*

"Holy cow cud!" I blurted as the murderous young man charged into the room, brandishing an eyebrow pencil like an icepick in his perfectly-manicured hands.

"What the...?" Betty-Sue squawked as well, scrambling up onto the backrest of the sofa.

"In the name of vacation days and medical coverage!" the disgruntled job-seeker shrieked as he lunged at our host.

Britt 2.0 had barely flinched when the door burst open, and was actually in the process of rolling her eyes as she spun around and delivered a powerful karate chop into her vengeful former-employee's clavicle and windpipe. He dropped to his knees with his hands clutching his throat, and gaped for air, but Britt 2.0 was not finished with him yet. She gave him a spinning kick to the jaw that dropped him onto his back, and then pounced on him with both knees landing squarely on his rib-cage. Seizing his stylish blonde locks with her left hand, she proceeded to deliver an unrelenting barrage of right-handed haymakers to the left side of his face for roughly thirty seconds, muttering angrily at him all the while.

"I figured one of you would flip out, Ekman," she growled, still pounding him relentlessly. "Honestly, I thought it would be Michaels. Never figured you had it in you. Please know that my continuing rain of blows is actually a sign of respect for your gutsy move. But you should also know that, legally speaking, you have accepted complete forfeiture of all severance and entitlements by coming back in here to exact vengeance, including the snazzy gift bag I had planned to give you. Was it worth it? Huh? Answer me, Ekman! You answer me, boy!"

When it became brutally clear that Ekman was in no condition to answer anymore, Britt 2.0 disgustedly leaned back and crossed her legs, still perched on the barely-conscious kid's sternum.

"Now you're going to walk out of here, aren't you, Ekman?" she said coldly, stroking the side of his battered face with her thumb. "And if you get any funny ideas about calling a lawyer or a press conference, all I have to do is make one little phone call of my own, and then no one's gonna help you. I've got these friends in Cincinnati...."

She let the sentence hang as she rose gracefully to her feet, stooping to wipe the blood from her hands on Ekman's expensive mauve silk shirt.

"Well, that was unpleasant," she stated, although she was struggling to keep a venomous smile from crossing her lips. "Why don't people raise their kids to accept job termination with grace and dignity? It's not his fault that it happened. Life just rolls that way, sometimes."

"Um," Betty-Sue and I replied, just as awkwardly as before.

"*Hoppy!*" Britt 2.0 roared out to the hallway. "Clean up this mess before you go, and I'll give you Ekman's severance and gift-bag cufflinks."

"Yes, Britt 2.0!" was the echoingly whiny reply from the kitchenette several doors down.

"Love you, you're the best stepbrother in the world," Britt 2.0 called back appreciatively, turning back to her cowering guests. "So, where were we? *Sweet Conformity*? They're probably tied up with the media right now, but I'm sure MC Morlock will love you every bit as much as I am. He doesn't like bright lights or colour, so he tends to stay off the red carpet. Wanna meet him?"

"Yes, please," Betty-Sue and I agreed in agitated unison. I'm sure we both wanted to go home, but disagreement with our host suddenly seemed like a really bad idea.

"Then off we go, Buck!" Britt 2.0 cheered, prancing toward the exit. "Ekman, be a dear and tell Hoppy to box up those lobsters and bring them to the dance studio, will you?"

"Yes, Britt 2.0," Ekman gurgled from the floor as we stepped over him on our way out the door, Betty-Sue sympathetically pausing to press a twenty dollar bill into his twitching hand.

I had never watched a full episode of *Canada's Next Top Best Dance Crew* that season, so I had yet to be introduced to the Gothic glory that was *Sweet Conformity*'s creator and manager, MC Morlock. Unlike most oddly-christened celebrities, he had not made the decision to change his name in any way in order to appear more edgy or commercial. His mother, Rosemary Bramford, rumoured to be an equally-mysterious cult priestess, had given him the name upon her deathbed, hoping that it would inspire her newborn son to live a life that was as creepy, despondent, and musically-appreciative as her own. It's a Goth thing, I guess, and, apparently, it had worked. Surviving the gritty world of New York City's underground graveyard scene, MC Morlock had grown into an emaciated, long-nailed, bleach-skinned, scarlet-and-purple-dreadlocked marvel of "New Age Goth" synchronized dance choreography. A firm believer in the mantra that "We are born the walking dead," his deadened white skin was habitually made to appear even deader through liberal applications of black eyeliner, lipstick, and nail polish. As if that wasn't bad enough, in his early teen years he had taken extensive vocal training from the world's most renowned creepy actor, Christopher Lee. Although Lee eventually dismissed his gifted pupil for the mind-boggling accomplishment of creeping him out, the damage was already done.

At the tender age of twenty-two, MC Morlock's passion for ice and bleakness had inspired his immigration to Toronto, Ontario, where he immediately became the driving force of artful creepiness in the Canadian film and music industries on the occasions when he wasn't skulking around the local graveyards, pleadingly whispering for death to stake it's rightful claim on him. The man was annually worshipped as a god at the MTV and Much Music video awards, and had also been named an honorary deathwill ambassador to the city of Salem, Massachusetts, before being hired to effectively creep-out the competition on *Canada's Next Top Best Dance Crew*. On a brighter note, he was also an accomplished sushi chef. Nobody could barbecue *unagi* like MC Morlock.

Had I been privy to any of this information at the time, I might have been more insistent upon skipping the meet-and-greet altogether in the interests of fewer subsequent nightmares, but blissful ignorance, and the ever-present need to keep my wife happy, led me down the hallway behind Britt 2.0 until we arrived at the double doors of the dance studio.

I should have known that something was wrong when Britt 2.0 had to bite her lip and take a deep breath before knocking on the door. I saw her flinch slightly when the ghostly voice of MC Morlock drifted through the door, bearing the challenge, "*Enter, ye who dare....*"

"Gosh golly, I wonder what's keeping Hoppy so long?" Britt 2.0 casually remarked, abruptly turning back the way we had come. "I'll go check on that. You guys have a nice chat, okay?"

Apparently, having minions comes at a price. Betty-Sue and I glanced cautiously at one another before swinging open the creakiest door I had ever heard and entering the studio.

I must admit that, aside from his somewhat startling appearance and tattered black clothing, MC Morlock didn't seem overtly creepy for the first few minutes, as he invited us to sit at a small table with him and have some of his homemade batwing tea, which was surprisingly tasty. He seemed like a genial host as he readily answered Betty-Sue's questions about how he managed to orchestrate such complex synchronisations from his dance crew.

"My methods are unique," MC Morlock admitted humbly, drumming his long fingernails against the tabletop, his five-foot-long dreadlocks hanging over the back of his chair and touching the ground. "Using a combination of hypnotherapy, sensory deprivation, larval-stage insects, and jazz theory, I am able to achieve within my dancers a near-catatonic state of focussed micromovement analysis. When my eye twitches, every one of my boys knows exactly what movement is going to follow, and they know exactly what reaction is expected of them. Perhaps you are familiar with my controversial *MC Morlock Punches People* tutorial YouTube video?"

"Yes, that was amazing!" Betty-Sue said excitedly. "You fake-punched that one *Sweet Conformity* dancer in the face, but all twelve of them reacted at exactly the same instant and got thrown back six feet into a brick wall. I thought it must have been computer graphics or something, but it was so real!"

"Fake-punched?" Morlock said, looking confused.

"And the way you made all that fake blood come from that guy's nose...." Betty-Sue marvelled. "So real."

Morlock smiled, his blackened eyes growing ever wider. "The reality makes it seem so much more real. Have you ever slept in a graveyard, curled up against the headstone of the mother who died giving birth to you?"

"Excuse me?" Betty-Sue said.

"Well, we've got to be getting back to the cows," I said loudly, standing and gripping Betty-Sue's hand. "It's been a pleasure meeting you, Mr Morlock, just like every other celebrity encounter in my life. Betty-Sue, please start inching toward the exit, without turning your back."

"There's something about the coldness of the stone," MC Morlock rambled, still never blinking his bloodshot eyes. "It reminds us that we are only the living dead before we die."

I was physically dragging Betty-Sue from her chair as I stated, "Okay Betty-Sue, I was aiming for subtlety, but I saw a metal bar on the exercise bench behind us, and I want you to pick it up as we continue to back away."

"Yeah, I was just thinking that," Betty-Sue admitted, easily keeping stride with me.

"The dead can only dance for so long, and then they must writhe for all eternity!" MC Morlock shouted after us,

pounding his clawed fists against the table, drawing blood from his palms with his fingernails.

"Congrats on the big win tonight!" Betty-Sue called back as we rushed out the door. "Good luck with the ... lifetime of morbid synchronized despondence thing." She slammed the door behind us and then asked, "Can we run now? I'm suddenly sweating like Roman Polanski's defence team."

"*Dang*, that guy was creepy!" I muttered, as we scurried down the hallway. (I suppose it goes without saying that MC Morlock also turns out to be evil in the final third of this book, but I'm going to say it anyway, so as not to offend all of the harmless and good-hearted creepy Goth people out there. I would also like to state for the record that I am sure there are plenty of non-evil celebrities in the world. They just never seem to meet me for some reason.)

We had made it back into the vacated auditorium when we heard Britt 2.0 calling for us to wait for her. We obligingly paused, although my left hand stayed in my pocket, feverishly clutching the polished casing of my folded castrating knife.

"You can't leave without your lobsters!" Britt 2.0 admonished us, as she rushed over to join us, carrying three takeout boxes. However, she did glance nervously over her shoulder and add, "Also, Hoppy just left, and I don't feel like being left alone with MC Morlock. I'm sure he'll make a great henchma– uh, I mean *manager*, but he takes some getting used to."

"We were about to make a panicked dash for our truck," Betty-Sue freely confessed. "You're welcome to keep up."

"Yeah, good plan," Britt 2.0 remarked, as we all charged out the nearest fire exit, ignoring the alarm we triggered as the door was bashed open. "Let's blow this yogurt stand."

We took a back alley to the parking garage, managing to

sidestep the red carpet, fans, and media in the process. Once we were all safely in my old truck with the doors locked, we relaxed a bit, and I even offered to drive Britt 2.0 back to her hotel, which she gratefully accepted in light of the fact that she had just fired her limo driver. We peeled rubber out of the garage and headed off into the darkening city night.

"Crap, I'm sorry you never got to meet *Sweet Conformity*," Britt 2.0 apologized through a mouthful of lobster. "If it's any consolation, MC Morlock's behavioural modifications have pretty much turned them into a brainwashed army of mini-hims, so you're probably not missing much. But I suppose that's better than most of these homegrown fifteen-minute teenage dance crews nowadays who are always BS-ing about how they're going to use their dance talents to change the world. Ha! In actuality, ninety percent of them won't be able to handle the newfound fame and will be in jail or hooked on meth in a couple of years. Yeah, I said it. You heard it. Off the record, of course."

"Cowboy's honour," Betty-Sue assured her. "So how have you managed to stay clean, if you don't mind my asking?"

Britt 2.0 cackled once more, which seemed to be a disturbing habit of hers. "Some of us strive for bigger things than spotlights, Betty. The blind focus of conquest.... It keeps me on track. Today, reality television. Tomorrow, the...! *Heh heh!* Anyway, Buck, I meant to ask you. As a career cowboy, would you say that you are well-versed in, shall we say ... the way of the cow?"

Betty-Sue and I exchanged shocked looks before I slowly replied, "I guess so. Have you read my book?"

"Book?" Britt 2.0 asked. "What book?"

"My autobiography of the night that Max-Ram Target saved my life," I clarified proudly. "*The Way of the Cow* was the title of the first chapter. By the way, if you're interested in learning the comedic truth of what happened that night, the book's called *Last Stand at Coyote Yelp Pass: The Tragic Cowboy Memoirs of Bucky Laroo, as dictated to Lane Bristow.* I think I've got a few copies in the backsea–"

"Bucky!" Betty-Sue wailed in frustration. "This is not the time! You know I hate it when you do that!"

"You know what I hate?" I remarked. "I hate that they took the '*as dictated to*' part off the cover. Now everybody's going to think that pizza-flipping hack was just making it all–"

"Silence, Bucky!" Betty-Sue snarled.

"Sorry, my little pickled sweet potato," I chuckled. "But I will say this. If I happen to write a second book, and they do it again, I'm gonna freak."

"Yeah, a second book," Betty-Sue sighed. "Brilliant, lover."

"You guys are hysterical," Britt 2.0 was laughing, tossing her lobster shell carelessly out the window.

"Thank you," Betty-Sue groaned. "But why did you want to know about the way of the cow bit?"

"Beats me," Britt 2.0 shrugged with apathetic honesty. "Some weird guy in a white lab coat paid me a million dollars to ask any redheaded northern cowboy with freckles about it while I'm up here, and report back to him immediately. Well, actually he wanted me to report a 'horseman from the northern sun,' or something like that, but it's all the same, I'm sure. Who can understand scientists, am I right, guys?"

"A weird who did what?" I asked, feeling my stomach twisting into a bowline.

"Relax, Buck," Britt 2.0 assured me. "I'm sure he was concerned with finding a cowboy who could somehow be deemed a threat to the entire modern scientific establishment, perhaps even fearing the unshakeable words of some sort of ancient prophecy. Of course, I'm just spit-balling here. And, honestly, I don't see how a cute and loveable loser like Bucky Laroo could ever be perceived as a threat to anybody. *Beep beep!*" she added, leaning across Betty-Sue to playfully tap a forefinger against my nose.

"Did you just say 'ancient prophecy?'" I asked as we pulled into the parking lot of the luxurious Tommy Haze's Let-Them-Eat-Cake Resort & Spa, where Britt 2.0 was currently residing. "What ancient prophecy? Cuz there was this blind prophet who showed up at our Harvest Potluck just last night, and he was all up in my face about some proph—"

"Bucky, don't dominate the conversation," Betty-Sue interjected, giving me a cautionary elbow to the ribs. "Show that much respect for our celebrity guest."

"*Tee hee!*" Britt 2.0 tittered, licking clarified lemon butter from her greasy fingers. "You two have got to be the cutest cowpoke couple I've ever seen. Tell you what. You are so awesome, I'm going to give you my personal cell number and email so we can keep in touch. Seriously, you guys call me up anytime."

"Holy horsehair!" Betty-Sue couldn't help blurting.

"Seriously?" I asked skeptically.

"Absolutely," Britt 2.0 grinned. "Here, let me see your cell phone, or any other electronic device with transmitting capacity that you carry on your person at all times."

Her wording was as unsettling as her frequent cackles, so I was a bit relieved to report, "We don't have a cell phone."

"Ha! I hear ya, Buck," Britt 2.0 laughed understandingly. "I've probably got eight. How many do you have?"

"We don't have any," I clarified.

Britt 2.0's smile was gone in an instant. She stared coldly at both of us for a moment before slowly replying, "Are you saying ... that you have zero transmissions that could theoretically be used to track your every movement via satellite? Is that what you're telling me?"

"Zero," I acknowledged. "But I do have a ballpoint pen. Just tell me your number and I'll write it on the back of my hand."

"Yeah, that's never going to happen," Britt 2.0 snarled, kicking open her door. "Get out of my sight, Pancho and Lefty."

Without another word, she swaggered out of the truck, slammed the door shut, and stormed into the hotel, pausing only long enough to drop the unsuspecting doorman with a well-placed kick to the shins.

Betty-Sue and I stared blankly at our angered guest until she was out of sight. Then Betty-Sue looked back at me and queried, "Did we offend her? I can't think of any term we might have used that could be taken the wrong way. I mean, 'ballpoint pen' is rarely heard these days in our increasingly-paperless society, but I don't think the meaning could have changed too drastically in the past ten years."

"She's a celebrity," I said dismissively. "Look at it this way. We got out of there with our lives, and we got free lobster. I call that a good evening. Can we go home now?"

"Fine," Betty-Sue sighed, slumping against my shoulder as I cut a U-turn in the parking lot. "But did you get the sneaking feeling that we were about to be tagged back there for the benefit of some weird guy in a white lab coat?"

"Tagged?"

Betty-Sue looked troubled as she insisted, "Why would she ask for my phone, and then get angry upon learning that we had, and I quote, 'zero transmissions that could theoretically be used to track your every movement via satellite?' That didn't seem in any way weird to you?"

"Beautiful famous women don't generally offer me their

phone numbers at all," I replied. "I thought that part was a bit weird."

"She offered it to both of us, dim-bulb," Betty-Sue growled. "Did you ever see that movie *I Love Your Work*? Giovanni Ribisi played a Hollywood superstar who gets so starved for normalcy that he starts stalking an average couple. Maybe Britt 2.0 was doing the same thing."

"That seems a bit far-fetched," I noted absently, pulling onto the Affluence Trail West and heading for home.

"What, you think she just really liked us?" Betty-Sue asked sarcastically. "You heard what she said."

"No, I meant the part about Giovanni Ribisi being a Hollywood superstar was a bit far-fetched," I corrected her. "His talent is undeniable, but he's kind of bogged himself down playing eccentric side-characters lately."

"What is wrong with you?" Betty-Sue had to ask. "Seriously?"

"You're overreacting, my little coconut-covered crab cake," I soothed her, putting an arm around her lovely shoulders. "Britt 2.0 is a sweet former-farmgirl with a humble upbringing, like every pop star claims to be. And I'm sure we both misheard her unsettling reference to a weird guy in a lab coat asking questions that seem to pertain specifically to me."

"Do you recall the last sweet former-farmgirl pop star we met?" Betty-Sue reminded me, again not without sarcasm.

"Of course I do," I said. "Her name was Minnie Marshmallow, and I chronicled the story of our tragic relationship in my autobiography, *Last Stand at Coyo*–"

"Stop that!"

"Sorry."

The truth was that my dismissive attitude was simply a ruse to keep Betty-Sue from knowing that I was even more bothered by the events of the past two days than she was. A blind prophet was trying to warn me about something, and an anonymous weird guy in a lab coat was paying celebrities millions of dollars to find me? What the heck? And what was all this talk about a prophecy? Weirdest of all was the fact that I wasn't even supposed to be in Affluenceville that night to meet the celebrity who had been paid a million dollars to report any sightings of me to a guy in a white lab coat. A man named Floyd Shorthorn had won the tickets, but he had blurted out enough information for me to find him, and then he had barely argued with me when I offered to purchase his coveted prize for a bizarrely low price. Could it be that I was somehow destined to meet Britt 2.0 and thereby learn more about some enigmatic ancient prophecy about me? What other explanation was there? It was all too close together to be coincidence.

In the past two evenings, I had been slapped in the face with an overwhelming amount of incomplete information, far too much for any one person to deal with. There was only one thing for a backwoods cowboy to do in the dark of night under such baffling circumstances.

"I'm swinging by Pollywog Wriggle Creek," I decided. "Let's go fishing."

Betty-Sue smiled at the therapeutic thought, resting her head on my shoulder and putting her cowboy boots up on the dash.

"Sounds like a plan, Bucky."

It was well past two o'clock in the morning when me and Betty-Sue returned to Cattle Poke Ranch, our lobster takeout boxes now filled with half a dozen good-sized perch. The angling break from the sudden oddity of our lives had been a welcome one, far more enjoyable than attending reality TV airings, but, unfortunately, the drama of the evening was not quite over.

When we pulled up to our cabin, Corky was sitting on the front porch, sipping from a glass of Old Bessie's milk.

"Hey Bucky, are you going to Kelowna?" he asked innocently, as soon as I stepped out of the truck and into the pale light of the moon and stars.

"Yes," I replied, surprising myself. But, somehow, it felt like the right thing to say.

"Serious?" Corky asked, raising an eyebrow.

I looked over at Betty-Sue as she stepped out of the cab, also studying my face curiously to see if I was serious. I smiled back at her. She deserved the trip down south, but she also deserved more. I decided right then that I was going to make the following June into a belated honeymoon that she would never forget.

"Yes, we're going to Kelowna," I stated. "I don't know why, but we are. Something weird is going on here, and somehow I get the feeling that it's all connected. If it's more tragicness, so be it. But we just inherited Cattle Poke Ranch, and my wife never got a proper honeymoon, so we're going. And you're not."

"Whoever said I was?" Corky replied, rubbing his hands together. "*Heh heh!*"

Betty-Sue's smile was as wide as I had ever seen it as she pounced on me with a huge, sloppy kiss.

"Well, I'm glad you're glad to hear it," I chuckled when she finally stopped to catch her breath.

"Don't tell me you sat out here all night just to ask us that," Betty-Sue remarked to Corky, as she took my hand and stepped onto the porch.

"Well, that was part of it," Corky admitted. "But mostly I needed your house-keys. Sassy locked herself in your cabin four hours ago and she won't come out. Is that lobster with clarified lemon butter I smell?"

THE MAN IN THE
MOON IS CRYING
◇◇◇◇◇◇◇◇◇◇◇◇◇◇◇◇◇◇◇◇◇◇◇◇◇◇

ASSY WAS SITTING CROSS-LEGGED on my kitchen table, surrounded by a dozen lit candles and incense when I unlocked the oak door and stepped into the darkened cabin. She didn't have any cowboy boots or socks on, her hair was hanging loosely over her shoulders, and she was tunelessly strumming her guitar, which appeared to have tacky fingerpainted flowers crudely scrawled all over it. My eyes bulged as I immediately recognized the visible symptoms.

"*Hippie flashback!*" I barked, quickly switching on all the lights and rushing to the fridge for a bottle of BBQ sauce. "Sassy, snap out of it!"

"I can smell them," she whispered, swaying back and forth like a willow in the breeze, her eyes wide and unseeing. "Potpourri and lentils and drain cleaner. Can't you smell them? Mommy?"

"Sassy!" Corky shouted, catching the uncapped bottle of BBQ sauce I had tossed to him and holding it under our sister's nose, while Betty-Sue began frantically shaking her by the shoulders. "C'mon, Sassy, you're stronger than this! Walk away from the floral wreaths! They're not real!"

"There's a centre to it all," Sassy murmured, still unblinking. "We're all part of the cosmic centre...."

"What happened?" Betty-Sue demanded, blowing out the candles and tossing the incense out the door.

"I don't know," Corky said, trying not to panic as he furiously swirled the steak sauce in front of Sassy's blissfully vacant eyes. "She was writing a song in the bus when Junior called on the sat-phone. I handed it to her, and the next thing I know she just hangs up and walks over here. She told me to bug off when I knocked, but then she stopped answering. I thought she had just fallen asleep."

"Get Junior on the phone, now!" I snarled, hurriedly throwing a frying pan on the stove and pouring a few glugs of canola oil into it, cranking the blue propane flame to high. As the oil began to heat, I dug through the freezer for the biggest T-bone steak I could find, quickly ripping off the brown paper wrappings.

"I tried calling him," Corky replied in frustration. "The hot-sounding Telus lady said the number was no longer in service."

"I have no idea what The Age of Aquarius is," Sassy sighed wistfully. "But I'm pretty sure this is it."

"Crap, the BBQ sauce isn't working!" Corky whined. "Bucky, we need that steak, *stat!*"

"Frozen steak in burning oil!" I announced, opening the kitchen window. "Gonna get a little smoky in here, baby! *Fire in the hole!*"

I dropped the icy chunk of red meat into the smoking oil and leapt back as the stove-top let out a deafening roar, spitting droplets of grease into the air. My Sunday shirt was instantly covered in grease spots, but the ploy worked. Sassy blinked for the first time in who knows how long, and began to sniff the air.

"Meat," she rasped, licking her dry lips. "Sassy like meat."

"Sassy love meat," Corky assured her, hugging his twin in sweet relief. "And shotguns and air pollution and establishments."

"What the crap happened to my guitar?" Sassy demanded, staring in horror at her garish floral instrument and the smudges of paint on her fingertips. "Where's my socks? Why am I on this table? Where'd my pigtail elastics go? *Bucky!* This is every bit your fault!"

"She's back," I said with confidence. "Just relax, Sassy. Your steak will be ready soon. We're going to make you all better."

Once we had her on the couch and gave her the steak, she began to recall the preceding events that had driven her to such a relapsed state.

"Junior's gone!" she wailed, still biting off as much steak as she could cram into her mouth at one time, ignoring her utensils completely. "He's gone and he's never coming back! I've lost my fiancé, band drummer/classical pianist, and business manager all in one night! What am I gonna do, Bucky? I'm a thirty-three-year-old single woman trying to make it in the music industry! I'm going to end up in a freakin' *laundromat!*"

"But Junior's been your fiancé for twelve years!" Corky protested. "Why would he ever leave you?"

"And the statement answers the question," Betty-Sue remarked, munching on her last cold jumbo prawn.

"That could explain why he kept giving me *The Book of Job* for our engagement anniversary every year for the past four years," Sassy admitted. "I had started to wonder about that."

"Look, Sassy," I groaned, "this is an easy fix. Call him, apologise to him, and then *marry him!*"

"I'll never find him," Sassy whimpered, sucking a mouthful of BBQ sauce straight from the bottle. "He said he was getting one of those hobo sticks with the bundle of stuff on the end so that he could go out to seek his fortune. And he's dramatic enough to mean it right now. He's *gone*, Bucky! Gone!"

"What happened?" the rest of us asked in impatient unison.

"Dumb ol' Flat Ed and Rita," Sassy said bitterly. "They pushed Junior to the brink last night with all their brainless bubbling about short engagements. And then the weirdest thing happened tonight. Some guy named Floyd Shorthorn called Junior and asked if I was there because he had a date with me! Junior said that was the last straw, so he left."

It took me a moment to realize that, for the first time in our lives, the predicament really was every bit my fault. I was the one who had promised Floyd Shorthorn a date with the lead vocalist of *Lost Cause Kin* in exchange for his backstage passes. Now, my beloved sister had been dumped, and I was to blame.

"Um, I'm sure this isn't your fault, Sassy," I said with a nervous laugh. "Not even close to your fault, actually. Why don't we chalk this one up to the old tried-and-true 'Bucky, this is every bit your fault,' and leave it at that ... without asking for anymore specifics?"

"What?" Betty-Sue said, squinting suspiciously at me.

"I couldn't do that!" Sassy declared, turning to put her BBQ-covered hands on my shoulders.

"No, really, I insist," I really insisted, glancing around the room to make sure that my volatile sister's cherished Bucky-Blaster shotgun was nowhere in sight. This seemed like an occasion when it might actually earn its christening.

"Forget it, Bucky!" Sassy sobbed, grabbing me in a crushing hug. "You are the awesomest, gnarliest, radicalest, bossest, most tubular, far-out baby brother in the world, and I'm not going to use you as my problem pincushion anymore! I brought this unspeakable horror on myself all by myself, and I'll work it out by myself, like a real man does."

I could always tell when Sassy was emotionally-unguarded, as she had a tendency to slip into extinct 80s lingo ... and refer to herself as a man.

"That's truly commendable, big sister," I gurgled, struggling to breathe in her smothering embrace. "But, just this once, this might actually be my fault."

"Silence, Bucky!" Sassy blubbered, her face a waterfall of lachrymose secretions. "I have to take responsibility for my own cataclysms. You've selflessly thrown yourself onto half of the grenades that I've fumbled in my lifetime, and I've dismissively thrown you onto the other half. I won't hear of it, ever again! Let me suffer my own flak for once, that I may learn and move forward, as a man should. Now, if you'll excuse me, I need to take this newfound sense of heartbreak and anguish to a place of seclusion and write a song with it."

"Wait, Sassy," Betty-Sue interjected, putting a gently-restraining hand on Sassy's arm, thankfully preventing my sister from reaching her guitar on the coffeetable. "Would it help if we all took the H2 up the old skid trail and watched the big one hundred grand rollover together? Family country fun time?"

"Actually, that would be really nice," Sassy choked, briefly brightening up before the next wave of hiccups and tears overtook her.

It really was a nice ride up into the mountains in the black of night, and the long-anticipated odometer rollover moment itself put most New Years Eve celebrations to shame.

In spite of the family country fun time pick-me-up, Sassy was obviously despondent over the following months, as fall turned to winter and 2010 drew ever nearer, but she bore it with an unusual dignity, never once blowing up or melting down. Well, at least not until she was in front of an international audience at the 2010 Winter Olympic Closing Ceremonies in February, but that's another story altogether. We all tried to cheer her up, but it wasn't much use. Junior had disappeared without a trace to "seek his fortune," taking only a long stick and a wheel of cheese wrapped in a handkerchief with him as he had promised, and we hadn't seen or heard from him since. Some experts say that it takes a third of the relationship's total duration time for the pain of a breakup to wear off, so I figured Sassy would be back to her old self by about 2014, unless the Mayan calendar interceded as predicted.

She did cheer up a little when Gramps unexpectedly announced that he was not going to let his retirement from ranching turn him into a useless rocking chair magnet, and that he was therefore going to assume the abandoned mantle of management for *Lost Cause Kin* that Junior had left behind. Sassy may have been heartbroken, but having a competent band manager at least meant that she would always have the salve of ready-available finances, and that was better than a horseshoe to the head.

It was a strange day when Gramps took the reins of management for my siblings' band. I had no idea that my passive, laidback grandfather had a caged tiger of ruthlessness inside him, just waiting to be unleashed on the country music world and its vastly under-prepared executives. (I distinctly remember overhearing one of his calls, wherein he told legendary music producer Elias Katzenberg, "It doesn't matter how I got this number. What matters is that my clients are not the lice-ridden street corner buskers you seem to think they are. Now get your boss on the phone!") Sure, I had never once seen him come out on the wrong end of a cattle sale or horse trade, but it was something else entirely when he showed up at the breakfast table on his first day of managerial duties. He still wore his usual jeans and western belt with the brass moose-head buckle, but the belt now held a lot more than just his Leatherman Super Tool pocketknife and a spare set of work gloves. His electronic accessories were truly impressive for a man who had not seen a touch-tone phone until the year 2002. My country grandpa, after demanding an exorbitant "seed money" advance payment from Corky and Sassy, was suddenly immersed comfortably in a world of pagers, PDAs, Blackberries, cell phones, a satellite phone, laptop computers, regular computers, and even a Kindle touch pad for some reason. As Coyote Yelp Pass still had no cell phone transmitter, Gramps' new trade tool of choice was the controversial Pakistani-made *Corn Popper 9000 Amp-Plus Bluetooth.* Its experimental self-contained micro-transmitter advancement offered to revolutionize communications technology by effectively eliminating dead-zones, but it had yet to meet the safety standards of North America, as all of the technicians developing the earpiece had an irritating habit of dying from sudden-onset brain cancer, making the *Corn Popper 9000* a highly-coveted contraband item in both Canada and the United States. (Gramps got his from a guy in a van.) Nobody on the ranch got brain cancer, but there were other unsettling effects of the earpiece, most notably the fact that lightweight metal objects seemed to continually gravitate towards Gramps whenever he entered a room. Old Bessie's milk began forming curds and whey before it even left the udder, and the old rabbit-eared television set in my cabin started picking up channels from Uzbekistan. Old Donald Budgekins was the first person in town to get a GPS in his truck later that month, and he would forever claim that the only thing the eloquent lady in it did was let out a single wail of "Abandon all hope, ye who enter here," just before the entire unit caught fire and melted into the dashboard. (On an interesting sidenote, a noted mathematician recently collaborated with a noted conspiracy theorist/dietician and a noted celebrity scientologist to calculate humanity's remaining time at the top of the food-chain. They concluded that human technology will never be able to advance beyond its three current pinnacles, namely the nursing-home favourite *Wood Curer 9000 Lifeless-Alert* pendant, the atomic particle accelerator, and microwaveable steam pouches of frozen cauliflower. Apparently, their calculations indicated that our ever-increasing exposure to the electromagnetic radiation being emitted by every known electrical device, combined with the likelihood of London smogs becoming self-aware and sentient within the next fifteen years, will result in sharp increases of early-onset cancers that will eventually overtake the global population growth curve. This, in turn, will result in future generations dying before they're old enough to get smart enough to figure out that their beloved wireless-electric O2 therapy masks are inadvertently irradiating their supplemental oxygen during every spa day at the day spa. Well, it made sense in the article. I don't want to be paranoid, but I've seriously been thinking about eating ants ever since I saw that *Medicine Man* movie with Sean Connery.)

The mellowest person in all of Coyote Yelp Pass during the first months of 2010 was Corky, and that, in and of itself, was enough to make me uneasy. For one thing, he had not mentioned the trip to Kelowna that Betty-Sue and I were planning since we had confirmed our intentions to him in the early morning hours of September 2, 2009. I would occasionally catch him in the middle of undertoned telephone conversations in Gramps' cabin or the tour bus, but he would just smile mellowly at me, and quickly hang up without even saying goodbye to whoever he was bargaining with. I tried not to let it bother me, choosing instead to deal with my daily chores and the upcoming calving season.

I also tried not to let the increasingly-distant words of both the blind prophet and Britt 2.0 bother me, and, admittedly, it got easier after a few days. I knew that it all couldn't just be coincidence, but I reminded myself of how many cattle tramplings I had endured over the course of my cowboy existence, and suddenly even the possible curse of an ancient prophecy didn't really bother me. Heck, after you've been trampled by cows a few dozen times, nothing really bothers you anymore.

They say that when March comes in like a lamb, it goes out like a lion, and the March of 2010 came in like a pink lamb with cotton candy wool who poops gum drops in a pasture of rainbows. Needless to say, the raging lion arrived well before the middle of the month, in the guise of a blizzard that lasted for roughly eighteen days and kept us scrambling to keep our newborn calves sheltered. However, May did bring the green of spring eventually, sometime around the 27th if I remember correctly, just in time for Betty-Sue and I to begin planning our long-overdue honeymoon. (I'm not sure if Kelowna is really a prime lovers' getaway, but, when you grow up in a town that still mass-produces and stores suet for the harder winters, any form of urban vacation begins to feel like a trip to The Big Apple.)

Gramps had assured us that he wasn't retired enough to let "his" cows go unattended, and so agreed to watch the ranch over the four-day weekend that we would be gone. Corky and Sassy, who hadn't had a concert since the Olympics debacle, (I'll get back to that in a minute.) casually said that they would help him out, if they had time. Then they had both laughed uproariously. I could only assume that to mean that Sassy had been let in on whatever plot Corky had been hatching for nearly a year. And Sassy's involvement in anything labelled as a 'plot,' particularly in her emotionally-unbalanced state, was enough to give me a peptic ulcer. However, my scheming siblings gave no other sinister vibes as the days rolled by, even pitching in and helping out with the ranch chores with more vigour than usual, and a lot less complaining.

All in all, it had just been a typical spring in Coyote Yelp Pass. The biggest news of the year thus far was that Sting Ripblood and Britt 2.0 had returned to Affluenceville, which was once again considered to be a suitable double for Los Angeles, to begin filming Sting's latest inevitable blockbuster, *Compound Fracture IV: Greenstick Pinch.* Apparently, Britt 2.0, like all pop stars, had decided to make a token movie, although a role in the *Compound Fracture* franchise was a considerably better deal than most of the vehicle flicks that so many other pop stars ended up with. As Corky had so eloquently wailed a few years before, "Seriously, Mariah Carey, what were you *thinking?*" (Corky wasn't the only one left wailing by a pop star movie. According to various media reports, the producers of *America's Next Top Best Dance Crew,* and series creator Nigel Wexworth, were once again devastated by the lost opportunity to have Britt 2.0 featured in their show that year. Disillusioned beyond all reason by the two-time dreamkill, Wexworth summarily abandoned his hit franchise in the interests of pursuing reality television that was in no way dependant on beauty or talent. He has since moved to Arizona, where he quickly found fulfilment and solace documenting irate senior citizens physically assaulting one another in seedy bingo halls, in the bestselling DVD series *The Wars of B-4: Sun City Nights.*)

The morning of the big day finally arrived, Friday, June 25th, 2010, and it was a beautiful, if oddly warm morning. I remember the warmth well, because I had to sneak into the barn in the darkened predawn hours to retrieve the silver bracelet I had hidden there as a surprise gift for Betty-Sue. I hadn't even been in the building since calving season ended the month before, and I was almost overwhelmed by a wafting, putrid stench, like rotting vegetables. The noxious smell made my eyes water, and I had to stumble back outside, coughing.

"What the heck?" I muttered, glancing back into the barn and shining my flashlight around for any sign of the offending odour's source. All I could see was oiled horse harnesses and the fresh straw that had been laid down on the floor after the last of the manure and afterbirth had been removed.

"Hey, Bucky," Sassy said, appearing suddenly from behind me. "What are you doing?"

"What are you doing up?" I coughed, wiping my stinging eyes.

"Ever since Junior left, I habitually walk the night," Sassy replied evenly, her hands in her overall pockets. "That MC Morlock guy might be onto something. What are you doing?"

"I hid a present for Betty-Sue in here," I replied. "What the sandhill is that smell?"

Sassy took a quick whiff, her discerning olfactory senses beginning their rapid computing before even she was forced to take a step back.

"Interesting," she gagged. "Smells like bad radishes."

"It's not bad radishes," I growled. "Bad radishes smell completely different."

"I'll get your present," Sassy offered, snatching my flashlight. "You hid it under the floorboards of the maternity pen, right?"

"How did you...?"

"I used to hide my owl pellet collection down there," Sassy said dismissively. "I'll be right back."

Before I could cautiously inquire as to what exactly an owl pellet was, my sister drew in a deep breath, charged into the barn, and returned twenty seconds later with the small cherry wood box, thankfully still sealed in a couple of clear zip-loc freezer bags.

"Good luck on your trip, baby bro," she said, after gasping for breath. "You'll have to tell me all about it when you get back, because, of course, I'll have no idea what transpired. *Heh heh!* Now, if you'll excuse me, I must walk the foggy predawn hour."

"It's not foggy out he–"

"Silence, Bucky. Don't ruin the moment for me."

I didn't feel like picking up anymore off-putting scent molecules before my big trip, so I decided to deal with finding and evicting whatever had died in the barn after I got back, as it wasn't currently in use anyway.

Even Corky was up by the time 4:00 a.m. arrived, and he and Sassy giddily waved at the departing truck until they thought we couldn't see them anymore. Then I caught one final glimpse of my siblings exchanging high-fives in my rearview mirror, and I thought I heard them letting out ecstatic rooster crows, which was rarely a good indication of what was to come.

"They seemed awfully excited, didn't they?" Betty-Sue speculated, putting her bare feet up on the dash in preparation for the long drive. "Isn't it exciting when they're all mysterious like that, Bucky? I can only imagine what kind of wonderful surprise they must be planning."

"Oh, I'm absolutely positive that they're planning a surprise," I said blandly. "I can only plead with God for it to be a wonderful one."

"I'll bet it's a present," Betty-Sue guessed eagerly. "They

probably feel bad about only getting us that ball of cow hair that they picked off the barbwire fence for a wedding present, so they're planning something spectacular to make up for it."

"Spectacular is very likely," I agreed, trying to relax my twitching left eyelid.

The trip into southern British Columbia was an all day venture, but very relaxing and peaceful, as no province in Canada can boast of more scenic splendour than ours. After the first few hours, the Rockies began to thin out and lower into the foothills of the Peace Region, and then a few hours later we drove into the more open cattle country of the Cariboo ranges. Betty-Sue's new digital camera was clicking and whirring every couple of minutes it seemed, documenting our belated honeymoon for posterity.

The night was well settled in when Betty-Sue spotted a large road sign and grew suddenly excited.

"Omigosh, that's it!" she blurted. "That's Kelowna! We're there!"

"How can you tell?" I asked. I had only glanced at the sign, but I was certain that it had not said Kelowna.

"Didn't you see the sign?" Betty-Sue said, gripping my forearm in excitement. "It had a picture of the Ogopogo, and it said '*Canada's National Monster Land, 25 km.*' We're almost there!"

"If you say so," I replied. "Everything south of Prince George looks like one big city to me."

Betty-Sue glanced at me skeptically. "You thought the icefields on the Yellowhead South through the Rockies looked like a city?"

"Comparatively," I said. "The glaciers moving through our backyard look way less urban than that."

"*Touché*," Betty-Sue admitted. "Why did Gramps build the ranch in that glacial trench, anyway?"

"Well, it's got great drainage if you can find a decent piece of bedrock. And the glaciers were eighteen miles away sixty years ago."

"That broken shale is not bedrock," Betty-Sue pointed out. "The woodshed was southeast of Gramps' cabin door when we started dating. Now it's due west. That cabin is moving downhill faster than the ice."

I had to think about that for a moment before recalling, "You know, I once told Sassy that I remembered hitching the horses on the other side of the woodshed, and she told me that I needed amniocentesis."

"Amniocentesis?"

I shrugged. "Well, she also thought that it had something to do with invasive removal of plaque from the blood vessels in the brain."

"Ooh! Ooh!" Betty-Sue was chattering again, eagerly pointing out the window. "There's another sign! We're getting closer."

I cringed as I read the monster-festooned sign aloud. "'*Welcome to Kelowna: Bloodthirsty Water Demon Capital of Canada.*' Is that an authorized municipal posting?"

"Municipalities love that kind of stuff," Betty-Sue said confidently. "It gives them a sense of identity. And it distracts tourists from the high murder and drug per capita rates.... For the record, I mean no disrespect to Kelowna specifically."

I looked strangely at her before asking, "Is that the official reasoning, or do you just have a really grim outlook on stuff like this?"

"Life is grim when you live in the trenches, son," Betty-Sue said darkly.

I was impressed. "Wow. Dramatic."

"I gave myself goosebumps," Betty-Sue giggled. "Hey,

there's another sign! '*Come Greet the Lady of the Lake Who Has Green Scales and Fangs.*'"

"You know," I had to comment, "I may very well be the worst writer in the world, and even I can tell that's just lazy scripting."

A couple of minutes later, the lights of Kelowna came into view, revealing it to be the largest city that Betty-Sue and I had been to since our ill-fated flight down to Vancouver for the 2010 Olympic Closi– Wait, did I mention that we had been to the Winter Olympic Closing Ceremonies that February? Crap, I'm a bad narrator. Sorry. Let's pause for a moment, stranding Betty-Sue and I on the outskirts of Kelowna, and rewind back a few months.

February 28, 2010 was a great day for Canadian pride as our country was able to claim more gold medals than any other nation in the history of Winter Olympics, including the first domestic gold medals ever won on Canadian soil. We even got to end the day on a glorious note, as Sidney Crosby scored his epic gold-winning overtime goal for Team Canada in the Men's Hockey Finals against the United States. It felt good to be Canadian that day, even though Betty-Sue and I only arrived into Vancouver International Airport in the late afternoon, with barely enough time to get a cab to BC Place for the Closing Ceremonies.

The entire trip was Corky and Sassy's treat, which was much appreciated. Corky had figured that a week in the city would do Sassy a lot of good, and help to get her mind off Junior, so the two of them had brought the bus down for the final week, leaving me and Betty-Sue airline tickets to join them on the last evening. We barely had time to find seats in the enormous centre before the spectacular ceremonies began, mostly because I was recognized by a female reporter from a noted Canadian news network.

"Bucky Laroo!" she was shouting as she charged through

the crowd with a microphone in hand and a protesting cameraman in tow. "Bucky Laroo! Oh, good heavens, I couldn't believe it when I saw you! Could we get a few thoughts on the games before the ceremonies start?"

The thought of more media publicity made me cringe, but there was no escaping the microphone that was being shoved in my face, so I agreed as Betty-Sue beamed proudly.

"Did you hear that, Lloyd?" the reporter excitedly chattered into her earpiece. "We've still got two minutes to fill, and he's ready…. Dang it, Lloyd, this is the Creepy Canadian we're talking about here…! Good, let's just roll it!"

"Okay, we're on live in five," the cameraman morosely announced. "Four … three … two … go."

"Well, Lloyd," the chipper reporter said into the camera, "there's no shortage of big names here at the 2010 Winter Olympics, but the event also draws its share of extremely small names that the world just cannot forget, no matter how much we all pray to. Some of you may recognize the cowboy beside me. On paper, he has been called the greatest fictional Canadian heroine with red hair since Anne of Green Gables…."

"Fiction?" I whispered irritably to Betty-Sue. "I told you that would happen!"

"Among those of us in the real world who bother to acknowledge his existence, he has been called the rule-proving exception to survival of the fittest," the reporter continued. "That's right, ladies and gentlemen. I'm live at BC Place with noted kidnapper, attempted murderer, and former ENRON executive, Bucky Laroo. Mr Laroo, do you have any thoughts on Sidney Crosby's gold-winning goal in the Men's Hockey Finals?"

"Um, it was pretty amazing," I sighed. "And I'm a cowboy. I was never an ENRON exec."

"Did you get that, Lloyd?" my interviewer blurted into the camera, clamping a hand over her earpiece. "Ladies and gentlemen, remember that you heard it here first! We have just received official confirmation of Bucky Laroo's kidnapping and attempted murder allegations!"

"What?" I demanded. "No! I'm not confir– You know what? That is just ... cheap."

"Mr Laroo," she explained patiently, "in the wake of your well-deserved notoriety, we received literally thousands of conflicting secondhand reports from people who were in no way involved with the event, but the one consistent factor in all of them is that you kidnapped iconic Hollywood action hunk Max-Ram Target, and then tried to kill him in order to ritualistically placate your cannibal impulses."

"That was the consistent factor?" I said incredulously.

"Okay, interview over," Betty-Sue snapped, snatching the microphone. "Lloyd, you're supposed to be better than this. Let's go, Bucky."

We found our seats, and the closing ceremonies began in grand fashion, including the unforgettable athletes march around the vast indoor arena. After final speeches from Canadian Prime Minister Stephen Harper and other distinguished leaders, the entertainment began with a crowd-stopping performance by Canadian music legend Neil Young.

"Omigosh, this is it!" Betty-Sue whispered after the standing ovation, barely able to contain her pride and glee. "Corky said they're up next! To think, your brother and sister are the second entertainment act of the greatest live show of the year! You must be so proud, Bucky."

"I am," I admitted, beaming involuntarily. "Corky's been telling everyone that Neil Young is his opening act. Look! There's Sassy!"

Corky loved being introduced, and so had agreed to

let Sassy appear first, rather than taking the stage together. Always one to make an entrance, Sassy was indeed drifting down from the domed roof in a glowing pink hot air balloon, illuminated by a dozen spotlights from all around us. The crowd cheered wildly as they spotted her, and she teased them with a few strummed bars of *The Old Pickle Barrel Song* on her guitar.

"This is the best day ever!" Betty-Sue whooped, waving both arms at Sassy, hoping my sister would spot us. "Sassy really needed this."

I had to agree, but I didn't, because I had noticed something else. Sassy was still blandly strumming her guitar, but was now close enough that I could see her face. Something was wrong. Her cheeks were flushed red, and her entire face was pulsating and contorting, as if she had been attempting to hold back a sneeze for the past ten minutes.

"Is she ... crying?" I asked.

"What?" Betty-Sue shouted back over the din.

"*QUIET!*" Sassy screamed into her headset, nearly deafening every international and domestic guest in BC Place. I have never heard that much silence fall so fast in a space that crowded. Tens of thousands were silenced in an instant, as well as hundreds of millions watching from around the world.

It was then that I realized that Sassy had actually been bottling up her emotions over Junior's departure for the past months, and had selected a very inopportune time to release them.

"What the crap are you all cheering about?" she demanded, vaulting over the basket rim and lightly dropping the last five feet to the ground. "Do you think Canada has anything to be cheering for? Who gives a dang if we won more gold medals than any nation in the history of the event? *Big freakin' deal!* Total medal counts are all that matter. That's it! Yeah, I can say what we're all thinking. It's Germany and America stealing the spotlight, people, just like it's World War II all over again. You think Canada's got something to brag about? Do you? We got *nothing*, Canada! *I hate you, Sidney Crosby!*"

She paused for a few moments to let sufficient shock and horror sink into the entire delegation of international athletes and dignitaries, casually strumming her guitar once more.

"I'd like to dedicate this first song to all you filthy traitors who won silver medals for Team Canada. Silver? Seriously, what were you all thinking? Seven silver medals that could have been gold. Hey, here's an idea. I heard a rumour that ten vampires and werewolves are planning an imminent invasion of Canada, so let's melt those seven silver medals down into seven silver bullets, and that way we'll be seventy percent less screwed when the day of bloodsucking judgement comes. I call this new song *If It's Not Gold, It's Frog Flop.* I hope you like it." She took a small sip of water from the bottle on her hip, and then began singing.

> *"I can smell the reek of silver,*
> *Taste the bitter burn of bronze...."*

That was as much as I could make out before the booing and screams for Laroo blood overwhelmed the sound system.

"I don't think it's a good time or place to be a Laroo," I shouted into Betty-Sue's ear.

"Yeah, let's get out of here," she agreed, clutching my hand and heading for the aisle. "If anyone asks, we're Buddy and Janis T. McKritch."

"Janis T. McKritch?" I echoed, as we ran up the stairs to the exit, fighting our way past the most zealous patriots who were charging down in ever-increasing numbers, converging on the arena where my sister still stood alone, blissfully strumming and singing.

"Oh sure, like you've never made up a secret agent name and prayed for a chance to use it someday," Betty-Sue retorted.

We made it safely to the performers' parking structure, and Betty-Sue had just spotted the Bucky-Paver tour bus when a renewed ruckus erupted from behind us. I spun around in time to see Corky and Sassy racing into the garage, clutching their guitars for dear life, and rightfully so. Legions of enraged Canadians were hot on their heels and gaining fast.

"Start the bus!" Corky was hollering at us. "They jumped the barriers and overwhelmed security! *Start the bus!*"

"Lover...." Betty-Sue said uneasily. "Start the bus."

"Run!" I shouted, yanking her by the hand and leading the charge to the bus, frantically and futilely clicking the stubborn auto-start pad on my key-chain.

It was a pretty glum twenty-hour drive back to Coyote Yelp Pass, especially for Corky. Only a couple of minutes after our narrow escape, he received a cell phone text message from none other than Canada's loveliest athlete, British Columbia's own ski-cross gold-medalist Ashleigh McIvor, who assured him in no uncertain terms that their planned date for later that evening was indefinitely postponed. It was a great day for Canada. Not so great for Canadians named Laroo.

With the clarity of hindsight, I can safely assume that Corky informed Sassy of whatever his devious plot was shortly after this unpleasant incident, as Sassy seemed as mellow and inscrutable as Corky was by the time we got back home. And they both stayed mellow as their entire spring touring schedule was cancelled within the next week.

(Ironically, their record sales simultaneously went through the roof in the United States and Germany.) They just dove right into their ranch chores with all the vigour that they had possessed in the days before *Lost Cause Kin* was even formed, smiling all the while with a quiet inner peace.

"Temporary setbacks, Bucky-baby," Sassy had calmly assured me after three months without a concert, or even a local honky-tonk performance. "The inevitable reclamation of our fame is at hand, so have fun in Kelowna ... not that the two are related in any way. *Heh heh!*"

Needless to say, her words were at the forefront of my mind as Betty-Sue and I finally arrived in the beautiful city of Kelowna late in the evening of June 25th, but I was still trying to ignore them. We parked at the rather upscale, albeit predictably monster-themed, hotel that the Hawkins Cheezies people had booked for us, and were greeted in the lobby by a polite young man named Gil, who stated that he would be our driver and tour guide for the remainder of our trip. We thanked him, then excused ourselves to the monster-themed restaurant for a romantic midnight meal before heading to our monster-themed room. That city was truly obsessed with monsters. (Our hotel room had an autographed portrait of Peter Lorre on the mantle instead of a television. It was weird, and kind of killed the romantic mood I had hoped to pursue.)

I admit that I was surprised to open our hotel door the next morning, only to find the well-dressed Gil asleep in the doorway, curled up so that his glossy leather shoes would not trip other people using the hallway in the middle of the night. I'm not sure if it was part of his job description to be at our beck and call, 24/7, or if he was just very devoted to his craft. I never asked.

Okay, I'm not sure if this makes me a bad writer, but I'm going to effectively gloss over the entire Hawkins Cheezies portion of our Kelowna trip. I am doing this partly because the events directly related to the ribbon-cutting ceremony have little relevance to the story that I am telling you, and also because Gil's meticulous seven-hour tour of the new Hawkins Cheezies factory was possibly the most brain-liquifying experience of my life. Nothing takes the joy out of junk food like finding out how it's processed and packaged.

Anyway, we managed to shake Gil off our tail around five o'clock, just in time for my big planned surprise of the evening. I made Betty-Sue wear a blindfold as I drove us out of the monster-muralled city, taking an old dirt road south along Lake Okanagan. You see, after deciding to take the trip to Kelowna, I had contacted an old cowboy friend of Gramps named Grits K. Yahoo. Like Gramps, Grits used to ranch around Coyote Yelp Pass, albeit on a considerably more well-to-do operation, but a tragic back injury had forced him to retire from the cowpunching world. He had moved to Kelowna in 1995 to run an exclusive dude ranch, where he specialized in romantic trail rides along the Okanagan shore. I had told him to have the full package waiting for us, regardless of cost, and he had more than delivered, being one of the few former Coyote Yelp Passians to remember me fondly. (Betty-Sue's mother, Stella, who lived in Affluenceville for many years after divorcing Bob Perkins, still doesn't put my name on our Christmas cards. I'm not sure if she even knows what my name is anymore. Mother-in-laws.... Be glad you can only legally have one at a time.)

Betty-Sue's lovely green eyes were wide and shining with astonishment when I led her out into the tall grass and removed her blindfold. Standing before us was old Grits, wearing a rustic western suit coat and his best black cowboy hat, his calloused hands holding the reins of two beautiful white Thoroughbred geldings. The steeds were about as fine an example of horseflesh as I would ever care to see, and the silver studding on their expensive black saddles and bridles truly completed the picture.

"Omigosh...." Betty-Sue whispered, instantly having to fight back a couple of tears. "Bucky, they're beautiful."

"You're beautiful, my little puffed rice marshmallow square," I assured her gallantly, stealing a quick kiss as I led her toward our mounts.

"Bucky, good to see you, boy," Grits said with a broad grin, shaking my hand. "And, I'm danged! You never told me your blushin' bride was little Betty-Sue Perkins! Gosh-golly, girl, you was knee-high to a grasshopper last time I seen you."

"Grits!" Betty-Sue said with the delight of abrupt remembrance, hugging the kindly old man. "I'd never forget that voice. You gave me my first mutton-busting lesson when I was three!"

"I did indeed," Grits chuckled. "But I'm sure you've got more to do than stand around jawin' with an ol' codger like me. If you'll step over to the tents o'er yonder, we'll get you all suited up and ready to ride."

We followed his pointed finger to a couple of large tents set up about twenty metres to the west of us, one pink and one blue. Betty-Sue was grinning broadly as she grabbed my hand and hauled me over to them, ducking inside the pink one. I couldn't help but smile as I heard her squeal with startled delight a second later. I stepped into the blue tent, where a western tuxedo, cowboy hat, and pair of pointy-toed cowboy boots were waiting for me, all exactly the right size. Grits had come through for me alright, and then some.

I was standing tall and shiny in my fancy new duds when Betty-Sue sheepishly emerged from her tent, her own pointy-toed boots complimented by an elegant blue evening gown, her typically ponytailed hair now hanging loose down her back. I tried to recall if she had even looked so beautiful in her wedding dress, but I just couldn't do it.

"Bucky...." she said, not knowing what to say. "This is too much."

"This is nothing," I assured her, taking her hand once more. "This is beginnings. Nothing more."

I escorted her to the slightly shorter gelding, and boosted her into the saddle, getting a strange thrill from seeing her ride side-saddle for the first time. I swung into my own saddle, and Grits pointed the way to the trail.

"You kids sure as heck don't need me taggin' along," he grinned. "You just follow them weeping willows until you come to a white gravel road. Ride on down that for a few miles until you reach the dock on the lakeshore. There'll be another surprise waiting for you down thattaway."

We thanked him again, and headed down the trail. The sun was dipping lower on the western horizon, but we didn't care. We didn't care if we were in those saddles til the sun came back up again.

"So, don't try telling me that you have no idea what the surprise down there is," Betty-Sue giggled, reaching across the short space between our steeds to hold my hand as we rode under the lightly swaying boughs of the weeping willows.

I knew exactly what the surprise was. It was a three-course supper which was being prepared on the docks by a local gourmet caterer, and featuring Betty-Sue's favourite dish, mandarin-glazed Cornish game hen with peppered asparagus tips. After our fine dining experience, we would spend the night in Grits small lake-house by the dock, where we would cuddle up in front of a fireplace with a bowl of popcorn, and watch Betty-Sue's favourite movie, *Rooster Cogburn*. But I wasn't going to tell her that. I just smiled.

"Bucky, this is incredible," she sighed. "I can be such a cow to you, and then you go and do all this."

"I married you knowing what a cow you could be," I assured her. "But you're usually a whitetail doe or a whitefeathered dove, so I'm not complaining."

She laughed and gave me a playful punch on the hip. The horses muttered back and forth at each other.

"Do you know how much I love you, Betty-Sue?" I asked, having a hard time keeping my eyes on the trail with a vision such as her riding beside me. "Before you moved back to Coyote Yelp Pass, I was becoming so comfortable with my paralysing loneliness that I was ready to just give up. I was going to move to Affluenceville, take a job as a night-janitor at a mini-mall, and happily die alone in a one bedroom apartment. That's how I was prepared to live out my days, with nothing more than a pet cat for company, as well as for insurance against my lifelong irrational fear of having an open-casket funeral. You changed all that."

"Omigosh," Betty-Sue remarked, looking impressed. "That is the most romantic thing I've ever heard you say. That must be a Laroo family first."

"Well, not quite," I admitted. "When Corky and Hollywood actress Jane Krakowski were dance-partner contestants on the hit NBC reality series *Dancing with the Upcoming and Outgoing* last year, he told her, 'I never noticed until tonight that the man in the moon looks like he's crying....'"

"Holy cheese, that is beautiful," Betty-Sue gasped.

"Yeah," I agreed. "And he claims that they ended up dating for nearly five days."

"Uh-huh," Betty-Sue said, looking a bit perturbed and biting her lip. "Um.... Yeah, I'm going to need you to say that to me. Right now."

"What?"

"What Corky said. I need you to say it to me, but say it like the exquisiteness of me and the moment just made you think of it on the spot."

"Betty-Sue, the sun is still u–"

"*Say it!*" she rasped, grabbing my collar and nearly pulling me out of my saddle.

I regained my balance, raised a debonair eyebrow, and crooned, "I never noticed until tonight ... that the man in the moon looks like he's crying. Dot dot dot."

"Omi-*gosh!*" Betty-Sue groaned, her eyes rolling back as she seized my collar again and planted a huge kiss onto my more-than-receptive mouth.

It took us a couple of hours to ride down to the rickety dock, but the sun was still in the sky to the west, and we could smell a truly indescribable aroma wafting up from the shore.

"You've got *food* waiting for us?" Betty-Sue exclaimed, sniffing the air hungrily.

"Possibly," I chuckled. "But that's the only hint you're getting."

When the winding trail led us down to the peaceful inlet, even my mouth dropped open in surprise, for the dock before us was nothing like what I had expected.

"You got a *yacht?*" Betty-Sue blurted as we beheld the regal vessel tied to the end of the wooden dock, its stern end emblazoned with the rather odd name *Cuz The Truck Got Stuck*.

"I got a *yacht?*" I echoed with equal incredulousness, while simultaneously praying, *Please Jesus, tell me that I didn't deliriously get caught up in the moment and get a yacht!*

"*You got a yacht!*" Betty-Sue screamed, nearly exploding with rapture, bouncing up and down in the saddle as if her patiently standing horse was trotting across uneven ground.

I could only nod dumbly and reply, "I got a yacht."

And that was when I saw them. Emerging from below decks were a man and a woman, both dressed in white tuxedos and white captain's hats. The man held an ice-filled champagne bucket, and the woman was setting a silver tray of appetizers onto a white dining table on the stern deck.

Even considering the undoubtedly exorbitant sum that this whole shebang was going to run me, it wouldn't have been so bad if the man and woman had been sailors or caterers, but it was fairly obvious that they weren't.

They were Corky and Sassy!

"Welcome aboard!" Corky whooped as he spotted us numbly approaching. "Just put your mounts in the corral, and climb up the gangplank! Have we got an evening planned for you!"

"An evening truly befitting the bestestest baby brother in the world, and the woman who tamed him!" Sassy called out boisterously. "We're your entertainment, servers, and helmsmen on this cruise, and the only rule is party til you drop!"

Please Jesus, tell me they didn't use my money to get a yacht....

"Bucky, you are insane!" Betty-Sue was laughing uncontrollably. "This is too much! And all that time you were pretending to be suspicious of what they were up to. Ha ha! You were planning this all along."

I could only give a weary shrug.

"I got a yacht."

We put the horses into the nearby corral next to the lake-house, and then crossed the creaking dock to the yacht, where Corky gallantly gave Betty-Sue his hand and helped her aboard as Sassy poured two glasses of fine champagne.

As soon as Betty-Sue's back was turned, I grabbed

Corky by the ear and hauled him to the prow, out of hearing range.

"What are you doing here, and why do I suddenly have a yacht?" I gurgled, shaking him by the shoulders to ensure that the words sunk in.

"Technically, it's a luxury forty-five-foot cabin cruiser," he corrected me.

"*Where did you get it?*"

"Relax, Bucky-charms," he said mildly. "It's a loaner. Sassy's little Olympic outburst may have put a damper on our celeb lifestyle, but I've still got a lot of friends with boats. We wanted to do something nice for you, okay? You've put up with us making money from lyrics about how much we hate you for the past seventeen years or so, so this is our turn to repay the favour."

"That's it?" I said suspiciously. "A yacht? Dinner? All out of the goodness of your hearts? And all those '*heh heh!*'s over the past year were just part of that?"

"Is that so hard to believe?"

"Where's the caterers?"

"Oh, them," Corky said dismissively. "I fired them and took their food. Now get back to the aft-thingy and charm your wife like this was all part of your plan. I've got to figure out how to drive this thing. I think I saw a manual in the cribbage board."

"Cribbage board?" I cringed. "Why do I have this horrible feeling that you meant to say 'bridge?'"

"Never could tell the dif," Corky remarked, clapping me on the back as he clambered up to the cribbage board to navigate the boat out onto the lake. "Just relax, Bucky. I think they've got lane markers set up. As long as we stick to them, we should be fine."

"Swimming pools have lane markers," I pointed out. "Not lakes. I never should have told you what I was planning!"

"But you did, Bucky," he called down over the banister. "And this is the path of convergence that four separate lives took. Look at it this way. Would you rather die here with your family treating you like a king for the first time in your life, or at the hands of some inevitable bounty hunter back on the ranch? Cuz those are probably your only options."

"Good point," I sighed, walking back to the dining table where my wife was waiting.

"What were you two talking about?" she smiled, sipping her champagne. "More big secrets to come?"

"I was just telling him not to kill us," I replied as honestly as I could. "We got a yacht."

Corky actually surprised us with his ability to handle the yacht, and Sassy seemed to be having a ball playing the part of the perfect hostess. She served us an undeniably delectable supper, and then serenaded us with her guitar. The atmosphere was as perfect as I could ever have asked for, so I seized the day and presented Betty-Sue with the silver bracelet I had spent a good chunk of my savings on several months earlier. The stunned silence and her cute O-shaped mouth made me the happiest cowboy alive.

As the sun set over the lake and darkness began to set in, Corky flicked on the running lights and Sassy lit a cute string of paper Japanese lanterns she had made. As if that wasn't enough, Corky came down from the bridge with a special present that Gramps had sent along with them for me. I opened the oddly-shaped wrapped gift, and found myself staring down at the weathered case of Gramps' own fiddle, the same one he had serenaded his grandchildren to sleep with on many a stormy night of my youth. I couldn't believe that he was giving it to me, but the plain white card inside simply read *It's yours, Bucky. Relax. I bought bagpipes. Invest in folk music. The industry's turning around. Gramps.*

"Well, don't just sit there, baby bro," Sassy quipped. "Play us a song; You're the fiddle man."

The only song I knew was Gramps' personal favourite, *The Orange Blossom Special*, but I played my heart out for my bride and my siblings, the flawless rendition carrying across the still of the dark lake. It may not have been much, but I played my best for them ... parum pum-pum pum.

When the song was finished, we all sat in peaceful silence with our backs against the hull railing, just drinking in the night and the last of our champagne glasses. Then Corky looked over at Sassy, smiled, and gave her a wink.

"Well, I guess it's time," Sassy announced, standing and downing her glass.

"It sure is," Corky chuckled. "Bucky and Betty-Sue, the biggest surprise is just waiting for you, and it's waiting downstairs."

He and Sassy chivalrously threw open the double doors leading to the cabin below decks, and waited for Betty-Sue and I to take the lead. Betty-Sue still couldn't stop giggling as she grabbed my hand and pulled me down into the darkened stateroom. We felt around for a light switch, and Betty-Sue finally found it. The light clicked on to reveal a truly luxurious bedroom/sitting room, but our gaze was immediately drawn to the twenty shiny steel barrels that were stacked around the room.

"I give up," I called out. "What are these?"

"I'll tell you when you wake up," Corky called back, strapping on a gasmask. "I promise. Fire in the hole."

Then he tossed a four litre glass bottle of chloroform into the cabin and locked the doors as soon as he heard it shatter on the carpet.

The lights went out as Betty-Sue and I slumped down onto the saturated shag rug. The last thing I saw through a glass porthole was the most glorious full moon in history shining in the clear sky over the lake. It really did look like the man in the moon was crying. I know I was.

POGO ON A STICK

◇◇◇◇◇◇◇◇◇◇◇◇◇◇◇◇◇◇◇◇◇◇◇◇◇◇

THE LIGHTS WERE STILL turned off when I regained consciousness some hours later, but the moonlight was bright enough for me to see the cabin I was sprawled on the floor of. I think the noise of the portable gasoline-powered pump running beside my head was what finally roused me, which is probably a good thing, since the exhaust was chugging straight into my mouth. I couldn't see Betty-Sue anywhere.

"What ... the ... crap ... just happened?" I growled, slowly sitting up and feeling the residual headache and dry tongue that has followed hard on the heels of every chloroforming episode in my life. And, yes, there's been more than one. Just read the first book.

I staggered to my feet, trying to shake the head-lightening gasoline fumes from my brain as I lurched unsteadily toward the stairs. I found the light switch again and clicked it on, the sudden illumination revealing a hose leading from one of the silver barrels, through the pump, and then out the door and onto the deck. Obviously, the barrels were being drained, but I still could not tell what was in them. However, all of them had been uncapped, releasing a smell like rotting fish into the air. Combined with the heavy-hanging gasoline fumes, it made the stateroom a very unpleasant place to be. I hurried upstairs, bashed open the ajar doors, and stumbled out into the clean air as fast as my shaking legs would allow.

I emerged into a slightly surreal environment, although that might have just been the gas fumes playing tricks on me. We were harboured in a small, round inlet shrouded from view on all sides by trees, a bit like a secluded lagoon with only a single narrow waterway leading back out to the lake, but that was as much as I could see of our surroundings. All of the running lights and Japanese lanterns had been extinguished, and all traces of our regal treatment from earlier that evening had vanished. In place of the dining table and champagne buckets, the deck was strewn with fishing nets, harpoons, power cables, old car batteries, and green metal ammunition boxes. At the far end of the aft deck was a large tarp-covered tube that looked sort of like a large telescope mounted on a tripod.

Corky and Sassy had undergone a transformation of their own. Gone were their spiffy white tuxedos and captain's hats, as well as their bright and chipper attitudes. They were now all furrow-browed business as they finished buckling and cinching on their black SWAT tactical gear, which I had been unaware that they owned, or was even legal to own.

"Ah, Bucky, you're up," Corky said, lacing his ankle-high combat boots. "Just in time, too. We're almost ready to begin."

"Well, I'm glad you let me coma my way through all the boring prep stages of whatever you're doing," I growled. "Where's Betty-Sue?"

"Who?" Sassy inquired.

"Wife, Sassy. We've been over this."

"Oh, right," Sassy said dismissively, strapping a couple bandoleers of shotgun shells onto her vest. "She's sleeping it off in the bridge. We were going to put you up there, too, but we forgot."

I dashed up the stairs to the bridge, and was relieved to discover that Betty-Sue was indeed snoring in the captain's chair, slumped against the helm and drooling on the control panel. It was a sweet sight, and I couldn't bring myself to rouse her until I had a better explanation. I quietly stepped back down to the deck, wondering how much unbrotherly violence God would oblige me against Corky under the circumstances. Maybe a dislocated shoulder, or a few minor rib fractures....

"You do realize that, in the process of forgetting to move me from below decks, you left me unconscious in a barely-ventilated confined space with an engine that was continuously pumping carbon monoxide into my face," I had to point out as I returned to the staging area.

"Yeah, it's a really good thing you woke up," Corky said absently, sliding a machete into the long sheath on his hip. "You would have missed the whole show."

"What show?" I demanded. "Is this some kind of domestic amphibious act of terrorism against the city of Kelowna? Because I kind of like Kelowna."

"Silence, Bucky," Sassy retorted, loosening the tarp straps on the covered tripod. "Just be grateful that you even get to be a part of this. We're claiming our rightful place in the history books. Just keep quiet and watch the water." She then gave the tarp a sharp tug, dropping it to the deck and revealing not a telescope, but rather an unusual ring of long, hollow steel tubes, joined at the end by a chambering mechanism with a long belt of ammunition running into it.

"Is that what I think it is?" I asked, knowing enough about modern weaponry to recognize the distinct design, but still hoping for the possibility that I was wrong.

"I honestly couldn't say for sure, Bucky," Sassy stated. "Historically speaking, you're pretty stupid, so this might not be anything close to what you think it is. But we really do love you."

"It looks like something I've only seen in movies," I clarified, "usually being carried by a helicopter, or by a guy with a cowboy hat and no shirt sleeves."

"That movie was so awesome," Sassy chuckled. "Close enough. It's an M134 Minigun. I wired it into that pile of old truck batteries we had up in the boneyard."

"Where in the sandhill did you get that thing?" I demanded, taking a quick glance in all directions, suddenly very anxious to know that we were alone. The Okanagan is a vast lake, more than one hundred thirty kilometres in length, but if there was ever an inopportune time for a cop to stumble across a secluded lagoon, this was it.

"The hardware store," Sassy replied, shaking her head as if the answer should have been the most obvious thing in the world. "It's just standard industrial-strength cable."

"The gun, not the power cord!" I snapped.

"What, this ol' thing?" Sassy said, surprised by such a trivial question as she gave the disturbingly wobbly tripod an affectionate kick. "Gee whiz, I can't even remember."

"Try a little harder," I growled.

"Umm, lemme see," Sassy said, pondering the understandably-vague memory. "Oh yeah, now I remember. I found it."

"You *found* it? Just lying on a street corner?"

"No, silly," she laughed. "Nobody leaves electric Gatling guns on street corners. That would be borderline irresponsible. Can you imagine the chaos that would reign if a 6000-round-per-minute weapon were to fall into the hands of someone unstable?"

"*Where did you get it?!*" I screamed.

"Let's see, it was about three years ago," Sassy recalled. "Do you remember that time when you tried to murder Max-Ram Target, and all those angry cops and assassins and pop stars tried pulling a *Smokin' Aces* on you in a last-ditch effort to save him from your diabolical plot?"

"I remember that version of it," I said dryly.

"Whatever," Sassy shrugged. "Anyway, I found this baby in the back of Klaus Klotzern's Humvee while the cops were busy arresting everybody. Figured it might come in handy someday."

After a stunned silence, I pointed out the problems with her logic.

"Three points of interest, Sassy. One: You stole police evidence. Two: You stole highly-illegal, highly-dangerous police evidence. And, three: You stole it from the most trigger-happy assassin in the history of East Germany, or any other form of Germany! Are you *insane?*"

"Chillax, Bucky-tooth tiger," Sassy dismissed my concerns. "Klaus is just a misunderstood old sweetie who loves good music. Once he found out we were the pickle barrel people, all was forgiven. He's even been sending me extra ammunition every Christmas."

"*What?*"

"Hey, I can't just buy that kind of heat in bulk, and he only left enough ammo in the Hummer for ten or twelve minutes of continuous firing. How long do you think that's gonna last? Five minutes, maybe?"

"You've actually been using that thing?" I said, appalled.

Sassy grinned. "2008 Alberta prairie tour, Bucky. Next time you're over there, ask anybody you meet how long it's been since they've seen a prairie dog. Or a prairie chicken, for that matter. They ain't seen one this year, I can promise you that. Hang on, I need to make sure the mounts are well-secured. Hand me that duct tape, will ya?"

"You still haven't told me what you're doing," I pointed out, obligingly handing her the silver tape.

"What we're doing?" Sassy said darkly, ripping off a four-foot section of tape. "Bucky, we're doing what every redneck does when faced with a groundbreaking, life-altering, world-shaking discovery: Kill it, stuff it, and probably eat it."

"Eat *what?*"

"I'm not at liberty to discuss matters of an ongoing operation," Sassy said, relishing the sound of her secret-agent lingo.

"So what's the deal with the pump and the barrels?" I asked.

"Bait for the prey, buddy-boy," Corky informed me, looking proudly at the belching nozzle of the hose, which was spewing the last of a pulpy red mixture into the lake. "That's the last barrel, so we should be at action stations any second."

"I don't have enough fingers to tally the federal laws you're breaking right now," I sighed. "What is that stuff?"

"I just told you," Corky remarked, ignoring the deeper aspect of my question. "This is how things get done, Bucky. Real discovery is the rape of the natural world. The guy on *Jurassic Park* said so."

"Yeah, but he meant that it was a *bad* thing," I had to explain, just as the pump ran dry.

Corky thought about that for a moment, but then shook his head and replied, "No, I really don't think he did."

"Okay, that's it," I snarled. "No more crap proceeding forth from the buttocks of bullocks. I want to know what's going on, right freakin' now!"

"Appreciate this, Bucky," Corky soothed me, putting an arm around my shoulders. "I've been planning this all year. Do you remember back last spring, when that vintage unplugged release of *The Old Pickle Barrel Song* was sweeping the international country-music charts, and I had that brief love affair with Taylor Swift as a result?"

"No," I said slowly, after fifteen to twenty seconds of stupefied silence. "I can say with a considerable amount of certainty that you never mentioned that. Ever."

"Whatever," Corky shrugged with the apathetic sincerity of delusion. "She took me yachting out here. Well, technically it wasn't a yacht. It was a luxury forty-five-foot cabi–"

"Corky!"

"Sorry. Anyway, we came here, to this very secluded inlet that we're in right now. This very spot, Bucky, on a night exactly like this one ... except that it was April, and it was raining, and it was two-thirty in the afternoon."

"A teenage American superstar who presumably spends the majority of her leisure time on the sunny Pacific coast, like all American celebrities, chooses an inland Canadian lake as a romantic yachting destination?" I asked, needing to hear the words, for entertainment value if nothing else. "On a rainy day in a region that probably still had snow on the ground?"

"I just said that," Corky replied patiently.

"Exactly how old was she at the time?"

"Silence, Bucky. Anyway, she went to defrost in the hot tub. I was standing on the prow, all alone in the rain, just me ... and my enormous Polaroid camera from the early 80s. And that's when I saw it."

"*Saw ... what?*"

"The future, Bucky," he said, quivering from the chills he was sending down his own spine as he handed me a worn Polaroid snapshot. "Yeah, I know what you're thinking. It's dark and grainy and my thumb's covering about a third of it, but you know exactly what that is, don't you? Welcome to the future, baby bro. It's the Ogopogo."

"Ogopogo?" I echoed skeptically, studying the photo in my hand.

Corky cackled gleefully, rubbing his hands together. "The Ogopogo, Bucky. The most famous North American sea serpent legend in the world, and you're holding the only real photographic proof of its existence right in the palm of your hand."

"That's it?" I said, trying to keep a tight rein on my gathering rage. "That's what this is all about? You gathered all this gear, and hijacked my honeymoon, and got a yacht, and chloroformed my wife ... all for a stupid monster hunt?"

"Bucky, just look at the photo," Corky instructed, growing impatient. "Seriously, the poop is in the pudding. That monster is real, and it's here."

That was my answer. After spending the better part of a year wondering what possible disastrous fiasco my delusional brother was planning, I had to admit that packing illegal heavy machine guns on a cryptozoological safari had never once crossed my mind. After nearly thirty years of siblinghood, you'd think that I would have learned to imagine disasters farther outside the box.

"And Taylor Swift will back your story?" I inquired, gently massaging my twitching left eye. "One hundred percent?"

"Who?" Corky said, looking confused, but then snapping his fingers as the forgivable mental lapse was corrected. "Oh. Right. Girlfriend. *Heh heh!* Honestly, I wouldn't bother her about it."

"Wouldn't dream of it," I assured him, handing his photo back. "That's an inner tube."

"What?" Corky said.

"It's the inner tube of a tractor tire," I explained more

thoroughly. "You see that glint of copper at the top? That's the fill valve."

"Are you sure?" Corky said, wearing the shocked expression that so frequently adorned his face in the wake of one of his brilliant schemes.

"Gimme that!" Sassy snapped, snatching the Polaroid from Corky's frozen fingers. She studied it for a long moment before turning her withering glare on Corky, and seething, "Are you telling me that I just polluted Lake Okanagan with nine hundred gallons of chum and pig blood to catch a stupid *inner tube?*"

"Hey, you thought it was the Ogopogo, too," Corky weakly pointed out.

"I'm the one who had to pay for all that slop!" Sassy shouted. "Oil drums included! All you did was borrow the boat!"

"And the big rig fifth-wheel to haul it," Corky defended himself. "And remember that last pit stop in Kamloops? Who paid for the pepperoni sticks and Swedish farmer's sausage, huh?"

Sassy, however, was inconsolable.

"Do you have any idea how many pigs and fish had to die to get three hundred gallons of blood and six hundred gallons of chum?!" she hollered, waving her arms in the air.

"Buying a two litre bucket of chum from a bait shop wasn't an option?" I couldn't help asking.

"Well, we're not turning back now!" Corky exploded, angrily cramming the Polaroid back into his pocket. "I don't care what I saw. Look at this place. There is no better cove for an Ogopogo to chill out in than this one. I've put in too much time and effort to just pull up the anchor and head for home! We're waiting it out, okay?"

"No, we're going back to the dock, and then I'm going

to try to revive my wife and convince her that she just had too much champagne," I growled. "Let's go."

"I've dedicated a year of my life to getting back here!" Corky yelled. "This has to be about destiny, Bucky. Seriously, what are the odds that you would get invited down here? Heck, what are the odds that the Hawkins Cheezies people would even put up a new factory here? And then you ignorantly plan a romantic trail ride within eight kilometres of where I spotted the thing? Trust me, Bucky. The angels want me to be here, right now. I just know it. Jeepers, guys, it's a year of my life, okay? Every hour of an entire year spent with the single-minded purpose of returning to Kelowna and capturing the great serpent. And now the day has come. Our day, Bucky."

"Inspiring," I muttered. "Last Thanksgiving you spent four days on the couch with a telephone in your lap while watching a marathon of HGTV's *The Unsellables*, because you couldn't remember the exact day that the radio station was airing their George Foreman Grill giveaway contest. You were just pretty sure that it was 'sometime over the long weekend, or next weekend.' Remember that?"

"That grill gives me meat, Bucky," Corky said, rolling his eyes with the exasperation of my perpetually missing the point. "Meat gives me protein, and protein gives me the perfectly-toned muscle mass with which to wrest the great serpent into submission, should it come to that. It's all connected. And can I help it if *The Unsellables'* Sofie Allsopp is insanely hot and British?"

"Fine," I groaned. "We're probably all going to jail anyway, so what's a few more minutes? We wait ten minutes, then we dump all this crap in the lake, and we get the heck out of here!"

"Deal," Corky sighed, shaking my hand.

We fell silent and stared over the port side for a long

moment at the chummy red water. The surface was still, aside from the rhythmic ripples emanating from around the hull of our lightly bobbing vessel.

"Well, this be boring," Sassy declared. "Corky, initiate Phase Two."

"Initiating Phase Two," Corky agreed, seizing me by the collar of my tuxedo. "Sorry, Bucky. There's a greater good to consider. Or, at least, a more cared about good."

I made a point of giving him one good punch in the eye before he heaved me overboard, but he had too much momentum, and I splashed noisily into the bloody water.

"*What the helicopter are you doing?*" I roared, when I finally managed to surface about thirty seconds later.

"Just keep thrashing, baby Buck-meister," Corky encouraged me. "We're simulating death throes, okay?"

"Pull me out!"

"No can do, Bucky," Sassy assured me, with an appreciated amount of emotional conflict in her voice. "Maybe Ogie likes carrion, or maybe he likes hunting live game, but love for the weak and wounded and stupid is universal. You can swim, right?"

"No!" I sputtered, frantically trying to figure out the art of treading water.

"Even better," Corky said. "Method acting. Would you stop that screaming? You're going to scare it off."

"Actually, I think the screaming helps," Sassy countered. "He sounds like a panicked baby harp seal. And what is the most commonly known fact about sea serpents?"

"Ah, of course!" Corky realized, snapping his fingers. "They love to eat baby harp seals! Everybody in the world knows that."

"I didn't know that," I whined. "Pull me out of here!"

"Fine, give him the inner tube," Sassy sighed. "Or

just wait for him to find the one *that you thought was the Ogopogo!*"

"Learn to let things go, Sassy," Corky advised, reluctantly tossing the rescue ring into my flailing arms. "Nobody likes a scab-picker."

I had just managed to get a good hold on the tube when a strange growling sound burbled through the water, freezing all of us in our tracks.

"What was that?" I had to ask.

"Holy cow cud," Sassy breathed, frantically chambering her confiscated Minigun. "It's here!"

"I'm a genius!" Corky cheered in an excited whisper. "Baby harp seal! I told you it would work!"

We all fell silent for a long moment, anxiously surveying the dark water. Then we heard it again, even louder than before. This time there was no doubt that the sound was coming from beneath the surface of the deep.

And then I saw it. An advancing trail of bubbles about fifty feet away quickly turned into a trail of ripples, and then an enormous dark hump broke the surface of the water, no more than fifteen feet away from me and closing in swiftly. Whatever it was, it was clearly animal, and clearly not the inner tube of a tractor tire.

I couldn't believe it. In that single moment of surface breaching, all the playful mythology of Lake Okanagan fell away, leaving behind only one glaring, obvious truth.

"Guys," I said uneasily, tightening my grasp on the rescue ring, "I think we just found the Ogopogo."

"*Holy—!*" Sassy roared. She may have been starting a panicked curse, but the roar of her firing Minigun drowned out anything else she may have impulsively blurted out.

The deafening stream of blazing bullets exploded into the water all around me, and the rounded hump instantly disappeared, diving for safety below the surface. Trails of bullet geysers shot up from the surface as Sassy frantically tried to maintain a grip on her nearly uncontrollable automatic cannon, her pigtails snapping and cracking around her face like twin bullwhips.

"Kill it! *Kill it!*" Corky was shrieking, cowering on the deck, which was rapidly being carpeted with hundreds of smoking brass shell casings.

Taking advantage of the strange clarity of mind that often presents itself in such chaotic situations, I made a concerted effort at keeping myself from utterly melting down into hysterics by dredging up my old Sunday School memory verses.

"'*I cried by reason of my affliction unto the Lord—*' STOP SHOOTING THAT MINIGUN! '*For thou hadst cast me into the deep, in the midst of the seas; and the floods compassed me about: all thy billows and thy waves passed over me.*' Jonah, Chapter 2, Verses 2 to 3. *Stop shooting that thing and get me out of here!*"

"Sorry, Bucky!" Sassy hollered back, her feet barely able to stay on the ground as the gun sprayed madly in every direction, including briefly into the boat deck. "I can't hear you over the deafening roar of one hundred rounds of 7.62x51mm NATO ammunition being discharged every second! And, honestly, I can't even speculate accurately as to what you might be saying right now."

The gun ran dry a second later, and the lake fell silent once more, except for the electric whirring of the still-rotating barrels.

"Did I get it, Corky?" Sassy called out eagerly, finally releasing the trigger and trying to ignore the residual heat emanating from the knee-high pile of shell casings she was wading in. "There's so much pulverized flesh in the water already that I can't tell. Oh yeah, and check to see if I shot

Bucky. That's probably important to know, too. Man, this brass is really hot...."

"No, no, I'm fine," I sarcastically assured her. "Just keep looking for the mons–"

Before I could even finish the sentence, I felt a steely set of jaws clamp onto my left cowboy boot, dragging me underwater before I could even cry out.

I was being dragged deeper and deeper into the blackness of the deep, my clawing fingers and kicking right foot not even slowing my descent. It had all happened so fast that I hadn't even had time to take a deep breath, and I didn't know how long I would be able to hold in what air I did have.

I'm not sure how long I managed to hold my breath, but I remember that I was about ready to explode when I suddenly felt myself being hauled upward, back toward the surface. My lungs were screaming profanities at me, demanding that the floodgates be opened, and I couldn't argue with them anymore. My mouth opened, and the water rushed in.

One second later, I felt myself bursting through the surface and into the merciful emptiness of air. But I barely had time to begin hacking the water out of my windpipe before my whole body was forcibly slammed onto a sloping gravel bank. The back of my head struck one of the larger rocks, and everything went black all over again. My last thought was a brief pondering of how many unconscious renderings a human body can handle before it starts to affect one's faculties. Over the course of my life I had passed out from cattle tramplings, blood loss, chloroform, taser guns, and now blunt head trauma. It was only a matter of time....

I'm not sure how much time passed before my eyes opened again, as no outside light could get into the sea cave that I was lying in, so I had no idea if it was day or night. I was just relieved that my eyes had opened again at all.

I was lying face-down on the wet shale of a surprisingly well-lit cavern, my cowboy boots still submerged in the edge of the glistening moon pool that I assumed the Ogopogo had dragged me up through. I wondered if I would be able to swim back out. The problem with that plan was the unknown depth of the cave below the water level, and also the fact that I still couldn't swim very well.

This was insane. I had just discovered the Ogopogo, and now it had dragged me down to this murky dwelling place to finish me off at its leisure. And my sister had been in possession of a military-exclusive M134 Minigun for the past three years. Oddly enough, I couldn't decide which discovery was the stranger one.

However, the bizarreness of the situation had apparently not even reached its ludicrous pinnacle yet, because it was about to become exponentially stranger. When I raised my battered face from the cold stone floor, I expected to maybe get a good look at the Ogopogo, or, at the very least, a brief glimpse of its gaping jaws filled with knife-like teeth as it bit my head off. Instead, I found myself staring at something else entirely.

He was a furry little biped, no more than fourteen inches tall, with highset eyes the size and shape of ping-pong balls, a physical attribute that we probably shared at the moment. His wooly fur was an unusual orange hue that covered his entire body, except for a wild mat of purple hair on the top of his head, and a purple tassel on the end of his long, thin tail. Strangest of all was the clothing that he wore, and that was what finally triggered recognition within me. The sight of his little brown vest and his red-and-yellow-striped turtleneck sweater filled my heart with both astonishment and a nostalgic delight that I had not felt since my childhood days in front of the television set.

"*Gobo Fraggle?*" I blurted, scrambling up onto my hands and knees.

"That's right, Bucky!" Gobo cheered. "Welcome! Welcome, you silly creature!"

"You *are* real!" I exclaimed. "I knew you were way too real to be just another one of Jim Henson's Muppets! I always knew it!"

"Well, after five seasons of unrelenting good times and great music, how could you *not* believe?" he laughed.

I couldn't believe this fortuitous turn of events. I have rarely known such joy.

"So, that must mean–" I sputtered. "I mean, I must be...!"

"...down at Fraggle Rock!" Gobo assured me.

"I can't believe it!" I whooped, leaping up and accidentally knocking over a Doozer construction at the same time. "*I'm down at Fraggle Rock!* This is the greatest day of my life!"

"What about your wedding day?" Gobo chided me.

"Besides that," I replied. "Hey, do you think it's weird that my first childhood crush was on Mokey? Of course, I was only four."

"Not at all, Bucky!" the Fraggle said dismissively. "A lot of you silly creatures found the soft-voiced persona of that pop-top earth mama endearing. On the other hand, it may have something to do with unresolved issues of your hippie upbringing. And I do find it odd that you ended up marrying a silly creature who has a lot more character traits in common with Red Fraggle than Mokey."

"By the way," I ventured, glancing up at the wobbly foam stalactites overhead, "I've always wanted to ask you something. Did something very traumatic involving dirty laundry happen to Boober, possibly at a young age?"

"Yeah," Gobo admitted, a bit glumly. "Yeah, it did. We would offer him support therapy, but that would go against our universal philosophy of only ever dancing our cares away. That is something you must learn in the days that follow, Bucky. It is highly dangerous to mess with the philosophies of comfortable people. Remember that, okay?"

"Um.... Okay," I said uncertainly. "But I am a bit curious. Why would the Ogopogo drag me down to Fraggle Rock?"

"Because, Bucky, you *are* the Ogopogo!" Gobo declared proudly, unslinging his gourd guitar from his back. "Here, let me sing you a little song about it that my Uncle Travelling Matt taught me...." He strummed a few notes, and then burst into toe-tapping melody, bopping back and forth as the music and lyrics swept him away.

> *"Ohhhhhhh, when your stinky feet turn into flippers,*
> *Don't get knots in your knickers–!"*

"This is a dream, isn't it?" I sighed, hating myself for even uttering the abominable words.

"You hit your head on a three hundred fifty pound slab of granite, Bucky," the Fraggle reminded me, annoyed at having been interrupted mid-verse. "And if there's one thing we've learned from television, it's that blunt-trauma induced loss of consciousness always results in fantastically vivid, and even retrospectively-prophetic, dream activity."

"Crap, I knew it was too good to be true," I muttered. "Oh well, I'd better wake up now. I have this strange feeling that my head may still be fully submerged underwater. Goodbye, Gobo. It was great to finally meet you. Tell Wembley I said hi.... And Mokey. Please tell Mokey that Bucky Laroo said hello."

"No!" Gobo panicked. "Don't wake up! I don't wanna cease to exis–!"

The cave was just as well-lit when I opened my eyes for the second time, but only because the dripping rock walls were thickly covered with a strange species of large blue glowworm. My head wasn't underwater, thankfully, but I was shivering as the chill air permeated my drenched tuxedo, and also as a result of the fact that I was trapped in a monster's lair, the last type of lair that I would ever have wanted to be trapped in. The lair of an evil scientist bent on wreaking havoc on the planet would have been preferable. At least the hero character can usually subdue an evil scientist with a single punch, if the movies are any indication of historical precedence, which I can only assume they are. Monsters, however, are a completely different story. One man alone can't stand up to a monster. I had to get out of there, fast.

I stood up and cautiously looked around the extensive cavern, but it seemed to be empty. There were several mounds of dried mud scattered around the rocky floor, and heaps of half-eaten fish, but nothing large enough to conceal a creature the size of the Ogopogo. Judging from the hump I had witnessed breaching the surface, I knew that the monster had to be at least fifteen or twenty feet long. However, the cave stretched quite a ways into the distance, and the glowworm light only gave off so much illumination, so I had no way of knowing if my captor was lurking in the shadows just beyond the nearest corner. The frightening possibility eliminated any option of searching for a way out farther up and into the darkness of the cave. My only way out was the way that I had come in. I would have to clear the underwater passage, and hopefully make it back to the lagoon without running out of air. I could only hope that the cave wasn't too deep below the surface, or too far away from the boat. Also, I could only hope that the boat wasn't already on its way down to meet me, as I was pretty certain that it had been taking on water through the various bullets holes in the hull, as a result of Sassy's panicked suppressive-fire.

I decided to make a break for the surface. This cave was most likely an historic find, but I was more than willing to leave the great discoveries and exploration to the scientists and adventurers. If they chose to give me a dust-jacket blurb, that would be all the credit I needed.

I turned to face the pool of water, and began steeling myself for the great plunge, possibly into a watery grave. However, the Ogopogo was coming out before I had a chance to go in.

The giant aquatic reptile burst from the moon pool, drenching me all over again as she bowled me onto my back. When she landed, she was straddling my prone form, her serpentine neck reared back so that her long, pointed, black head could glare down at me with glittering sea-green eyes. Her thin tongue licked forward like a snake smelling the ground, and she let out an ominous hiss. I realized that in spite of the extensive bath I had just taken, I probably still reeked of chum and pig's blood, which was probably a bad combination of things to smell like in the presence of anything with teeth that looked like ivory arrowheads. I tried to wriggle free, but the sea dragon's massive football-shaped body, paddle-like flippers, and long tapered tail were immoveable. I was pinned fast, and it was getting increasingly hard to breathe. The Ogopogo was lowering her face toward mine, and her jaws were now gaping wide, dripping hunger-induced saliva onto my cheeks.

"I'm not a fish!" was the only thing I could think to gurgle in protest, silently praying that this was not one of the notoriously incommunicable *Quebecois* Ogopogos.

Fortunately, fish are generally a silent bunch, so the sound of one crying out for mercy was a startling auditory experience for the blue-and-black-striped dragon that was perched on top of me. She immediately scrambled back as fast as her flattened limbs would carry her, ending up half-submerged back in the water, ducking her head low to stare in astonishment at me, her small green eyes growing wide.

"*Brooble brooble*," the creature muttered with her mouth underwater, sending up bubbles to the surface.

"I'm not a fish," I repeated slowly, carefully rising to my feet. "Please don't eat me. I'm supposed to be on my honeymoon. Hence the chum-covered rental tux that I'm definitely not getting a deposit back on."

The Ogopogo silently slid farther back into her watery comfort-zone, dropping her head until only her eyes, nostrils, and the striped hump of her back were visible. She seemed to be considering whether or not I was a threat. By then it must have been fairly evident that I was not a fish, and I had managed to keep my explanation low-voiced enough to rule out baby harp seal. She did not know what I was.

"Calm down," I said as soothingly as I could, taking a tentative step toward the equally-wary dragon. "Let's just be ... multicultural. We're all Canadian here, and that's what being Canadian is about. I think."

"*Mrawr?*" the Ogopogo queried, raising her neck from the water and tilting her dripping head inquisitively to the right, staring intensely at me with a glittering left eye.

"I'm not going to hurt you," I said, continuing to slowly step forward. "And I'm hoping you'll return the favour."

The Ogopogo raised her head until it was at eye-level, then craned her neck forward to get within sniffing distance of me, her long, slit nostrils fluttering around the edges as she tried to determine friend or foe or food.

"*Meh*," she said, as if anticipating a response. "*Meh.*"

"I'm not a fish," was the only thing I could think to say once more. "I'm just a cowboy."

The sea dragon was almost nose-to-nose with me, but her mouth was still tightly closed, which seemed to be a good sign, given the circumstances. Those jaws could have engulfed my head with ease.

The next thing I knew, her long tongue was being eagerly wiped across my face, soaking it with drool as she licked me like a happy dog. She certainly wriggled and whined like one as well, seeming delighted to have made a new friend in the lonely cave. I could only hope that the seemingly affectionate display was a friendly greeting, and not some form of bizarre mating ritual. How was I supposed to know what was going on in that Ogopogo brain?

"Um, it's good to meet you, too," I gurgled as the giant reptile began nuzzling her two-foot-long jaws against my tuxedo, smearing it with saliva. Her breath was nauseating, but I was just glad that I wasn't smelling it from halfway down her gullet, as I could only assume that it smelled worse down there. I carefully reached out my hand to scratch the Ogopogo behind where her ears would have been if she'd had any, and her lapdog nature seemed to enjoy that. The dark skin on her head was hard and bumpy, with a spiky protrusion over each eye, but, aside from that, her body was as sleek and smooth as the harp seals she reportedly dined on. (For the record, there are no harp seals, baby or otherwise, to be found anywhere in Lake Okanagan, so I'm not sure where exactly that particular report came from, although I'm apparently the only person on the planet to whom it is not common knowledge.)

"*Meh, meh! Boof!*" the Ogopogo mumbled as she waddled past me with movements that were also very much like a seal's, looking back as if expecting me to follow her. I decided it would be impolite to refuse. (Never argue with a carnivorous host.) I walked behind her swishing tail until she stopped before one of the mud mounds that I had seen. Then she just stood and looked into it. It was darker in this part of the cave, so I grabbed one of the larger belligerent glowworms from the cold stone wall, and held its clammy body ahead of me to illuminate the path. Once I was alongside the Ogopogo's long neck, I could see that the mud mound was actually hollow in the centre, almost like a birdnest. And inside was a single pale-blue egg, nearly the size of a football.

"It's your baby?" I asked. The proud manner in which the Ogopogo lowered her head to nuzzle the egg with her smooth snout answered the question.

It was at that moment that I remembered how many mud mounds I had seen when I first regained consciousness. I quickly ran to the nearest cave wall and grabbed half a dozen more of the protesting bioluminescent grubs and held them aloft, lighting up a large portion of the cavern.

There had to be a dozen nests in that cave, some with as many as four or five eggs, far too many to have been laid by the lone Ogopogo who stood beside me. I realized the truth even as I spoke it.

"This is a communal nesting ground," I said, startled. "Do you all live here? All the Ogopogos?"

"*Meh,*" the Ogopogo grunted. I didn't know if she was agreeing with me, but the cave was certainly large enough to house at least a couple dozen of the creatures at a time. I could have used the space as winter feeding grounds for fifty cows, no problem.

"So where are the others?" I asked, glancing nervously into the darker side-tunnels.

As if in response, we heard a loud splashing coming from the moon pool, and turned toward the sound. However, it was not a pod of Ogopogos rising to the surface. It was two scuba-geared warriors, coming to my rescue. Corky and Sassy charged into the cave as fast as their flippered feet would carry them, spitting out oxygen regulators and drawing their weapons.

"*Get away from our baby brother, kraken spawn of the murky abyss!*" Corky roared, sliding his goggles onto his head, and brandishing his machete like a Samurai. "I swear I will cut your gargouille off!"

"No!" I protested, jumping in front of the Ogopogo with my arms outstretched. "She's friendly! She's a ... scaly dog that lays eggs."

"Did you hear that, Corky?" Sassy said sharply, dropping her underwater flashlight and cocking both barrels of the Bucky-Blaster. "That demon siren of the deep has Bucky under her spell! Cover your ears before her hypnotic song takes you too!"

"Do you hear any hypnotic song?" I said disgustedly. "She's not a kraken, or a siren. She's just the Ogopogo, and she's friendly. Here, watch this."

I released my glowworm prisoners and picked up a small, mostly-intact trout from the cave floor. The Ogopogo sniffed the air excitedly as the decaying fish was waved in front of her nose.

"You want this, girl?" I teased, dancing around her with the dangling fish. "Who wants the fish, huh? Who wants the fish? Does my girl want the fish?"

The Ogopogo seemed delighted by this game of keep-away, wriggling and hopping back and forth, her tail lashing about like a hunting lion's.

"*Meh! Meh!*" she cheered. Even Sassy seemed to be persuaded by then, lowering her shotgun in astonishment.

"You want the fish?" I whooped, tossing it up in the air. "Go get it! Get the fish!"

For a flippered quadruped on land, the Ogopogo

surprised all of us with her light-footed agility. She reared up on her back flippers and lunged nearly fifteen feet into the air, snatching the fish from the skies with her sharp teeth, and swallowing it in a single gulp.

"Awesome!" Sassy hollered gleefully as the dragon crashed back to the cave floor, and Corky and I shouted our agreement.

The Ogopogo, however, did not look awesome for some reason. As soon as she had all four flippers back on the ground, her entire body tensed up rigidly. Her small eyes bulged, and her massive jaws gaped wide, but no sound came out. She was completely motionless, aside from the occasional convulsion running down her neck and into her tail.

"What's she doing?" Corky asked, voicing the question that was in all of our minds.

"Probably just savouring the fish," I guessed, a bit uncertainly.

"I don't think she's savouring the fish," Sassy had to state, and I couldn't really argue with her. The Ogopogo looked more as if she was turning to stone, frozen and silent.

"Um, I think the fish is stuck in her throat," Corky said slowly, after a few awkward moments. "Yeah, I'm pretty sure the fish is stuck in her throat."

"No, that can't happen," I assured him. "It was just a little one."

"Can't?" Corky retorted. "Remember all of those fateful occasions on the ranch when we would say, 'The cows can't go down that wrong road?' The cows always went down that wrong road!"

"The fish isn't stuck in her throat," I snarled. "This thing chugs down fish for a living."

"Are you sure?" Sassy remarked. "Cuz I can see a fish-shaped lump halfway down her neck, and it ain't going down."

"That's not a fish-shaped lump," I declared with confidence. "Sheesh, Sassy, after a lifetime of me being right every time you start overreacting about something, would you just trust me for once?"

Before the final word had passed my lips, the Ogopogo's head pitched forward and slammed onto the rocky floor. Then her cramping muscles slowly relaxed, and she never moved again.

I had just killed the Ogopogo.

"Hmm," Sassy pondered. "Corky, what's that word for when something is more than just ironic?"

"Manganesic," Corky replied without missing a beat.

"Wow, Bucky, that was really manganesic," Sassy commented, putting a hand on my sopping, chum-and-saliva-covered shoulder. "Didn't think you had it in ya, baby bro."

"I just killed the Ogopogo," I said aloud, hoping that the statement would wake me up for the third time that night.

"Yeah, that was really something," Sassy said absently, lowering the hammers on her Bucky-Blaster, and slinging it back onto her shoulder. "I always figured that something that spends its life hiding in a lake would have better breath control. You know, Corky, it's times like this that just make me wonder.... Do you think Lindsay Lohan will ever make a theatrical comeback?"

"Actually, Sassy," Corky ventured, "that's a very good question, and one that requires some amount of deliberation. On the one hand, she's made some very bad lifestyle and career decisions which have led many executives to consider her a studio risk. But it's hard to deny that she has a star power and raw talent that leaves many of Hollywood's hot new faces in the dust. And, while I was initially appalled that anyone would dare to tamper with a Stevie Nicks classic, I have to admit that Lilo did a credible version of *Edge of Seventeen*, giving it a life of her own while being faithful to the vision and spirit of the original. So, to answer your question, I would say that Lindsay Lohan just needs to take on a few less-commercial roles to solidify her in the public eye as a competent leading lady, perhaps in independent films driven by storytelling. Personally, I believe that if she can just keep herself out of trouble until sometime around July 20th of this year, she should be fine."

"Yeah, those were my thoughts exactly," Sassy agreed. "To be sure, that whole *I Know Who Killed Me* debacle will be hard to live down, but– *Holy crap!* Bucky just killed the Ogopogo!"

"No!" I blurted in horror, running to the noble beast's side. I frantically shook her fallen head, but it only lolled limply in my hands, her tongue flopping out onto the rocks. The dragon of the Okanagan was dead.

In the interests of young readers, I'm going to gloss over what I said as I kicked the cave wall in frustration, but, unfortunately, what happened as a direct result of that kick is kind of crucial to the rest of the book, so I am obligated to give you all of the details. Apparently, my furious cowboy boot drove straight into a stress-crack that was already under considerable weight of overbear. As the echo of my unrepeatable explosion was still bouncing about the cavern, the cave wall began to split, leaving a long black crack that zig-zagged up to the cave ceiling, and quickly began to carve its way around several large stalactites. Small rocks began pattering down on our heads as we stared up at the rapidly-widening crack.

"*Cave in!*" Sassy bellowed, tossing me over her shoulder and charging back toward the moon pool, with Corky hot on her heels. She tossed me ahead of her like a torpedo, and I belly-flopped noisily into the water, although the sound was minuscule in comparison to the roaring of the collapsing cave roof. Corky and Sassy dove headlong into the water behind me, and the three of us plunged below the surface as rocks of all sizes rained down around us.

When we finally resurfaced, gasping for breath, the damage was done, and a cloud of dust hung heavily in the air. I could see that most of the cave was still intact ... except for the dozen or so stalactites that had dislodged and buried the Ogopogo. Only her head and neck were still visible, protruding from the base of the rocky rubble. And, as we all watched helplessly, one final knife-like stalactite gave way and plummeted to the cave floor, neatly severing the poor beast's head from her neck.

"Okay," Corky said, looking a bit green, "I've routinely pulled aborted calves out of cows, sometimes three weeks after the fact, and they came out of the womb as amorphous blobs of grey matter with a smell that could make your eyeballs bleed ... but *that* was the most terrible thing I've ever seen. Nice work, Bucky."

"Yes, I'm equally appalled and filled with contempt for Bucky," Sassy agreed emphatically. "Corky, give me that plastic bag. I want to take the head home."

"*I killed the Ogopogo!*" I screamed. "What is wrong with me?"

"Been askin' the Good Lord that for nigh on thirty years, Bucky," Sassy muttered, shaking a few invasive drops of water out of the large black garbage bag Corky had handed her. "Corky, get your Polaroid ready. Let's do this properly and get back to the boat while it's still salvageable. And before that blonde chick in the bridge drowns in her sleep. I suppose that's important, too."

"Well, good thing it's only a loaner," Corky cackled, then suddenly turned glum. "But I'll tell you one thing. Corb Lund is going to lay an egg when he sees it."

"Who's laying eggs?" I had to ask.

They ignored me.

THE BALLAD OF BUCKY™
(PART TWO)

Ian Tyson:

> *"The serpent bade him welcome*
> *When he surfaced from the bog.*
> *For, although she was a monster,*
> *She was kind as an ol' hound dog.*

> *"Hospitality was a trait*
> *That ran deep in the Pogo line.*
> *But offering goodwill to Bucky...*
> *That's casting pearls before the swine.*

> *"The pleas of sobbing children*
> *Couldn't melt his heart of stone.*
> *Hard as peanut brittle,*
> *He claimed the serpent's life his own.*

> *"With evil glee in flaming eyes,*
> *And spittle on his chin,*
> *He roared, 'Your head's mantle decor!*
> *Now face your extinction!'"*

Corky and Sassy:

> *"With his steed and shining blade,*
> *He bumbles 'cross the plains!*
> *A hero for our time,*
> *Except he's clinically insane!*
> *Don't cry out for the Air Force!*
> *Don't call the Armada!*
> *Just call on out for Buckyyyyyyyy...!*
> *Dragon Butcher of Canada!"*

Everyone is Going to Love Me

◇◇◇◇◇◇◇◇◇◇◇◇◇◇◇◇◇

OUR CHEEZIES-DESIGNATED TOUR GUIDE, Gil, was in a panicked frenzy by the time I trudged back into the hotel lobby at about three o'clock in the morning, dragging a barely-conscious Betty-Sue behind me. I'm sure we were a sight to behold, still dressed in our worse-for-wear evening attire, which I had been obligated to purchase from Grits for more money than I care to write down right now. Unlike the slack-jawed staff behind the reception desk, Gil didn't seem to notice our dishevelled appearance at first.

"Where have you been?" he whined, rushing over to us. "You were supposed to be at the plastic bag factory at six o'clock for my four-hour lecture on how the Cheezies get into the bag."

"Lost track of the time," I growled, heading for the elevator. "Excuse me."

"What's wrong with your wife?" Gil asked, finally noticing the flaccid woman in my arms, who was alternately snoring and giggling.

"Too much champagne," I sighed. "And chloroform."

"Is that a French red?" Gil asked.

"I like ice cream!" Betty-Sue tittered in her sleep. Betty-Sue hasn't been chloroformed as many times in her life as I have, so I guess her tolerance to the stuff isn't up to my level yet.

I had left Corky and Sassy alone at the dock to deal with their floundering craft, which was sitting so low in the water that Betty-Sue and I had gotten drenched as I carried her across the awash deck. All of Corky and Sassy's hunting gear had been washed into the lake, including Sassy's beloved Minigun, much to her chagrin, but I didn't care. I didn't want to tell the world about the Ogopogo, and I didn't want to tell Betty-Sue about why she had been chloroformed, and I didn't want to stick around and help Corky and Sassy perfect the story they were planning to tell Canadian country music star Corb Lund. I just wanted to get in my truck and go home. So I had thrown Betty-Sue over her saddle, deadman style, tying her hands and feet to the stirrups before leading her horse back to the ranch, where the ranch owner was less-than-thrilled with the sight of his rented formalwear. Grits didn't send me a Christmas card that year.

Our hotel phone rang just as I was putting my new tuxedo in the bathtub to soak, figuring that fresh blood/chum/saliva stains might be exceptions to the dry-clean only rule. I had already put my still half-drugged wife to bed, but the jangling phone didn't even make her twitch. When I answered on the third ring, Sassy asked if I had any cooking pots in my truck that were big enough to boil the Ogopogo head in, as she wanted to preserve the skull.

"No I don't have cooking pots in the truck!" I exploded. "What were you thinking? Seriously, do you two ever think about anything?"

"Bucky, me lad," she soothed me, "in matters of wildlife, it should only ever be about the shooting, not the thinking.

Especially monsters who add nothing to the food chain. Can you honestly tell me that an Ogopogo ever contributed to society? Aside from a feeble attempt at painting Canada with some semblance of mythological culture?"

"I don't think that argument's going to hold up in court," I growled. "Greenpeace is going to eat us alive if they ever find out."

"Walk it off, baby bro," Sassy said dismissively. "When all the whales in the world are dead, we finally get to lop a couple bucks off the price of shrimp. It's going to be a day of days, Bucky. Dead whales and cheap shrimp." Then she hung up.

Betty-Sue had a splitting headache in the morning, and that was probably why she didn't protest much when I informed her rather shortly that the honeymoon was over, and we were heading back to Coyote Yelp Pass. She just kissed me, took two aspirins, and began packing, muttering something about never touching alcohol ever again.

Gil was still aghast when we tripped over him in the doorway on our way out, and he begged us to stick around for his five-hour tour of the cornmeal mill that was scheduled for that morning.

"Sorry, Gil," I said, prying his fingernails off my old duffel bag as I tossed it into the back of my truck. "Kelowna's left a bad taste in my mouth. And it tastes like chloroform and carbon monoxide fumes and chum."

"No, you can't leave!" Gil protested, trying to block Betty-Sue as she skilfully danced around him and climbed into the passenger seat. "Do you have any idea what kind of people actually run W.T. Hawkins, Ltd? I'm going to get fired or worse if they think you were disappointed by your all-inclusive trip, even if you are the Creepy Canadian who tried to kill Max-Ram Target. I can't fail them, or I'm a dead man!"

"Seriously?" I asked, raising a curious eyebrow.

"No, probably not," Gil sighed, slumping against the tailgate. "I'm just a textbook overreactor-slash-voluntary whipping boy. My therapist had a clinical word for it, but I can't remember what it was."

"Relax, Gil," I said, patting his sagging shoulder. "Trust me, this isn't your fault, or Kelowna's, or Hawkins Cheezies's. We had a moderately great time in your company. We're just ranchers, that's all. We can only go so many days without being trampled by a cow. And I think the clinical word you're looking for is 'wimp.'"

"I hear you," Gil said glumly. "We all have our little soul-salves, I guess. Believe me, I get a lot antsier than this if I can't find a woman in a black catsuit who's willing to put a dog collar on me at least once a week and swat me with a rolled-up newspaper because I've been such a bad puppy. It's those little tics and quirks that help us to get through the day."

"Uh, yeah," I said, withdrawing my hand from his shoulder and wiping it on my jeans. "Hey, on an unrelated note, can I see that piece of paper I gave you with our home phone number on it? I think I gave you the wrong one."

He obligingly handed over the small scrap of paper, which I quickly stuffed into my mouth and swallowed. Then I wrote 1-250-555-5555 on another sheet, and handed it to him.

"Thanks," Gil said appreciatively, rubbing the paper between his tense fingers. "I'll call you guys. Frequently."

"I bet you will," I muttered under my breath, getting into the cab and slamming the door.

"We should change our number anyway," Betty-Sue advised me, locking her door.

"Yeah, first thing when we get back," I assured her,

gunning the engine. "Just do up your seatbelt and roll up the windows. That guy might chase us."

"What about Corky and Sassy?" Betty-Sue asked. "Are they coming home, too?"

"I think they said something about taking a detour to visit Canadian country-music icon Corb Lund," I replied, pulling out of the parking lot, as Gil waved frantically in the rearview mirror.

"Could we go with them?" Betty-Sue asked eagerly. "I love Corb Lund! What's that song he does about the trucks?"

"It's probably not a good day," I cautioned her. "Corky and Sassy can have weird effects on people. Like filling them with murderous rage, for instance."

"How can you say such things?" Betty-Sue gasped. "They gave us the greatest night ever last night, and you stab them in the back like that!"

"And, oddly, I'm at peace with it," I remarked.

I knew that I would have to tell her the whole truth very soon, but I also knew that she would want to return to the Ogopogo's cave as soon as I did, and I just wanted to get back to my cows. I decided to tell her once we were back in the saddle in the company of cows, and pray that she wouldn't divorce me over a measly sixteen hour delay.

I was in a fairly lousy mood, but the trip turned out to have a nice little turnaround at the very end. As we were driving northward through the surprisingly heavy Sunday morning traffic of the city of Kamloops, red and blue lights flashed behind us, and we were pulled over by an RCMP cruiser. After speculating to one another about what traffic laws we may have broken, (Although my agitated mind was secretly focussed more on firearm and environmental laws.) we watched as the most morbidly-obese police sergeant I have ever seen squeezed his way out of the sagging car, and oozed across the hot pavement toward us.

"Son, do you know why I've pulled you over?" he drawled, stooping to admire his handlebar mustache and bald head in my sideview mirror, the metal siding of my door creaking and buckling as his belly was pressed against it.

"Did I miss a red light?" I guessed. I could think of nothing else that I might have done wrong.

"Busted taillight, boy," he growled. "License and registration. Nice cowboy getup, by the way. Little early for a Hallowe'en party, ain't it?"

"We're real cowboys, Officer," Betty-Sue pointed out.

"No lip from you, little missy," the sergeant muttered, accepting the driver's license I handed to him. "I'm not in the mood."

He stared hard at my license for a long moment, his diminutive eyes growing wider with each passing second.

"Bucky Laroo?" he said. "That's your real name?"

"Always has been," I assured him.

"*The* Bucky Laroo?" he clarified, sticking his face within a couple inches of mine, his breath reeking of Bavarian creme filling.

"You've read Max-Ram Target's book?" I ventured with a sigh.

Suddenly, the massive sergeant was laughing uproariously and shaking my hand.

"Heck, no, son!" he blurted. "I've read yours! *Last Stand at Coyote Yelp Pass: The Tragic Cowboy Memoirs of Bucky Laroo* is the best book I've ever read!"

"Are you kidding me?" Betty-Sue cringed.

"No way!" he assured us. "I read it fourteen times last year alone! I can't believe this! Bucky Laroo! And you must be Betty-Sue Perkins!"

"Betty-Sue Laroo now," she corrected him.

"That's so beautiful," the sergeant whispered, clutching a hand over his heart as his eyes brimmed with delighted tears. "I was pulling for you two right from the first chapters."

He nearly suffocated me as he squeezed as much of his massive girth into the driverside window as he could manage in order to shake Betty-Sue's hand.

"Name's Burbank Mudford, ma'am," he said by way of introduction. "You've married one of the greatest overlooked heroes in Canadian history. It's a real honour."

"Why, thank you, sir," Betty-Sue giggled. "I've always thought so. Bucky, isn't it great to finally meet a fan?"

"*Mmph*," I replied, my face mashed somewhere in between my first fan's armpit and nightstick.

"I'm so sorry for pulling you over," Sergeant Mudford apologized profusely, bracing his feet against the asphalt and popping back out the window like a cork. "But I'm so incredibly honoured to have finally met you. My daughter's a big fan of *Lost Cause Kin*, but I've always told her that the real hero was the man behind the lyrics."

"No need to apologize," I assured him, trying to remember how to breathe again. "You were just doing your job."

"Well, actually I kicked out your taillight when I walked over here to make up my weekly quota," Mudford admitted, readjusting his service belt which had gotten a little tangled up in my face. "Sorry about that. But this is even better, because now I get to give a couple of real salt-of-the-earth types the royal treatment they deserve. I'll get you through this traffic in no time!" He grabbed the radio on the shoulder of his armoured vest and excitedly announced, "Calling all units, this is Car 87-Maple Glaze at the intersection of Highway 97 and Vicars Road. We have

Lane Bristow

a 10-13-945-2816-Honey Cruller-94 Diplomatic to Coyote Yelp Pass in progress. Requesting a full escort."

"*Copy that, 87-Maple Glaze,*" the radio immediately squawked back. "*Car 21-Apple Fritter, en route.*"

And that was how we left Kamloops, with red tape over the left taillight and six police cars plowing the road and blocking every intersection. When we were well outside the city limits, Sergeant Mudford pulled our truck over once more and gave Betty-Sue and I a crushing farewell group hug, ordering all of his subordinate constables to gather around and join in. It always feels nice to be on the right side of the law.

The remainder of the drive home was thankfully uneventful, but I knew the peace would be short-lived. Sure enough, it didn't last thirty seconds after we got back to the ranch that night. Apparently, Corky and Sassy had decided that Corb Lund could figure out what happened to his boat without a personal touch from them, because they managed to get back to the ranch ahead of us, parking the Bucky-Paver at its usual askew angle beside Gramps' cabin. I didn't realize that they had been in my house until Betty-Sue walked in the darkened doorway ahead of me, switched on the porch light, and let out a startled scream.

Evidently, she had never seen a bleached sea serpent skull on the kitchen table before. I know I hadn't.

"Surprise!" Sassy whooped, leaping out from behind the sofa with a fistful of balloons. "Happy Ogopogo Memorial Day! I boiled it with bleach and ammonia in an old wash basin in the bus on the way back. I can only imagine the kinds of dreams I'll have tonight."

"*Fweeeeee!*" the noisemaker in Corky's mouth agreed.

Of course, there was no hiding the truth after that. Fortunately, Betty-Sue took the news quite well, having been trampled by her share of cows as well in the past couple of years, and Corky and Sassy only had to tackle her to the floor and pry her hands off my neck two or three times before the belated tale was finished. About an hour later, she finally settled down enough to put the full blame on Corky and Sassy, where it belonged, and banished them for all eternity from our kitchen.

"Sorry, lover," she sighed, slumping into a chair and staring blankly at the massive skull on our kitchen table. "I guess I wouldn't have known what to say either."

"No problem," I croaked, massaging circulation back into my carotid arteries. "So now what do we do?"

"Well, we have to tell someone," Betty-Sue decided, tapping a fingernail against the skull's tapered snout. "Like a scientist or a reporter."

"You should take it to Dirt Harry!" Sassy blurted, popping up against the screen of the open dining room window. "That's the way to get the story done right!"

Betty-Sue irritably slammed the window shut and drew the blinds, but had to admit, "She may be right. We should take it to Dirt Harry."

"Who?"

"Hal Herald," Betty-Sue explained. "They call him Dirt Harry. He's an investigative journalist for *The Affluenceville Profit*. He's a great reporter, Bucky. He's the guy who exposed the Max-Ram Target elephant tusk smuggling story to the world."

"Yeah, nine billion dollars did seem like a pretty high net income, even for a movie star," I recalled. "Poor Mort.... Oh well, what the heck. Let's give him a call. Although, for the record, I still think we all might go to jail for this, and I'd much rather just bury this dang thing with Mrs Quivercake's jellied salad under a few kilograms of lye and sulphuric acid. But it's your choice. The skull is apparently a present for you, Corky and Sassy being the sentimental fools that they are."

The next morning, Sassy reassured me that Dirt Harry was the answer to breaking the Ogopogo story to the world.

"He never backs away from getting the truth," she said reverently. "He's like the reporters in all the Capra movies."

"That was never a good thing," I reminded her. "Even when they weren't all in the pocket of a fat man in a three-piece."

Sassy stared at me, and then skeptically inquired, "Are you absolutely *sure* that we're talking about the same movies?"

"Honestly, we're probably not," I sighed.

I called the offices of *The Affluenceville Profit* just after breakfast, and they agreed to connect me to Dirt Harry after I assured them that my story had monetary significance. I'm not sure why I suddenly felt the need to be secretive, but I could only bring myself to confide to Dirt Harry that I had made the biggest scientific discovery of the new millennium. I guess his shrewd reporter nose could smell a major story even over the phone, because he said that he believed me, and agreed to meet me that morning.

Of course, getting to Coyote Yelp Pass is never going to be as simple as saying, "Meet me in Coyote Yelp Pass." As I mentioned earlier, the route to my hometown is slightly more complex.

"Okay, you might want to write this down," I instructed Dirt Harry over the phone. "Take the Affluenceville Trail West until you pass the garbage dump. On the southwest side of it, you'll see an old sign that says '*Danger: Quicksand Bogs.*' Ignore that, they're mostly dried up anyway, but you're going to want to keep your wheels moving at all times, just to be safe. Don't stop until you're at the base of the canyon walls. They're not vertical in the ninety degree sense, but you're going to want to use the power winch mounted at the top to keep your engine from blowing out.

"If you make it to the top, you'll be on the Slash Trail, and it's a sixty-five degree road about seven feet wide, so you're going to want to keep your speed up around eighty-five, pull your passenger-side mirror in tight against the door, and hug the cliff wall on your right. You're not too attached to your paint job, are you?

"Anyway, that'll take you down to the Honest Kim Tributary Barge. It's great, you don't even have to get out of your car anymore. Just drop fifty cents into the tin can receptacle, reach out the window, and hand-over-hand the rope until you're on the far bank. Of course, as soon as you're on the other side, you're going to want to roll that window up real quick, because you'll be driving through our proudest landmark, the largest natural hornets nest in North America.

"A couple klicks farther down that trail, you'll see another sign for a Bed and Breakfast, and a kindly-looking old man sitting on the front steps of a rickety hovel, playing a banjo. Do not stop. No matter what you do, do not stop until you get to Pine Beetle Glen. Once you're there, you'll see a big metal box on a flat rock with a chainsaw in it. Use that to buck up any dead trees that are too big to drive over. Just top up the gas and oil when you're done. It's an honour system. Oh yeah, and that rickety hovel is within earshot of there, so if a kindly-looking old man with a banjo shows up, offering to help you.... Well, you've got a chainsaw.

"After the glen, you'll reach The Great Washout of '32. We haven't had time to fill it up again this year, but we did build up either side a bit like ramps, so you just need to floor it as soon as you see the warning sign. You'll get a bit of air, but you should be fine.

"Now you're in the homestretch, just have to survive Humpty's Great Falls. There's a bunch of old cider barrels and rope at the top, so just lash one to each corner of your car, and it should give you enough buoyancy to.... Okay, that was a joke, ha ha. Coyote Yelp Pass is half a klick past The Great Washout of '32. But, seriously. The old guy with the banjo.... Don't stop."

Apparently, Dirt Harry was a good note-taker, because his mud-caked silver Crown Victoria slogged its way into the ranch yard a couple of hours later. The sporty-looking young man met me by the machine shop, where I was welding together the framework for a new silage wagon. He stepped from his car, wearing a double-breasted navy pinstripe suit and a perfectly angled brown fedora. The man knew how to put together an outfit.

I had obviously expected a surprised reaction from Dirt Harry, but his response surprised even me. When I led him over to my truck box and showed him the Ogopogo skull, which was in an old cardboard box that used to hold rolls of baler twine, he nearly blew a gasket.

"Do you know what this is?" he kept squawking, waving his arms and jumping in the air. *"Do you know what this is? This changes everything! This changes it all! You and me are going to be the most famous people in the world, and everyone everywhere is going to love us!"*

"Really?" I said skeptically. "That doesn't sound much like the way my life works."

"Bucky, your life has been busted and rusting compared to the way it's going to work from now on," he gloatingly promised me. "I'm talking about fame, money, women, product endorsements, biopics, rehab stints, the whole shebang! We're the men who found the monsters. Now there's your *Time Magazine* cover caption!"

Shortly afterward, he got me to make a short testimonial statement which he videotaped for posterity.

"Welcome to Coyote Yelp Pass," I said, trying to smile on behalf of the billions of adoring fans whom Dirt Harry had promised would reverently view the film for years to come. "I'm holding the skull of a recently deceased Ogopogo, taken from a sea cave in Lake Okanagan two days ago. I would like to state for the record that I really did not mean to kill it ... and I probably shouldn't have said that. I'm just a cowboy. I don't know much about this biological crap aside from cowpies, but I think this was a plesiosaurus. Is that the right name? You know, those half-snake, half-walrus dinosaur things? Anyway, I think that's what it is. Isn't that nuts? Hi. I'm Bucky Laroo."

Dirt Harry was barely able to see through his joyful tears as he drove away an hour later, but he promised to return that evening with a paleontologist to verify the find, after which we would issue an official press release and become the most beloved people on the planet. I could not help reiterating that I found his blind optimism unnerving.

I have always found it wise to trust in my unnervings. I was hardly surprised when Dirt Harry did not show up that evening and could not be reached by phone, even though he had given me the numbers for all three of his telephones and all four of his pagers. In my experience, falling off the face of the earth is an inevitable consequence of overconfidence.

"You don't think he stopped at the old banjo guy's place, do you?" Betty-Sue queried nervously after I had called all of Dirt Harry's numbers.

"Banjo guy hasn't moved or changed clothes in the last six trips we've taken to Affluenceville," I pointed out. "I'm pretty sure he's dead, but, of course, I'm not getting close enough to check."

"Oh, of course," Betty-Sue quickly agreed. "That's how alligators get you. With patience."

The next morning, Betty-Sue was listening to Affluenceville FM 302.7, *The Trump*, when a news story was aired about a noted reporter for *The Affluenceville Profit* being arrested the night before. I turned up the volume just in time to hear that "since his arrest last night, famed journalist Hal Herald, aka Dirt Harry, has been tried and convicted of numerous counts of serial arson, insider trading, heroin trafficking, selling military secrets to North Korea, anthrax production, attempted reconstruction of the Berlin Wall, hate crimes against the nation of Cambodia, donkey hunting in Arizona, out-of-season donkey hunting in Mexico, the assassination of Hollywood actor Steve Buscemi, plagiarizing the literary works of Karl Marx, and serial polygamy." No definite jail term had been released to the public, but Dirt Harry's subdued attorney had officially stated that, "Anybody who had dinner party plans with Dirt Harry anytime in the next few decades.... Well, hopefully you kept all your receipts."

"Hmm," Betty-Sue said uncomfortably. "Well, that explains that...."

"That's it," I snapped, switching off the radio. "We're burying that skull in the backyard and forgetting about it. This is getting way too weird."

"I think you're overreacting about an innocent coincidence, Bucky," Sassy commented, having barged into my kitchen and helped herself to my cheese omelette.

"It doesn't strike you as odd that the radio hasn't mentioned anything about the assassination of Steve Buscemi until now?" I asked. "Not one word?"

"Not even a little bit odd," Sassy shrugged, still chewing

a mouthful of cheesy eggs. "I don't think you could have ever actually called the guy an A-lister. B-plus, maybe, but even that was only in the late 90s. He hit his stride in *Armageddon*, but that awful *Domestic Disturbance* really sunk him. Seriously, what has John Travolta been thinking lately?"

"Well, that fully explains it," I groaned. "I'm getting rid of the skull."

"I hate to get all territorial on you, lover," Betty-Sue stated, "but you did say that skull was mine, so, technically, I make the final call on what happens to it."

"Wait a second," I said, suddenly realizing the obvious fact that had evaded me until that moment. "Sassy, why the heck did you give that skull to Betty-Sue?"

"Don't give it another thought, Bucky," Sassy said mellowly, slurping down the last of my coffee. "Me and Corky got our own souvenirs. *Heh heh!*"

In retrospect, I really should have grilled Sassy a little harder as to what she meant, but I was unfortunately distracted by Betty-Sue suddenly tearing up and whimpering something about, "You don't think I'm good enough to be given a dinosaur skull!" And, while I was trying to convince her that I had only been questioning my sister's historically sinister/diversionary motives, the phone rang.

"Hello, this is Bucky Laroo," I sighed.

"Indeed it is," the male voice on the other end said gleefully. "Voice print's confirmed. It's him."

"What?" I said. "Who is this?"

"Sorry, Bucky, you weren't supposed to hear that," the voice sheepishly apologized. "I'll come right to the point. My name is Dr Kay Argo, and I'm Director of Research at the Affluenceville Through-The-Nose Mummification, Archeology, and Palaeontology Science Centre."

"Odd," I said. "I drove past the museum on my way

home a couple of nights ago, and the sign still said that Dr Grubwell was Director of Research. I remember it distinctly, because Grubwell is an unusual and funny name, and it makes me giggle like a ninny every time I drive past. My wife can testify to that."

"It is funny, isn't it?" Argo's voice agreed. "Unfortunately, there have been a few, shall we say, shakeups in the science centre in the past twelve to sixteen hours, and Dr Grubwell is all tied up at the moment ... metaphorically, of course. *Heh heh!*"

"Sorry, what was that?" I said. "I didn't quite catch your last two syllables."

"I can see that you're a man to whom time is a precious commodity, Bucky, perhaps even more so than you could possibly imagine, so I'll come right to the point ... again. Shortly before his arrest, Dirt Harry came to me with a little story about a most peculiar artifact in your possession, possibly the last decent thing he ever did before his secret life of villainy so dramatically caught up with him. Aren't you relieved that we didn't also fall victim to his madness?"

"I'm not sure," I replied cautiously. "I've had my share of run-ins with the criminally insane, and this Dirt Harry guy just didn't seem to fit the profile. He was too ... joyful."

"Well, that's the tricky thing about the most sociopathic of evil masterminds," Dr Argo explained. "Sometimes you can be talking right to them and never be the wiser. *Heh heh!*"

"Look, I hate to sound rude, but Dirt Harry did say that he was taking the story only to Dr Grubwell," I pointed out. "Can I speak to him?"

"Well, if you've been listening to the news, you must know that dishonesty would certainly not be below Dirt Harry. Trust me, he contacted me, not Dr Grubwell. *Heh heh!* Anyway, I was wondering when would be an opportune time for me to examine the skull. Obviously, we would like to have this unusual matter swept under the ru– Um, I mean, *resolved* as quickly as possible. Can we come out there sometime in the next five to fifteen minutes? Believe me, we would have been out there before you even knew about it, but we were unfortunately unable to locate Coyote Yelp Pass on any maps or GPS coordinates, and it is my understanding that you have zero transmissions that could theoretically be used to track your every movement via satellite."

There was something about his familiar phrasing and occasional cackling that made me uneasy, although it would take me some time to remember where I had heard similar patterns of speech. I decided that it was best not to give him directions to my home, even though I let myself believe that it was just the way scientists talked. Instead, I offered to bring the skull to the Science Centre after work that evening. I had already lost enough work hours because of that dang skull and my dang torpedoed honeymoon. Argo genially, albeit reluctantly, agreed to the brief postponement.

Corky, who had considered Agriculture to be the only science course he needed in high school, showed a surprising amount of interest in the fact that I was going to meet scientists, and begged to come along. After the disturbing sequence of events that had befallen Dirt Harry, reportedly within four hours of speaking to me about the Ogopogo, I decided that having a little backup wouldn't hurt, although I couldn't imagine a bunch of scientists being much of a threat to anyone. I had seen all the movies.

Before leaving that night, I asked Sassy, her Bucky-Blaster, and Gramps to stay with Betty-Sue at my cabin until I returned, and they agreed, although they didn't quite seem to grasp the gravity of the situation. (Gramps' response to seeing the skull of the legendary Ogopogo for the first time was, "That musta been one ugly 'gator. Bucky, your horse needs new shoes.")

"Thanks for coming along, big brother," I said as we headed off toward Affluenceville in his Hummer, the skull still in its baler twine box in the back seat. "I don't know what this whole deal with Dirt Harry is about, but it can't be good."

"Don't you worry about a thing, baby bro," Corky said confidently. "I got your back. I'll defend you from all foes, no matter how lecherous and unsavoury."

"Relax," I replied. "We're just going to see a bunch of scientists."

"Even better," Corky said. "But you've gotta drive back. We're hitting the town after we see these science guys."

"You'd better behave," I warned him. "I don't care how much of a celebrity you think you are. If your pants come off and get jammed into a jukebox again, I'm leaving you under the pool table."

"You clearly don't understand the sanctity of a barroom dare," Corky said, rolling his eyes.

When we arrived at the massive and lavish Science Centre, we were blocked from entering the main doors by an apparent old hippie who introduced himself as Dr Kay Argo. He was a surprisingly fit gentleman in a white lab coat, with a trim white beard and long white hair tied back in a ponytail.

"Where is the specimen?" he inquired, donning a pair of latex gloves after we had cordially introduced ourselves.

"It's in an old cardboard box in the backseat," I replied, gesturing at the Hummer in the parking lot behind us. "Want us to bring it inside?"

"Actually, no, you'd better not come in," Argo decided, quickly stepping out of the doorway and locking the oddly vacant building behind him. "I'll just examine it out here."

"Are those bullet holes in the walls?" Corky asked, looking at the reception area through the glass doors, which were also strangely fractured and perforated.

"Renovations," Argo said evenly, pressing a button on his keypad which dropped the steel security doors in front of the glass ones, blocking our view of the building's interior. "Shall we?"

When I showed him the skull, he didn't say anything for a long time, and I'm not sure that he drew in a breath for about a minute and a half. He just stood there with his lips pressed shut, his eyes bulging, and his face turning purple. I wasn't sure if it was the skull itself which had reduced him to that state, or the fact that the legendary discovery was being stored in a tattered cardboard box stained with axle grease.

"Mr Laroo," he finally said very slowly, and through clenched teeth. "You have made an amazing discovery. Unfortunately, I don't think it's something that anybody anywhere is ever going to be interested in. I would advise you to leave it with me. I might take a few samples just for the hey of it, and then dispose of it properly."

"Excuse me?" I said. "Doc, this is the Ogopogo."

"Well, we tried," Corky said dismissively. "Bucky, let's hit the town."

"I'll take it now, if you don't mind," Argo said, his tensely clawed fingers already reaching toward the backseat.

"Love to, but I can't," I assured the oddly-behaving man. "It's my wife's, and she wants to keep it for now. You're welcome to take some samples, though."

"Samples are worthless," Argo said darkly, the veins on his temples growing more prominent by the second. "I need the whole thing."

"That is a strange thing for a scientist to say," I noted, carefully stepping in front of him and closing the box.

"Especially after you just said that you were going to take samples. Nice meeting you, Doc. We're going home now."

"No, wait!" Argo blurted, but then apparently thought the better of it. He smiled passively and said, "Corky, you were planning a night out? May I recommend the Convoluted Science of Mixology Lounge? It's just around the corner on Profits of Current Treatment Avenue. You should stop by and get a taste of the science nightlife."

"You have one of those here?" Corky blurted in delight.

"One of what?" I asked.

"Scientist bars!" Corky exclaimed. "This is going to be great! Let's go."

"*Scientist* bars?" I asked incredulously.

"Of course," Argo replied. "The university, the natural history museum, and the research hospital are all on this block as well. You're in the Affluenceville Science Triangle. We all need someplace to congregate and relax after a hard day of ... sciencing."

"They have actual scientist bars?" I had to ask again.

"Don't waste my time, Bucky, just move!" Corky cheered, clambering into the cab. "You're the best, Doc."

Argo's quiet smile and folded arms told me that we were being dismissed, but I persisted, "Are you sure that nobody is going to be interested in the skull? It does seem like something that people would be interested in."

"I can assure you, Bucky," he chuckled, putting his hands on my shoulders. "Nobody is even going to have a chance to be interested in it."

"What?" I said, confused, and a bit chilled.

"Let's go, Bucky!" Corky was insisting, beeping the horn. "I can't cut loose without my designated driver. Whoohoo!"

"Go, Bucky," Argo said, smiling. "Have fun. Enjoy life while you still can."

I decided that scientists were just a seriously weird bunch, so I got in the Hummer, and Corky began driving to the nearby bar.

"I don't care what he said," I stated. "Somebody is interested in this skull. It's the only explanation for what happened to Dirt Harry."

"Forget about the Ogopogo, Bucky," Corky advised. "I know it's already distant history to me. Tonight is all about good times. We are gonna have some fun!"

"What are you so excited about?" I demanded. "The guy just mentioned a scientist bar and you almost blew your appendix."

"Hey, I've only heard legends about them," Corky said excitedly. "But they sound wild. Apparently, they're just like singles bars, but no one has a snowflake's chance of actually hooking up, because they're all so smart and boring. That puts their frustration level through the roof, so you're almost guaranteed to see some action. The desperate Alpha-male factor with these guys is unbelievable. They go ballistic. Get ready to rumble, Bucky."

"What did I tell you about picking fights with scientists in seedy bars?" I snapped.

"Nothing," Corky countered smugly. "And, as such, it would be hypocritical of you to try to stop me from doing something that you have never even had cause to warn me about before."

"Good point," I conceded. "Corky, if we ever end up in a scientist bar, don't pick fights with the scientists."

"*Touché*," Corky muttered, hating it when I managed to outmanoeuvre his logic. "But, if anything does happen to go down, by the random die roll of fate, I brought an extra roll of Loonies. Say the word and it's yours."

"What the heck would I need a roll of Loonies for?" I asked.

"Bucky, Bucky, Bucky," Corky laughed softly, patting my shoulder. "You're so cute and innocent and ignorant. Norman Rockwell would have loved you. Our code word for backup will be 'Help me, Bucky, there's too many of them, bring a pool cue.' Can you remember that?"

"Even if you paraphrased it," I sighed, pulling my cowboy hat down low over my ears.

"That's my baby bro!" Corky chuckled, giving me a rough hug.

The scientist bar looked a lot like any other upscale lounge, except for the fact that it was completely devoid of patrons. The only person in sight was the lean young bartender with curly brown hair, who smiled pleasantly as we entered.

"Welcome to Mixology," he greeted us. "Archie Aptrick at your service. Complimentary lab coats are available at the coat-check if you would like the novelty of making yourself one of our primary clientele for the duration of your stay. What's your toxic distilled substance?"

"Hey, where's all the scientists?" Corky demanded. "I heard this is supposed to be a scientist bar."

"Well, the evening rush hasn't started yet," Archie explained. "Most scientists work crazy hours, you know what I mean?"

"I'll have a coffee," I said, slumping onto a barstool.

"And for you, sir?" Archie asked Corky.

"What's the largest size drinking vessel you have available?" Corky requested, glumly sitting beside me. Evidently he needed to drink away the disappointment of not having any scientists to pick a fight with.

"That would be the large bottles that the higher-content alcohol is stored in before it's served, sir," Archie replied.

"We'll take four of those," Corky said morosely. "One brown, one red, one clear, and one ... off-tone yellow-brown."

"Sealy, we need a four gallon mix of the good stuff!" Archie called back to the storeroom.

"I'm on it, Archie," a perky female voice called back.

"Hmm, sounds cute," Corky said, cheering up slightly and trying to peer around the open door behind the bar to catch a glimpse of our waitress. However, before he could see her, and before my coffee was even poured, the main doors burst open and a muscular, shaven-headed, and odorous young man stormed into the bar, dressed in tattered street clothes, and obviously incensed.

"Okay, who's the wise-guy who parked a Hummer where I wanted to park?" he demanded with a drunken belligerence that almost struck me as being a bit over the top. He pointed an accusing finger at Corky and stated, "When I come here to relax and unwind in intellectual company, neatly compensating for all of my educational shortcomings, I don't want to have to work my way around a bunch of out-of-town rednecks who think my streets are theirs to do with as they like. I want to know who took my parking space. Was it you, hoss?"

Gramps once told me that the one surefire way to psyche out an idiot who was trying to pick a fight with you in a bar was to rip off your shirt and throw it on both sides of the room. Lately, I've been wondering how much hassle could have been avoided if I had recalled his advice that night. Probably not much, but I still wonder.

"Corky, go move the Hummer," I groaned. "Somebody needs to park a stolen bicycle there."

"See, Bucky?" Corky chuckled, ignoring my request and playfully elbowing me in the ribs. "Desperate Alpha-male factor. Told ya!"

"Oh, good grief," I muttered, putting my head in my hands. "My stomach hurts."

"Do you want the Loonies or not?" Corky asked, deftly sliding his hands into his bulging jacket pockets.

"Corky, that's not a scientist," I sighed.

"First you take my parking spot, and then you try to *ignore me?*" the intruder shouted, clenching his fists angrily.

"Calm down, buddy," Archie whimpered at the hostile vagrant, cowering behind the bar. "We don't want any trouble."

"Exactly," Corky said coolly. "We're just here to get wasted, which is historically synonymous with not wanting or causing any trouble."

"You'd better move that rig out of my spot, pard!" the man roared, stepping threateningly toward us. "Nobody parks where Theo Gapps wants to park!"

"You have a *car?*" I said incredulously, although admittedly judging the book by the cover.

"Hey, lots of angry homeless people have cars," Archie pointed out defensively. "Sheesh, this is Affluenceville, okay? Most of our street people have RVs."

"Can it, barkeep," Theo Gapps snarled. "I want my parking space, and I'll take it if I have to."

"We parked half a block away in a metred space, in front of a flower shop that closed six hours ago," I reminded him. "There's free parking spaces vacant right in front of the door you just walked in. What's the big deal?"

"The flowers remind me of my grandmother's country garden in the summer nights of my youth, planting seeds in the light of the moon," Theo admitted. "The sight of them takes me back to a simpler time, when the world made sense, and relief from it all was only as far away as my imagination."

"Oh," I said. "Actually, that was a better answer than I expected. Corky, go move the Hummer."

"*I'll* move your Hummer!" Theo snapped, recovering from his momentary state of emotional vulnerability in an instant. "Fork over the keys, cowboy!"

"Last chance, Bucky," Corky whispered gleefully to me. "I've got an extra roll."

"Let's just go," I growled, standing from the bar. "This is starting to feel like a dream I had once."

"You're not going anywhere until I've beaten my lack of parking inconvenience out of you!" the furious patron declared, shoving me back into my seat.

"Hey, that's my baby brother you're messing with," Corky snarled, lunging out of his seat with a coin roll in each fist. "To be sure, I've made my fortune by exploiting an arm's-length disdain of him in front of an international audience, but that's just good business sense. You're making this unnecessarily personal, hombres. Now why don't we all just sit down and have a couple of rounds? First one's on me."

Without waiting for a reply, he slammed a hard fistful of one-dollar coins into Theo Gapps' jaw, dropping him onto his back.

"Well, that's round one," Corky growled, shaking his tingling fist. "Who's up for round two?" He then turned to me and smiled as he held up his gold-filled fist. "See, Bucky? Loonies. Never go into a bar without them."

As he was speaking, he didn't notice Gapps lunging to his feet behind him and grabbing a pool cue from a nearby table.

"Corky, duck!" I shouted.

Corky's barroom brawl instincts were at high alert, and he immediately hit the carpet rolling as the cue whistled over his head.

"It's just you and me now, buckaroo!" Gapps roared, charging toward me with the cue raised high over his head.

I have always believed in turning the other cheek, but not in matters concerning wooden staves that can cave your skull in. I took a quick step back and drew back a fist to defend myself. Unfortunately, in doing so, I unknowingly drove my reared-back elbow hard into the left eye of the dark-haired waitress who had silently emerged from the backroom with Corky's drinks, and her dark-rimmed glasses did little to cushion the blow. She was immediately knocked unconscious, and the four bottles flew from the tray in her hands as she toppled to the carpet, which really wasn't thick enough to make a decent landing pad. She never flinched as the glass bottles shattered on the floor all around her, spraying her with four gallons of alcohol.

"Uh-oh," I cringed. "That was at least partially my fault."

"Bucky, this is every bit your fault!" Corky corrected me emphatically.

"Sealy!" Archie cried out, appalled as he rushed to his fallen coworker's side.

"Oh shoot, that ain't good," Gapps said in a suddenly panicked voice, quickly wiping his fingerprints from the pool cue with his shirt sleeve as he turned and ran for the door.

"Nice going, Bucky!" Corky snapped, rising from the floor and watching our would-be attacker flee the premises. "You just ruined what could have been a beautiful bar brawl. Everyone knows that the saloon girl always has a comedic role to play. She could have been smashing a beer bottle over your head right now!"

"It was an accident!" I whined. "You know I don't hit women. Sure, I tasered one multiple times and threw a kitchen chair at another one's head on the night that Max-Ram Target saved my life, but that was under completely different circumsta–"

"*Shut up and get out of my bar, you cowboy freak!*" Archie bellowed, kneeling beside the waitress and trying to revive her.

"Hey, that's profiling," Corky admonished him, although, after shooting a skeptical sidewise glance at me, he had to admit, "But I can sort of see where you're coming from...."

It wasn't until that moment that Corky absently looked down and got a good look at the young waitress sprawled on the floor, and a strange transformation came over him. I had seen him bring giggling groupies home to show off to Gramps, and I had heard his boastful, if generally unsubstantiated, claims of the beautiful female celebrities he had dated, but I had never once seen such a look of enrapturement come over his slack-jawed face as the one that appeared when he first laid eyes on the still and lovely form of Sealy the waitress.

"Good gravy, Bucky," Corky said breathlessly, his eyes bulging. "First you kill the Ogopogo, and now you kill an angel. God is not letting you into Heaven anymore."

"She's not dead, she's unconscious," Archie muttered, checking the young woman's pulse and then scrambling to his feet. "I'm calling an ambulance."

"Wake up, pretty lady," Corky whispered, kneeling reverently by her side and taking her hand as Archie dashed to the phone behind the bar. "Okay, Bucky, we're clearly running short on options here. Shoulder-shaking and hand-patting haven't worked. We give her another two minutes to come around, and then I'm Snow Whiting her."

"You can't kiss an unconscious woman," I said, revolted

by the very thought. "Do you have any idea how sick and disgusting that is?"

Corky looked at me strangely, and then replied, "Are you suggesting that Walt Disney packaged perverted and possibly dangerous ideas in the guise of harmless family entertainment? I suppose the next thing you're going to try to tell me is that his production company's predominant theme of always listening to your heart is bad advice."

"No, I'd never suggest that," I assured him. "I'm sure Idi Amin never once listened to his heart. That was the whole problem."

"Obviously," Corky remarked, patting Sealy's hand. "Come on, princess, nap time's over. I'm not going to let my nasty baby brother hurt you anymore. Wake up."

"What happened?" Sealy whispered as she began to stir, her eyelids fluttering open. Corky's eyes bulged even wider as the girl's beautiful dark brown pupils were revealed, even though her left eyelid was changing colour faster than the average chameleon.

"Ma'am, you were horrifically assaulted by an unstable cowboy in a scientist bar," Corky managed to say without stammering noticeably. "I regret to admit that he's a blood relative, but I can only hope that it will not tarnish your opinion of all members of the generally-noble Laroo clan. We're an honourable, gentlemanly bunch, with one glaring exception."

"I love you, too, big brother," I said wearily.

"Laroo?" Sealy said curiously, gazing hypnotically into Corky's eyes. "Did you ... rescue me?"

Corky was getting more tongue-tied by the dark-haired beauty every minute, but managed to give a short nod, and then introduce himself.

"Hi. I'm Corky Laroo."

Don't Bring a Camel
to a Gunfight
◇◇◇◇◇◇◇◇◇◇◇◇◇◇◇◇◇◇◇◇◇◇◇◇◇

H ER NAME WAS SEALY Kent. She did not want
to go to the hospital, but for the next three and a
half hours, I was forced to wait in the Hummer as
Corky persuaded her to "walk it off" with him around the
vast city block. Not that Sealy required much persuading, as
it was fairly obvious that she was just as taken by my brother
as he was by her. Archie the bartender just seemed relieved
that his waitress was not in a coma, and readily gave her
the rest of the night off, even going so far as to close down
the bar, which I thought was an odd move for a responsible
business owner. But I didn't voice my curiosity. I figured
that the more Archie and Sealy were allowed to forget about
my existence, the less likely they would be to have me sued
or arrested. So I just waited in the darkness of the truck with
the skull of the Ogopogo that I had murdered, watching my
brother occasionally walk past with the waitress I had nearly
murdered. I missed my cows, and I had only been away from
them for six hours.

I must have dozed off, because I didn't realize that
Corky had returned until he was shaking me vigorously by
the shoulders to rouse me.

"Yeah, I'll make the coffee, baby," I yawned, sitting up.

"Shut up and wake up!" Corky said exuberantly. "Bucky, she's perfect. She's like a Canadian Sofie Allsopp. We have absolutely everything in common!"

"That's quite a claim," I noted, rubbing my eyes with a thumb and forefinger. "Not quite on par with dating Jane Krakowski and Taylor Swift in the same year, but it's still impressive."

"Did you see her eyes?" Corky marvelled, his own eyes vacant with the blindness of love. "Like black onyx stones forged in kiln fires."

"That ... doesn't make any sense."

"And those sexy librarian glasses with the dark rims...." Corky continued wistfully. "I was just waiting for her use that husky voice to start lecturing me on late fees."

"And the imprint of my elbow in her left lense wouldn't have diminished the effect?" I ventured, unable to resist goading him.

"Murderer," Corky growled.

"Yes, she was very pretty," I obliged him. "Can we go home now?"

"Very pretty?" Corky said disgustedly. "That's all you can say? Canadian gold medalist Ashleigh McIvor was very pretty. Sealy is ... exquisitely Victorian."

"I don't think that's an actual measurement on the beauty scale."

"Zip it, Buck-of-the-draw," he growled, shoving a crumpled sheet of paper in my face. "Read it."

"'Our Mutually Cherished Things,'" I read the title aloud, squinting in the dim illumination offered by a nearby streetlight. "Oh, that's cute. She made the M in 'Mutually' look like a heart. She's a keeper, bro."

"*Read it!*" Corky rasped, barely able to contain his glee. "We're solvates!"

"I'm going to guess that you meant 'soulmates,' but I had to do more than my share of the homework on that one," I replied. "Okay, I'm reading, I'm reading.... 'Favourite song: *Can't Fight This Feeling Anymore* by *REO Speedwagon*. Favourite movie: *Bill Cosby, Himself*. Favourite food: Cornbread with jalapenos and taco beef. Favourite hobby: Base-jumping over alligator-laden waters in the Florida everglades....' Wait a second. These are *mutual* favourites? She likes your Mexican cornbread, too? And the alligator thing?"

"What did I tell you?" Corky cheered. "And, before you even say it, she wasn't just agreeing with everything I said. We couldn't believe it at first, so we picked a category and we'd both write down our favourite at the same time. Two lists, Bucky, and they both matched all the way down. It's true love, Bucky! This is even better than a fight with a bunch of lab coats would have been!"

"'Favourite movie villain,'" I continued obligingly, now actually growing a bit curious about the shocking similarities. "'Hans Gruber, *Die Hard*. Favourite movie hero: Bruce Willis's feet, *Die Hard*. Favourite possible tongue-in-cheek depiction of the Nixon Watergate scandal aftermath: *Marvin K. Mooney, Will You Please Go Now!* by Dr Seuss....' Seriously?"

"Read it again with the mind of the times, Bucky."

"Okay, this is creeping me out," I confessed, handing the paper back to him. "Can we go home now?"

Betty-Sue was understandably surprised the next morning when I told her about Dr Argo's lack of interest in the skull, and I didn't even bother telling her about his oddly creepy behaviour. After our random encounters with Gil and MC Morlock in the past months, she did not need any more creepiness introduced into her life for the next couple of years, regardless of how intellectual the source. Creepy is just universally creepy, no matter what kind of doctorate supposedly justifies it.

"Well, we tried," I said as cheerfully as I could manage at the breakfast table. "Let's just put the skull on the mantle, and it'll make a great conversation piece whenever we get company ... if we ever get company."

"All right, listen up!" Sassy announced from the head of the table, where she had habitually positioned herself almost every morning since Junior left, generally after sleeping on our couch. "Tomorrow is Canada Day, which means I'm going to be tied up all day assembling my homemade fireworks, and I don't want any extra chores getting in the way. We've got a big day ahead if you guys want the show of a lifetime tomorrow, so lets divvy up the empire, shall we?"

"Sassy," I commented, "as a thirty-three-year-old woman with the residual wealth of a previously-stellar musical career, have you ever contemplated getting your own place? Maybe even your own couch? We would help you build a cabin out here."

"Why would I want another place?" Sassy said irritably, missing the point as usual. "Between this place, and Gramps' cabin, and the Bucky-Paver, I can hardly remember whose couch I'm crashing on anymore. Anyway, if I didn't have your couch, I would have nothing to store my fireworks under. Now be silent, loser laps, and let's go over the agenda for the day."

"You know something, Sassy?" Betty-Sue growled. "I don't know how you can call yourself a good Christian when you're so dang meanspirited."

"I am not," Sassy said, looking offended.

"Seriously?" I cringed. "Remember when Mr Hayashi

was getting all nostalgic a few years ago, after the doctors thought they found that tumour? He was wishing that his daughter would settle down and have a family, since he didn't want to die without seeing a grandchild, and you said, 'Relax, Mr Hayashi. Amanda's holding a beer in front of a campfire and flipping the bird in 90% of her Facebook photos. I'm sure she'll be pregnant in no time.' Remember that?"

"Mr Hayashi has a daughter?" Sassy marvelled. "Ain't that something.... Where's Corky?"

"He said he was going to be up all night in the bus, writing sonnets," I sighed. "See, Sassy, that's a good example of utilizing one's own domestic property. As the bus is Corky's official bought-and-paid-for place of residence, it only makes sense that he would reside there ... and sleep on his own couch."

"You're losing me, Bucky," Sassy said absently, unfolding the day-plan she had drawn up. "Okay, we've got nothing but short grass left in the second section of the lease line, so somebody's got to move the herd up to the second junction. That's going to be an all-day gig, but it's a fenced stretch, so it shouldn't take more than one person. Who's up for it?"

"I'll do it," Betty-Sue volunteered. "Porkchop's been needing a good workout. I'll get her saddled up right after breakfast."

"*Sucker!*" Sassy gloated. "Man, I love being the delegater. I should have thought of this years ago. Okay, Bucky-Go-Lightly, that leaves you and me to reinforce the uprights on the new grain shed, and then we'll take a ride up to the sacrificial rock at the edge of The Spirit Realm and put out the monthly placation offering to keep the hostile mountain spirits off our backs."

"Oh, come on, Sassy," I groaned. "We've been over this. They're not hostile mountain spirits."

"I'll tell you what they're not," Sassy snapped. "They're not afraid of my M134 Minigun. And do you know why? Because *you* let it get washed off Corb Lund's boat into the middle of the Okanagan! I don't care what they are or aren't. That Minigun was our best defence against them, and I'm not taking anymore chances, so gather up the first-fruits of our labours!"

The first-fruits of our labours were actually the overripe crabapples that had fallen off the scraggly little grove behind the barn, which even Waggy the pig wouldn't touch. After sweltering for the day in the confines of the new grain shed, and finally finishing it, Sassy and I loaded up as many of the putrid orbs as we could cram into a black garbage bag, threw it into the back of the Hummer, and hitched the horse-trailer onto the back fender ball-hitch. Then we saddled up my old white gelding, Homestretch, and Sassy's three-year-old chestnut filly, Kelly Clarkson, and put them into the trailer for the rough drive up to "The Outer Rim" of Banshee Screech Peak. (The sacrificial rock was less than half a mile from where the trail ended, an easy walking distance, but most of the locals considered it prudent to have something a little faster than a pair of cowboy boots underneath them when venturing that close to The Spirit Realm. There was always the off-chance that the hostile mountain spirits would not look with favour upon your offering, choosing instead to look with delectable favour upon you. I'm not superstitious, but I'm not taking any chances, either.)

After a pleasant, if habitually ominous, ride to the edge of the vast murky bogs that surround the mountain's base, we laid out the placation offering without incident and spurred our mounts back toward the Hummer.

"So how are the fireworks this year?" I asked. "The ones that I just learned are under my couch?"

"Even more volatile and unstable than last year," Sassy gloated. "Them babies are gonna blow the lid off the town. Did you pick up that birdshot for me?"

"Yes, they're in your bus," I replied. Sassy was usually exclusive in her use of double-ought buckshot or slugs in her 10-gauge shotgun, but, in the interests of tradition, she would obligingly switch to the lighter birdshot shells every July 1st. After all, Canada Day just wouldn't be Canada Day without the Coyote Yelp Pass Annual Owl Hunt. It's the heartwarming little traditions like that which make the holidays something to be remembered.

The sun was still up, but had dropped below the treeline, its light filtering through the leafy boughs ahead of us as we rode westward to the vehicle. It was then that I noticed that Sassy had become strangely silent, and was glancing around in an agitated manner. Usually, my sister was in her element on a horseback ride through the mountains, often singing or telling me stories about wonderful things she had done. That day was different. Her eyes were wide, as were her nostrils, and she was breathing through her mouth. Her right hand was gripping the stock of her Bucky-Blaster in the scabbard under her leg, causing me to unknowingly grasp the stock of my own 30-30 deer rifle.

"Are you okay?" I finally asked, not knowing what could have driven her to such a state. I hadn't seen or heard anything out of the ordinary.

"Silence, Bucky," she replied, and it wasn't in her usual belligerently high-octave voice. For the first time in my life, I had been silenced because somebody actually needed to hear something!

Sassy reined Kelly Clarkson to a halt, and I instinctively stopped Homestretch alongside her. Sassy seemed to be alternately straining each individual sense as hard as she could. First she plugged her ears and closed her eyes so that she could devote her full olfactory senses to the smells of the air around us. Then she opened her eyes, but held her breath, allowing her keen eyes to achieve their full potential in the fading daylight. Finally, she took another deep breath, closed her eyes, and took her fingers out of her ears, letting the minute sounds of the silent forest pour into them.

"What the heck is wrong with you?" I finally demanded, unable to bear the suspense anymore as I grabbed her by the shoulder.

Sassy jolted slightly as she opened her eyes, and then stared hard into the woods directly ahead of us for another long moment.

"There's something in those trees," she muttered.

"Is it them?" I asked, suddenly nervous in spite of my professed skepticism.

Sassy did not reply.

"Sassy?"

I looked over at her, but found myself instead staring into the void which my sister and her horse had occupied only a moment before. Sassy had ghosted into the trees without so much as stirring a bristled coniferous bough.

"Uh ... Sassy?"

A lone wolf chose that moment to contribute to the eeriness of the moment by letting out a mournful howl in the distance.

"Oh, perfect," I sighed. "Homestretch, I want my boring back."

Homestretch muttered an unintelligible reply, having grown accustomed to my whining for the solace of mind-gelling monotony a long time ago. Without waiting for the urging of my spurs, he began plodding back toward the truck once more. The old gelding was getting close to retirement age, but he still loved nothing more than going home.

You learn to spot subtle variations in your daily routine and surroundings when you live in the stillness of the mountains. It's not like city living, where every moment of every day brings a different psychedelic collage of smells, sounds, sights, and prickly sensations, some of which have actual relevance to you. On the ranch things often don't change for months or even years at a time, my twenty-plus-year-old pickup truck being a prime example, so you tend to sit up and take notice when even the slightest change occurs, even if you arrive at the altered locale well after the fact.

Such a change had taken place when I returned to the clearing at the end of the trail where the Hummer and horsetrailer were parked, and it was of sufficient variance from the longstanding norm to prompt immediate verbalization of the discovery to my patient steed.

"Why the crap is there a Bactrian camel in my horsetrailer?"

Again, Homestretch didn't have anything useful to say, nor did the camel who ignored me altogether, choosing instead to hang his head out of the open side window and focus all of his efforts on determining how much frothy green slime he could lather up onto his massive lips and jowls with perpetual chewing motions. Man alive, camels disgust me.

My hand cautiously reached for my rifle stock once more, only to discover that it had ghosted away as mysteriously as Sassy had a few minutes earlier.

"Nice piece, *monsieur*," a chilling voice said from behind me, or, rather, as chilling as a heavy French accent can be.

I gave Homestretch's reins a slight tug to the right, and he obligingly turned me around to face the source of the French voice.

He was a very thin man with an even thinner moustache and skin whiter than my own, what was left of his brown hair buzzed into a rigid military brushcut. He seemed much more at home in the woods than most strangers I had seen in this part of the world, French or otherwise. He wore a blue and white camouflaged jumpsuit and a forest green beret, along with an armoured vest and pouches of ammunition. Obviously, his nationality did not affect his choice of weapon, because he had a Belgian-made FN P90 assault rifle slung under his right arm, and my considerably less shiny American-made Winchester Model 94 Trapper in his hands.

"In response to the question you asked, as well as to the obvious one that you haven't, my camel is in your horsetrailer because he is tired from our long and arduous trek into the mountains in search of you," the Frenchman explained, checking the barrel and lever-action of the rifle he had taken from me without my even knowing that he was there. "I reasoned that after I killed you, I could let him rest in there while I stole your H2 and drove it back to civilization."

"Ah, so we get to the meat and potatoes of the matter," I said knowingly, nodding my head. "I thought you had that whole marrow-frosting assassin-esque look about you. Mind if I ask what I did this time? Is it the dead dinosaur, or is Mort trying to get his spotlight back again?"

"Who?"

"Max-Ram Target."

"No, he has nothing to do with this one. You are being killed now because of the Impossible Lie."

"Excuse me?" I said uncertainly. "Look, if you want the stupid skull, it's in a cardboard box in the backseat. I really should take it inside, I suppose."

"No, no, I kill you either way," the man said. "You are not scared, yes?"

I shrugged acceptantly, rubbing my twitching left eye.

"Well, it's kind of like anything on a rote pattern. You get used to it. Like chronic dermatitis."

"You use the topical antifungal cream?"

"Yeah, it helps."

"So, it is true, you have no fear of death," he said admiringly. "You should know that I could have laid in wait and shot you from the saddle without you ever knowing I was here, but I needed to look on the face of the legendary Bucky Laroo, the only man in history valiant enough to make the great Klaus Klotzern back down in reverence."

"Hey, how's he doing?" I had to ask, still feeling an odd twinge of affection for the ice-blooded East German who had spared my life on the night that Max-Ram Target saved it.

"Oh, he's fine," the assassin assured me. "He sent, how do you say ... newsie letter with his *Noel* card last year. He's raising goats now. Apparently, it's the best Feta you ever eat."

"Well, that's real good to hear," I acknowledged. "Tell him I said hi ... with my dying breath."

"Certainly, Lucky Bucky," he genially agreed. "You know that is what they call you, yes?"

"That's not an accurate description," I had to point out. "Before I married Betty-Sue, the closest I ever came to winning the lottery was that time I nearly choked to death on a pearl in my can of smoked oysters."

"He even has defeats the power of the killer shellfish," the Frenchman said, shaking his head in stunned admiration. "*Bon fromage*, how I have dreamt of this day! Every assassin to operate in this hemisphere in the past three years has dreamt of this day, but it is all mine! Killing the legend will only make me the greatest legend of all."

"Oh, for the love of horseshoes, just pull the trigger!" I growled. "Do all you assassins talk so much?"

"Only to those who are worthy of our time," he coldly assured me. "Let us at least part as acquaintances. You will begin, please."

"Hi," I sighed. "I'm Bucky Laroo."

"You may call me The Sickle," my cordial murderer replied, bowing slightly.

"Do you actually use one of those?" I said hopefully. "Because I've always had this irrational fear of open-casket funer—"

"Yes, I have a sickle, but, no, I would never use it on the great Bucky Laroo. Noble warriors such as yourself deserve to die clean, with no more than a single bullet to the heart."

"Gee, thanks," I said glumly. "There goes the whole dying wish bit...."

"Sorry, but I would be desecrating my own values as well as your hallowed memory to make a mess out of you, like I have done to so many meaningless others. I regret that your end can't be as you would prefer, but at least it's as you deserve."

"Well, I'll take what I can get," I admitted. "Also, your adorable French accent takes a bit of the bitter edge off the pill, so.... Whatever. Thanks for being so upfront about it. Cowboys appreciate that."

"You are most welcome," The Sickle said graciously. "And don't worry. In the unlikely event that Heaven exists, it won't be lonely, because I have to also whack everybody in your immediate family, since you've most likely spread word of the Impossible Lie to them as well."

"Okay, I get it," I muttered, wearily stepping down from the saddle as I suddenly found myself burdened with the responsibility of staying alive, now that my family was being targeted.

I was out of options. In spite of his eccentricity, it was

obvious that The Sickle was a trained killer. My horse wasn't as fast as his trigger finger, and Sassy had the keys to the Hummer. I could think of only one way to delay the inevitable.

"Tell you what," I offered. "I'll give you the ultimate honour, Sickle-Joe. You get to put down those guns and kill me with your bare hands. We'll live or die as equals. How does that flip your waffles?"

"You don't playing games with my heart, no?" The Sickle said, his voice shaking with sudden emotion. "Because already I am very vulnerable-static."

"I think I understood that," I said agreeably, unbuttoning and rolling up my plaid shirt sleeves, while still keeping a careful hand on Homestretch's reins. "No tricks. Just two skinny guys having a toe-to-toe slugfest until someone's heart explodes from the sheer manliness of it all. What do you say?"

"You do me such much honour," The Sickle whispered, joyful tears rolling down his sunken cheeks as he hurled both of his weapons to the ground and began warming up by twisting his lithe body into a reef-knot. "That flips my *crepes* very well. *Let's get ready to rumba, cowboy!*"

"Again, I think I know what you meant," I groaned. "Sassy, anytime you're ready."

"*Yaaah!*" Sassy roared as she and Kelly Clarkson burst from the trees to the south at a flat-out gallop, no more than twenty feet away.

"*Sacré poulet!*" The Sickle gasped. "*Saboteur!*"

He tried to make a dive for my rifle, but it was too late. The ever-unstoppable Kelly Clarkson plowed into The Sickle like a locomotive, sending him flying about sixteen feet through the air before he was intercepted by the base of an unyielding spruce tree.

"Run for it, Bucky!" Sassy shouted, whipping the Bucky-

Blaster out of its scabbard and charging after our fallen attacker. "Get the skull! I'll save or avenge you, depending on how this plays out."

"Sassy, get back here!" I yelled, snatching my rifle and springing back into Homestretch's saddle.

The Sickle had not been stunned for more than a second, and his elite training had kicked in just as suddenly. In a flash, he had somersaulted around the base of the tree, and disappeared into the thick brush behind it, shouting what may have been French obscenities back at us.

"Sassy, don't follow him in there!" I warned my sister, who, unfortunately, was already in highset juggernaut mode.

"Never fear, Bucky," she admonished me, as her charger raced headlong into the foliage. "These are the woods in which we are at home. *I'm coming, Frenchy!*"

"Crap," I growled, having no choice but to spur Homestretch into a gallop and follow my deranged sister into the green maze. "Sassy, killing people makes Jesus sad! *Do not kill him!*"

"No promises," Sassy called back, already hidden from sight by the trees. "I've been in a bit of a mood lately...."

Homestretch can still outrun just about any other Quarter Horse in British Columbia, especially when heading in the direction of home, which, coincidentally, we were. As such, we managed to catch up with Sassy in a matter of seconds, but held a few feet behind her, allowing her to utilize her superior tracking skills.

"He's heading for the switchback notch!" Sassy shouted. "Stop running and face the fiddler, little rabbit."

I almost rear-ended Kelly Clarkson when Sassy abruptly drew back on the reins and the filly slammed on all four horseshoe brakes simultaneously. Sassy sat up tall in the saddle, her eyes bulging and sweeping the woods in every direction.

"Sassy...?" I ventured, pulling Homestretch up alongside her.

"Son of a donkey spit!" Sassy squawked, whirling her horse around and heading back the way we had come. "He doubled back to the Hummer! The slippery frog is going for his camel!"

"Actually, I'd guess that he's going back for the bullpup assault rif–"

"Silence, Bucky! *Move!*"

We galloped back through the trees, our faces getting assaulted from every angle by clawed branches. My mouth and eyeballs were filled with pulpy leaves, which may have been why I didn't see The Sickle, or his retrieved assault rifle, until his camel collided headlong with Homestretch, knocking both of us out of the saddle. We hit the ground in a tangle of limbs and guns, and rolled across the forest floor, trying to untangle our entwined rifle barrels. In the process, I was forced to neglect the number one rule of riding the aptly-named Homestretch, ("Don't drop the reins.") and he was already distinguishable only as a billowing dust-trail pointing directly toward the ranch.

Sassy's superior sense of situational awareness had given her the foresight to swerve her horse around the oncoming camel at the last second, and she was already whipping around with the Bucky-Blaster in firing position. Unfortunately, she couldn't get a clean shot at The Sickle without blowing my face off as well, so she held her fire, which was actually a bit of a relief, as I had always wondered if such an occurrence would bother her all that much.

"*Die, Bucky!*" The Sickle rasped as he clobbered me across the face with my own rifle butt, easily torquing it from my feverish grasp. He probably could have turned the weapon on me in a more efficient manner, but was interrupted by the panicked hooves of his camel, which was equally determined to dispatch at least one of us in the confined space between the tree trunks. We both rolled clear in opposite directions, leaving my gun in the churned dirt beneath the camel's belly.

The Sickle rolled to his feet with the agility and grace of a lethal ballerina, but Sassy had bailed off Kelly Clarkson and tackled him before he could raise his weapon. He casually judo tossed her across the small clearing, slamming her into me as I tried to regain my footing among the tree roots, and knocking both of us into the dirt. I tried to roll away and grab Sassy's fallen shotgun, but The Sickle was too fast, stepping between me and the 10-gauge weapon with the FN P90 in his hands.

"And so ends the great Bucky Laroo," The Sickle gloated, raising his weapon as he stood over me.

Out of the corner of my eye, I could see Sassy slowly getting to her feet, just beyond The Sickle's peripheral vision. I had to keep him distracted, for just another moment.

"Wait!" I blurted as I stood up and held my hands out toward him, my mind racing. "Before you kill me, there's one thing I need to know."

"What?" he demanded.

Sassy was on her feet by then, and beginning to stealthily advance from behind The Sickle.

"Uh, how exactly did you ever manage to...?" I stammered, having no idea where my question was going.

Sassy sprang forward like a leaping gazelle, bypassing The Sickle altogether and slamming a hard fist into my jaw. I was knocked onto my back once more, roaming points of light doing the tango in my eyes.

"Sorry about that, Bucky," Sassy apologised, shaking her tingling fist. "But you were probably going to ask something retarded like, 'Who hired you, and why?' and I couldn't bear the thought of such cardboard dialogue. There's only one thing I want to know before we're toast. Who brushes your teeth when you're in a coma? And how do they keep you from aspirating on the toothpaste?"

"Cowboys...." The Sickle said disgustedly, taking up the trigger slack on his automatic rifle. However, the overwhelming resonance of Sassy's deftly presented question had caught up with him, and would not allow him to pull the trigger.

"You have to admit, it makes you wonder," Sassy said smugly, folding her arms.

"Perfectness," The Sickle muttered, keeping us covered with the bullpup weapon as he drew a satellite phone from his fatigues and punched an eleven digit number into it. "Now that is just going to eat me up all day."

He held the phone to his ear, the booted toe of his right foot tapping impatiently against the loam as he listened to the ringing tone.

"Who are you calling?" I asked.

"My sister-in-law," he replied briskly. "She works in radiology department. Hang on."

I could hear the phone stop ringing and a garbled voice answered.

"Hey, Nancy," The Sickle said cheerily. "It's Vasil.... Fine, fine.... Hey, I was just wondering.... What...? No, I did call.... No, I did. Ask Mom. She can tell you.... Hey, I told you I had to work that night.... Fine, Nancy, I love your cooking, I just had to work! *Bon* grief.... Look, this has been bugging me. Who brushes the teeth of the comatose patients? Or do you put some kind of attachment on their breathing tube...? Uh-huh.... Uh-huh.... Okay, that was all I want– What? Yeah, I'll call her. I love you, too.... *What...?* Oh yeah? You get real job! Little Miss Perfect, giving people cancer while you hide behind your prissy lead apron– Hello?"

He hung up and pocketed the phone.

"She said there's specially-trained nurses and orderlies who do it," he reported. "Okay, where were we?"

Sassy was choking back giggles. "Your name is Vasil?"

"*Shut up, you stupid rednecks!*" The Sickle screamed, raising his gun once more.

"Wait!" Sassy protested. "You didn't tell us how they keep the patients from aspirating!"

"Oh, crap," The Sickle sighed, obligingly drawing the phone from his pocket again. However, before he could tap *Redial*, a charging Sassy had hurled a rock at his face, cutting the call short, and following it up with a flurry of furious punches to the assassin's face and solar plexis.

"Bucky dies when *I* make the call, not before," she growled, giving the assassin her specialty Sockeye Salmon Sucker left hook across the face, and then clamping her teeth onto his right ear, recalling the technique that Gramps had allegedly used to defeat the intruding hostile mountain spirit in the fall of '78. The Sickle was screeching like a startled owl as the two grappling Titans seized the FN P90 and fought for sole possession of it, noisily discharging every one of the fifty-one rounds into the air in the process. When the weapon ran dry, Sassy was straddling the supine assassin, her strong legs wrapped around his throat and right arm in a triangular *Sankaku-Jime* chokehold, and he was rapidly running out of air. I took advantage of the momentary diversion to seize a large fallen branch and break it across the back of Sassy's head.

Obviously, I had meant to hit The Sickle in the face, but that French guy had the reflexes of one of those snakes that eat mongooses, even trapped in a chokehold with a decreased SpO2 level. He managed to jerk away from my double-handed swing, pitching Sassy forward and leaving her suddenly exposed pigtails to absorb the blow and snap the heavy stick in half.

"Bucky, you're a dead man," she managed to snarl before her eyes glazed over and she slumped to the ground.

"Sorry about that, big sister," I whined as The Sickle and I both lunged for my rifle, which the camel was still trying to stomp into the ground. I managed to grab it first, but The Sickle hit me in the chest with a flying karate kick, sending both of us, and the camel, tumbling down a nearby steep slope toward Besa River. I don't think either one of us managed to land a punch the whole way down, but having a bellowing camel as the sandwich filling between us did more than enough damage, to say nothing of the boulders we were bouncing off and dislodging. Neither one of us could even stand by the time we reached the rocky bank at the bottom and splashed into the river shallows. Nobody had a rifle by then, and we were bleeding from more cuts and scrapes than I cared to number. The camel seemed least affected of the three of us, lumbering to its feet and wandering off down the riverbank.

I tried to rise, but my head seemed to have become clogged with horseshoe nails at some point during the prolonged tumble, and weighed a metric tonne. The Sickle came to more quickly, shakily standing and drawing a long curving sickle from the sheath on his back.

"Now you die, cowboy," he gurgled, holding the harvesting tool over my face.

My eyes had glazed over to the point where the only thing I could make out was blurry moving shapes in the filtered sunlight. I could not even see The Sickle, only a looming shadow growing ever larger in the centre of my vision. However, the one thing I could see was the multiple cuts on his blurred face, letting the smell of his foreign blood into the air.

I heard a twig snap faintly in the distance.

"One more question," I ventured, managing to sit halfway up, my head pounding. "Do you eat a lot of jellied salad?"

Before he could answer, his blurred shadow was blotted from my view by a lightning-fast, and much larger, shadow which swooped out of nowhere with a fearsome screech. The Sickle only had time to let out a considerably less fearsome screech of his own as he was snatched away into the trees. His sickle clattered onto the bare rocks where his feet had been a second before.

After that, there was nothing but stillness, and the sound of the unruffled camel burping up its cud.

I sat up again, rubbing my eyes to clear my vision, and trying to ignore my pounding head. When my vision cleared, I could see no trace of The Sickle, or the fearsome shadow that had spirited him away. All I could see was the camel, and my upside-down cowboy hat, which was just beginning to float downstream. I groggily stumbled into the river and snagged it before it could catch the rapid current midstream. However, no sooner had I clapped it back onto my head than I heard another sound, one which was rather unusual in our area. It was the sound of a low-flying helicopter.

The sleek black attack aircraft appeared around a bend in the river, no more than twenty feet above the face of the water, close enough for me to hear the *Air Wolf* soundtrack that was blaring dramatically over the public address system.

"*Get back!*" I hollered, frantically trying to wave them off. "You're not local! It's not safe!"

"*Attention, redheaded cowboy with freckles!*" an

authoritative voice echoed over the PA. *"Are you Mr Bucky Laroo?"*

"Yes, I'm Bucky Laroo!" I screamed back. "What is going on here?"

The only response was a single tranquillizer dart that slammed into my right ear, plunging my world into blackness all over again. And I could add one more cause of unconsciousness rendering to my ever-growing list. It's not easy being a cowboy.

LUCY
◇◇◇◇◇◇◇

THERE ARE FEW THINGS worse than shattered anticipation. I had secretly been looking forward to seeing how much of Coyote Yelp Pass would be demolished by Sassy's homemade fireworks again that year, and I ended up sleeping right through Canada Day! My best guess is that my eyes closed on Wednesday, June 30th, and didn't open again until sometime around Friday, July 9th. Wonderfully relaxing stuff, those tranquillizer darts, and they don't leave you with the hangover headache of chloroform. I decided right then and there that, henceforth, I only wanted to be rendered unconscious by tranq guns, my new KO agent of choice. However, a lower dosage would have been appreciated. I do so hate being in a chemical coma on Canada Day.

I could hear piano music drifting in from a long way off, but that was officially the only thing that was registering. My eyes did not want to open, my limbs did not want to move, and my tongue did not want speak until it had been fully re-hydrated, a process that I estimated would not take more than a week or two of continuous submersion in water. Yeah, parched does not even begin to describe it.

I was lying in what seemed to be a massive bed under the most glorious comforter I have ever felt. My chin felt oddly prickly as my head lolled slightly to the right, brushing my jawline against my clavicle.

"Silk pajamas?" I croaked, patting my supine body just to be sure. "Betty-Sue? When did I get silk pajamas?"

"She's not here, Bucky," a young girl called out from somewhere beyond the room I was lying in, her voice carried clearly by the two-way baby monitor that was sitting on the night-table beside the bed. "Are you getting up or what?"

I opened my eyes. I was in a mansion. Either that, or I was in a master bedroom that had once been part of a mansion. However, when I looked at the partially ajar door leading out to an enormous hallway, the second possibility became much more unlikely. I was in a mansion. A really, really big mansion.

My brown plaid shirt and Wranglers had been washed and folded, and set on the corner of the bed, along with my cowboy hat and newly-polished boots. Even my folded castrating knife was perched on top of the pile, its worn faux-ivory handle nicely shined. I got up, got dressed, and cautiously ventured out into the hallway, after slurping down the thoughtful glass of water that had been waiting at my bedside.

I'm not much for scenic descriptions, but I do recall that the gold trim on the wallpaper seemed to be made of real gold, as was the gold trim on all the furniture, sculptures, and wall hangings. The sum total of my life's earnings might have been able to buy an armrest off one of the smaller sofas in that hallway.

I followed the sound of the piano to a spiral staircase that was wide enough to drive Corky and Sassy's tour bus down at highway speeds. The endless staircase led to a rotunda sitting room, filled with even more jewel-encrusted furniture, luxury apparently being an acceptable substitute for comfort in the world of rich people. I descended the staircase to the ground floor, a process that took no more than eight minutes, and that was where I saw the backside of the piano, or thought that I did. I had never seen a transparent grand piano before, and I wouldn't have believed it if I hadn't seen the slightly distorted shape of the young pianist sitting on the transparent bench on the other side. She was approximately half a football field away, but it was obvious that she was an elegant young girl in a casual white blouse, green plaid skirt, and black knee socks, her red hair tied back into a neat braid. Standing vigilantly at her side was an imposing bearded man in a tuxedo, his jet black hair slicked back tightly against his skull with a rare form of styling gel that poor people are imprisoned for even knowing the brand-name of.

"Ah, good, you're up, Mr Laroo," the child said graciously. "Carlos and I were beginning to worry."

"Where's my sister?" I demanded, glancing uneasily at the unfamiliar tropical greenery that was visible through the thirty-foot-high windows, beyond a marble veranda.

"She's fine," the child said simply. "She's back at your ranch, with the rest of your family, and none the wiser."

"Where's my horse?"

"You dropped the reins. Same story."

"Where am I, and why do I seem to have a full beard?"

"I do apologise for that," the eloquent girl said regretfully, standing from behind the piano and taking a step toward me. "But please understand that mistakes do happen. All it takes is one little mixup with the placement of a decimal point, and suddenly the tranquilliser rifle is loaded for a ten day nap, rather than a ten minute one. I assure you there is nothing to be overly concerned about. As penance for his mistake, Carlos here has been working your muscles regularly to prevent atrophy, as well as keeping you bathed and groomed. Again, I'm really sorry."

"I don't have the words to express how creeped out I am right now," I confessed, rubbing my twitching eye.

"You're a hard worker, Bucky," the girl pointed out. "A man who devotes his life to providing food for the world. Such a man deserves a good week-and-a-half nap at least once in his life. And you need not be concerned by the fact that your heart stopped three or four times during the first couple of days.... Was it four times, Carlos?"

"Five, ma'am," Carlos replied promptly.

"Of course," the child said, slapping her forehead. "But don't worry, Bucky. We got it started back up again every time before there was much significant tissue death."

"Would you mind defining 'significant' in this instance?" I requested. "Yours might not be the same as mine."

I was only about twelve feet away from the small girl, and the shake of Carlos' head told me not to come any closer. The girl, however, smiled and curtsied politely.

"My name is Lucy," she introduced herself, carefully stepping over a small iguana that was scurrying across the polished stone floor. "Welcome to my summer home, Bucky. Well, welcome to one of them. I've got three or four."

"Five, ma'am," Carlos corrected her. I wasn't sure if I had seen the man blink yet.

"Dare I ask if I'm even still in Canada?" I had to ask. "There's not a lot of iguana's in my region. Or in my longitudinal hemisphere."

"Where exactly you are is none of your concern, Bucky," Lucy said coldly, but then had to think hard for a moment before admitting, "Shoot, actually I can't remember what country we're in. I lose track. Carlos?"

Carlos leaned down to whisper in his principle's ear. Lucy cringed.

"What the heck are we doing there?" she demanded. "Did I *ask* for that?"

"You were adamant, ma'am."

"You don't realize how lucky you ugly, poor people are, Bucky," Lucy sighed. "You forget what day of the week it is once in a while. I forget what continent I'm on."

"Who are you?" I asked.

"I already told you. My name is Lucy, and this is my security chief, Carlos. What more do you need to know?"

"I don't need to know if that piano is made entirely out of real diamonds," I admitted, "but I really want to know."

"No, silly," Lucy laughed. "The work that would have to go into something like that would be absolutely mind-boggling. Simplify, always simplify. It's just carved out of one really big diamond."

"See?" I said. "Kick me. I need to just go with my first instincts from now on."

"She's a beaut, isn't she?" Lucy said admiringly, stroking the clear keys. "She was my birthday present last year. Not what I'd asked for, mind you, but I got over it."

"Yeah, I can empathize," I remarked. "My sister used to give me balls of cow hair for my birthday. But a solid diamond piano is cute."

"Yup, I've come around to it," Lucy smiled, patting the piano cover. "At first, I was just going to donate it to the citizens of Mexico to pay off their national debt and aid in their fight against political corruption, but now I'm getting a little attached. Every girl likes her shiny things, right?"

"Why am I here?" I asked irritably. "Who was that Sickle guy who was trying to kill me?"

"We only know him as The Sickle," Lucy admitted. "We tried to get to you before he did, but his people had more lead time. You'll be happy to know that we've spread the word about you brutally annihilating him to the appropriate circles. That should buy you a bit of time before they try again, so rest assured that your family is safe. They're even more scared of you now, Bucky. You can use that to get out of this alive."

"I didn't annihilate anybody!" I growled.

"Illusion can be power, Bucky," Lucy assured me. "In your case, it's probably your best bet. Anyway, The Sickle was a very unpleasant man, even by French standards."

"Was?" I queried, feeling a sinking in my gut.

"It would seem that the swamps around your Banshee Screech Peak are not good places for strangers to wander lightly in," Lucy noted. "Carlos' men searched briefly for The Sickle after securing you, but there was little sign of him. In fact, the only sign of humanity to be found was.... What was it again, Carlos?"

"A femur, ma'am."

I was going to reiterate my innocence in the potentially grisly matter, but was shocked to realize that my Ogopogo skull was no more than fifteen feet away, mounted neatly on a short marble column between two gold-trimmed sofas.

"Hey, that's my Pogo skull!" I exclaimed, rushing over to it.

"Yes, it is," Lucy affirmed. "I thought we should bring it along for safekeeping until you were recovered. That's why you're here, Bucky. That is why The Sickle is trying to kill you."

"He could have just asked for it," I pointed out. "I didn't want the dang thing, anyway."

"He wasn't trying to steal your discovery, Bucky," Lucy corrected me. "He didn't want the discovery to exist. His first move after killing you would have been grinding that skull to powder."

"That's crazy," I said. "Who wouldn't want to know that a monster really existed?"

"You didn't discover a monster, Bucky," Lucy noted. "Once it's out of the cushy realm of mythology, it becomes just another animal, and, as it turns out, this animal is one that we've known about for years. It's called ... a plesiosaurus."

I couldn't understand why she had turned a bit green and seemed to be choking on her own words.

"Yeah, that's what I told Dirt Harry," I recalled. "It looked like what I've seen in books, anyway. Are you confirming that my Ogopogo is a leftover dinosaur?"

"No, you idiot, I'm confirming that your Ogopogo is a leftover prehistoric aquatic reptile that lived at the same time as the dinosaurs," Lucy snapped. "Now it's living at the same time as people, and that is really going to screw things up."

"Well, technically, it's not *living* with people," I had to point out.

"Carlos?" Lucy quipped patiently, folding her small hands in front of her skirt as Carlos drew a collapsible cattle prod out of his tuxedo pants and gave me a stern electrical jab with it.

"*Owch!*"

"I don't appreciate rhetorical responses, Bucky," Lucy muttered. "Get off the floor. You're going to squash the iguanas."

"Sorry," I croaked, stumbling back to my feet and trying to shake the excess electricity out of my brain.

"Listen carefully, carrot head," Lucy cruelly instructed me. "Here's the essence of scientific discovery in a nutshell. The person who discovers a magical, winged, fire-breathing dragon is going to be an international hero. The person who discovers a living dinosaur, or cohabiting aquatic reptile, is just going to get The Sickle. Got it?"

"No."

"Oh, good grief," Lucy groaned. "Okay, try to keep up here. Isolated as you may have been all your life, I'm sure that you've still had time to learn about the ultimate scientific truth, namely a system of orderly biological progression known informally as the theory of evolution. You are familiar with it?"

"It's been mentioned once or twice," I acknowledged.

"Do you believe it?" Lucy persisted.

"Not really," I said. "Sorry, I was King James raised."

"Eek, this is even worse than I thought," Lucy cringed. "You just set off a hand grenade inside a brand new can of worms, Bucky."

"What?"

"Science doesn't like people like you, Bucky," Lucy stated, "because science likes to play God. By establishing set legal parameters requiring knowledge to be something that can be visually observed, tested, and reproduced in a laboratory setting within a closed system, science effectively does not allow for the possibility of anything bigger than itself. Hence, science is the official outer limit, and, hence, science is God. The fact that we haven't been able to reproduce a single aspect of the evolutionary process in lab tests is considered to be a minor speed bump."

"Well, that's kind of a narrow-minded viewpoint," I said.

"True enough," Lucy freely admitted. "After all, if science is simply a set of dimensional laws created by a higher being in order to orchestrate time, space, and matter, then it stands to reason that true creation cannot readily confirm or deny a creator. However, human nature makes flat-out denial a lot less scary than confirmation, so that's what The Establishment prefers to do."

"What does this have to do with my Ogopogo?" I asked again.

"Science set some pretty rigid boundaries, Bucky," Lucy explained. "Every first-grader on the planet can tell you that there's sixty-five million years of buffer protecting them from getting eaten by a dinosaur. You screwed that up. When the first innocent child gets eaten by a dinosaur on their way home from school, you will have to live with the knowledge that it's every bit your fault."

"How the heck is that my fault?" I demanded.

"Duh!" Lucy retorted. "You can't get eaten by something that hasn't been discovered yet. You found the Pogo, and you survived, so you officially opened the door. Any blood that follows is on your hands. But that's not even the biggest problem."

"Sorry, but I'm still not following you," I interjected. "How can any future eatings be my fault, when we don't know how many people have already made the discovery over the years, but either got eaten in the process or were just dismissed as perpetrators of some kind of hoa—"

"Silence, Bucky!" Lucy barked. "Leave the rationalizations to your betters. Just take the flak."

"Got it," I sighed. "Historically, I'm pretty good at that."

"By the time this is over," Lucy said ominously, "you're going to wish that you had been eaten by a dinosaur. The Sickle was just the start. They're all going to come after you."

"Who?"

"Everyone who understands the moral and, more importantly, financial backlash of rewriting every modern science, biology, and natural history textbook on the planet. They are going to kill you, either physically or socially. Probably both."

"What?" I protested. "I just discovered the Ogopogo! If

anything, I'm going to be famous. I'm not trying to brag, but this is big stuff."

"*Silence, Bucky!* Don't you get it? They are not going to let that happen! Look at your interview with Dirt Harry. Do you honestly think it was just impossibly bad timing for you? Your story got quashed, and The Sickle came knocking to make sure it stayed that way."

"How the heck do you know all this?" I asked. "You look like you're twelve."

"Eleven, actually," the child replied evenly. "I was nine when I got my PhD in communications and biotechnology from the University of Persian Purr Crossing, Florida, and I was ten when I created and patented The Big Shiny Thing That Replaced The Internet."

"That was *you?*" I gasped, stunned and awed.

"Quite frankly, Mr Laroo, I don't generally give out this information to peons, and especially not to cowboys from Canada, so keep it tucked under that Stetson, got it? I am a member of a very old family which is on the opposite side of every social, intellectual, and financial spectrum curve that you might be on, if we're even on the same curve at all. International banking, technological innovations, political puppeteers.... You name it, we're probably it. Along with a dozen or so other families, we form the global intellectual elite that has kept this planet ticking properly for centuries. There is not a thing that happens that we do not know about and regulate."

My eyes narrowed as I fully comprehended the bold statement. "So ... you guys knew that Uwe Boll was going to take advantage of that German tax shelter to make his films, and you just let it happe–"

"That was a rule-proving exception!" Lucy snapped indignantly.

"But you are saying that the entire global intellectual

elite knows that I found the Ogopogo, right? Did you guys send The Sickle after me?"

"Similar measures were extensively discussed," Lucy confessed, looking a little sheepish. "But no. We believe that The Sickle was working for an international cabala of scientists who think they own the planet. They're a fanatical bunch who we call The Establishment. They're the ones who make sure that the most mind-blowing discoveries never get a chance to blow anyone's mind. There is no level they will not stoop to in order to ensure that textbooks only have to be sporadically updated, rather than comprehensively rewritten. That's why we came looking for you. We feared that your discovery, codenamed *Impossible Lie*, might be unsettling enough to rattle even the most devout of The Establishment's fanatics, a small core group known as the Galapagos Brethren. They're a virtual cult of scientists, Bucky, and they will stop at nothing to save on the cost of printer ink for new textbooks. Look at Affluenceville. The Galapagos Brethren couldn't figure out where Coyote Yelp Pass was, so their North American standby operatives initiated a hostile takeover and lockdown of the nearest urban centre. They needed to control every scientific mind within two hundred kilometres in an effort to contain the damage."

"Oh," I said, thinking back. "So Corky and I really did see bullet holes in the walls of the science centre."

"They're all fine, of course," Lucy assured me. "Cowboys are easy enough to rub out, but people start to ask questions when hundreds of scientists and professors go missing in the middle of the night. They'll just be in intensive subliminal deprogramming for the next four to six weeks. By the time that science centre opens up again, nobody who works there will remember ever having heard the word Ogopogo. And the scientist bar you went to? Why do you think it was so empty? Trust me, most scientists are wasted 24/7, because of their extremely high desperate-Alpha-male factor. That place should have been packed by 9:30 on a Tuesday. Kay Argo may be a paleontologist, but my bet would be that his real specialty is professional cleaner. He sent you to that bar to get you away from your vehicle, so that his hired goons could tag it and figure out where you lived. They figured that would be smarter than just icing you in the middle of the city, but they won't make the same mistake twice."

"Ah, now it all makes sense," I realized. "So the guy who came in to pick a fight was just a hired thug sent by Argo to make sure we were distracted while the tracker was fixed to the Hummer. I thought his belligerence was a bit over the top. Or is he one of The Sickle's crew? I mean, no matter how fanatical a bunch of evil scientists are, they must have hitmen or mercenaries on their payroll to take care of real-world business outside the lab, right? The Sickle was like French Special Forces or something. If such a thing exists."

"I can't tell you who their muscle is," Lucy reluctantly admitted. "We've never been able to figure out who they outsource their dirty work to. One thing about scientists. Their nerd factor is high enough to conceal paper trails very well. We know they must be hiring someone, but we have no idea who. The Sickle is one of the few names we've come up with, but it's not a known alias."

"He called himself Vasil on the phone to his sister-in-law," I supplied, remembering how the name had made Sassy giggle.

Lucy nodded. "We'll look into it, but it's likely an alias, too, and 'sister-in-law' is probably code. Trust me, Bucky. No matter what kind of pansy-pant lily-livers the scientists themselves might be, they wouldn't take a chance on hiring anyone but the very best to wipe out all traces of you. Cowboys don't get to change the world, Bucky. A lot of people have made sure of that."

"So the entire scientific establishment is secretly terrified of me right now?" I clarified. "Cool...."

"You don't know the half of it," Lucy said confidently, striding to the nearest wall, which was no more than an eighth of a mile away, and unveiling a small hidden safe from behind an original Van Gogh hanging. "Even if you had given the skull to The Sickle, he still would have whacked you. Your discovery has effectively threatened the most closely guarded scientific staple on the planet, one that my own family once worked hard to establish as unassailable in the global subconsciousness."

She completed the numeric combination and biometric security on the safe, and it let out a hiss as the heavy alloy door opened. Reaching inside, she carefully drew out a very old-looking roll of brown parchment, and held it out for me to see as she began the long walk back to the piano.

"In 1859," she monologued authoritatively, "my ancestors nearly bankrupt themselves by launching one of the largest-scale advertising campaigns in recorded history, in order to promote a radically original book entitled *On the Origin of Species by Means of Natural Selection, or the Preservation of Favoured Races in the Struggle for Life*, the compiled life's work of a brilliantly angry little man named Charles Darwin."

"Did you really just use the words 'little' and 'angry' to describe one of the leading scientific revolutionaries of the last thousand years?" I had to ask.

"You have a lot of freckles, Bucky," Lucy marvelled, "and I think those freckles are the reason that everybody everywhere wants to punch you in the face as soon as they meet you, if not one of the primary reasons that so many of them actually want to kill you. They don't compliment your face or your hideous red hair at all. You just look like you got sneezed on by somebody who was having a nosebleed."

"You know, you're a redhead with freckles, Lucy," I couldn't help replying. "I don't know why I'm stating the obvious right now."

"I'm not freckled," Lucy said passively.

"Yes, you are," I assured her. "Your entire face is covered with them."

"No it's not," Lucy returned. "Every time I run crying to my bodyguards, chauffeurs, extended domestic staff, or pampering parents, they all assure me that it's not. Carlos?"

"Your face is the hue of an unblemished peach, ma'am," Carlos said promptly.

"Thank you, Carlos." Lucy smiled appreciatively. "And my hair...?"

"Gold woven on the loom of Rumpelstiltskin, ma'am."

"Okay, I think that might just be a perk of affluence," I remarked.

"No it's not," Lucy chuckled.

"Yeah, I say that a lot, too," I noted. "Okay, fine, Darwin had issues. But I'd imagine your family made good on their investment. I hear the book sold pretty well. My autobiography, *Last Stand at Coyote Yelp Pass: The Tragic Cowboy Memoirs of Bucky Laroo*, only sold fifty copies in its publication year. Isn't that sick? I'm starting to think that the subsequent upsurge in Cheezies sales was unrelated."

"Silence, Bucky," Lucy groaned. "Believe it or not, my family's integral pride eventually takes precedence over our wealth. Sometimes, it just takes a century of so. Unfortunately, in that time, the facts haven't consistently supported the theory of evolution, or even old-age cosmology. It turns out that chemical combinations mixed with electrical current do not create the foundations of life; radioisotopic dating is bogus; natural selection has only ever demonstrably decreased genetic information, rather than increasing it as one would expect in an evolutionary process; the Grand Canyon probably formed in about twenty minutes, evidenced by wall height, formations, directionality, and sedimentary deposits, indicative of rapid flood-cutting; the Galapagos iguanas are hybridized; archeopteryx is just another stupid bird; space grime accumulation on the moon and rings of Saturn is non-existent, contraindicative of billions of years of formation; equivalent temperatures of known cosmological boundaries are indicative of a repetitive ricocheting of photons across the breadth of a rapidly expanding universe in defiance of a set speed of light; the Pangaea model is ironically discredited by the very existence of the Mid-Atlantic Ridge; the decaying lunar orbit would have wreaked havoc on prehistoric tidal patterns; erosion and salination rates should have allowed much saltier oceans to reclaim the planet about a billion years ago; so-called rule-proving exceptions to the Geologic Column are discovered every five minutes; high-altitude fossilized and non-fossilized inland shell beds, including Mt Everest, are indicative of recent global flooding, which, in turn, probably formed Mt Everest and all fold-mountain formations, including the majority of your precious British Columbia; reducing atmospheric conditions increasing in density over long time periods does not allow for the evolution of plant life, to say nothing about supporting the enormous sizes of prehistoric flora and fauna; the relative youth of the sun wouldn't have allowed any form of sustainable plant life to survive even a few millions of years ago; dissipation of galaxial arms should have occurred a few billion years ago due to uneven orbital velocities; every known vestigial formation has demonstrable function, forcing scientists to relabel them as being 'reduced in size-slash-function' rather than their previously debunked labelling of 'useless,'; and, finally, global legends of dragons within diverse and vastly unconnected cultures are indicative of dinosaurian coexistence with man. And that's just a chip off the iceberg, Bucky."

"Do you need a glass of water?" I had to ask. "For the record, I didn't understand a word you just said."

"*Silence!*" Lucy roared, pounding a fist on her diamond piano. "You still have no idea what you've done, do you? The entire world has pounced on the evolutionary theory, no matter how porous, and they're not going to give it up just because some stupid cowboy found the world's first unfossilized dinosaur bone. Soft-tissue is one thing. Completely unfossilized is quite another."

"Just to be clear, you are an evolutionist, right?" I asked, not certain if that was the implication I was meant to infer.

"Of course," Lucy snapped. "All atheists are. What's your point?"

"Nothing," I said. "What's with the parchment?"

"This parchment," Lucy said with bridled patience, "dates back to November 24th, 1889. It was written by Darwin's little-known older twin brother Zigfried Darwin on the night that he died, exactly thirty years after the first edition of *Origins* was published. This is the reason they're all going to come after you. This is the most feared writing in the history of modern science. Those who dare to speak of it in the dark and secret corners call it ... The Zigfried Prophecy. *Narrator!*"

A closet door on the east wall immediately swung open, and a distinguished, elderly black man strode out with a small podium tucked under his right arm. When he arrived at Lucy's side about two minutes later, he graciously accepted the parchment roll from her outstretched hands, erected the podium, and spread the weathered paper upon it. After quietly clearing his throat, he began reading aloud in a baritone voice that resonated with Shakespearean authority:

> *"Now this is the Law of the Jungle—*
> *As old and as true as the sky;*
> *And the Wolf that shall keep it may prosper,*
> *But the Wolf that shall break it must die.*
> *As the creeper that girdles the tree-trunk,*
> *The Law runneth forward and back—*
> *For the strength of the Pack is the Wolf,*
> *And the strength of the Wolf is the Pack."*

"That's Rudyard Kipling's *The Law of the Jungle*," I pointed out.

"Shoot, you're right," Lucy said sheepishly. "Flip the scroll, Narrator. I just scrawled that on the back, cuz it's so awesome I didn't want to forget it."

The familiar-looking narrator obliged, and began again:

> *"Beloved and yet loathed,*
> *By all and by none,*
> *A horseman arises*
> *From the far northern sun.*

> *"With natural smallpox*
> *Bridged over his nose,*
> *And Orangutan's mane*
> *On his head and his toes.*

"He saddles the Great Horse
Of Truth for the ride.
No man can yet slay him,
Though most will still try.

"So blessed with halfwit,
The dullard rides unaware,
Not yet knowing the way,
Nor impending despair.

"While all the world cries,
'Wondrous monkeys are we!
Darwin has released us!
Origins set us free!'

"But the day soon approaches
When all science will bow
To the gift of a monster,
And the way of the cow."

Upon completion of the chilling recitation, the narrator silently handed the parchment back to Lucy, then tucked his podium under his arm and returned to his closet.

"Always such a private man," Lucy said admiringly, watching the narrator leave.

I pondered a few moments on what I had just seen and heard, but I eventually did have to ask, "Was that Roscoe Lee Browne?"

"No!" Lucy said very quickly. "It wasn't. Roscoe Lee Browne is completely dead. *Heh heh!*"

"Are you sure?" I pressed her. "Because that guy looked and sounded exactly like the late, great actor, Roscoe Lee Browne."

"Let's focus on the prophecy, Bucky," she said dryly. "Any thoughts?"

"Are you saying they think it's about me? I'm the horseman from the northern sun? Because there was this weird blind guy who showed up at our Harvest Potlu–"

"Silence, Bucky, and think about it. Natural smallpox and an orangutan's mane? I'm looking right at it. They've been watching every redheaded Canadian cowboy with freckles for the last hundred and twenty years. Heck, they've probably been watching you like a hawk ever since the night Max-Ram Target saved your life. Beloved and yet loathed, by all and by none? It all makes sense now, anonymous pickle barrel boy who tried to kill a revered Hollywood icon."

"You know," I groaned, "as fascinating as it is to hear the historical words of Darwin's twin brother, especially from the mouth of a guy who seriously looks and sounds like Roscoe Lee Browne, I can't help being just the slightest bit skeptical. That's the reason that a conglomeration of paranoid scientists are trying to kill me? A conveniently-rhymed parchment prophecy? They seem to be putting a lot of stock in that, considering it was supposedly written by a twin brother that nobody anywhere has ever mentioned before. Ever."

"Ah, you know how the old shunning routine goes when somebody screws up the family legacy," Lucy said with a dismissive shrug. "How often did your parents talk about your mom's creepy brother Julio after he was arrested in that petting zoo in Duluth?"

"What?" I said, puzzled. "I don't have an uncle."

"Yeah, that's what Darwin's kids said. Science has always been terrified of what it can't explain, Bucky, and there are forces protecting this scroll that science cannot explain. Sure, for the first few years, everybody just said that Zigfried was a nut, as evidenced by his use of parchment in the late 1800s when paper was pretty much setting the trend, but it just kept on surfacing. They've all tried to destroy it. Before the Sacred Order of Ginger put it under my family's protection, Thomas Huxley himself passed it through fire and water, and it came out as pristine as you see it now."

"The Sacred Order of what?" I asked uncertainly.

"Silence! Are you even listening? Fire and water combined can't touch this thing!"

"Tell me something," I requested. "Did they pass it through fire and water at exactly the same time? It's unlikely, but they might have, you know, cancelled each other out...."

Lucy had to think about that for a long while.

"Hmm," she said. "I know that when Eugenie Scott's crew briefly captured it in 1998, she used a fire hose and a flamethrower. It might have been both at the same time...."

"Did anyone try passing it through fire and water separately?" I had to ask. "Or through scissors?"

"Don't rush me," Lucy mused, still thinking hard.

"Look, I know that you prefer my silence, but did you say that Zigfried was the older twin? Because I do have some experience with rhymes inspired by the loathing of younger siblings. I might even be called the world's leading expert on the subject."

"No, that's Donnie Wahlberg," Lucy assured me.

"Seriously?"

"Listen between the lines, Bucky."

"Okay, so I'm the Canadian leading expert. Either way, I'd say they're making a whole lot of something out of nothing."

"These are the people who developed the Big Bang, Bucky. It's kind of what they do."

"So why are you helping me?"

"Hey, I may be a devout atheist, but I have some minor sociopathic attributes as well. Sometimes, I just like to poke a stirring stick through the upper crust and see what stinks underneath."

"Well, the world's only ever benefited from people like that," I acknowledged. "Can I go now?"

"You can leave," Lucy granted. "But you do need to understand what you're up against. There are a bazillion different religions out there. Atheism, monotheism, polytheism, pantheism, Buddhism, Wicca, Val Kilmer.... And do you know what every one of them has in common?"

"Live debate entertainment value?"

"They're comfortable, Bucky. They're entrenched, and they all think that everyone else is out to get them. The Christians think the atheists are destroying their sacred values, the atheists think the Christians are mobilizing to take over the world, and you don't even want to know what an eye-twitching wreck Val Kilmer is these days. Did you ever see *The Chaos Experiment*? Of course you didn't. No one did. But I think it got into his head."

"Why do you keep referencing Val Kilmer as a religion?"

"They don't call dwindling fanbases 'cult followings' for nothing, Bucky."

"I still maintain he's underrated."

"Whatever you say, Freckleberry Finn," Lucy snorted. "I'm just trying to warn you of what's to come. It's your skull, and it's your flak. Joanne Whalley and Drew Barrymore will join hands and sing songs about how much they hate you by the time this is all over. You want my advice? Run and hide. I can set you and your family up with fake IDs, and a little plastic surgery could only help someone like you."

"Thanks, but I think I'll take my chances with the

truth," I decided, lifting the Ogopogo skull from its pedestal and tucking it under my arm. "Thanks for starting my heart when it stopped, and for your assurances that my life is going to be a living hell from this moment on. Which way is Canada?"

"Carlos will take care of your travel arrangements," Lucy promised. "Good luck, Bucky. You're like me in at least one way, I think. You like to smell what stinks under the crust, too. Ride hard, cowboy. Carlos, please see the gentleman out."

"Certainly, ma'am," Carlos conceded, drawing back a huge fist and driving it like a pile-driver into my left eye, slamming me to the floor. The last thing I saw before blacking out was yet another curious iguana crawling onto my face.

"He's out, ma'am."

Aren't We All
Just Radishes?
◇◇◇◇◇◇◇◇◇◇◇◇◇◇◇◇◇◇◇◇◇◇◇◇◇◇◇◇◇◇

I WOKE UP JUST AS I was being roughly thrown out of a helicopter with the Ogopogo skull still in my arms. I was about five kilometres south of Cattle Poke Ranch and, amazingly enough, still about eighty feet above the forest floor. It was roughly 7:30 a.m. on Saturday, July 10, 2010, and I didn't even know that much at the time. I was about to die without even knowing what day it was.

My shrill, girlish screams probably woke up the entire populace of nearby Coyote Yelp Pass as I tumbled into the unwelcoming foliage of the coniferous trees below, but, with the exception of a single blue spruce needle which I am convinced is still lodged up under my left eyelid, I made it to the spongy loam floor without serious injury. Unfortunately, that same spongy loam concealed the burrow of a highly unreasonable raccoon who proceeded to viciously maul me for the next three to four minutes, until I was able to stab him with a broken stick.

"I brought supper," I announced wearily as I trudged into the cabin an hour and a half later, plunking the skull and dead raccoon unceremoniously onto the kitchen table, about half a second before Betty-Sue pounced on me. Corky and

Sassy had both invited themselves over for a late breakfast, and scarcely glanced up from their pancakes as they each gave me a welcoming grunt. It's nice to be missed.

"So I guess this means you'll be wanting your living room back," Sassy mumbled through a mouthful of scrambled eggs. "Fine, I'll have all my stuff moved out by the end of next week."

"You were moving into my house?" I said in disgust, still being suffocated by Betty-Sue's tearful embrace.

Corky snorted, gesturing irritably at Betty-Sue. "Do you think it was easy, what with this stick in the mud not wanting to move out? You'd think she was a blood relative or something."

"Bucky, what's going on?" Betty-Sue cried, finally relaxing her bear-like grasp. "We had the whole town scouring the woods, looking for you! You were gone for ten days! Why are people trying to kill you again? Where were you? Where's that Sickle guy? What do we do? Who do we call? What's happening to us?"

"This," I replied, taking her trembling palm in my left hand, while grabbing my fishing rod from the porch rack with my right. "Let's fish. Corky, you should check your Hummer for some kind of tracking device. Sassy ... thanks for saving my life ten days ago. Skin that coon and put it in the fridge for tonight. I'll be back in six-and-a-half to nine hours."

"This is no time to fish!" Betty-Sue protested. "We need to figure this out before that French killer comes back."

"He's not coming back," I assured her grimly, leading the way back to the front door. "As much as I hate to lend credence to the local mythology ... I think the hostile mountain spirits got him. Or maybe it was just a bear."

"Told ya," Sassy chuckled, holding out an expectant

hand toward Corky, who grumbled under his breath as he handed over a ten dollar bill.

"Bucky, we need to prioritize here," Betty-Sue cautioned me. "There's more important things than fishing right now!"

"Cowboys figured out what's important a long time ago," Corky defended me. "And fishing trumps just about anything else. Anyway, you can't eat raccoon without salmon. That would be like eating cougar without owl. Sassy, do we still have that jar of chokecherry jelly?"

On the banks of the Besa River, I told Betty-Sue the whole story of The Sickle's attack, and my subsequent abduction by the eleven-year-old inventor of The Big Shiny Thing That Replaced The Internet. As proof that there really is a God, Betty-Sue believed me, and it was she who came up with the idea that would eventually save all of our lives.

"Celebrities," she decided.

"What?" I said, not sure that I had heard her correctly as I reeled in my second brown trout.

"You talk like the Scientific Establishment is an untouchable force that's bigger than us all," Betty-Sue rightly deduced. "But it's not. There's one force out there that even they can't control, at least not fully. Hollywood. Nashville. We need celebrities, Bucky. Once they've got our back, we're the untouchable ones. But we need to go big. Corky and Sassy are becoming national icons, but we need to break out the big guns. The cops will never believe us. We can't get to the media on our own. We can't get to the scientists. And we can't just destroy the skull anymore. It may be the only insurance we have. We need celebrities."

"I know exactly what you're getting at," I replied. "And the answer's no."

"Bucky, we don't have time for your ego right now,"

Betty-Sue chided me. "You have to put it behind you if we want to get out of this mess."

"I put ego into a stew and ate it when I was four," I reminded her. "I just know that it's not going to work. Anne Murray is a lone wolf, and a lone gunslinger, and she only takes on the fights that land on her own doorstep. Everybody knows that."

"I was talking about Max-Ram Target," Betty-Sue said, rolling her eyes.

I cringed.

"I'm not calling Mort."

"Lover, we don't have a choice here."

"We do have a choice," I corrected her. "We have the choice to not call Mort."

"We need him. He said you're his best friend at our wedding. He owes us."

"We have no idea how far gone Mort is," I pointed out, casting my line into the still waters again. "Aside from that Michael Moore documentary, the guy has not done a movie in more than six years. Being deprived of his precious spotlight for that long could have seriously thermal-shocked his mind, and he was enough of a freak already. At my bachelor party, he tried to convince me that his childhood nickname was Grendel's Mother, and I think he seriously wanted to believe it."

"You had a bachelor party?" Betty-Sue asked suspiciously.

"Let's stay focussed here," I said hurriedly. "The repercussions of hippie abandonment onto the doorstep of Hollywood are mind-blowing. I say this with absolute sincerity: If we ever decide to abandon baby Rusty, we're abandoning him with a hip-hop music producer who's survived being shot by drug dealers before we abandon him to Hollywood."

"Why would those words ever come out of your mouth?" Betty-Sue demanded, appalled.

"I'm just saying that Mort is a man who has taken narcissism to levels that even Mike Gladue Jr never dreamed of."

Betty-Sue had to think about that for a moment before confessing, "I don't get that reference."

"Sure you do," I reminded her. "He was that drunk epileptic guy who put in the stained-glass murals at Stagnate's Pub and Taxidermy."

"Oh, right, him," Betty-Sue recalled. "Good comparison. But I still say Max-Ram's our best shot. Nobody argues with Hollywood action hunks. Not even scientists."

"And I still say no, he's a freak."

"You can't just pass judgment like that," Betty-Sue scolded me. "You eat the tails off deep-fried prawns!"

"And they are crunchy and delicious," I said defensively.

"It is the weirdest thing I have ever seen you do," Betty-Sue stated. "And I once saw you rack an imaginary shotgun and make a '*chk-chk*' sound to psyche yourself up before going into the bank to ask for our building loan."

"Fine," I admitted. "I rack imaginary shotguns and eat shrimp tails. And, yes, I forgot to put both of those oddities on that *List of Weird Stuff I Do* that you made me write out before we got married."

"You regularly do the shotgun thing?" Betty-Sue queried skeptically, baiting her hook with a fresh ladybug.

"Only when I'm nervous, and usually in front of a mirror."

Betty-Sue squinted suspiciously at me, and stated, "You disappeared into the public outhouse for nearly twenty minutes when I made you audition for that play at the Community Lean-to."

"It was short notice, and it was *Swan Lake*!" I reminded her. "You need to steel yourself for something like that."

"And there was a mirror in the outhouse?"

"Actually, there was a real shotgun in there. How weird is that? Anyway, I don't remember seeing anything on *your* weird stuff list about inserting a superfluous letter 'x' between the first two letters of the word 'especially.' Yeah, I can say it properly. Especially, especially, especially!"

"*Touché*," Betty-Sue grudgingly admitted. "But I still think Max-Ram could help us. Exspecially if he really wants to be your friend. We still have the number he gave us with his wedding present. He's still thinking of you, anyway."

"Can you make him stop?" I sighed. "I didn't want his snowglobes at our wedding, and I certainly didn't want his autobiography last year."

"Don't complain, lover," Betty-Sue commented. "A good book can save your life. Remember that spring blizzard, when Oprah's autobiography saved your life?"

"I started a fire with it," I pointed out. "And the only reason I even had it was because Sassy thought that it would be hilarious to put it in the saddlebag where my winter coat and Epi-pen were supposed to be."

We still hadn't agreed on anything by the time we returned to the ranch that afternoon, but I secretly had to admit that Betty-Sue had raised a good point. Hollywood was the one place that The Establishment didn't fully have in a chokehold yet, although they had been discreetly influencing most major studio releases for the past forty years. However, rigid adherence to science generally translated into lame cinema wherein the car chases never ended in explosions, and nobody knew that better than Mort. The appalling pseudo-science presented in his dozens of big-budget action movies had rivalled that of the black-and-white B-monster movies of the 1950s. Betty-Sue was right. If we needed someone untouchable, we needed Morton Lincoln von Justin, aka Max-Ram Target.

Corky and Sassy had finally gotten around to searching for the tracker on the H2 when Betty-Sue and I pulled into the ranch yard after a nine hour absence, evidently not considering the task as much of a priority as I did.

"It's real simple," Sassy was explaining, as the two of them leaned against the giant propane tank beside Gramps' cabin, facing the Hummer. "It's probably well-hidden, but I read about this kind of stuff in one of the *Alias* novelizations. All we need to do is find a guy with an older model pacemaker and nothing left to live for. We get him to slowly walk around the perimeter of the truck, and wherever he goes into cardiac arrest is the general area where the transmitter was affixed. After that, all we need is a cattle prod and a Pez dispenser to deactivate the–"

"Fine, I'll call Mort," I decided, snatching the small black box with the antenna and blinking red light from the Hummer's back bumper and grinding it under my boot heel. "Let's get this over with."

"Oh, you're back, Bucky," Gramps said, leaning out the front door. "Good to know the French guy didn't vaporize you like the RCMP forensics team concluded. You know I had to unsaddle and brush down Homestretch for you, don't you?"

"Sorry about that, Gramps," I sighed. "Won't happen again. Sassy, I need to borrow your sat-phone. I happen to know for a fact that you stole it from Shania Twain four years ago, so maybe it's a well-guarded enough secret to not be bugged. I don't trust my own phone anymore."

I took the satellite phone back to my cabin, where Betty-Sue had retrieved the card Mort had included with his wedding-gift snowglobe collection. I reluctantly accepted it.

"'Dear Bucky,'" I obligingly read aloud, "'give me a call if you ever need anything, ol' buddy. Betty-Sue, give me a call if you ever divorce Bucky. Please divorce Bucky. Sincerely, Max-Ram Target.' I can't read it without getting misty-eyed."

"I don't care if you have to do the freaky shotgun thing," Betty-Sue said. "Just call the freak so we can get our boring back."

"*Chk-chk*," I replied glumly, dialling the number on the back of the card into the sat-phone.

The phone on the receiving end only rang once, and then a cheerful young woman answered.

"Melinda Carp Talent Agencies, this is Kitty."

"Uh ... hi Kitty," I replied, confused. I had met the rather frightening Ms Melinda Carp on several unpleasant occasions when she was acting as Mort's manager/bodyguard, but I had no idea why he would have given us her agency number. "I'm Bucky Laroo. I was given this number to contact Max-Ram Target."

"Mr Target asked Ms Carp to forward all of his calls to our agency during his absence," Kitty chirped. "Can I put you through to his fan voice-mail?"

"Actually, I've been told by my wife that I need to talk to Max-Ram directly, and with some amount of urgency. Do you have contact information for him?"

"I can't give out that information, sir."

"Then could I please speak with Ms Carp?"

"Is she expecting a call from you?"

"I'm a ... friend from Canada," I explained. "She tasered me a few times when she was visiting my ranch in 2007." (Just read the first book.)

"I'm afraid I'd own my own agency if I had a nickel for every time I've heard that story, sir," Kitty said dryly. "You'll have to be more specific."

"Her only true love used to call her Mellie," I expounded, feeling a little guilty for passing on information given to me in presumed confidence. "Then he cheated on her with a cheerleader in a wading pool filled with chocolate pudding and guacamole."

There was a moment of silence, and then Kitty replied, "I'll put you right through, sir."

"You're a peach, Kitty," I assured the obliging receptionist.

I had to listen to a few seconds of elevator music before Melinda picked up her extension.

"Melinda Carp," she said coolly, her authoritative voice the result of dealing with Hollywood's most spoiled stars and starlets for the past ten years, and also from her previous years of hard-bitten service as a Sergeant in the United States Marine Corps.

"Hey, Melinda," I said, unable to keep a slight crack out of my voice. "It's, uh, Bucky. How have you been?"

"*Laroo*...." she gurgled. "What do you want, cowboy?"

"Very little," I promised. "I don't want to talk to you. And I seriously don't want to talk to Mort."

"Then why are you tying up my line?"

"I need to talk to Mort."

"I don't represent that drooling pinata-head anymore," Melinda said cruelly.

"So why are you taking his calls?"

"Because he's my friend," she snapped. "Professional loathing doesn't change that."

"You just called him a drooling pinat–"

"I don't know where Max-Ram is," Melinda declared. "I don't care. His second non-fiction book was a disaster, sort of like your first one, so he said he needed to go find his true inner author. That's all I know, and that was five months ago."

"Do you have any idea where he might have gone?" I asked. "It's kind of important that I find him."

"All I know is that he said something about his greatest source of literary inspiration. His Canadian Walden, whatever that meant."

I felt as if a lightning bolt had gone out of the phone and into my ear.

"Canadian Walden?" I repeated.

"Yeah, that's what he called it. I can't find it on any map, so I'm assuming it's a Thoreau reference."

"Wow," I said, feeling numb, and also disgusted with myself for not figuring out the truth earlier. "Always a pleasure talking to you, Ms Carp."

"Tell Corky his bubble-boo says she misses hi–!" Melinda was blurting as I hung up, obviously still retaining romantic feelings for my suave older brother.

"Did she try to give you a message for Corky?" Betty-Sue asked, staring across the kitchen table at me.

"Yes," I said, standing and putting on my cowboy hat. "I'm not going to tell him."

"Where's Mort?" Betty-Sue wanted to know as I headed for the door.

"He's living in our barn loft," I sighed, stepping back out into the warm July sunshine. "Excuse me for a few minutes."

"He's where?" Betty-Sue called out, quite certain that she had misheard me. "Did you say Ashcroft?"

"I wish I'd said Ashcroft," I said, closing the door behind me and making a beeline for the barn.

In all the excitement of finding and killing the Ogopogo, and having disgruntled interest groups trying to find and kill me, I had completely forgotten about the strange stench which Sassy and I had come across the last time any of us had been in the barn. A smell like rotting vegetables. I had never known Mort to smell like that, but, somehow, I knew that he was the cause.

The July heat had not helped matters any, and my eyes were watering by the time I began ascending the ladder to the loft, the same loft that Mort and I had fled into during the night that he saved my life.

"Ashcroft," I muttered as I climbed. "The quaint town of Ashcroft, British Columbia. It's lovely this time of year. Why couldn't you go to Ashcroft?"

And that was when I heard the rhythmic humming, a moment before my head poked through the loft hatch like a groundhog looking for its shadow.

The legendary Hollywood action hunk, Max-Ram Target, was sitting cross-legged in the centre of the loft, surrounded on all sides by piles of blank writing paper and half-eaten vegetables. I had never seen him in such an unkempt state, and I doubt anyone else in the world ever had either. Mort was well aware of the fact that he was the worst actor alive, which meant that his best shot at staying in business was shocking headlines and looking really, really good. Apparently, the transition from action hunk to non-fiction author had changed all of that. His custom-made, uber-cool black clothing was long gone, and he now wore a simple burlap tunic and knee shorts, handsewn together with orange baler twine. In place of his standard North Korea-made brand-name footwear, *Max-Ram Kicks*, he now wore hairy mukluks that seemed to be made from weasel pelts. His perfect apple fritter tan had not been maintained very well in the unlit loft, and I guessed that his skin was now pastier than my own, although the thick layer of barnyard grime that he was coated in made it impossible to be conclusive about that. What I could tell was that the lifelong bodybuilder had lost a good bit of his perfectly-chiselled physical "Oomph," as Sassy so admiringly referred to it. Apparently, barn lofts aren't a great place to keep up a rigorous fitness regimen. To be sure, he was still an imposing, muscular specimen, but it was clear that his muscle-mag cover days were over, and the fact that he now sported an unmanageable blonde Grizzly Adams beard didn't help matters much. Only his blonde hair, his golden crown of glory, remained unchanged: Perfectly cleaned, barbered, and swept back into his trademark *Max-Ram Slick-Back 'do* that so many other blonde celebrities had imitated, but never managed to perfectly re-create. I didn't want to know how he had kept it clean, but it occurred to me that Sassy's cherished exhibition calf had been going through our supply of *Happy Horse Hop Lather* livestock shampoo faster than usual that summer.

His back was turned to me, but his head was cocked slightly to one side, as if he was listening intently in spite of his incessantly peaceful humming.

"Mort?" I ventured, stepping into the loft.

"Shh, Bucky, shh," he replied soothingly, rocking ever-so-slightly back and forth. "You're disturbing the balance."

"Please tell me you're not stuck in some kind of hippie flashback," I said, slowly approaching him. "I've been having a hard enough time keeping Sassy grounded these past few months."

"With every care-laden syllable, you fracture the balance," Mort teasingly scolded me. "The intricate balance between man and paper and ... a pile of putrid apple cores."

"Yeah," I said, stepping around to study his serene face. "Those are radishes."

"Bear with me, brother," Mort requested, finally opening his blue eyes and smiling up at me.

"Oh crap," I remarked. "This is exactly what I was afraid of. You've lost it."

"My life of Walden is new to me, Bucky," he confessed.

"It's the vastness of nature. So much to learn, to discover.... Who can even begin to comprehend it all?"

"It is a bit daunting at first," I said cautiously. "That's probably why we invented categorization. For example, when you dig something purple out of the ground, categorization tells us that it's not an apple. It's a radish."

"Aren't we all just radishes, Bucky?" he answered mellowly.

"Mort, what are you doing in my barn? What are you doing in my country?"

"Living a life of perpetual wonderment and revelation, Bucky. As an example, I just found out that I've been eating radishes for the last five months. May I recommend putting a few more cows in the barn every night next winter? The end of February was still a bit nippy up here."

"What, burlap and baler twine aren't an insulating combination?" I asked sarcastically. "Seriously, Mort, it's amazing that your fingers aren't shrivelled black nub– Is that a wedding ring?"

"What?" Mort said, jolting out of his mellow haze for the first time. "No. Why would you say that?"

Even as he was protesting in denial, he was frantically trying to remove the gold band from his left hand, but had a lot of accumulated finger grit to work past.

"Left hand, gold band, third finger," I noted. "I took a leap."

"Rumor's, Bucky. Nothing else."

"Rumours?" I said. "What rumours?"

Mort finally managed to painfully twist the ring from his finger, and quickly dropped it into the leather medicine bag he wore around his neck.

"That is so weird," he commented, embarrassed. "What are the odds of my lucky cosmic unity hole falling out of here and getting stuck on my finger? Unfathomable. So tell me all, Bucky. How're the book sales going?"

"Well, it hasn't hit any bestseller lists yet," I assured him. "And it hasn't stayed at number one for more than two years."

Yes, as I mentioned before, Mort had written his own account of our last encounter, and he had entitled it *The Purity of Redemption: The Night That Max-Ram Target Saved His Soul While Saving Bucky Laroo's Life*. He had sent me a copy the previous spring, and the first page of the hardcover masterpiece had been autographed as a token of his gratitude for my real-life contributions:

> *Hey Bucky,*
>
> *I figured I should at least send you a comp copy, as my shameless exploitation of your life added the gritty factor necessary for me to retain the number one slot on the New York Times Bestseller List for the past twenty-one months. I owe you, buddy. My regards to your wife, who could have been mine had I chosen to invest a little more effort into that particular venture. I love you and Canada.*
>
> *Max-Ram Target.*

"Did you even read it?" Mort inquired.

"Forgive me if I don't feel like reading your justification of the events that almost got me killed," I retorted.

"Hey, at least I actually wrote mine," Mort scoffed, "rather than farming out copyediting duty to some barely-literate stretcher jockey because I'm too insecure to trust in my own typesetting."

"A lot of people still get 'then' and 'than' mixed up," I said defensively. "I'm a cowboy. I'm not a writer."

"Well, neither is he. That many split infinitives.... It's unforgivable, Bucky."

"Really?" I countered. "And was it your lack of split infinitives that led to your second book selling a grand total of thirty copies in its first year? Mine sold nearly twice that many."

"Don't knock my sophomore work, Bucky," Mort protested. "Do you have any idea how significant that book was? I wrote about the men who changed the face of America! A stirringly poignant biographical look at the life and trials of a dozen of the greatest overlooked heroes of the African-American civil rights movement. It's time that their stories and sacrifices were made known!"

"Inspiring subject matter," I readily agreed. "And did anyone even try to tell you that *12 Angry Black Men* was a really bad title?"

"Bucky, have you learned nothing?" Mort sighed, standing and stretching his sore legs. "Nobody ever tells celebrities that they're on the wrong track. Did you hear Liam Neeson's German accent in *Schindler's List*? No one said a word. And do you have any idea how many studios backed *Wyatt Earpp* over the vastly superior *Tombstone*, just because Kevin Costner wanted more spotlight? It made sense at the time."

"The sands really shifted there, didn't they?" I remarked. "Look, Mort, I've been trying to get a hold of you, and Melinda said you were incognito. You're seriously doing the Walden thing?"

"I've had nothing but frills since the age of six, Bucky. I lived my life like one of those lizards that run across the water. I finally stopped, for just a second, and I've been floundering in the water ever since, trying to figure out who I am."

"Well, the essence of who you am is hanging noxiously

in the air," I dutifully reported. "So I'm guessing that the last time you floundered in literal water was about ... five months ago?"

"It's called roughing it, Bucky. You don't know the gritty side of life until your skin is just as gritty."

"That's beyond gritty," I informed him. "Is that a barnacle on your wrist?"

"I've been wondering about that," Mort admitted, glancing at the scaly growth on his right arm.

"You're taking a shower," I stated. "Let's go."

"I'm in Walden, Bucky!" Mort insisted. "You can't make me leave."

"You're squatting in my barn," I corrected him. "Legally speaking, I could shoot you and carry you out. Speaking of squatting, how have you been ... you know...?"

"The outhouse behind the barn," Mort replied dismissively.

"That's not an outhouse," I said uneasily.

"Four walls and a bucket, Bucky. Four walls and a bucket."

"And no roof," I pointed out. "It's the box from an old dump truck."

Mort snickered.

"Are you five?" I demanded.

"Hey, you're the one who introduced the word 'dump' into the conversation," Mort giggled. "Why were you trying to call me?"

"People have been trying to kill me again," I said. "Betty-Sue thought that the combination of you and your money could make it stop."

"Odd assumption," Mort noted. "Historically, people have tried to kill you because of me."

"That's what I told her. Can you help me or not?"

"I'd do anything in my power to help you, brother," Mort

said kindly, putting his crunchy hands on my shoulders. "If there is one thing that I have learned from my banishment in Walden, it's that I must dedicate my life to the atonement of my wrongdoings."

"How exactly can you atone for your sins by locking yourself in a barn for months at a ti– Okay, when I say it out loud, the question kind of answers itself. Never mind."

"Well, rest assured that you will henceforth be benefiting from the benefactor that is the new Max-Ram Target. My sentence in Walden has opened my eyes to a new–"

"This isn't Walden," I interrupted. "I don't think you're using that word correctly."

"Whatever," Mort said airily. "Anyway, it's over. It's time to step back into the world and do great things for my fellow man. Every one of the considerable resources at my disposal is now at yours. I will not rest, Bucky, until I have saved your life once more. Tell me what you need."

"Ideally?" I said dryly. "I need people to stop trying to kill me."

Mort cringed at the impossible goal. "Okay, that's a pretty tall order. Let's baby-step this thing, shall we? What's your backup goal?"

"No backup, Mort. People are trying to kill me."

"Alright, we'll focus on that one for now," Mort reluctantly conceded. "But I must emphasize that most business models recommend starting with the little problems and working your way up, as the little problems generally form the foundation that the major ones are built upon."

I had to think about that for a moment before stating, "That doesn't sound like a real business strategy."

"Maybe you're right," Mort admitted. "Actually, that might have been an ant poison commercial. But if you do happen to think of smaller problems, let me know, and we can get started on them right away."

"No smaller problems, Mort," I assured him. "People are trying to kill me."

"I'm going to need some thinking time," Mort said. "You mentioned a shower?"

"Yes, I'm about to pass out in here," I replied, guiding him gingerly toward the ladder. "And I've smelled everything."

"Can I bring some radishes?"

"Leave the radishes."

We left the barn, and stepped into the mercifully fresh air. Mort took a few moments to regain his "dirt legs," and then we headed back up the lane toward Gramps' cabin.

"So you're really trying to be an author now?" I asked, trying to make an effort at civil conversation.

"Not much choice," Mort replied. "The acting still hasn't panned out. I haven't had a movie offer in ten years. Do you know what it's like to workout for seven hours a day for ten years, knowing that the only stuff-strutting you're going to do is on the sidewalk? I got so depressed that I recently started working out only five hours a day."

"Really? Because you're looking kind of, um...."

"I know," Mort sighed. "Apparently, a diet of radishes and chicken scratch isn't ideal for maintaining a bodybuilder's muscle tone. And the only meat I've had is a couple of stillborn calves you guys lost during the spring."

"Wow," I said. "I really didn't need to know that."

"Yeah, I should have kept that one tucked away," Mort confessed.

We arrived at the front porch of Gramps' cabin, and I pushed Mort inside, directing him to use as much soap, shampoo, shaving cream, toothpaste, and steel wool as was required to be presentable, and then to come over to my place to hear the whole story.

Only a few seconds after I had slammed the door

behind him, it was yanked open again, and Corky and Sassy stumbled out, choking and gagging.

"Did you even take the time to say hello?" I ventured mildly.

"What the crap?" Sassy gagged. "Bucky, a blonde Sasquatch just walked into the cabin!"

"It smelled so bad!" Corky howled, rubbing his stinging eyes. "So bad! Aagh!"

"That wasn't a Sasquatch," I sighed. "How many times do I have to tell you that there's no such thing as Sasquatches? It was just Mort."

"Who?" Sassy said, utterly bewildered.

"Guys, we've been over this," I groaned. "Seriously. Morton Lincoln von Justin. That's his real name."

"I'm not following you, Bucky," Corky said, still confused.

"Max-Ram Target," I clarified.

"What the held-underwater is he doing here?" Corky demanded. "Did you kidnap him again?"

"No," I promised. "He's just been seeking literary alignment of the cosmos in the barn loft for the past few months."

"You're lying," Sassy protested. "No way the El Paso Oak would have voluntarily shrivelled up into that pudgy blonde gibbon who just walked in there."

"Guys, take it easy," I said. "He's still pretty ripped. He just looks smaller without the California tan and sheen of olive oil. However, I think we need to start buying a higher-protein chicken scratch."

"You'd better not be going anywhere near my chickens, Bucky-off-at-the-whistle," Sassy said, glaring suspiciously at me.

"What?" I said.

"That was Max-Ram Target without a tan?" Corky said,

still aghast at the thought. "He looked like an uncooked slice of French toast. It's almost like...."

"...he's mortal?" I guessed.

"You bite your tongue!" Corky said savagely, his undying devotion to his favourite action hunk not bothered in the least by Max-Ram Target's decade-long sabbatical.

"I don't know, Corky," Sassy said, almost numb from the dawning comprehension. "Maybe the witless boob actually has a point. Seeing Max-Ram like that for the first time, all pasty and smelly.... It's lifted a veil from my eyes. I think I need to take this newfound sense of revelation and disillusionment, and write a song with it."

"You should do that," I blandly encouraged her. "I'm going to go shovel some radish pulp out of the loft. Apparently, he's been living off them."

"Oh," Sassy said. "Well, there goes another veil. I've been blaming the hostile mountain spirits for cleaning all the radishes out of the root cellar."

"Why do we always plant them in such enormous quantities every year?" Corky had to ask. "Does anyone in this family even like radishes?"

The sun was setting by the time I finished mucking out the loft, and Betty-Sue climbed the ladder to join me with a mug of coffee and a bowl of raccoon/fish gumbo.

"I can't believe this," she said. "He's been here the whole time?"

"Only since February," I replied, sipping from the offered mug. "You've seen him?"

"Corky and Sassy brought him over for supper. Why didn't you come over and tell me first?"

"I didn't know what to say," I said wearily. "Last time we heard from him, he still wanted to marry you."

"Well, I don't think you need to worry about his intentions," Betty-Sue chuckled. "He's been calling me

Cindy-Lou for the last hour. I guess he forgot about me after he got married."

"He is married?"

"Well, he was. He married Minnie Marshmallow after she tried to kill the two of you, but then she left him for that horror movie hunk, Brad The Impaler. So I think he married Ashley Olsen after that, but it only lasted a couple weeks. Then he married one of the Kennedy's, but I'm pretty sure they went Splitsville, too, after he lost the bid for governor of one of the blue states. Sheesh, do you read any of those celebrity gossip magazines I bring home? Anyway, the important thing is that I told him what's happening, and he says he's got a plan."

"So he's seen the skull?"

"And Corky's photo of the inner tube. He's a believer. But he's also been an on-and-off Scientologist for the last couple of years, so maybe that makes him an easy convert."

"Why do I still have this flickering instant of surprise whenever I learn something new about Mort?" I asked, shaking my head. "Assassins and bounty hunters don't surprise me anymore. And I await his plan with bated breath."

"Oh, and I told him to wait until this mess is taken care of before telling you his theory about you being a lizard king from the planet DC-8," Betty-Sue added.

"I love you so much when you anticipate me," I smiled, sitting down on an inverted grain pail and digging into the delicious stew.

"Right back at ya, lover," Betty-Sue chuckled, giving me a peck on the cheek. "You really need to shave."

By 4:00 a.m. the following morning, Mort and I were on the road in my old pickup truck, heading south to meet our destiny. Unfortunately, we weren't quite travelling alone. Let me explain.

Our plan was fairly simple, although it had taken a few hours of debating the night before to come up with. It was Sassy who first suggested that the man we needed to get the skull to was the legendary Canadian paleontologist and, more recently, Kelowna's leading cryptozoologist, Dr Harmon Megiddo. Sassy reverently compared him to the Fair Witness characters from Robert Heinlein's novel *Stranger in a Strange Land* for his seeming inability to draw conclusions. Rather, he only meticulously recorded facts, which terrified most of the intellectual guests on his Monday evening television program, *This Week In Science Up Until Our Submission Deadline Of 6:00 p.m. Saturday, with Harmon Megiddo.* (I sarcastically expressed amazement that Sassy would be caught dead watching informational programming, but she calmly replied that people habitually underestimated her intellectual capacity as they were generally too overwhelmed by her beauty and musical talent.) Apparently, Megiddo's televised guests had a tendency to suffer psychotic breaks during interviews with him, as did various political and scientific participants in live debates that he moderated. They just became overwhelmed by the obviousness of their own personal biases. He sounded like another creepy guy to me, but Corky, Betty-Sue, Mort, and even Gramps were all familiar with the man's life-goal of pure objectivity, (Admittedly, a rather odd goal to carry into the often straw-grasping field of cryptozoology.) so I agreed to take the skull down to his studios in Kelowna. We didn't know if we would be able to get onto Megiddo's show, but we figured that as long as we could get the skull into his hands, he could help us.

"You're going all the way back to Kelowna?" Corky couldn't help asking. "Why don't we just go door-to-door in Affluenceville with the skull?"

"It's too risky," I sighed. "According to Lucy, the whole

city's in lockdown, and half the people wouldn't believe us anyway. We need to get to an expert, and we need to get on the air. If The Establishment can ruin someone like Dirty Harry, they can ruin anyone, even the cops. The only way we can keep innocent people safe from scientists is to let them all know the truth, all at the same time."

"Like in *The Matrix*," Sassy realized. "One second, you're checking out the hot blonde in the red dress, and the next second Hugo Weaving's got a Desert Eagle pointed at your head."

"That's closer than your comparisons usually are," I granted her, "but it's not quite what– Never mind. You're right. It's like *The Matrix*."

"'*Do you hear that, Mr Anderson?*'" Sassy drawled. "'*That's the sound of inevitability....*'"

"Ha!" Corky laughed, loving Sassy's spot-on impression of Hugo Weaving's ominous character from the movie. "I could listen to you do that all day."

"And so could I, on any other day," I admitted. "For now, though, can we get back to our life-saving plan?"

"'*Humans aren't a species, they're a disease....*'" Sassy continued, unable to quickly shut down once she was in Agent Smith mode.

"Okay, I think we're sidetracking here," I had to interject.

"So?" Corky countered. "People sidetrack all the time. That's what keeps conversations rolling, even in dire times. What, do you think we're bound by some form of editorial rule-set that stipulates all conversations must relate in some way to a plot-line or central theme?"

"I guess not," I sighed.

"Good," Corky said with a victorious nod. "Because I still have an extensive piece yet to speak in regard to Hollywood director Michael Bay's so-called storytelling ability. You see,

Max-Ram, ever since I was a small boy, seeking inspiration from whatever media I could find it in...."

It was my suggestion that we utilize Mort's incalculable wealth to fly down to Kelowna, but he pointed out that flights of any kind were much easier to track. He said that our best bet was just to drive south, avoiding major cities and highways as much as possible, and only paying cash so that our credit cards could not be traced. I reluctantly agreed to this, and accepted Corky's generous offer of five thousand dollars in cash that he had buried under the chicken coop six years earlier and then forgotten about. But I insisted that I would not allow anyone in my family to be put in harm's way. I told Betty-Sue that I wanted her to stay at the ranch until the skies were clear again. Only Mort refused to be dissuaded, adamant about keeping a vigil at my side til the very end.

We got up at 3:00 the next morning, loaded up my truck with sleeping bags, a change of clothes, food, my deer rifle, and the cardboard box with the Ogopogo skull, and then I bade an emotional farewell to my family. Even Sassy was in tears as she offered me one of her cherished Shocking Silly palm-sized cattle prods for protection. I didn't accept it. I know how much the gift must have meant to Sassy, but I also know that she tends to forget about such vital components as grounding wires and non-conductive casings when she gets to tinkering.

Mort and I were on the road by 3:30, and we were alone. However, that was not to last.

I'm not sure what tipped me off. I hadn't been given a lot of clues, so I'm kind of surprised that I managed to put it all together so quickly. We had just driven out of the ranch yard when two simple historic facts popped into my head: 1) Sassy had uncharacteristically stated that Betty-Sue could have the Ogopogo skull, as she and Corky had "other souvenirs," and 2) Sassy had uncharacteristically told me to stay away from her chicken coop, even going so far as to dig up the five thousand dollars from underneath it by herself so that I wouldn't have to.

I think Mort had already dozed off again in the passenger seat when I abruptly slammed on the brakes, cut a U-turn, and raced back to the ranch. I pulled right up to the chicken coop, ignoring Mort's startled questions, and ran for the door. As I pulled it open, I saw Sassy emerging from the tour bus, and her eyes grew wide as she screamed for me to get back, but it was too late by then. I had seen everything.

The orphaned Ogopogo egg was being nested by one of Sassy's chickens!

I'm going to gloss over the high-pitched chaos of the next twenty-five minutes or so, as my throat still hurts from all my screams of, "What were you *thinking?!*" and I don't want to relive that anymore than I have to.

Sassy's eventual calm response to my red-faced barrage of demands was as typical as any that I had come to expect from her.

"Why have beef when you can have veal?"

"It was Sassy's idea!" Corky blurted when I turned my clawed fingers toward his throat. "I was against going back to the cave for it the whole time. I never planned it out with Sassy when you were out of hearing range!"

"Corky, you're an idiot," Sassy growled in response to the betrayal.

"But an idiot who will always be eight minutes older than you," Corky replied smugly.

"I swear I'll outlive you by nine minutes if it's the last thing I ever do," Sassy snapped.

"Isn't outliving someone by a set amount of time the very definition of the last thing you'll ever do?" Mort asked, which, in turn, was the best point that I would ever hear him make. "Anyway, how exactly were you planning to raise an aquatic reptile to veal age in the northern Rockies? You don't even know what to feed it."

"You know something, Max-Ram?" Sassy replied coldly, staring without expression at her one-time idol. "Ever since coming to terms with the fact that you are both mortal and a has-been, I find myself increasingly revolted by you. I look at you, and I want to punch you in the throat. When you fall to your knees, silently clutching your collapsed trachea and gaping like a beached crawdad.... I can't even describe the euphoric surge that my parched soul will be flooded with when that happens. Or maybe it's just because you're fat now. Dude, you are *so* freaking fat.... You know what? I can't even stand to look at you. It's making me tense and nauseous. I'm going to go back to the bus and get The Big Shiny Thing That Replaced The Internet to give me a back rub."

So that's why Mort and I weren't alone when we left the ranch again at 4:00. We had a large blue egg to keep us, and its mother's skull, company all the way back to Kelowna. I couldn't bring myself to just smash the dang thing with a sledgehammer, so we were now faced with the considerably more time-consuming task of putting it back.

THE BALLAD OF BUCKY™ (PART THREE)

Ian Tyson:

> "With the serpent lying at his feet,
> Bucky hatched another plot.
> Though the Ogopogo was growing cold
> Her clutch of eggs was not!
>
> "Bucky wasn't satisfied,
> Just sending a monster to her grave.
> He said 'The egg is mine, it'll hatch just fine,
> Into an omelette or a slave!'
>
> "We cried, 'Bucky, you know James Cameron
> Would want you to put that big egg back!'
> But he saddled up for his hometown,
> And the egg was in his pack.
>
> "As he galloped t'ward the sunset,
> He screamed defiance to the sky:
> 'You'll do my chores, baby dinosaur!
> And, when you're old, you'll be a pie!'"

Corky and Sassy:

> *"With his steed and shining blade,*
> *He bumbles 'cross the plains!*
> *We tried to stop him, Mama,*
> *But your baby's off the chain!*
> *We wanted to change the chorus,*
> *But nothing rhymed but Armada!*
> *So call on out for Buckyyyyyyyy...!*
> *Dragon Butcher of Canada!"*

STUNG BY STING

◇◇◇◇◇◇◇◇◇◇◇◇◇◇◇◇◇◇◇◇◇◇◇◇

WE HADN'T EVEN MADE it through Coyote Yelp Pass before Mort requested a stop to make a phone call, arguing that a pay phone was not likely to be bugged. I decided that I had to trust in his help if I was to get through this mess, so I obligingly pulled over at the livery stable outside of Stagnate's Pub and Taxidermy, where the town's only pay phone was located.

"What is livery, anyway?" Mort asked as he stepped out of the truck.

"Nobody knows," I assured him as we entered the stable. "There's horses in here, an old jukebox, and bags of concrete mix, for some reason."

"Why is the town's only pay phone in a horse barn?"

"Ninety percent of the town's injuries happen there," I explained. "Keep your back to the wall, and watch out for Mr Slappaloosa."

"Mr Slappaloosa?"

"Dapple grey, fourteen hands high, and he's the only horse with tusks. But don't worry. They're filed. Well, at least one of them is. Just be quick."

"Why are you following me?" Mort inquired, dropping a quarter into the dusty phone.

"That's the cost of using my quarters. And almost getting me killed by an East German assassin three years ago."

"I knew you were going to bring that up," Mort sighed, dialling the phone. He waited until a garbled voice on the other end replied, and then he exploded, "*Hey, knuckle face!* Yeah, I'm still alive, you sodden sheet of single ply, and guess what? I'm on a dangerous real-life mission to Kelowna with monsters and assassins and desperados and–!"

I had snatched away the receiver and slammed it down before he could finish his rant.

"What the sandhill was that?" I demanded. "We're trying not to get killed here, remember?"

"Sorry, Bucky," Mort said sincerely. "That one's been building for the past few months."

"You were supposed to be calling one of your resources," I angrily reminded him. "Who was that?"

"Ashton Kutcher," Mort replied evenly. "You know, that skinny guy who married Bruce Willis's ex-wife, ol' what's-her-name...?"

"I know who Ashton Kutcher is, Mort," I growled. "This is serious crap we're in here, okay? There could be more assassins coming after me, or my wife, and this time I don't have Sassy or Gramps around to bite off ears for me. I have you, and your so-called resources that are supposed to be helping me out. Thus far, I feel more like I've picked up a hitchhiker with really great hair who has no intention of splitting the gas bill. Do I consider you God's punishment for everything I haven't repented of yet? I'm not ruling anything out at this early stage of our very long journey. Do not make anymore phone calls to your enemies. Do not tell anyone else what we're doing, or where we are, or where we're going. I would have no problem with leaving you on the side of the road at the nearest radish farm, except for the knowledge that you would be closer to my house than you will be if I actually go through with this. Get in the truck!"

"You never run out of breath, Bucky," Mort said admiringly. "That's always amazed me. I was always gasping and purple during my monologues. Actually, my intense purple face was the only reason that so many people thought that I could really act for so long."

"I went through an operatic phase when I was sixteen," I admitted as we returned to my truck. "The vocal warmups kept the cows calm. But it wreaked havoc on the goat for some reason."

In spite of our shaky start, the first few hours on the road were peaceful enough. Both Mort and I were shaved and showered, and dressed in fresh clothes, although he had initially been reluctant to part with his burlap garments, possibly fearing that, after five months of continuous skin-contact, they would be equally reluctant to part with him.

By the time we hit Highway 97 South, Mort had finished doing his "pared-down essentials workout" of two thousand pushups in the truck-box, and we managed to make pleasant small talk in the cab, mostly about the Ogopogo. However, as is often the case in the company of has-beens, the topic eventually drifted back to Mort's previous acting career, although it soon became apparent that this was a bit of a sore spot for him as well, in spite of his professed love of non-fiction authorship.

"So why haven't you tried to get back into the movies?" I asked as we drew near Prince George later that morning. "Did you always want to be an author?"

"Not really," Mort said glumly. "I mean, it's great, but I only really thought of it after I put out the autobiography and everybody loved it. I missed being loved. Heck, I even missed being loved to hate. Actually, my second career choice had always been senior air traffic controller, but that didn't work out so well, and neither did my beekeeping career, so I figured I'd focus on writing. Yes, *12 Angry Black Men* could have used a little critical input, but I've learned from my mistakes, and I have great hopes for my next work. Just the thought of bringing literary inspiration to the world is so rewarding, isn't it?"

"What are you writing about this time?" I inquired.

Apparently, that was the wrong question to ask. Mort's eyes instantly began brimming with tears, and his face began performing a series of contortionist gymnastics that would have put Chinese ballet to shame.

"*Heep!*" he squeaked, biting his lip to hold back the sobs.

"Um ... Mort?"

"*Snrrk!*" he sniffled, his eyeballs bulging and straining as if he were attempting to suction the tears back into their respective ducts.

"Mort, you're crying in my truck," I said uneasily. "Why are you crying in my truck?"

"Because I've got nothing, Bucky!" he blurted, pounding a frustrated fist against the dusty dashboard. "*Nothing!* I sat in that barn loft for five months, humming and meditating and interpretive dancing, and the only idea I got out of it was for a biography called *One Seriously Scary Black Man: The Tony Todd Story.* I can't write that, Bucky. I can't write anything! I need to get back into the movies, or I'm going to go nuts! *Waaah!*"

"You can't get back into the movies, Mort," I said, deciding that brutal honesty was the best defence at that point. "You are the worst actor alive. I'm not going to sugarcoat it. You know those brown-pompadoured actors in the mid 80s with the big glasses and full beards? I'd put you in their category, at best. The one-man army genre is over, and it's not coming back."

"Hey, do you think I didn't want to be taken seriously?" Mort exploded. "Do you think I didn't want to be a great actor? Do you think I didn't want to be a kung fu master? Do you think I wanted to look as if I had never held a gun before in every single one of my movies? Shooting assault rifles from the hip? Do you think real soldiers and cops and reluctant hero clichés can actually hit anything shooting from the hip, or holding their handguns sideways? No! But that's all my directors ever let me do. *Waaah!* All I could do was look good. I wanted to train. I wanted to be an actor. But my old manager, Rick, he always told me, 'All you have is your body, Max-Ram. That's all you'll ever have.' And I'm eight years old at the time, so I took it to heart, and devoted myself blindly to my incredible physique for the next fifteen years. Every time I started thinking about acting lessons or combat training, some fashion article would come out about me actually having a body fat index, and Rick would just send me back to the gym. Then they'd stuff a gun in both of my hands and say 'Just dive sideways through the air, Max-Ram. Just dive sideways through the air.'"

"You did do that a lot," I recalled. "However, you did it very well. It actually got a patent, didn't it? The Max-Ram Lateral Corkscrew Power Dive®, or something like that."

"I do have that to my credit," Mort said with repressed pride, wiping away his tears. "But, after fifty movies, even that isn't enough. I didn't contribute a thing to the world of cinema."

"You could have made time, Mort. You spent half of your life partying."

"I was tired, Bucky! Do you know why I partied? Because it was easy. Partying is the easiest thing in the world. You just drink and drive and shuffle around on the dance floor, and the slower you move, the more people assume that you know what you're doing. Nobody in Hollywood could dance slower than me."

"'I was tired?' Does that excuse still work in Los Angeles?"

"I'll tell you what, Bucky. Spend the next couple of decades devoting as much as three hours a day exclusively to your rear deltoids, and then get back to me."

"*Touché*," I acknowledged. "Well, if the movies mean that much to you, why didn't you try flexing the old acting chops a bit more? Lower budget independent dramas or student film projects would have loved to work with somebody like you. And you would have learned a few things about actual storytelling."

"I did try that, Bucky," Mort sighed. "It didn't work. I just couldn't commit to anything but action cinema. I even grew a ponytail and tried to make it as the next king of the direct-to-DVD market. I could have been the next Lorenzo Lamas, but nobody would give me a shot. After redefining the brainless action genre of the 80s and then burning out, dramatic roles were just too much to try out for. I even tried writing my own last year, but my self-referential tongue-in-cheek biographical parody drama called *MXRT* got threatened with lawsuits from Brussels. After that, I just gave up. I was finished. Heck, I never even bothered to dream about starring in those critically-lauded movies that win all the awards for no other reason than that they exclusively feature male nudity."

"The angels weep with you, Mort."

"I never got real awards, Bucky! You know the only award I ever won in my last ten years in the movies? The Tissue Paper Shirt Medal at the 38th Annual Lonely Housewife Movie Awards.... Well, I guess I can sort of be proud of that. Actually, I still hold the unrivalled distinction of wearing a shirt for only 18% of my total recorded screen time, with a mere 11% of that time spent in a shirt with intact sleeves. And because of my incredible muscle mass, and the fact that all other male actors were contractually obligated to wear suits or turtleneck sweaters whenever we shared scenes, no one could say that it was gay. Some of us actually learned a few lessons from the shower-room scene in *Top Gun*."

"Yes, that was a defining aspect of your movies, wasn't it?" I agreed. "You could never keep your sleeves, and your female co-stars could never keep their buttons. The formula seemed to work, but it never really gave you a chance for meaningful interactions."

"And that's not even the worst part," Mort groaned. "I had some great dramatic opportunities, but I always chickened out because I didn't want to make a fool of myself. Even when people started figuring out how bad an actor I was, a few long-sighted directors saw dramatic potential in me. In the late 90s, I got several offers to play the leads in the incredible true stories of music teachers-slash-basketball coaches who teach groups of self-centred inner-city kids to respect themselves. Oh, but get this, there's a twist. One of the kids has an emotionally repressed parent who disapproves of them pursuing their dream, rather than the family business, but then, in the final playoff-slash-recital scene, the kid looks out at the audience, and, sure enough–"

"I saw it," I interjected drearily.

"Really?" Mort said. "Which one?"

"All of them," I assured him. "Every single one. Just out of curiosity, did you ever see that movie where the coach teaches a group of self-centred inner-city kids to respect themselves, and they succeed in winning State, and then go on to a professional sports career wherein they perpetually get away with drug use-slash-trafficking, solicitation, impaired driving, and statutory rape?"

Mort had to think carefully before replying, "No, I

don't think I've ever seen that one. That is so weird, come to think of it. Have they actually made that one yet?"

"I'm sure somebody has. But, if it really means that much to you, why don't you try again? Perhaps after taking a few acting and kung fu lessons, or maybe doing a stint in the Marine Corps. I mean, you just spent five months living in my barn, so I assume you've got some spare time on your hands these days. You could devote the next five months to honing your craft ... if we get out of this whole dragon debacle alive, of course."

"Bucky, don't you get it?" Mort sobbed. "It's not just about the training. It's about the comeback odds."

"What?"

"The odds, Bucky. Do you think I'm under any illusion? I know the odds of an 80s child action star making a comeback, and I'm talking about odds pertaining specifically to me. They've done studies on this. You've got a better chance at making a comeback than I do. I've got a better chance of being eaten by a shark while scratching a winning lottery ticket in a laundromat than I do of making a comeback. Bill Paxton has a better chance of playing a non-arrogant character who survives a *Predator*, *Alien*, or *Terminator* franchise than I do of making a comeback."

"Oh, come on," I remarked. "Nothing's that impossible."

"I'm not kidding here, Bucky. These are actual Max-Ram Target comeback study results, compiled by some of California's leading mathematicians. Halle Berry has a better chance of actually deserving an Osc–"

"Okay, I get it," I grimaced. "So, obviously, the only solution is to give up in total despair and languish away until you lose all will to go on."

"Well, that's been working so far," Mort agreed morosely.

"I have one of those cyanide capsules in my synthetic right molar."

"*What?*"

"Yeah, you know, just in case I'm ever surrounded and hopelessly outgunned by a domestic terrorist faction, while mentally carrying information that could jeopardize my nation's security if leaked. You've gotta be prepared for stuff like that."

"That's the *only* reason you have a cyanide capsule in your synthetic molar?" I asked cautiously.

"Yeah, I don't even know why I brought that up," Mort said dismissively. "Why do you ask?"

"No reason.... Don't think about that one too hard, okay?"

"I never do," Mort said absently. "Are you hungry? We should stop for lunch."

"Sure thing," I readily agreed, anxious to distract my emotionally-unstable travelling buddy from thoughts of his suicide pill. "We'll find something on the other side of Prince George. I don't want to stop in any cities."

It was nearly noon when we found a small roadside eatery south of Quesnel. Well, technically, it was a gas station-carwash-laundromat-grocery store-café-bakery-antique shop, wherein the friendly proprietor instructed us to call him "Pop." Mort kept his head ducked the entire time that we were inside ordering, and insisted that we get our burgers to go, as he didn't want to be recognized for fear of starting a riot. None of the fifteen patrons and staff recognized him.

We took our food out to the truck, and I lowered the tailgate for us to sit in, enjoying the fresh air and warm sunshine. As we were in the process of tucking into our grub, a rather unusual thing happened. A black old-model Bell 47G bubble-dome helicopter began circling the parking lot, and then landed no more than thirty feet from my truck, the rotor wash sending my onion rings flying across the highway. Mort was the first to identify the chopper's sole black-clad occupant, and he nearly choked on his burger, which was a real shame, because Pop made just about the best blamed burgers I've ever tasted. Mozza *and* cheddar!

"What?" I queried, still munching my burger. "It's just a helicopter. The guys who are after me come on camels."

"Bucky!" Mort sputtered, his eyes nearly popping out of their sockets. "That's ... that's ... *Sting Ripblood!*"

"Seriously?" I said over the roaring engine, trying to get a better look at the glowering young man behind the bubble glass. It certainly looked like the action hero I had seen on the stage of *Canada's Next Top Best Dance Crew* the previous fall.

"He hates me!" Mort whimpered. "How did he find me? And what the crap is he doing in Canada?!"

"He's filming the latest *Compound Fracture* installment in Affluenceville," I informed him, trying to catch the few onion rings that had landed in the truck box. "Didn't you know that?"

"No!" Mort protested. "How is that possible? *Greenstick Pinch* is supposed to be set in Los Angeles, like the rest of the series!"

"Apparently, somebody thought northern British Columbia was an economical stand-in," I said dryly. "Wait a minute. You actually watched the last movie and you couldn't tell that it wasn't really Los Angeles? Have you been to an optometrist lately?"

Sting Ripblood, the musclebound pinnacle of Hollywood's A-List, was out of the domed cockpit and striding purposefully toward us before the helicopter even began to power down. He didn't even duck his head as he passed under the shrieking rotors, almost daring one of them to dip low and take his head off. The man exuded shiny black coolness from head to toe, from his shiny black shoes to his shiny black leather trenchcoat, and all the way up to his perfectly-sculpted head of jet black hair, shining with Brille cream. Blackest and shiniest of all were his glaring eyes, peering at us from over his shiny black *Matrix*-esque sunglasses. In summary, he was by far the coolest, shiniest, blackest white man I had ever seen.

He stopped about ten feet away, and stood before us like a gunfighter, widening his stance and pushing back his trenchcoat with his thumbs, revealing his shiny black silk shirt and pants, and the ornately-patterned leather of his shiny honey-mustard belt. (Even in my star-struck stupor, I thought that last part was a bit weird.)

"Target," he said in a voice that was every bit as dark and cool as the rest of him.

"Hey, Sting," Mort whined.

Sting raised a skeptical shiny black eyebrow as he studied the quaking form of his apparent nemesis.

"You're looking very ... like that."

"Thanks," Mort gulped. "Just eating my purple vegetables."

"The little birds are singing about you doing a lot more than that, Max-Ram," Sting said coldly. "Getting some big Hollywood plans for the next few decades?"

"What?" Mort said, puzzled. "I'm done with the movies, Sting. You know that." Looking miserable, he added, "I'm focussing blindly on my promising career as a non-fiction author."

"I believe you," Sting growled. "I read the article in *Forbes*."

"My name was printed in current media?" Mort said, even more surprised. "My full name?"

"And this must be Bucky Laroo," Sting said, a bit more

genially as he glanced at me. "The same Bucky Laroo whose life you reputedly saved through great acts of valour and sacrifice. That doesn't sound much like the Max-Ram Target I knew. I guess anyone can still surprise us, no matter how well we may think we know them."

"*Ta-da*," Mort said weakly.

"Pleasure to meet you, Mr Ripblood," I said, standing and extending my hand. "Big fan."

"Britt 2.0 told me all about you, Laroo," Sting said, ignoring my hand but snatching my brown cowboy hat off my head and obligingly autographing it with a permanent marker. "To think, you were within my grasp last fall, and you slipped away. From me, and from justice."

"What?" I said.

Sting ignored me, slapping my hat crookedly back onto my head as he brushed past me, making a beeline for Mort. With his comfort bubble being invaded, Mort tried to casually scootch farther back into the truck box, but his pants snagged on the rusty tailgate hinge beside him, preventing his escape.

Sting was eye-to-eye with Mort when he finally spoke again, his black eyes narrowing as Mort's baby blues bulged ever wider.

"Did you really think I wouldn't be monitoring Ashton Kutcher's phone calls?" Sting said menacingly. "Did you really think I wouldn't find you?"

"How did you find me?" Mort had to ask.

"Because you told Ashton Kutcher that you were on your way to Kelowna, you idiot!" Sting reminded him. "This province may be huge, but Highway 97 is still the only one between Kelowna and the pay phone you used."

"Good point," Mort said.

Sting only glared harder as he replied, "I should have known you would be lurking around Coyote Yelp Pass. If I'd known where that was, I would have found you five months ago, wouldn't I have? The next time you leave a cryptic message about retreating to your Canadian Walden, make sure you visit a few other Canadian locations first. I happen to know that the only Canadian soil you've ever set foot in is Coyote Yelp Pass, and a couple of airports that brought you there."

"Duly noted," Mort acknowledged.

"It's been a long time coming, hasn't it, Max-Ram?" Sting said irritably. "You know what I'm talking about."

"My imminent butt-kicking?" Mort ventured.

"Take another guess," Sting snarled.

"Hey, you didn't even like that horse!" Mort protested.

"Always the coy one, eh?" Sting said, putting an icy hand on Mort's shoulder. "They discussed it for so long in secret, we all thought it was a myth. Apparently, we were wrong."

"What are you talking about?" Mort demanded.

"*Do not play games with me, Target!*" Sting shouted, grabbing Mort's Adam's apple. "I want to know how you got on that list! Aside from the fact that your films have grossed a quarter of a trillion dollars worldwide, it doesn't make any sense at all. That top slot should have been mine!"

"What list?" Mort gurgled.

"What list?" I echoed.

Sting froze, and a quiet smile began to work its way across his lips.

"You really don't know?"

"I've never heard about any list!" Mort insisted breathlessly. "Unless it's the hit list that me and Bucky are probably on, but I can't imagine why you'd want to be on that one."

"Is there a problem here?" I inquired.

"Silence, Bucky!" Mort instinctively snapped, his face turning from crimson to violet.

"Fine with me," I said with a shrug, wiping a dab of mustard from my chin. "I'll just sit here in silence and finish my burger. Man, this place makes a good burger."

"Yeah, it smells awesome," Sting admitted, never relaxing his grip on Mort's windpipe. "Is that bacon *and* mushrooms I smell?"

"And two patties and two kinds of cheese," I pointed out. "Want me to get you one? We can all sit down and discuss our issues over a plate of meat, as God intended for men to. And maybe you could stop strangling Mort?"

"Please?" Mort added.

Sting finally released Mort with a shove, and then began pacing in front of the tailgate, ominously popping his knuckles. Mort gasped for breath.

"Okay, I'm still confused," he finally wheezed.

"Holy cow cud, this is a good burger," I had to remark once more, still chewing.

"You know, Max-Ram," Sting gloated, stretching his bulging muscles in preparation of Mort's apparently imminent butt-kicking, "you have no idea what a delight it was to learn off the grapevine that The Establishment was looking for your little buckaroo here. After that, I knew that it was only a matter of time before you surfaced, and you didn't disappoint. I mean, I always knew you were an idiot, but to also be a known cohort of Canada's most-wanted eco-terrorist was just too good to be true. And, yet, here we are: The two most coveted action hunks in Hollywood history, and the infamous Bucky Laroo, the EnCana Bomber."

"Bucky's the what now?" I asked in mid-chew.

"Oh, it's going to be all over the news by tomorrow," Sting assured me. "Once The Establishment finishes identifying, or possibly planting, sufficient incriminating evidence around Cattle Poke Ranch, your reign of terror in BC is over."

"Yeah, that takes time," Mort agreed, having some experience in such things. Just read the first book.

"I'm the EnCana Bomber?" I demanded.

"Could you say that again into this digital audio recorder, but without the question mark?" Sting requested, holding the device up to my face.

"I am not the EnCana pipeline bomber!" I insisted.

Sting shrugged as he clicked the recorder off. "Well, that 'not' part should be easy enough to edit out. Thanks, Bucky."

"Sting, what are you talking about?" Mort asked. "How does Bucky's history of known eco-terrorism help you?"

Sting was chuckling as he gave Mort a rough hug. "It makes my argument that the two of you require a more permanent form of disqualification much more compelling."

"Disqualification?" Mort said, confused. "Disqualification from what?"

Sting jovially clapped us both on the back, but ignored the question.

"Well," he chortled, "the smell of those burgers is making me absolutely ravenous, so, if you'll excuse me, I'm going to go grab one, and perhaps indulge myself with a decadent banana split as well. I will eat them at my leisure, whilst giving the two of you a sporting head-start. I'd put it to good use if I were you, for what little good it will do."

Then he turned and strode into the café. There was an auditory gasp from within as every patron and staff member instantly recognized him.

Mort and I sat in frigid silence on the tailgate, staring after the departed Hollywood Titan.

"Fascinating," Mort said blankly. "To the best of my

knowledge, we're both straight, but you just can't help but watch that man walk away."

"It's like watching the Batman in slow motion," I agreed.

We sat in silence for a few moments, listening to the sounds of the highway.

"He's planning to hurt us when he comes out again," I said. "That's what I got from what he said, unless he was being insanely cryptic."

Mort nodded. "We need to leave. Right now."

"Yeah," I sighed, stuffing my burger back into the takeout bag. "We have enough survival to attend to already."

I had pulled out my keys, but Mort was suddenly in a blind panic, snatching them from my hand and scrambling into the driver's seat with a shout of "*Reverse shotgun!*" I barely had time to get the passenger door open before he gunned the engine and spat gravel across the parking lot. My old truck careened onto the highway and sped southward once more, with Max-Ram Target furiously weaving around both outgoing and oncoming traffic.

"If you insist on driving, can I finish your burger?" I asked mildly, digging mine out of the bag once more.

"How can you eat?" Mort squawked, blasting the horn at a moose in the ditch. "We're going to die!"

"Statistically, one hundred percent of people who don't eat die," I replied. "Seriously, I'm going to eat that thing if you don't."

"So impending death doesn't bother you?"

"No more than it did yesterday. Or three years ago, for that matter."

"Okay," Mort said, trying to sound calm, "just for the sake of clarification, what exactly do you think Sting Ripblood is going to do to us?"

"Mort, Betty-Sue is a celebrity gossip junkie. I know you

and Sting aren't friends. They were running stories about your feud on *Egress Hollywood* a couple years ago."

"Possible understatement," Mort said glumly. "Now I know how you must have felt for all those years, Bucky. It is seriously discombobulating to have someone pointlessly hate you for years on end."

"It wasn't pointless," I reminded him. "You stole his girlfriend, and you ran over his prize Arabian stallion with a back-hoe."

"Hey, at least one of those was an accident," Mort said defensively.

"Which one?" I asked curiously. "The horse or the girlfriend?"

"Irrelevant," Mort said after a moment's hesitation. "He's overreacting."

"It was the girlfriend, wasn't it?"

"I said it's irrelevant!"

"It's an Oath of Enmity, right? You found someone new to drop an Oath of Enmity onto, didn't you?"

"Hey, I'll have you know that he dumped that load on me, not vice versa!"

"Please rephrase that."

"He's going to kill me, Bucky!"

"Okay, calm down," I soothed him. "So you deliberately murdered one horse. If it was a Quarter Horse, maybe I'd be mad at you, too, but it was just some prissy Arabian. What's the worst that can happen? Sting doesn't know about the Ogopogo. He just thinks I'm an eco-terrorist. So he'll catch up with us, he'll kick the stuffing out of us, hopefully focussing more on you, and then we go on our merry way again. Yes, he does know fifteen different martial arts which I am not looking forward to having demonstrated on my face, but it's like getting a flu shot. Suck it up and cinch it up, and it's over before you know it."

"Oh Bucky, you just don't get it," Mort said mournfully, pressing the gas pedal as far into the floorboards as he could. "Don't you know his story? He's as real as they come."

"I heard a bit about it," I admitted. "No one knows where he's from, except that it was one of those Eurasian military states where all the ambulance paramedics carry machine guns."

"That's not the half of it," Mort said nervously, craning his neck to watch the sky. "Sting Ripblood is no hippie kid with abandonment issues. He was found bundled on the doorstep of a Los Angeles dojo in a Little Tiananmen neighbourhood in 1985. He had a dead stork underneath him. For the next twelve years, he was raised by a sensai named Ki-Lang Yu, never once setting foot outside. He learned *seventeen* different types of martial arts, not fifteen. He's a killing machine, Bucky."

"They kept an abandoned baby locked up in a dojo for twelve years?"

"Yeah, there was a bit of a media uproar over that one," Mort admitted. "It's weird. I've seen the exact same thing happen in dozens of kung fu movies, and none of those sensais got deported when they revealed their protege to the world. What is wrong with America?"

"Okay, so we'll seriously get the stuffing kicked out of us," I granted him. "Just think of the great story it'll make to tell my kids. For the record, I didn't say 'our kids' because it sounds weird, and because I pray every day that you never have kids."

"*Bucky, he's an assassin for the Irish mob!*" Mort blurted.

"Excuse me?"

"He kills people for the Irish mafia!" Mort repeated. "I'm not even supposed to know about it. Nobody's supposed to know, but I walked into the wrong bathroom in Boston this one time, and Sting's standing behind this bug-eyed Italian guy with one of those wire things, with the handles...."

"He ziplined a guy in front of you?" I said incredulously.

Mort nodded sharply, still scanning the skies as we raced down the highway. "He said only poser action hunks just pretend to kill people. And then he said that he'd inject a 50cc syringe of oxygen into my superior vena cava while I slept if I ever told anyone. He must think I told you, and that's why he's coming after us."

"Did he say what he'd do to the person you told?"

"He did, actually. But you don't want to know that."

I stared at him. "You're not kidding, are you?"

"Look at my flushed face and brow perspiration, Bucky! Am I capable of this quality of acting?"

"Oh crap, he is going to kill us," I said, instinctively looking to the sky. "They must have leaked the whole EnCana Bomber story to him so that he'd kill me, too."

"That doesn't make any sense, Bucky," Mort protested. "You have red hair and freckles and a frog-belly complexion. Nobody on Tommy-Gun O'Flannagan's crew is going to have a beef with you."

"I was talking about The Establishment."

"Oh.... Yeah, that does make more sense, given the circumstances. He must work for them, too."

"No wonder Lucy couldn't figure out who The Establishment's muscle is," I realized. "They've been hiring movie stars to do their dirty work! Come to think of it, that Sickle guy did look like he could have been Jean Reno's brother. I'll bet you anything that he's a French action hunk."

"But you said he was pasty and skinny with bad teeth and a severely receding hairline," Mort pointed out.

"Do you watch a lot of European cinema, Mort?" I said,

disgusted by his lack of culture. "That's what action hunks look like over there."

Before he could reply, an unusual shrill whistle pierced the cab, just before a propelled grenade slammed into the road ahead of us, exploding into a massive ball of fire and flying chunks of pavement.

"*Fish poop in a bowl!*" Mort roared, spinning the wheel and swerving the truck around the smoking crater.

"What was that?" I demanded.

"Hmm," Sting's garbled voice chuckled. "Perhaps I should have gone with the laser-guided Hellfire missiles, but it's just so hard to find a 1Z Viper assault helicopter on short notice."

"He's in our heads, Bucky!" Mort panicked. "I always knew that wasn't beyond him."

"I'm in your right jacket pocket, numbskull," Sting replied irritably.

Mort quickly dug into his jacket and produced a small walkie-talkie.

"Crap," he muttered. "I thought there might have been some genuine respect and affection when he hugged me, not just a handoff." Keying the mike, he snapped, "Sting, what are you doing? They're going to have to send a road crew to fix the pothole you just blasted!"

"I'm so glad you've started considering the burden of the common man," Sting said mildly. "Maybe you'll actually die worthy."

"*Are you insane?*" Mort shouted back. "It was just a horse!"

"It amuses me to think that you'll die believing that," Sting's voice cackled.

"Bucky, you're the thinker!" Mort reminded me. "Think!"

"He's a hired gun," I shot back. "Buy him off!"

"Sting, name your price," Mort urged the radio in his sweaty fist. "Let's work this out."

A second grenade smashed into the ditch directly beside me, showering the truck with dirt as we sped by. A moment later, the old bubble-dome chopper shot overhead and flew down the road ahead of us. Sting was expertly piloting the aircraft with his right hand, while aiming a handheld M32 Multiple Grenade Launcher out the cockpit with his left.

"How do you like my six-shooter, cowboy?" his chilling voice jeered.

"Sting, come on," Mort urged him. "This is business. Make me an offer."

"Keep your enemies closer, Max-Ram," Sting scoffed. "Your money is peanuts to me."

"Well, that didn't work," Mort said, instantly accepting defeat. "Any more ideas?"

"Yeah, try offering him his girlfriend back," I growled.

"I can't anymore," Mort confessed. "She's married to Ryan Reynolds."

"She's what?"

"Nothing."

"*Die, Bucky!*" Sting rasped over the radio. Three more grenades slammed into the road all around us before we managed to race underneath the hovering craft once again, the concussion of each blast nearly lifting the truck onto two wheels.

"I am getting so sick of celebrities trying to kill me," I snarled, hanging onto the doorhandle for dear life, watching the chopper wheel around to give chase in my sideview mirror. "What is the deal with that, anyway?"

"You know what I'm getting sick of?" Mort remarked, passing a logging truck on the right side of the road, the passenger-side tires biting into the packed dirt of the ditch.

"Sympathy invites to dinner parties at Dwayne Johnson's house. They're just horrible."

"*What does that have to do with anything?!*" I exploded.

"Hey, maybe you've smelled what The Rock is cooking, but you've never had to eat that crap," Mort said evenly. However, he was only able to keep a straight face for another second or two, and then he had to snort back a laugh.

I stared at him in disgust.

"You thought up that stupid joke months ago, and you've just been waiting for a chance to use it, haven't you?"

"I was alone in a barn for five months," Mort quipped. "I needed to use it before I die. And I'm about to die!"

"Okay, that's fair," I admitted.

"Just pull over and hold still, Bucky," Sting's voice encouraged me. "Everyone ends at some point, and this is your point. All is fleeting. Why does everybody think that everything's going to last? It never does. Do you remember the summer of 2005, when Anne Heche escaped from Whitney Houston's basement, and no one saw her again until three weeks later when she was hit by an oncoming car while riding a segway down a one-way street in Raccoon City? Of course you don't remember! And they were calling that one the entertainment news story of the decade. It's all fleeting, Bucky. Just accept it."

"What city did he just say she was in?" I asked.

"*Die, Bucky! Die, Max-Ram!*" was Sting's raspy reply, as his final grenade slammed into my tailgate. Mort and I ducked as the back window shattered, spraying us with fragmented glass.

"It's gotta make you feel kind of good, doesn't it, Bucky?" Mort guessed, still spinning the steering wheel in a vain attempt to lose our airborne pursuer.

"No, it doesn't make me feel good!" I yelled. "What part of this is supposed to make me feel good?"

Mort shrugged. "Just knowing that he wants me dead as much as he wants you dead."

"Hey, I heard that, and it's not true!" Sting snapped. "Your career gave me something to aspire to, Max-Ram, rivals or not. I can respect you for that. But a Canadian cowboy moonlighting as an eco-terrorist? How many oxymorons can you cram into one job description? Trying to save the environment, while simultaneously ignoring the fact that every time one of your cows breaks wind, six of your own unborn grandchildren die!"

"What?" I said. I said that a lot when trying to make sense of my celebrity dialogues.

The truck was nearly knocked off the road as Sting swooped low and began bashing his landing ski against my door, ripping off the sideview mirror. Unable to reload his grenade launcher and fly at the same time, he was now concentrating on destroying my truck by the sheer weight of his helicopter.

"Man, I hate this place," he was muttering, as Mort fought to retain control of the truck. "I don't care about the studio economy. This is the last time I'm substituting anything in Canada for Los Angeles. British Columbia has got to be the biggest waste of real estate this side of Baltimore. With the space you Canadians are tying up, we could pave over the whole dang province, put in three or four brand new great states of Texas, and start pumping out some real cowboys."

"What do you mean, real cowboys?" I demanded, snatching Mort's radio.

"The kind who drink and fish and cut records in Nashville," Sting barked. "The kind who don't upset The Establishment. Honestly, I don't know what you actually did, but if the scientists of the world want you dead, then you must deserve it. Cowboys don't get to change the world,

Bucky. It's never too late to learn that lesson, even if you don't have the option of living long enough to apply it."

"Hey, you don't know that cowboys can't change the world," I reminded him irritably.

"Be serious," Sting scoffed. "Can street-corner mimes ever truly make their parents proud? Can any form of arachnid make a good house-pet? Can Ben Affleck play a remotely likeable character? It's all the same, Bucky. You should've just stayed home and plucked a banjo and sang songs about the old glittering gulch."

"The old what?" I cringed.

"That's a cowboy thing, isn't it?"

"I don't think that's even a regular thing," I commented.

Sting was now flying so low alongside us that I could look him in the eye. He smirked at me, and pulled out an Uzi submachine gun, aiming it directly at my window.

"I'll show you a cowboy thing," I growled, leaning over and seizing the steering wheel. In spite of Mort's resistance and squeals of protest, I hauled the wheel hard to the right. The helicopter's landing skis screeched across the roof of the truck as we swerved directly under them and into the right-hand ditch. Mort frantically fought to keep us from rolling as we plowed our way down to the fallow plowed field below, while Sting swung the helicopter around, firing a quick burst from the Uzi into our plummeting wake. Then he effortlessly managed to fly the aircraft underneath the roadside powerlines, and the chase continued.

"*What the heck, Bucky?*" Mort yelped as we crashed through a flimsy board fence.

"Just relax, and floor it!" I ordered him. "Gramps did this on the way to his wedding rehearsal with Grams sitting right next to him, holding their wedding cake on her lap."

"Were they being chased by a helicopter, too?" he

inquired sarcastically as we slammed into the bumpy dirt, the chopper still hot on our tailgate.

"No, it was more pest control," I recalled fondly, crawling over the backrest into the backseat. "He was trying to run down a coyote. Keep swerving. We need to kick up the dust."

"What are you doing?" Mort demanded.

"Blinding him," I replied, tossing my cowboy hat onto the seat, and taking a moment to ensure that the Ogopogo egg in the baler twine box was still intact. "He's too low. That's a short range sub gun. If he pulls out of the dust, he'll be shooting wild."

"That's your whole plan?"

"He's stopped shooting, hasn't he?"

"Very clever, Bucky," Sting's voice gurgled. "But no cowboy's gonna make a fool out of me. You just put yourself in open terrain!"

"Bucky, just shoot him!" Mort squawked. "You've got that 30-30 right there!"

"Killing people makes Jesus sad," I sighed, pulling on a pair of leather work gloves as I climbed out the shattered rear window.

The truck box was still filled with various farm implements, including a thirty-foot logging chain. I wasn't sure if I was just being insane, or if I had just seen too many movies, but I didn't have any better plan. I quickly hooked one end of the chain around the heavy 5th-wheel trailer hitch in the centre of the box. However, before I could do anything else, Sting made a low strafing run from directly behind us, bullets pelting into the tailgate. Mort swerved hard to get away, and I lost my balance. I managed to grab hard onto the logging chain as I was pitched over the right tire rim, and then I was in the dirt, being dragged behind my own truck.

"*Mort!*" I bellowed, clinging to the chain for dear life as my lean body cut a new furrow across the field. "Stop the truck!"

"Mop the duck?" Mort called back.

"Absolutely!" I screamed. "Mop the duck! While you're at it, slop the muck, crop the Canuck, and *stop the truck!*"

"Is that code for something?" Mort wanted to know, driving faster.

It took me a minute to hand-over-hand my way back to the tailgate, setting fire to what muscles were in my arms in the process. However, I managed to heave myself back into the truck box and reel the chain in after me. In spite of the imminent overhead peril, I had to take a moment to look at Mort, and then down at the chain in my hands, which was oddly reminiscent of "one of those wire things, with the handles" at the moment. I closed my eyes and shook off the homicidal impulse.

"Keep Jesus happy, Bucky," I reminded myself, looking to the sky once more. "Keep Him happy."

An instant later, I was forced to drop onto my back as Sting dove down from above, attempting to land on the cab. I could hear Mort hollering as the roof began caving in around him, all but drowned out by the screech of the buckling metal.

"Bucky!" Mort roared. "I think Jesus understands extenuating circumstances!"

"Suck it up and cinch it up, cowboy!" I shouted back, lunging up and hooking the free end of the logging chain to the nearest landing ski, which was only a couple of feet above me. None the wiser, Sting began ascending upward in preparation for his next great flying pile-driver, dragging the heavy chain into the air below him. With no time to spare, I reached into the backseat, seized my Winchester Trapper, and emptied all seven rounds of 30-30 hollow-point into the tail rotor, which was buzzing less than six feet over my head. At least five of the rounds found their target, and smoke and hydraulic fluid began pouring from the helicopter's tail. My job was done. Dropping the empty rifle, I scrambled back to the cab, and fell back into my seat.

"He's landing on us!" Mort whined as we continued to tear across the field, with the smoking helicopter now on a short leash.

"So call the obvious police," I snapped. "I need you to slam on your brakes, as hard as you can, on three."

"*What?*"

"Just do it!" I yelled. "Three! Two! One! *Brake!*"

"You said on three!" Mort snapped.

"Sorry, I meant one. *One!*"

Mort obligingly mashed the brakes through the floorboards, and the speeding Chevy slammed to a halt, the bubble-dome chopper shooting straight over us at full speed.

"Oh, one more thing," I said, reaching over to unclip his seatbelt as the physics of the situation suddenly caught up with me. "Duck."

"Duck?" Mort clarified.

"*Duck!*" I squawked, grabbing him by the shoulders and pulling him into the seat cushions.

The heavy chain connecting the helicopter to my truck box snapped taut an instant later, ripping through the metal uprights of the cab, just above the base of the windows. The unstable chopper was yanked in a sideways circle, dragging the chain through the cab just over our heads and turning my beloved Chevy Sierra into a convertible. The entire roof was torn off like the lid of a sardine can, and every window exploded, showering Mort and I with glass once more. A couple of seconds later, the peeled-off roof hit the dirt next to the driver's door, and the spinning helicopter gouged a trench into the field at almost the same instant, the main rotor snapping off and sending up a blinding cloud of black topsoil.

Then there was silence, so much so that we could actually hear the fine rain of dust settling all around us.

Mort and I cautiously sat up into the fresh air, one on either side of the chain that was running lengthwise through my truck cab and down the centre of the hood. It was still held fast to the crumpled remains of the bubble-dome, which lay on its side with its belly facing us, no more than twenty-five feet away.

"You ... *planned that?*" Mort whispered incredulously, shaking from the pumping adrenaline.

"Well, actually the cab removal part only occurred to me as you were hitting the brakes," I confessed, shaking a fair bit myself. "Better late, right?"

We stared in silence at the demolished helicopter for a few moments that felt like hours.

"Um," Mort mumbled, licking his dry lips. "Do you think he's dead?"

"No, he auto-rotated in pretty softl–" I was assuring him, just as the entire aircraft exploded into a raging ball of flame.

"Oops," Mort said.

"Yep," I said. "He's dead."

"Come on!" Mort yelled, scrambling over the hood and running toward the flaming wreckage, managing to lose one of his shirt sleeves in the process. "Get to the chopper!"

We ran as fast as we could, but the heat was unbearable, and we couldn't get close and were finally forced to withdraw to the truck.

"Whoa," Mort said, blinking a lot. "The Wall of Fire *deja vu.*"

"What?"

"Crap!" Mort snarled, kicking angrily at the dust. "They've already started releasing pre-production teaser trailers for *Compound Fracture IV*, and it looked like it was going to be awesome!"

"It did look kind of awesome, didn't it?" I remarked. "You just can't go wrong casting Alan Rickman as the villain."

"'Let me reset that for you!'" Mort quipped, doing a pretty fair impression of Frank C. Pound's signature line.

"No, it's more gravelly and staccato than that," I couldn't help correcting him. "Like this: '*Let me reset that for you!*'"

"That's really good, Bucky," he replied, quite impressed. "Shoot, why couldn't I ever get great lines like that? Or great franchises, for that matter? Seriously, how is it possible that I made fifty big-budget action movies, and never had a single sequel? Even Seagal had a Ryback sequel. *Seagal!*"

"Maybe your habit of consistently putting your special effects director in charge of script revisions was a bad idea in the long-run," I suggested. "I know that Michael Bay's been doing it for years, but– *What are we talking about?!* We just killed Sting Ripblood! We're going to jail!"

"Calm down, Bucky," Mort soothed me. "I'll take care of everything."

"Hollywood's leading action hunk is turning into a charcoal briquette right in front of us!" I shouted. "You can't just make that go away!"

"Sure I can," Mort asserted, pulling a small white card out of the medicine bag hanging from his neck. "I've got the cadaver contingency playbook for celebrities. You see, Bucky, at some point in the lives of roughly 67% of movie stars, and 100% of pop stars, we find ourselves alone in a dark alley or Iowa cornfield with one or more dead bodies. We need to know the basics of forensic misdirection."

"This is the playbook?" I said, snatching the business card from his hand.

"Everything you'll ever need to know," Mort said confidently.

"'Step one,'" I read aloud, squinting to make out the single line of fine print. "'Burn it. The end.' That's it?"

"That's it," Mort said smugly. "Never fails. All we need is an ignition source, and some form of high-temp accelerant to incinerate the body and its immediate surroundings...."

His voice trailed off as he noticed my unblinking glower aimed in his direction. Then he looked over at the fireball, and sheepishly took his card back, dropping it into the medicine bag.

"Anyway, it works. Don't knock the system, Bucky."

"Behavioural modifications in cults 'work,' Mort, quite efficiently, I hear. That doesn't mean that they're something to be modelled after. We go to the police, we tell them what happened, they don't believe us, and we both go to jail, knowing that Roman Polanski is still skiing in luxury Swiss resorts. Because that's the way it works for the Bucky Laroos of the world."

We were interrupted by a hoarse cough, and looked up in time to see a singed Sting Ripblood staggering out from behind the fireball. Most of his cool black clothes had been reduced to charred threads, but he still held the Uzi in his trembling hands.

"Good enough for me," I said.

We turned and charged back toward the truck, diving into the open cab just as Sting opened fire, shooting out my left headlight. I landed behind the steering wheel and slammed the truck into reverse. The wheels spun, but we weren't moving.

"Unhook that chain!" I roared, keeping my head low as Sting emptied his clip into my coolant reservoir.

Mort wriggled into the truck box, but the chain was too tight to release. Sting seemed to be experiencing some sort of inner-ear disorder, but he was still gaining momentum as he lurched toward us, tossing aside his submachine gun, and drawing a small dagger from his belt, which was the only fully-intact article of clothing that remained on his body.

"I need slack!" Mort yelled back at me. "Roll forward!"

"Oh, that is a really bad idea," I grimaced, reluctantly obeying as Sting broke into a gallop, driven beyond his shocked state by a lifetime of combat training, and a newfound murderous rage.

The truck chugged half a foot forward, and the chain began to droop. Mort gave it one more powerful heave, and the hook came free, sliding over the side of the truck to the furrows below. I slammed the stick shift back to reverse and punched the accelerator, just as Sting made a dive for the hood, the icepick blade of his dagger scraping the chrome from my bumper as he crashed into the soil. Then we were gone, driving backwards as fast as the truck would carry us, and leaving Sting lying face-down in a cloud of dust in the centre of a four hundred acre field.

Once we were flying down the highway once more, trying to ignore the bugs pelting our faces, Mort finally marvelled, "And she still runs?"

"Never underestimate a 1990 2-wheel-drive Chevy Sierra extended cab long-box," I said, licking the spattered remains of a couple mosquitos from my teeth. "And how did your shirt get shredded so fast? Mine didn't even get a tear, and I was the one getting dragged behind the truck!"

"I thought it was always like this," Mort remarked, glancing down admiringly at his clearly visible pectorals.

"Why would you possibly think that?"

"Who cares about my sexy shredded shirt?" Mort

shouted in agitation. "I am genuinely frazzled, okay? I don't like real bullets, Bucky, so forgive me if I'm going a little cuckoo for Cocoa Puffs right now!"

"That must be a regional expression," I noted. "Because I've never had any clue as to what it means."

"You're not helping me to calm down, Bucky!"

"Impromptu musical number?" I offered, reaching into the backseat and pulling out my fiddle case.

Mort contemplated that for a moment, and then inquired, "Do you know *My Immortal* by *Evanescence*?"

"No."

"*Lucky* by Britney Spears?"

"No. Actually, I only know *The Orange Blossom Special*. And *Hot Cross Buns*."

"Dang it, Bucky, I need soul-soothing, not toe-tapping! Crap, we're gonna die. He's going to find us, and then we're going to die."

"We just crashed his only local mode of transportation," I reminded him. "By the time he's mobile again, we'll be long gone. We'll have to deviate from our planned route a bit more, but we'll be fine."

"Sting knows where we're going, Bucky! He heard me say Kelowna."

"He's stranded in a field, a mile from the highway," I said. "All of his gear and most of his clothes got burnt up. Chill out. It's going to take him a while to get back to civilization and refit, if he even decides to keep chasing us at all. We probably put a good scare into him, so he should just go back to his film set."

Mort fell silent as he considered that possibility, and he stayed that way for the next fifty kilometres or so. However, it was obvious that he was unable to fully relax, and, in fact, he seemed to be getting more agitated with each passing minute.

"Um," he finally said, his voice still shaking a bit. "I'm sorry, Bucky, but can you stop the truck, please? Seriously, I need you to stop the truck."

"It's perfectly natural," I assured him. "Just hang your head over the side. We need to put some more distance between us and him."

"Bucky, I'm a high-functioning alcoholic. Nothing can make me vomit. But you need to stop the truck."

"Why?"

"Sting Ripblood is going to be looking for this truck," Mort carefully explained. "So do you know where the best place for me to hide is? Anywhere but in this truck!"

"Calm down, Mort," I muttered, wiping a dragonfly out of my eyebrows. "Where are you going to go?"

"Look, I said I'd help you with this quest," Mort reminded me. "And if it was just a bunch of pansy-pant scientists and their regular hired assassins hunting us, I'd fight beside you to the end. But this is Sting Ripblood. There's a big gaping difference between nobility and futility, Bucky. Let's just cut our losses and go live in a cave somewhere. After seven years, Betty-Sue can have you declared dead in absentia, and she'll be free to marry some other nice man. And everyone's happy."

"That's the worst plan I've ever heard."

"Bucky, please," Mort said, now squirming in his seat like a toddler trying to hold it until the next rest stop. "Stop the truck."

"No."

"Bucky, stop the truck."

"Mort, let's just take a minute, collect our breath, and figure this—"

"I asked you nicely!" Mort shouted, scrambling onto the seat and vaulting over the passenger-side door at speeds well in excess of the posted limit. "*Aaaaiiiieeeeee!!*"

Fortunately, we were in the middle of the bridge over Grizzly Snuffle Creek at the time, so Mort's fall was broken by a twenty foot drop into semi-deep water, rather than pavement.

"Holy cow cud!" I blurted, slamming on the brakes.

By the time I had pulled over and ran to the concrete railing-girders, Mort had found the current and was swimming furiously downstream.

"*Mort!*" I hollered down at him. "Are you out of your mind? I was doing a buck twenty!"

"I'm alive, freckles!" he shouted over his shoulder, still clawing at the swift water. "And I'm staying that way! Tell the authorities that my body vaporized in a hot-spring geyser!"

"Mort, get back here!"

"You'll never take me alive!" Mort maniacally cheered, slogging to shore. "*Bahaha!*"

"Oh, for the love of pigtails," I muttered, scurrying back to my topless truck. I pulled onto a gravel turnout on the far side of the bridge, and followed a battered ATV trail down the riverbank until I spotted Mort running ahead of me like a madman. I stopped the truck, bailed over the side, and pursued him on foot.

"Mort, stop!"

"You'll thank me for this one day!" Mort replied in a deranged voice.

"You're a Hollywood action hunk, Mort," I called after him, hurdling fallen logs. "You have zero applicable life skills. You'll never survive out here!"

"I've played *MacGuyver*-esque roles!" Mort yelled back, plowing through dense underbrush. "I'll improvise tools of survival from animal bones and peat moss!"

"*MacGuyver*-esque tools of survival don't work, Mort. They did an episode of *MythBusters* on it."

"*Craaaap!*" Mort wheezed, finally glancing back at me. "Are you gaining on me? How are you gaining on me?!"

"I've been outrunning killer cows since I was five," I reminded him. "I'm as light of foot as a wild roe."

Mort burst into a shaded clearing on the riverbank, and spun around to face me, ripping a green branch off a small deciduous tree and brandishing it like a leafy spear.

"Turn thee aside to thy right hand or to thy left!" he shouted, his eyes bulging with fanatical desperation. "*Don't make me kill you, Bucky!*"

"You're not going to kill me," I said, skidding to a halt with my hands passively raised. "If you really need to blow off some steam, these woods are full of squirrels and rocks. There is nothing more therapeutic than murdering a squirrel with a rock."

"Step back!" Mort warned me. "I may be the least qualified, and most overrated, action hunk on the planet, but I will cudgel you if you come any closer. There is very little technical expertise required for the discharging of a tree branch!"

"My three main food groups are steak, beans, and starch, Mort. You've been eating radishes for the past five months. I'm not bragging, but I don't think you have the protein stores to take me down right now."

"I'm not going back there to die, Bucky! I am the most worthless human being that I know. Do you really want me to die like that?"

"And you think living in a cave is going to make you worthwhile?" I coughed, slowly approaching him.

"Reverting to an animal state, in perpetual balance with nature? According to the hippies and Free Masons and Biodiversity Treaty and eco-terrorists, I'm a hero!"

"Mort," I said patiently. "You are coming back to what's left of my truck with me. We are going to find someone who will listen to us, and they are going to tell the rest of the world not to kill us anymore. Then we are going to get rid of that stupid lizard egg, and go on with our lives. And you are going to star in the biggest action blockbusters of the new decade."

"Really?" Mort said, beginning to lower his stick.

"No. I made that last part up. But I can't do this alone. Come on, put down the branch. Just console yourself with the knowledge that you're actually needed for once in your life, no matter the outcome."

"You really need me?" Mort said, clearly touched by my words as the tip of his spear lowered into the bed of pine needles he was standing in.

"An hour ago, I would have said no," I admitted. "But, yeah, I need you, Mort. I've always tried to do everything on my own, and it's not working this time around. Sometimes, even I need someone to steer the truck while I lasso the helicopter."

Mort thought about that for another moment, but then grew suddenly uncomfortable again.

"Um ... is this, like, one of those ... male bonding moments?"

I had to ponder the definition for awhile before confessing, "It's almost starting to feel like one, isn't it?"

"Yeah," Mort growled. "What's your angle, Bucky?"

"Fine, we'll do it your way," I sighed. Then I punched him in the face and tackled him to the forest floor.

"I'm not going back!" Mort shouted, trying to gouge my eyes out with his fingernails.

"Yes, you are!" I snarled, strangling him.

Mort's groping hand found his fallen stick, and he clobbered me across the head with it before scrambling to his feet and making another dash for the woods. I managed to shake off the pain and charge after him, my flying tackle sending both of us over the bank and into the river. The current was even stronger there than at the bridge, and it quickly swept us away, still kicking and clawing at each other.

After a few more moments of manly negotiations, I was briefly carried beyond the reach of his flailing fists, and I had to ask, "Hey, do you think that maybe we're fighting right now because we still have unresolved issues from all those years we spent hating each oth–"

"*Die, Bucky!*" Mort rasped, socking me in the eye and dunking my head underwater. I managed to break free just as we were washed over the precipice of Grizzly Snuffle Falls. We most likely would have died on impact with the lower rocky tier of the falls if our drop hadn't been cushioned by the pillow-like backside of a young bear, waiting for spawning salmon. It let out a startled yammer and began running in panicked circles, as Mort and I tumbled/rolled/plummeted the remaining thirty-seven feet to the deep pool at the bottom of the falls.

Mort was the first to surface again, his shredded shirt now completely gone, and I can't really blame him for incredulously asking, "Did we just land on a grizzly bea–"

"*Die, Mort!*" I snarled, socking him in the eye. "That's for trying to steal my wife before she was my wife!"

The current was picking up speed again, and our fight soon raged right past a stunned camping family of five, the father and young daughter of whom were fishing along the riverbank. Showing an impressive instinct for improvised weaponry, Mort seized one of their fishing lines from the water as we went past and whipped the hook at my face, sinking one of the barbs into my cheek.

"*Yeeowch!*" I screamed through clenched teeth, just as I found my footing and charged for the safety of the shore. However, Mort lunged out of the water right behind me, tackling me into the muddy bank and trying to pin me down.

"Don't just stand there, little girl!" he snapped at the slack-jawed nine-year-old. "*Kill him!*"

He was trying to strangle me with the fishing line that was still attached to my face as the slick mud carried us back down the steep bank toward the water, but I managed to seize a small scaling knife from a nearby icebox, and sever the lightweight test line. I had to elbow Mort in the throat before I could get free and clamber up the bank on my hands and knees, but the blow scarcely slowed him down. With mud smeared all over his face, hair, torso, and pants, the shirtless muscleman scooped up a large salmon from the icebox and charged after me with a bloodcurdling war-cry, swinging the rose-coloured fish around his head like a mace.

"*Yaaah!*"

I was still on my knees, but, at the last possible second, I reached up and wrenched the large metal tackle box from the father's quaking hands and swung it double-handed into the side of Mort's skull with a resonating *KLONG!* He was instantly knocked off his feet and onto his back, out cold and snoring before his body slammed into the rocky soil.

"Sorry about that, Mort," I cringed, after checking his pulse to make sure that I hadn't made Jesus sadder than necessary.

In the stunned silence that followed, I shakily rose to my feet, nearly as mud-covered as Mort, and trying to ignore the hook, lure, and small carp that were still dangling from the side of my face. All I could think was that I now had at least a mile of uphill terrain to carry Mort's deadweight body over before we could get back in the truck.

"It's okay, folks," I wheezed, waving placidly at the huddled family, even as I felt the penetrating barb of the fishhook beginning to jab my tongue through my buccal pouch. "I'm a US Marshal. This man is a federal fugitive.... Okay, that was a lie. Hi. I'm Bucky Laroo. Do you have a pair of wire clippers that I could possibly borrow?"

Sting Ripblood and Lucy had both assured me that cowboys don't get to change the world. At that point, I was seriously hoping that they were right. However, there was no time for such wishful thinking. Mort and I had been detected en route, and that meant that it was time to initiate my contingency plan. But I'll tell you about that later.

THE BOOM BARN

◇◇◇◇◇◇◇◇◇◇◇◇◇◇◇◇◇◇◇◇◇◇◇◇◇◇

ORT WOKE UP LESS than seven hours later, so I don't think his condition could have been classified as a very serious coma at any point of its duration. By then, I was fairly certain that my truck was illegal to operate on public roads, so I had detoured onto a rocky side-road a couple hours north of Kelowna. I finally stopped for the night on the forested outskirts of the tiny town of Buffalo Borborygmus Pass, a place that made Coyote Yelp Pass look upscale cosmopolitan. I didn't even want to risk a hotel at that point, so it seemed that we were going to have to use my devastated truck for shelter, a difficult goal to meet without a roof or windows.

Mort didn't say much when he came to, but he did sheepishly inquire if I was alright, and he didn't try to jump out of the moving vehicle again, so I figured that was a good sign. We made a small campfire in a forest clearing as night fell in, and munched on some of Sassy's homemade owl jerky for supper.

"Sorry for freaking out, Bucky," he finally said, gingerly rubbing the goose-egg on his right temple. "I guess impending death is a lot scarier for those of us who have wasted our lives, like all celebrities."

"It's okay, Mort. I was scared, too. And are you sure you

don't want another shirt? I packed an extra fleece in case it got cold."

"No, I'm better like this," Mort said passively, apparently most relaxed when in a shirtless state. "So what do we do now?"

"I'm working on it," I said, trying to brush my own shirt clean of some of the dried mud that we were both caked in. "There's a public campground a couple kilometres from here. Once it gets a bit darker, I'll use the pay phone there to make a couple calls. Unless you have some more resources to bring to the table, that is. And I use the word 'more' in spite of the fact that I really haven't seen any yet."

"All in good time, Bucky. A ground-based, cash-only plan is still our best shot. Are you going to call Megiddo?"

"No," I said, shaking my head. "I want to call him on as short a notice as possible. We can't afford to give The Establishment any lead time. We're only an hour and a half from Kelowna, so he should be able to meet us pretty quickly. We'll pick a good rendezvous spot in the morning, and call him on Shania Twain's sat-phone. And, once this is all over, we should probably call Shania Twain and give her back her sat-phone."

"Did you have a rendezvous in mind?"

"I think I saw a good spot on the way in."

"Do you think I should wear my Fu Manchu disguise? It's in my medicine bag."

"We want Megiddo to know who you are, Mort. Why would you need a disguise?"

"No reason. I just love wearing it. I never knew what I was missing from never having facial hair until I moved into your barn. And I just love the way the Fu Manchu's feathery lightness tickles the lateral edges of my filtrum. It makes me think of how the birds must feel."

"As birds are so well-known for their feathery lips?"

"Exactly," Mort said, looking a bit nostalgic as he gazed down admiringly at his muscular, mud-smeared torso in the flickering firelight. "I always envied them that. But my facial insurance clauses always stipulated that nothing was to obstruct the camera's view of my face. Why do you think I patented the sweptback look for my hairstyle? It kept my perfect ears and perpetually acne-free forehead exposed. A face as beautiful as mine needed to be in the clear."

"Is that why you only ever wore camouflage up to your throat in all your jungle combat movies?"

"Only until '95. That's when I began actively enforcing my neck clauses."

"That's all fascinating and immediately relevant, Mort, but right now you've got to tell me anything else you know about Sting. If he really is working as a hitman for The Establishment, I need to know what else he's capable of."

"Are you kidding me?" Mort said. "You can't even blame Sting for what he is. Sure, he whacked a few dozen Italian and Colombian wiseguys in Boston, but most of them were other mafia cartel dudes who probably had it coming, anyway. Compared to what he is now, Sting was an honourable warrior back then."

"So what changed?"

"Bucky, what do you think changed? He started dating a pop star. Pop stars are literally the most horrible people on the planet, and Britt 2.0 is the worst of the worst. She is pure evil."

"Do you know her?" I asked. "Me and Betty-Sue met her last year, and she had nothing good to say about you."

"Yeah, I knew her," Mort said glumly. "I knew her before she was famous, and I'm starting to think that she might have been secretly evil back then, too. Most pop stars get famous and then become evil. Britt 2.0 had a head-start. I should have seen it, but I didn't, and I helped her find the path to stardom. You might even say that she only made it as far as she has because of me ... so now I've got that on my conscience, along with everything else. But, trust me, if Sting Ripblood wants us dead, Britt 2.0 was probably the one who put the idea in his head. She's more connected than The Establishment itself. And now that she's got *Sweet Conformity* and MC Morlock as her muscle.... Gee-whiz, Bucky, she's going to be unstoppable. I'm not going to lie to you. I may have gone into your barn to find literary inspiration, but I made the decision about an hour after I heard that she was bringing a new crew of creepy synchronized dancers and MC Morlock home to California. Hollywood just didn't feel safe anymore."

"Well, she's in BC again, Mort," I remarked. "So maybe Hollywood is the safest place to be, for the first time in history. But she must not know about the Ogopogo. Either that, or she just didn't tell Sting. He kept talking about you being on a list that he should have been on. Do you have any idea what he meant?"

"No," Mort sighed. "Not a clue."

After Mort was asleep, I snuck into the public campground, and called Betty-Sue from the pay phone there. I had wanted to sever all communications with home until this mess was cleaned up, but the plan had to be adapted to the circumstances.

After assuring her that Mort and I were fine, without mentioning that the truck was going to need a little detailing when I got back, I casually suggested that she should "take a mosey around the barnyard first thing in the morning, looking for out-of-place odds and ends."

"What did you lose now, Bucky?"

"I'm not sure, exactly," I replied without lying. "Maybe some short sections of polyvinyl chloride piping ... some bags of ammonium nitrate ... a large supply of diesel fuel. Stuff like that."

"Bucky, that stuff's been strewn all over the ranch ever since we were kids."

"Well, somehow I'm thinking that you may find them all in one centralized location," I admitted. "Perhaps with some coils of insulated copper wiring and a bunch of windup alarm clocks. Maybe a threatening letter or two against the EnCana Corporation...."

There was silence on the other end of the line for a few moments, and then Betty-Sue stated, "Somebody's setting us up as the EnCana Bomber, aren't they? That's how they're going to justify killing us."

"On a hopeful note, I did hear it from what might have been a misinformed secondhand source."

"That's it," Betty-Sue snapped. "I'm calling the cops. Do we still have the number for that Mudford guy?"

"The cops are going to be coming out there, anyway," I assured her. "And I'm sure that anonymous sources within The Establishment have already given them quite an earful about me. You and Gramps have to make sure they don't find anything."

"Bucky, I can redistribute PVC and fertilizer and diesel to look innocent. But what if they've just planted boxes of dynamite, or crap like that?"

"You blow it up," I said, hating to have to state the obvious.

There was an embarrassed silence before Betty-Sue admitted, "Okay, I would have thought of that in another minute."

"I know you would have," I consoled her.

"The cops are going to be asking where you are," Betty-Sue pointed out. "What do I tell them?"

"Just tell the truth," I sighed. "At the end of the day,

that's probably all Baby Jesus expects of us. But, hopefully, this will all be over with by the time they get there. I passed an old barn on the side-road about eight klicks north of Buffalo Borborygmus Pass on the highway 97C offshoot. Tomorrow, Mort and I will barricade ourselves inside, and then make the call. If the skull's as big a deal as I think it is, we'll probably get a live press conference by tomorrow night. That won't give The Establishment much lead time. Once we get the skull onto people's TVs, it's a done deal, and we get our boring back."

"Bucky ... be careful, okay? I love you."

"I love you," I said, smiling at the comforting mutual thought. "I'll call again when it's all over."

As soon as I had hung up, I was dialling another number.

"*Potpourri and Lentil, Incorporated*," Sassy's voice answered cheerily.

"Hey, big sister, it's me," I said. "By the way, when you steal a satellite phone, you probably shouldn't try to use it as a business line."

"Where are you?" she demanded. "We're right on schedule. And you still haven't told us what's going on."

"I'll tell you everything later," I promised. "Sorry I'm so late. For now, all you need to know is that my truck is suddenly running slower than I had anticipated when I first called you. People were trying to kill me again."

Sassy killed the phone battery for about twenty seconds as she was overwhelmed with hysterical laughter at the comedic image.

"I was being serious," I added, once she had calmed down.

"I know. That's what makes it so funny. Anyway, you should be used to that by now, Valley of the Gwangi. When do you want to do this?"

"ASAP," I assured her. "How far away are you now?"

When I returned to the campsite, I couldn't help but spend an hour or so sitting in the backseat of my truck, just watching that football-sized egg nestled amongst old bath towels in the baler twine box, next to its mother's skull. I wondered if it was warm enough. The sea cave had seemed cool, but I had been soaking wet, so I really had no idea. I put my hand on the bumpy surface, and thought for a moment that I felt a kick. I decided right then and there that I needed to have a kid of my own. When I started getting paternal instincts around a lizard egg, it had to be indicative of some sort of gaping hole in my life. It was seriously time for imaginary baby Rusty to become a reality.

"Hey, baby Pogo," I said softly, trying not to disturb Mort who was snoring in the truck box. "Sorry I killed your mama before you could meet her. She was a real sweetie. But I've got a plan to get you back home, and maybe make your mama famous in the process. Anyway, I'm going to try my best not to get you killed. Hopefully, you'll be able to return the favour by the time this is all over."

I placed another towel over the egg's leathery shell before closing the box again.

Mort and I spent a moderately restless night in the box of my truck, but it didn't rain very much, so it wasn't that bad, especially after Mort finally gave in and accepted the loan of a warm sweatshirt. Around nine o'clock the next morning, we drove out to the long-abandoned and dilapidated barn that I had seen through the trees on the way in, and hid the truck behind it, out of sight of the overgrown dirt lane. We went inside with the baler twine box and my rifle, and bolted all the doors. There was a large pile of rough-cut slabs stacked inside the barn, probably from a renovation project that never got off the ground. Although many of them were beginning to warp with age, they were still useful for our purposes, and so we spent the next few hours digging in and fortifying our position with the boards and a rusty can of spikes. The barn was sagging and leaning in all sorts of directions, and the buckled roof looked as if the world's largest pumpkin had dropped onto the middle of it, but the walls were made of old railroad ties, which would serve well as bullet-stoppers, should the need arise.

By the time we were certain that our position was secure, having left only the front door as an access point, it was nearly noon. I used Shania Twain's stolen sat-phone to call the television studio, and asked to speak to Harmon Megiddo. When I told the receptionist that I had verifiable proof that cryptozoology had become palaeontology, he connected me to Megiddo's office.

Although a very solemn-sounding man, Dr Harmon Megiddo lived up to his objective reputation by not immediately dismissing me as some kind of hoax when I told him that I had an Ogopogo skull in my possession. He was immediately intrigued, and agreed to make the drive out to Buffalo Borborygmus Pass to meet us as soon as possible that afternoon. However, he insisted that he needed to be quick, as he had promised to take his three children to see Canada's greatest brother-and-sister country-music duo, *The Fighting Mackenzies*, in concert in the nearby city of Kamloops that night.

"And I anticipate that they will kill me if I bail on them," he gravely assured me. "Literally. I woke up with little Natalie holding a DeWalt jigsaw to my throat after I had to cancel our Florida trip to Disney's Celebration Village last year."

"That is disturbing," I said. "And, although I am bound by family loyalty to inform you that *The Fighting Mackenzies* are a bunch of overrated Socialists, I will try to be as brief as possible." (Actually, I hated to speak ill of the beautiful twin siblings, Ronnie and Cherie Mackenzie, whom I had met on various occasions, and who seemed like fine people, even for celebrities. In particular, I liked the way that they dedicated almost every concert and album to their beloved baby brother, Plucky, whom they claimed had been the inspiration for all of their most heartwarming songs. Of course, Corky and Sassy had unambiguously assured me that Ronnie and Cherie were actually incarnate manifestations of Screwtape and Wormwood.)

"Very well, I anticipate endeavouring to be there by two o'clock," Megiddo's deep voice stated. "Verification of authenticity of a quality specimen is anticipated to take no more than twelve to fifteen seconds beneath a trained analytical eye, and, if confirmed, I anticipate arranging for a six o'clock national press release while on my way back to town ... while safely using my hands-free cellular device, of course."

"I can't thank you enough for this, Doc," I said. "We'll be waiting."

"I have done nothing for you at this time," he quickly reminded me. "And I can give no assurances that anything can be done. All I can tell you is my current anticipations. What I have told you is based upon historical calculation, and that is risky to say the least, as the exceptions disprove the rule in my mind. Anything could happen between now and noon. The world could have ceased to exist, as an example. Good day, Mr Laroo, and goodbye, just in case the world does end, thus preventing our meeting."

He hung up.

"And there's the creepy part," I sighed, pocketing the phone. "You know what's really sad, Mort?"

"The fact that my last cell phone had four different takeout places on speed-dial?"

"No, I was going to say that it's sad how we can spend

our entire lives devoted to study and knowledge, but, in the end, we're all just…. Wait a second. Four?"

"Yeah," Mort said with a shameful nod. "Pizza, Chinese, sushi, and the other pizza. Not even the good sushi, either. When I was in my Hollywood prime, I only ate food at black-tie establishments. The closest thing to takeout that I ever had was seven-star delivery that arrived at my door in a luxury double-decker bus with an onboard wait-staff, a saltwater aquarium for the lobster, and a live cow for the freshest butter you've ever dunked a dead aquatic invertebrate in. What happened to me, Bucky?"

I had to stare at him for a moment before reminding him of the obvious. "You moved into a barn loft for five months. Once you go home, you can have it all again."

"Oh, of course," Mort said, snapping out of his nostalgic reverie with a nervous laugh. "Everything will be fine when I'm back home. Why would I even ask such a foolish question? Ha ha."

We took turns napping and standing guard for the next couple of hours, but Megiddo still hadn't shown up. It was nearly three o'clock when Mort started getting antsy, pacing the barn nervously and pondering aloud what type of fateful detour had befallen our scientific guest.

"He probably just underestimated the driving time," I pointed out. "Buffalo Borborygmus Pass isn't exactly tied to the freeway."

"Trust me, Bucky," Mort said darkly. "It's never that simple."

I really hate it when Mort's right.

He turned around and began walking toward the east wall of the barn for the fortieth time in the past five minutes. All of the windows had been carefully boarded up, but we had left a narrow space between two of the boards on the east wall, so that we could peer through, and spot anyone who might have been attempting to enter the abandoned barnyard via the lane. However, Mort never made it to the window. The floorboards under his feet squeaked, and something about the sound made him stop. It was an odd sound, in retrospect. The floorboards were heavy planks set deep into a dirt base. Floors that solid weren't supposed to squeak.

"Bucky?" he said, freezing and staring down between the two slats he was straddling. "Why is there something ... blinking and whirring in a hollow under these floor boards?"

He slowly took a step back as I approached, and we stared down at the floor together. Sure enough, there was a strange whirring sound coming from beneath those floorboards, and a tiny red light could just be seen blinking in the narrow space between them.

There wasn't much to say for the next couple of minutes, so we just stood there like idiots, looking down at the rotting floor, and the blinky thing beneath it.

Mort was the one who finally had to break the silence with another statement of the obvious.

"You know that's a bomb down there, right, Bucky?"

"Yeah," I said, nodding slowly. "Yeah, that's a bomb."

"Huh," Mort marvelled. "That is so weird that there would be a bomb here."

"Seriously weird," I agreed.

"So why aren't we running right now?"

"I was just wondering that, myself."

"Do you want to run?" Mort persisted.

"Yup," I said, nodding once more. "I really do."

"Are we going to run?"

"Well," I ventured, "there's always the age-old issue of trigger versus timer to consider first. Until we figure out something on that front, I think standing really still might be a good idea."

"In the short-term," Mort pointed out.

"Yeah, that's what I meant," I said. "Jeepers, scientists and their celebrity hitmen are diabolical. Who do you think they sent this time? Sting can't have regrouped this fast."

"It's hard to say," Mort replied. "Believe it or not, most celebrities aren't evil, so I could only speculate. As much as I would hope for it to be somebody super cool like Carl Weathers ... it's probably just one of Britt 2.0's crew. Have I ever told you how much I hate synchronized dance moves, Bucky?"

"No, you never mentioned that."

"I hate synchronized dance moves!"

We stood for another silent minute, watching the hypnotic blinking of that little red light.

"Are you hungry?" Mort asked, putting his hands in his pockets.

"An odd question, under the circumstances."

"Hey, I'm just cutting the tension.... Are you?"

"Starving, actually," I admitted. "Could really go for a nice steak right about now."

"How did they know we were going to be here?" Mort demanded. "We were here before we told anybody!"

"Eek," I said through gritted teeth. "Uh, actually, that one might be on me."

"What?"

"I called Betty-Sue last night. And I may have accidentally told her exactly where we were going."

"Bucky...."

"Just say it."

"Bucky, this is every bit your fault!"

"That's been said a lot," I noted. "But it's actually been true a lot lately. That is so weird."

"You know what's funny?" Mort growled. "I always figured that you and I were destined to die together, and it would be my fault. What the heck, Bucky? I haven't been this disillusioned since the day I figured out that the lonely girls in the commercials aren't the same ones who actually pick up the phones."

"Look, I'm having a bit of an off-year," I said. "I'm sorry."

Mort sighed and rubbed his weary eyes.

"Don't be," he decided. "It's actually a real load off my shoulders. You're the one who has to answer to God for me now. I'm off the hook."

"Glad to help," I groaned.

"Hey, I just thought of something," Mort said. "Did they know when we'd be here?"

"No," I realized. "I didn't know when Megiddo could get here. I didn't even specify morning or afternoon."

"Then we can probably rule out a timer," Mort said. "The bomb probably went active when we opened the front door. But it didn't go off when we closed the door, or in the last few hours that we've been walking around in here, so we can rule out motion triggers within the barn. But there could still be a trigger that trips if we try to leave, or we could have tripped a preset timer, in which case we have no idea how much time we have left. But that comes with the risk that we'd leave before the clock ran out, and nobody with half a brain would risk that. So it all comes down to a trigger, probably on the exits."

"How do you know so much about bombs?"

"Kathryn Bigelow," Mort quipped. "She was one of those directors who saw dramatic potential in me. A couple years back, she wanted me to be in her Academy Award-winning war epic about an American EOD team disarming roadside bombs in war-torn Iraq."

"You could have starred in *The Hurt Locker*?" I said incredulously. "Why didn't you take it?"

"Because I've only ever listened to my commercial instincts," Mort said irritably. "I was too busy trying to convince James Cameron that Sam Worthington was a talentless buffoon, because everybody and their dog kept gushing about what a Best Picture shoo-in his dang *Lord of the Smurfs* was going to—"

"Rivetting," I interrupted. "Did you learn anything about disarming bombs?"

"I remember the '3-Ds,'" Mort recalled after thinking hard for a moment. "Don't get close, don't activate, and don't use satellite phones."

"Okay, we're doing great so far," I said. "Anything else?"

"Yeah. Don't try disarming a bomb if you're not a certified bomb technician."

"Probably good advice," I conceded.

"But whoever planted it didn't have much time," Mort pointed out. "Six hours, tops, to get here, find this place, and rig it. There's no way they could rig every exit. They probably just put triggers on the doors. I'd say our best egress point is the loft. But then there's the spotter to consider."

"What?"

"Seriously, Bucky, think like an assassin for a minute. In a place this remote, do you really think a celebrity hitman is going to just drop off a bomb and drive away? He's watching this place right now."

"How do you suddenly know all this stuff?" I had to ask again. "You didn't even take the role."

Mort snorted derisively. "You don't make fifty low-watt dim-bulb action movies without figuring out the obvious right way to do stuff. You know how the villain would always lock me in a chamber with the Rube Goldberg device, and then just walk away, laughing hysterically?"

"Yeah. Sassy did that to me a few times when we were kids."

"Well," Mort said patiently, "we have to assume that a bunch of cheesed-off scientists would only hire the most brilliant celebrity hitmen, i.e., somebody smarter than the bunch of pill-popping B-grade Hollywood action screenwriters that I always got stuck with. Trust me, somebody's watching the door. And I know what you're thinking, Bucky. Surely all action screenwriters can't be a bunch of pill-popping Hallmark rejects. But they are. All of them. Pill-popping, fart-brained, slack-jawed, unhygienic–"

"Mort?" I felt compelled to interject. "Bomb? Come on, you were really on a roll a second ago."

"The bomber doesn't have a remote detonator or a listening device," Mort said confidently, instantly focussed on the mission once more. "If he did, we would've been dead as soon as we stepped inside, or as soon as he realized that we were aware of him. We weren't supposed to see anything until it was all over, so he's probably just watching the front door from somewhere near the lane. A lone assassin makes more sense than an entire hit squad, so there's a good chance that the west side where we parked the truck isn't being watched. There's no way he had time to set up a decent perimeter on a place this size. I'd say the west wall is our blind spot. If we can get into the loft, we can just jump through that rotten roof and into the truck."

"Little problem, Mort," I pointed out. "There's no trampoline in the truck box. No soft hay, no bags of cotton balls, and it's at least a ten foot drop. The only thing in the truck box is an iron 5th-wheel hitch, a couple of spades, a bunch of branding irons, a pitchfork, a box of six-inch spikes, a box of fencing staples, multiple glass root beer bottles–"

"Are you coming or not?" Mort demanded, already halfway up the loft ladder with the box under his arm.

"Yeah, let's do it," I said acceptantly, but could not help beginning an undertoned recitation. "*Now I lay me down to sleep....*"

The barn roof was so rotten that we were almost certain to be visible as soon as we climbed into the loft. Not wanting to test Mort's theory about the bomber not having a remote detonator, we simply made a dash for the nearest gaping hole over the vicinity of my parked truck, and dove out into the air. I held my rifle in my hands, and Mort held the baler twine box, and we clung to them as we plummeted toward my truck.

Well, I've had softer landings than that implement-laden truck box, but, fortunately, I've had harder ones, too. Both of us had tingling feet as we scrambled into the cab, but at least our feet were still working. My right foot worked just fine as I gunned the engine and stomped the accelerator. The tires only spun on the overgrown grass for a moment, and then we were racing for the lane, bracing for an explosion behind us.

Nothing exploded behind us.

"Huh," Mort said as we hit the lane and shot out toward the main road. "That was kind of anticlimactic. I really wanted to see a real explosion. The movie ones are so lame. All fire, no shockwave-propelled debris...."

"It's a shame, to be sure," I agreed, cranking a hard right onto the road and heading back toward Highway 97C. "We're going to have to try to meet Megiddo somewhere else. Try getting him on the phone again."

Mort was still watching the road behind us, even then

hoping that the barn might blow up before we were out of sight.

"Uh, Bucky?" he said weakly. "I think I was wrong about one thing."

"What?" I said sharply.

"I said a lone assassin made more sense than a hit squad," he bravely confessed. "I don't think a lone assassin would bring five black Suburbans."

I took my eyes off the road to follow his gaze in our wake. Sure enough, five black vehicles were bearing down hard on us, their drivers hidden from sight by devious tinted windows.

"Oh, crap," I muttered, punching the accelerator again. "I love this truck, but she's not running optimal after yesterday. I don't think we can outrun them."

"Nope, we can't," Mort assured me, approximately two seconds before the lead pursuit vehicle rammed into my tailgate, driving both of us hard into our seats.

"Hang on!" I shouted.

A second vehicle had pulled alongside us, and I had no room to swerve on the narrow country road. Before I could think of anything, the tinted passenger-side window beside me rolled down, and a gun barrel poked out. Whoever was behind it was a pretty darn good shot, because Mort and I had both taken a tranquillizer dart in the neck an instant later.

"Hmm," I said, instantly feeling drowsy. "Sorry, Mort, but I think we need to pull over. Safety first on the road, you know?"

"Yeah, good idea," he said groggily, pulling the feathered dart out of his neck and staring at it in chemical-induced fascination. "Nice knowing you, Bucky. I don't think I've ever been knocked out by a tranq dart before."

"I have," I remembered, as I obligingly hit my right turn

signal and eased onto the shoulder of the road. "They're great. They don't give you the hangover headaches like chloroform does."

"I'll never get to say goodbye to her," Mort said, voicing his last regret as he pitched forward and bonked his head on the glove compartment.

"Who's her?" I managed to ask as I shifted my beloved old rig into park and pocketed the keys, but I was asleep before I could even figure out if he had answered.

CREEPY PEOPLE
IN CLOAKS
◇◇◇◇◇◇◇◇◇◇◇◇◇◇

I NEVER WOULD HAVE SUPPORTED the notion of separation of the classes until after I found myself inexplicably spending time in the company of celebrities. It only takes a few hours of such company to convince one that a segregated system of elitism really is in everybody's best interests. We need financial buffer zones.

In the wake of my encounters with Mort, Minnie Marshmallow, Sting, Britt 2.0, and even Corky and Sassy, I have come to the realization that peons like me need as much insulation from celebrities as possible. Having them filtered appropriately through movie screens, televisions, and radios is a good start, but I'm also beginning to support the idea of building a two-hundred-foot concrete wall around California with coiled razor wire and broken glass on the top. Seriously, we'd all be better off. People still talk about how much they love Elvis, but that's probably because most of us never met the dude. Honestly, I'm willing to bet that he smelled bad toward the end. Even a bodybuilding nut like Mort occasionally smells like warm cheese.

Even before I discovered prehistoric aquatic reptiles, I suppose I could have laid claim to an unusual life, at least on occasion. Aside from the whole running-gag of celebrities and assassins infrequently trying to kill me, I have also had more than my share of abductions by creepy people in cloaks, which apparently happens only one to zero times during the lifespan of the average person.

The first time I was abducted by people in cloaks, the moonlit mob turned out to be led by none other than Coyote Yelp Pass's leading expert on paranormal culture and Chinese cuisine, Mr Hayashi. He told me that my abduction and subsequent three days of unlawful confinement in a cave behind Sabertooth Falls was for my own good. In response to the next obvious question, he explained that they needed to exorcise the river poltergeist whose wreaking of great mischief had taken over my physical body, trapping my living essence in a crystal monolith which the devil had given to me as reward for some unspecified past-life service. I was six at the time. (Evidently, small mirrors were considered to be something of a taboo item in Coyote Yelp Pass at the time, and some of the more devoutly superstitious locals still don't trust them. As a direct result, Mr Hayashi prides himself on being able to shoulder-check like no one else on the planet.)

During the process of growing up, I had patiently endured close to a dozen other episodes featuring people in cloaks, which is probably why I wasn't quite as petrified as Mort was when we woke up surrounded by several of them about three hours after our escape from the barn. In a strange way, it was a soothing reminder of home to me.

"*What the crap?*" was the first thing I heard Mort blurt, his volume and blind panic jolting me from my tranquillizer-induced slumber. My bleary eyes opened into very dim lighting, and took in the bizarre scene in a brief, groggy moment.

Mort and I were duct-taped to a couple of dining room

chairs in the middle of a vast, sawdust-covered room, which I quickly recognized as the unfinished convention hall of a luxury hotel that was still under construction. Very little light could get through the boarded-over windows, but, with the aid of several creepy red candelabras, I could make out the white forms of four hooded and cloaked entities standing in a really creepy ring around us. A jewel-encrusted communion chalice was being passed around the circle, with each creepy cloaked person in turn accepting it, and then partaking of the thick yellow liquid, which I would later conclusively identify as banana smoothie. It was too dark to make out their faces, but we could hear them well enough as they continually droned out an ominous, undertoned chant:

> *"Apes we were once;*
> *Apes we ever shall be.*
> *We split the banana.*
> *Monkey chow, make us free."*

Yes, fanatical atheists can be just as unnerving as fanatical fundamentalists on the right occasions, and I think I can safely say that their coven rituals qualify. Evolutionary ascension of consciousness may be a noble life-quest destination, but the means of getting there can really creep the pants off you.

"Accept our communion, O Great Amnyed!" the apparent leader of the cult cried out in a voice that was oddly familiar, raising the goblet over his head with both hands. "Inflator of all confusion and inconsistency! Deflector of all doubt and legitimate questioning! Lineator of all circular reasoning!"

"Amnyed?" I said. "Mort, who the heck is Amnyed?"

"Atheist deity," Mort said promptly. "We're in big trouble, Bucky."

"An *atheist* deity?" I cringed. "How does that work?"

"I don't know," he admitted. "Conformity, maybe? Also, having a central figure of adulation makes congregant gatherings seem a lot less pointless, but I'm just spit-balling, of course. The fanatical atheist cult was one of the few that I never got around to being a part of. I was planning to convert back in the fall of 2004, but then Buddhism started making a comeback with all the hottest girls, so I jumped on that bandwagon inste—"

"*Silence!*" the cult leader thundered, sloshing the last of the communion goblet's contents onto Mort's face, as if expecting it to react like holy water on a vampire. "Both of you! Cowboys and brainless Hollywood action hunks are equally unworthy to speak in the non-presence of the almighty Amnyed! Although, for the record, Max-Ram Target, I'm a big fan, and it is truly a shame that your stellar career officially ends tonight."

"I'll settle for that," Mort admitted. "Ebert and *The Chicago Sun-Times* were saying that my career was over before the Soviet Union was."

"That was kind of harsh," I noted. "How old were you back then? Seven?"

"Eight," Mort said glumly. "He's ruthless, Bucky. He's like a thumb-flicking dream crusher." Although saddened by the painful memory, Mort cheered up slightly as he lapped his tongue over his splattered lips, tasting the yellow slop that had been thrown on him and reacting with delight. "Hey! I love banana smoothie! Do you guys have any more of that? We haven't eaten yet today."

"*Apes we were once....*" the cult continued to quaver in unison.

"Whatever you're doing ... it's working," I commented

uneasily. "Say, Mort, what's the technical term for that clicky board thing with the stripes that they click in all the movie outtakes, when the director says 'Action,' or 'Marker,' or whatever it is that they say?"

"Why would that possibly be in your head at this very moment?" Mort asked, staring at me.

"It was swirling in my subconsciousness as the tranqs were filtering through my kidneys," I said. "I have no control over that. It is the kidneys, right?"

"I thought it was the liver," Mort noted, still trying to reach the blotches of banana smoothie on his cheeks with his tongue.

I had to think about that, but eventually decided, "I can't remember, but I'm sure it's not the liver. Lungs, maybe? They're ... spongy, filtery things, right?"

"Bucky, trust me, I know about livers. I spent most of my preteen years trashing my first one."

"You know more about livers than clicky boards?"

"I also know about textile manufacturing," Mort offered. "And the fine art of Korean cooking."

"Really?" I said, surprised. "I never knew that about you."

Mort shrugged, as much as his duct-tape bindings would allow. "I've got skills, Bucky."

"Okay, it's not scaring them!" another familiar voice snapped from beneath one of the hoods. A second later, the hood was irritably pushed back to reveal a beautiful dark-haired woman with dark-rimmed librarian-esque glasses.

"Sealy the waitress?" I exclaimed.

"That's Dr Kent to you," she snarled, mopping a copious amount of sweat from her lovely brow. "Seriously, guys, what's the point of hand-sewing these things? Heavy white felt in the middle of July? Whose idea was that?"

"You're a *scientist?*" I said incredulously. "I thought you were just a waitress at a scientist bar."

"They have those up here?" Mort asked, immediately interested. "I've only heard stories."

"They're not all they're cracked up to be," I dutifully informed him. "Sealy, what are you doing? Don't tell me that you're the one who's been sending hitmakers and bombmen after us."

"I'm going to guess that you meant hitmen and bombmakers, you idiot," Sealy snapped. "And the answer's no. We didn't send anybody after you."

"Oh, that's a relief," I said. "Can we go now?"

"You're not going anywhere," the familiar-sounding leader assured me. Then he nodded to the remaining two cultists, and they all lowered their hoods together.

The first one I recognized was Theo Gapps, the belligerent young man who had tried to pick a fight with Corky in the scientist bar. The second was Archie the bartender, and the leader turned out to be none other than Dr Kay Argo, the scientist who had apparently lied about not being interested in my Ogopogo skull.

"I'm just gonna throw a couple words out there," I ventured. "Let me know if they mean anything to you.... Galapagos Brethren?"

"Very few people find out that name and live," Argo said coldly. "And, trust me, you're not one of the few."

"So you *are* trying to kill me," I clarified. "I'm confused. You said you didn't send anyone after us. Does that mean your thugs rescued us from the guys in the black Suburbans? Why would you do that if you were just going to kill us?"

"We didn't rescue you," Argo replied, rolling his eyes. "We captured you."

"So those *were* your thugs in the Suburbans?"

"There weren't any thugs, Bucky," Theo Gapps stated irritably.

"Fine, so they're not thugs, they're celebrities," I corrected myself. "They still walk like a duck."

"Celebrities?" Gapps said. "What are you talking about? We don't hire thugs, okay? And we certainly don't hire celebrities, whatever that's supposed to mean."

"What about Sting Ripblood?" I pointed out.

"What about Sting Ripblood?" Sealy countered, looking as puzzled as I was.

"You didn't hire him?" I said. "Then who did?"

"What are you talking about?" Sealy demanded. "We brought you in on our own."

"No, no, you don't understand," Mort said patiently. "What Bucky's trying to say is that if you're all scientists, and you don't hire outside muscle to do your dirty work, then who were the guys in the black Suburbans who planted the bomb?"

"Obviously somebody pretty dangerous," Archie Aptrick growled.

"So ... bear with me for a minute," I said, still not catching on. "You didn't send anybody after us, and you don't have any thugs, celebrity or otherwise, but some thugs in black Suburbans just randomly tried to kill us, and then ... what? How'd we get here? Did they just steal my truck, and you guys found us on the side of the road?"

"Every time," Argo was muttering, shaking his head. "We have to go through this every time."

"I'm giving you one more guess, Bucky," Sealy seethed, her naturally rosy cheeks turning slightly more volcanic.

"You lost me," I admitted.

"We were driving the Suburbans, Bucky!" Sealy exploded. "Do you understand now? We were driving the Suburbans! All those fancy, advanced-driving techniques, and pinpoint firing accuracy on moving targets.... That was us."

"No, we're talking about the *black* Suburbans," Mort clarified, still as lost as I was. "The ones that were chasing us."

"*That was us!*" Sealy screamed. "*We* chased you from the barn! *We* planted the bomb! *We* shot you in the neck at ninety kilometres per hour! It was all us! Every attempt on your life, from the minute you first found the Impossible Lie.... It was us!"

"But you said you were scientists," I reminded her.

"Of course we said we're scientists!" she wailed in frustration. "Bucky, get a clue!"

"Okay, I think I get it," I said, finally beginning to understand. "So where are the *real* scientists? You really had me going for a minute there, *Doctor* Kent. Ha! And you, *Doctor* Argo, you had me sold from the second I met you. You should have been an actor, man."

"Every time," Argo was still repeating through clenched teeth. "Every single time.... Fine, forget it. Dr Kent, it seems that Mr Laroo is anticipating being apprehended by quote-unquote 'thugs.' Kindly oblige him, will you?"

"Gladly," Sealy muttered, drawing a small riding crop out from under her cloak and slapping me across the face with it.

"*Owch!*" I yelped, feeling a thin, stinging welt already forming across my left cheek. "What was that for?"

"Where's the Impossible Lie, Bucky?" Sealy demanded, raising the crop threateningly once more. "Talk! Who's your protector?"

"Hey, you leave my best friend alone!" Mort shouted bravely, struggling to loosen his duct tape.

"If you insist," Sealy said coolly, hopping onto Mort's lap and beginning to punch him in the face repeatedly. "Who's protecting the cowboy, Target? Is it you? Or someone intelligent?"

"*Ow, ow, ow!*" Mort yammered with each successive blow.

"Talk!" Sealy rasped, desisting her pugilism and grabbing Mort by the throat. "Are you or are you not the one who's been protecting him?"

"Protecting him?" Mort winced. "Are you kidding me? I'm starting to think that I'm the sidekick in our harrowing-yet-comedic escapades."

"*Where's the skull?*" Sealy barked, twisting Mort's right ear.

"What do you mean?" Mort demanded, looking sharply at me. "Bucky, where's the skull?"

"Sorry, Mort," I said. "It's better if you don't know. That box you were carrying only had a big rock in it."

"Where is it?" Sealy shouted. "Why did we only find a pig's skull in your truck? Did you honestly think that evolutionist scientists would be stupid enough to mistake any part of a pig's head for something completely different and prehistoric?"

"Oh, that's my fault," I admitted. "For the record, it wasn't an attempt at misdirection. I've been meaning to throw that thing away for months, but I just keep forgetting. But, yes, I knew there was a risk of interception, so I left the real skull in a safe place until I was certain that the coast was clear. You want my plesiosaurus? You've gotta let us go first."

"*It's not a plesiosaurus!*" Archie screamed.

"Alright, everybody calm down!" Argo snapped. Then he smiled venomously and said, "So you don't feel like talking, eh, Bucky? Very well. Dr Gapps, would you be so kind as to bring in ... *The Extractor!*"

The other cult members and Mort all gasped in horror at the diabolical request.

"Has it really come to this?" Sealy whispered, aghast.

"Bucky, tell them where the skull is!" Mort whined, his face turning whiter than a winter-coat weasel. "Trust me, do it right now!"

"What's going on?" I said, instantly anxious. "What's The Extractor? Mort? Tell me what The Extractor is!"

"Uh, boss?" Gapps said reluctantly to Argo. "Little problem there."

"What?" Argo asked.

"Um, well, I ... couldn't get The Extractor," Gapps admitted. "We've only got eighty-five bucks left in our mission budget as it is."

"I told you I wanted an Extractor!" Argo shouted. "Did you or did you not get my requisition form before we left?"

"Yeah, I did," Gapps growled. "I also told you to make sure that we held onto enough petty cash for a decent interrogation kit, and *you* said that we absolutely had to have fully-loaded black Suburbans with full circumference tinted windows! I told you that there was plenty of room for all of us in my mom's station wagon, but you were all like, 'No, we need need *need* black Suburbans!'"

"*Waaaaait* a second...." I said, realization finally dawning on me. "You guys were driving the black Suburbans? A bunch of scientists?"

"*Yes!*" Sealy roared. "What do you think we've been saying this whole time?!"

"Honestly, you haven't been making a whole lot of sense," I confessed.

"That's it," Sealy muttered, stepping toward me with the riding crop in her trembling fist. "I'm opening up a can of whoop—"

"Easy there, Dr Kent," Argo soothed her. "All in good time."

"Okay, I think I'm starting to follow what you're saying here," I said, not without lingering uncertainty. "So you're saying that you're real scientists ... but you can actually, like, *do stuff?*"

"Yes, Bucky," Argo said with a patience that had to squeeze past his clenched teeth. "We're a lot more capable than you, or anyone else, seems to wanna give us credit for. We're the Galapagos Brethren, baby. The most lethal, elite scientists on the freakin' planet!"

The dramatic introduction lost a lot of its effect when Mort noisily had to snort back a laugh.

"You seem to think that's funny, Kindergarten Commando," Archie growled.

"Look, people," Mort snickered, "I grew up in an era that revitalized and redefined the B-movie formulas, and I know the categories that all scientists fall into. There's only two, actually, and both of them are about as intimidating as any form of Italian military action. First, we have the good scientists who equip the cop or soldier or reluctant hero cliché, and then cower in the lab until he saves the day. Then there's the glass-jawed mad scientists who the cop or soldier or reluctant hero cliché eventually subdues with a single punch. And you guys are trying to tell us that you're ... what? *Action* scientists?"

"Mort, I'd stop talking now," I quietly urged him, noting the reddening of our captors' faces. However, even I finally had to choke back a laugh, and girlishly giggle, "Action scientists! *Tee hee!*"

"Nice try," Mort chortled mockingly. "Oh no! Better get Paul Revere to ride through town, yelling, '*The Whitecoats are coming! The Whitecoats are coming!*' Ha! Sure, the hot chick got in a couple lucky shots, mostly owing to our duct tape and old-school chivalry, but let's be serious, dudes. In the real world, the best you can hope for is that your attacker hurts his hand by accidentally punching you in the pocket-protector. Action scientists! What a gas!"

"Har har!" I laughed with him. "Good one, Mort. Tell you what, lab coats, if you're so lethal on your own, why would you send that Sickle guy to my ranch instead of doing the job yourselves?"

"Can I assume," Gapps snarled, "that you are referring to our brother, Dr Vasil 'The Sickle' Clouseau Croissant, world-renowned palaeontologist, and curator of *Le Nouveau Grande Poulet Museum Histoiré Naturel*, the scientific jewel of *Valleé de la Coassar Grenouille*, France?"

The laughter of Mort and myself was immediately cut short.

"Oh," I said blankly. "Okay, I didn't know that."

"*Sacré creux dans le beignet!*" Mort whispered in astonishment. "Bucky, you told me that Sickle guy was a gunslinging super-soldier who oozed lethality."

"I never used any of those words," I countered. "I said he knew how to take care of himself."

"And he was one of these guys," Mort said slowly, "which, by association, should mean that–"

Before he could finish his thought, Sealy had drawn an HK-MP5 submachine gun from beneath her cloak, brought the bolt-action up to her mouth with a quick kissing motion, and then pointed it at Mort's forehead, all within the span of half a second.

"Holy crap, did she just chamber that thing with her *tongue?*" I blurted.

"*Don't kill me!*" Mort cried, closing his eyes. "I believe in action scientists! *I believe!*"

With a triumphant smile, Sealy gestured between us

and the weapon, mockingly introducing us. "Fish, this is barrel; Barrel, this is fish."

"Uh, one discrepancy," I ventured, hoping to distract her. "In the fish in a barrel analogy, wouldn't the gun just be ... gun?"

"That's actually a good point, Dr Kent," Gapps agreed. "The cowboy and Max-Ram Target are the fish, and the chairs and duct tape, or even the overall condition of immobility, are the barrel."

"Do not unmix my metaphors, Dr Gapps," Sealy said ominously. "I swear, it's people like you who are going to tank this organization. If it hadn't been for that affirmative action program telling us to recruit steady-boat theistic evolutionists, you never would have made it through the door."

"Deal with it, my child," Gapps chuckled, kissing his rosary.

"Wow," I said, still shaking my head as all of my former wimpy nerd illusions began to fade away in the wake of reality. "Holy cow cud, Corky was right. We really did get into a barroom brawl with scientists."

"Dang right you did, you literal rule-of-thumber," Sealy said sourly, tapping a finger against her blackened left eye to remind me of my own villainy. "Now focus, Bucky. You are going to tell me where the skull is, or you get to watch Max-Ram Target die for the first time, in life or any of its simulated variants."

"Really?" I said, glancing at Mort. "You never died in any of your movies?"

"Personal sacrifice for a greater good was never a theme I encouraged," Mort admitted. "And I always got the girl. Actually, I usually got two or three."

Sealy was clearly disgusted as she muttered, "No wonder Sting Ripblood completely swept the final traces of your memory into the void as soon as he burst onto the scene. He is a real hero. During Hurricane Katrina, he rescued a stranded bunch of elementary school children from a rooftop, using nothing more than a floating bookcase and several lengths of licorice whip. You can't compete with that."

"I can't even argue with that," Mort readily assured her. "He's the only action hero since John Wayne to actually deserve his hallowed status. And his jawline.... Seriously, that mandible is like a locomotive cow-catcher. You could split firewood with that thing."

"Okay, you just lost the right to live," Sealy growled, pressing the sub gun's muzzle between Mort's eyes.

"Hey!" I snapped, clamping my tongue between my teeth. "Deal wiff thith!"

"What the chuck-roast are you doing?" Archie asked.

"I'm theriouth!" I slurringly warned them. "Ith you kill him, I bithe oth my thongue, and then you'll neveth thind the thkull!"

"That is disgusting," Sealy said. "I'm killing them both, and we take our chances finding the skull. Everybody agreed?"

"Stop," Argo ordered her. "The information Laroo has is bigger than all of us."

"Wow," I said. "That is the most awesome thing anyone's ever said to me."

"I said it to her, saddlebags," Argo snapped.

I shrugged. "I'll take what I can get at this point."

"We're done here," Argo decided. "Sealy, you're the only one who can stand screaming and the sight of copious amounts of blood, so take them somewhere conveniently out of sight and hearing range, and get the information! Can you handle that alone with no immediately available backup?"

"Of course," Sealy promised. "After all, they're tied up and I'm insanely self-confident."

"Are you sure that's the smartest plan?" Mort had to ask. "I have literally starred in dozens of films that featured this exact same formulaic escape setup, and it never ends well for you guys."

"Mort, I will kill you if they don't," I rasped. "I swear by various unholy artifacts."

"Just take them away," Argo said in disgust.

"So this is what it comes down to?" I protested. "Persecuting me for what I believe?"

"You wish," Argo scoffed. "The privileged few get persecuted for their beliefs, and the world can respect them for their suffering and perseverance. You're just a stupid cowboy who got dragged into the wrong sea cave by the wrong dinosaur."

"Prehistoric aquatic reptile," I corrected him.

"Silence!" Argo barked. "The hard reality is that we don't care what you believe in, Bucky.... Hmm.... Actually, I don't even remember what it was that you believe. Gapps, you're our token religious guy. What was in the file?"

"It's a grey area," Gapps dutifully reported, flipping through a copy of my autobiography, *Last Stand at Coyote Yelp Pass: The Tragic Cowboy Memoirs of Bucky Laroo*. "At various times, he considers a life in the monastery and references his grandfather calling on Saint Michael, both of which are indicative of Catholicism, but then he mentions attending a Baptist church and once refers to himself as 'Baptist-raised.' And his parents were hippies. This book is a denominational mine-field."

"Best guess?" Argo queried.

Gapps shrugged, tossing the book away. "Let's stamp him as generic Christian and get on with killing him."

"Good enough," Argo conceded. "See, Bucky? There's

nothing but impartiality in this room. Who cares what you stand for? We're here because of one stupid word that you said without pondering consequences. You're being persecuted for the random roll of the fateful die. Without thinking, you blurted the word 'plesiosaurus' to the media in reference to a recently-deceased animal, and that crap-brained blurt is what brought you to this. So, in the bloody and agonizing hours to come, don't blame yourself, or your faith. This could have happened to anybody. It's only happening to you because you're unlucky, really stupid, and because there's something about you that makes us all detest you. Probably your freckles."

"Yeah, my vote's on the freckles," Mort concurred.

"Are you crazy?" I demanded of everyone in the room. "Doesn't your precious theory of evolution have safeguards in place for this kind of contingency? Punctuated equilibrium, evolutionary stasis, that kind of thing?"

The entire coven roared with laughter at the suggestion.

"And he said it with a straight face, too," Sealy gasped, wiping away mirthful tears. "Evolutionary stasis, Bucky? Have we gotten that desperate already? That was a safeguard we made up when we kept finding lobe-finned fish and gracilis ants that were supposed to have died out a bazillion years ago. We can gloss over stuff like that, and even twist it around to make it seem like a rule-proving exception, but this is a dinosaur we're talking about here."

"No it's not," I said. "But what about punctuated equilibrium? You could put that theory into demonstrable parameters for the first time ever by telling people that a plesiosaur-like creature emerged spontaneously from the egg of a turtle or other repti–" At that point, my own hysterical laughter finally overwhelmed me, and I had to admit, "Okay, you're right. That is pretty funny once you spell it out."

"And we even got it into the textbooks!" Argo laughed. "Face facts, Bucky. We make the theories for the sole purpose of answering questions without all the hassle of control tests or finding evidence. We tell the masses that all this crap magically happened a billion years ago, and then we leave them on their own to find a way of arguing with it. Being a scientist is actually really easy after that."

"Scientists believe in magic?" I asked.

Argo shrugged. "We prefer the term 'a mechanism not yet discovered.' But it boils down to pretty much the same thing. The Big Bang was an amazing magical event wherein nothing exploded and created everything. The upcoming Bucky Bang will be an equally magical occurrence wherein the memory of you, Max-Ram Target, and the Impossible Lie will explode into nothing, and create everybody else's happiness. Of course, that's only if you promptly tell us where the skull is. If you don't, your fate will be a lot less ... clean."

"Cowboy cleanup on aisle six," Sealy quipped, smirking.

"Ha!" Mort laughed. "That's awesome. Get it, Bucky? It's comparing your living dissection to a grocery store that sells a form of contained, but potentially messy, cowboy product that somehow gets dropped and splatters onto the walls and floors, so they have to–"

"I got the joke, Mort."

"Who is Mort?" Sealy wanted to know.

"However," Mort continued, "all joking aside, I do have to wonder how you, as impartial scientists, can put such stock in your theories when the very radioisotopic dating methods which supposedly back up your claims have been called into question so many times. It's common knowledge that a mass of radiocarbon equal to the mass of our planet would be decayed away to an unmeasurable state in well under a million years. And, yet, radiocarbon is still found in diamonds which supposedly formed during the Carboniferous Era, one to four billion years ago. And don't even get me started on Potassium-Argon dating, the same dating method that told us the eruption of Mt St Helens took place as much as 2.8 million years ago, rather than in 1980, the year that I was born. Actually, on the very day that I was born. Now, I don't know if Bucky's King Jimmy has all the real answers, but I do find it interesting that it is the only ancient religious writing that had apparent knowledge of such scientific staples as the symbiotic interdependence of time, space, and matter, and the existence of the Coriolis Effect, facts that the rest of the civilized world was thousands of years away from being aware of. I specifically cite Genesis 1:1, and Ecclesiastes 1:6. That Solomon dude knew his stuff."

"Ha!" Sealy guffawed. "Monkey Year baby!"

"Wow," I remarked. "That was sort of an impressive scientific and religious tirade, Mort.... Wait a second. You were born on May 18, 1980? I thought your birthday was July 2nd."

"Yeah, my first televised appearance was actually in an ash removal documentary," Mort affirmed. "I had the date legally changed when I moved to Hollywood."

"You changed your birthday?" I incredulously asked.

"No volcano was going to steal my thunder, Bucky," Mort said darkly.

"You raise some very good points, Max-Ram," Argo acknowledged. "Dr Kent, would you care to address the issues at hand for our celebrity guest?"

"Certainly, Doctor," Sealy agreed, drawing a taser gun from the sleeve of her robe, and zapping Mort in the throat with it. He only had time to let out a startled, *"Aak!"* before slumping into his seat, unconscious once more.

"You present a very convincing counter argument," I admitted. "You know, I really hope that you guys aren't representative of all atheists and theistic evolutionists in any way, because that would seriously make me reconsider all of those movies and TV shows I've seen where they're the most sympathetic and rational characters."

"*Mwa ha ha!*" Argo thundered triumphantly. "Take them away, Dr Kent! Get the location of the skull! And the rest of you ... it's Monday night! So get your phones ready to call in your votes, because *Canada's Next Top Best Dance Crew* starts in five minutes!"

The coven let out one last delighted roar as they charged into the adjoining hallway, which was presumably where their TV was located.

"Can one of you put in a vote for *Peach-Zee N Cream*?" I called after them. "I promised my wife."

"Yeah, I'm voting for them," Archie obliged me. "Always the dark horse runner, isn't it?"

"Always," I agreed. "Thanks, Doc."

After the others were gone, Sealy demonstrated an impressive physical strength for a slender woman as she strapped me and the still out-cold Mort onto a double-wide dolly, still tied to our chairs. Then she wheeled us out of the improvised communion sanctum, and hauled us to the half-built swimming pool room on the far side of the building, which was apparently to be our improvised torture chamber. Starting in the shallow end of the empty pool, she rolled us down to the eight-foot deep end, presumably for ease of cleanup while containing any inevitable splatter. Several steel tables were already set up around us and covered with improvised instruments of torture, mainly power tools, butane torches, and various odds and ends, some of which seemed to have been pilfered from the back of my truck.

"Well, well, well, Bucky," Sealy mused, stripping off her

heavy white robe to reveal a rather attractive black skirt and long-sleeved black tee shirt underneath it. Then she casually pulled on a white lab coat in preparation for the grisly task that awaited her.

"Sealy, I think you're crazy," I pointed out. "But unless you're certifiably insane, you should let us go, right now."

"Honestly, I would," Sealy ventured, plugging a handheld angle grinder into a nearby surge protector. "Unfortunately, this is just too darn fun. Question one: Who is protecting you? Townes was one of our best. Max-Ram Target seems to have some kind of preset loyalty to you, but he's just too flat-out stupid to have sandbagged Townes."

"Who?"

"You know dang well who! After The Sickle failed us, we stopped to reevaluate what we were dealing with. However, our conclusions still came back to what we had suspected all along: You're just a troublesome halfwit who seriously needs to get dead. So we sent our most brilliantly psychopathic scientist, Dr P.L. Townes, to finish the job yesterday morning. But *somebody* tipped off the RCMP about a scientist smuggling a dismantled stealth fighter and assembly kit across the Montana border into BC. That means that we're out the cost of a perfectly good F-22 Raptor, a Vulcan cannon, and a full compliment of AMRACM B-Blaster missiles. You think that crap is cheap? Plus, we had to disavow our top hitter, and reconfiguring a satellite to remotely activate those cyanide molars cost a fortu– But I've said too much. The bottom line is that now we've been required to mobilize in force, something that we haven't had to do in decades, and I don't intend to be the one who fails for the third time. *Who spilled the beans, Bucky?*"

"Somebody took out one of your hitmen?"

"Quit playing dumb, and start talking," Sealy snarled, lowering the angle grinder down to my cowboy boots. The coarse sand wheel quickly buzzed through the pointed toe of my left boot, and began filing my big toenail.

"Wait a second!" I yelped. "Okay, Sting Ripblood attacked us yesterday around noon. He seemed determined to kill us himself. We thought he was working for you, because, believe it or not, celebrity assassins make more sense than scientist assassins. Maybe he wanted the job all to himself."

"Sting Ripblood?" Sealy said in disgust. "You really expect me to believe that?"

"Hey, you know that he's in BC, and everybody knows about what Mort did to his horse."

"Your lies offend me, Bucky," Sealy stated, tossing aside the angle grinder. "An overdone pedicure is too good for you. You're getting the same treatment you've been inflicting on defenceless animals all your life. Like calves, for example. This wouldn't happen to be a castrating knife we found in your pocket, would it?"

Sure enough, she held up my ivory pocketknife.

"Yep, that's it," I said warily.

"Psychotic instrument of torture," Sealy muttered, gingerly setting my knife down on the table again. "But we'll save that part for last. And then I'm melting it down and giving it back to the earth."

"Don't do that!" I protested. "Do you have any idea how much that thing cost?"

"How much?"

"Okay, it was a giveaway when we bought a New Holland bidirectional tractor."

"Brilliant defence, Bucky," she smirked, holding up one of my CPR branding irons. "And look what else we found in the back of your truck. All I need now is a shot of 8-way to give you the full Branding Day treatment."

"You know, I never thought I'd hear myself say this," I

commented. "But I'm starting to miss the good old days of religious fanaticism."

"That's the shifting sands of time, Bucky," Sealy said with a shrug, sparking one of the butane torches and holding the blue flame to the lettered end of the branding iron. "Like a cat sneezing in a litter box. The persecuting-slash-killing strokes may come from different hands, but the basic principles haven't changed. After a period of bigoted tribulation, revolutionary thinkers in the fields of religion, science, finance, and government slowly become popular. Eventually, their ideas form the basis of patriotism and government, their egos spin madly out of control, they become the string-pulling elite behind the national power structure, and they are then free to persecute and kill anyone who presents new revolutionary thoughts. Sometimes, they'll even reach a point where they're willing to kill people who are doing nothing more than following after their own revolutionary ideals. The diehard patriots who would have drained their own lifeblood to rewrite the American Constitution, if all of the original copies were destroyed as the world simultaneously ran out of ink, were the same patriots who waged the pure evil side of the Civil War in order to deny the same freedom chronicled in said constitution to their slaves. Following this example into the twentieth century, corporate greed predominantly began determining who got whacked, whether by mobsters, the CIA, or big oil. But the one constant factor thus far is that the hitters are always safe until public opinion turns against them by way of popular media. Once Hollywood doesn't like you anymore, the gig is up. But that is never going to happen to The Establishment, because we are the smartest people alive, which means that we know exactly how to manipulate the overblown egos of Hollywood in order to maintain our place at the top. Hence, science is the ultimate be-all end-all in every movie, even if that science is presented as off-the-wall Roland Emmerich disaster movie bull-crap. It's the system that works, Bucky, and it's not going anywhere anytime soon. The only possible threat to us is ego-less peons like you, who keep screwing up life with reality and are completely non-manipulable. The only recourse for us is to kill you, which is usually regrettable, but in your case is going to be so darn gratifying that I can barely contain myself."

"I really appreciate your comprehensive explanations," I said.

"Thank you," Sealy replied, blowing on the end of my branding iron which was now glowing with red heat. "Well, I'd say we're about ready to begin. I'm going to brand you until it comes out the other side, as my father once said to our most evil cow back on the ranch in my sweet farmgirl days."

"You were a *cowgirl?*" I cringed.

Sealy flushed at the shameful admission, and quickly brushed it off. "I've said too much. *Bottoms up, Bucky!*"

"I can't believe Corky actually has a thing for you," I growled.

"Really?" Sealy said, instantly giddy. "How did you know? Has he ever talked about me? What did he say?"

"That you're a Canadian Sofie Allsopp."

"That hot British chick from HGTV's *The Unsellables*?" Sealy gasped, obviously flattered by the comparison.

"You are insane!" I shouted. "I'm not trying to introduce any new ideas. I never have been. *I just discovered the Ogopogo!* That's it!"

"Nobody's arguing with that," Sealy quipped. "You're too stupid to come up with anything original, and cowboys don't get to change the world. You see, Bucky, it took awhile, but for the last hundred years we've had people right where we want them: At a point where they believe that what science tells us and what scientists tell us is exactly the same thing. It's an incredible, very comfortable system, or was until you showed up. The problem with you, Bucky, is not new ideas, but rather something much, much worse, namely dredging up old ideas long-thought to have been discredited. Trust me, very few people want to listen to new ideas. But absolutely nobody wants to know that the old ideas that preceded the new ideas which have since become the current ideas were right all along. Especially science ideas. No matter how cyclical our reasoning might be, our textbook progression *must* be linear, even if that means building up on a bull-crap theory for another hundred and fifty years. The breach of a comfort zone is the most terrifying hypothetical in the western world. Even more so than the mid-season cancellation of a reality television show."

"*Never say those words!*" Mort roared in horror, abruptly jolting awake beside me.

"Ah, good morning, sunshine," Sealy greeted him. "We were just discussing science ethics prior to your dismemberment and death. Any thoughts?" She teasingly rested the glowing iron against the toe of Mort's shoe, filling the air with the smell of cheap burnt plastic.

"Nope, I'm good," Mort said meekly. "But, all kidding aside, if you guys have anymore of that banana smoothie that you threw in my face, I am seriously hungry right now."

"Sealy, you still haven't told me why you're doing this," I pointed out, hoping to keep her distracted until the iron in her hand wasn't quite as luminous. "I mean, you've explained your motives very thoroughly, but I still don't get why a bunch of scientists are doing their own dirty work, aside from an obvious sensitivity about being perceived as weakling nerds. Why don't you just outsource dirty work like everybody else on the planet?"

"Outhires are loose ends, Bucky," Sealy patiently explained. "Nothing else. Also, our overblown egos and rampant paranoia prevents us from trusting anybody but ourselves, like all scientists."

"Oh," I said. "Actually, that makes sense."

"And, of course, psychotic bloodlust transcends even the universally-perceived buffer zone of intellectualism," Sealy gloatingly added. "Hurting people is fun!"

"That also makes perfect sense," Mort noted. "I dated this one super-model Mensa Society chick in Flagstaff, and, when I started dating her little sister behind her back, she threw an astro-physiology textbook at my head."

"Shut up, Mort," I tearfully whispered. "For the love of T-bones, just shut up, *please!*"

"You brought this on yourself, Bucky!" Sealy yelled, beginning to advance toward me with the hot iron. "Do you have any clue about the ramifications of finding a living dinosaur? The ramifications of proving they didn't die out sixty-five million years ago? Visualize the headache you get from trying to decide whether to put your paper-shelled bubble mailer in the paper or plastic recycling bin. Now multiply that by about a bazillion. And when you add in the fact that we found Shania Twain's stolen sat-phone in your truck.... All I'm doing is ridding the world of a monster. I guess we have that much in common. Ha!"

"Did you just ask me to visualize a headache?" I asked.

Sealy just smiled evilly, pointing the end of the iron at my face.

"Time to reboot that memory, Bucky."

"Reboot *this*, you uber-sexy nut-job!" Mort shouted, lashing out his right foot. His right shoe came off with frightening speed, spinning through the air and catching

Sealy under the jaw, sending her flying back against one of the steel tables before collapsing amidst her own instruments of torture. The branding iron which had been knocked out of her hand landed at my feet a second later.

"Thank you," I croaked.

"I used to do that at parties," Mort said with a touch of pride. "I learned all my best stunts when I was wasted. Let's get out of here."

He began lurching sideways as hard as his bound limbs would allow, finally succeeding in toppling his chair onto its right side with a resonant crash, the duct tape-swathed armrest landing right on top of the smoking branding iron. The air was filled with smoke as the tape began to melt and burn, and Mort grimaced against the pain of his right forearm's proximity to the heat.

"Bucky, I'm not going to lie to you," he muttered. "I'm going to start crying like a little girl in about five seconds."

"Go to an angry place," I urged him. "Think about Canadians."

"But I love Canadians!" Mort winced through clenched teeth. "I hate Bulgarians now."

"Your national profiling is still disturbing, but use it for now. Focus on the rage."

"*Yeeeeooowwwww!*" Mort squalled, finally ripping free from his half-melted bindings. He did a power roll to get away from the pool of flaming tape, and then quickly began to peel off my layers of silver adhesive.

"So what did the Bulgarians do to you?" I couldn't help wondering.

"Actually," Mort replied, "there was just this one Bulgarian shepherd kid from this tiny town called *Chakal Ligavene Kanyon* outside of *Blagoevgrad*. We got into a brass *stotinki* toss over the last *kavarma kebap*, and he—"

"You know, it's like I could tell you the ending before

you even say it," I interrupted, standing and ripping off the lingering strands of tape.

"Did I tell you this one already?" Mort asked.

"In another life, so it seems," I sighed.

"*Die, Bucky!*" Sealy rasped, abruptly reviving and whipping the MP5 out from under her white lab coat.

Without thinking, I gave the nearest steel table a hard donkey-kick, smashing it onto its side and sending its contents flying in Sealy's direction just as she opened fire. Her first volley punched into an incoming can of red spray-paint and the butane torch, both of which exploded in a ball of flame and red pigment. All three of us were knocked off our feet, Mort's shirt was instantly disintegrated, and Sealy was covered from head to toe in paint. We all lay on the pool floor, coughing and covering our ringing ears. The fire from the burnt duct tape was beginning to spread to the layers of sawdust on the floor, which was quickly increasing in combustibility by the various liquid chemicals that I had knocked off the table.

"Who's freckled now?" I snarled at the stunned Sealy as I groggily crawled to my hands and knees.

"That's the best one-liner I've ever heard!" Mort said in horrified awe. "Gosh golly gee-whiz, Bucky, I really am the sidekick."

"Why is my shirt still completely intact?" I demanded, staring at the tattered remains of the new sweatshirt I had loaned Mort. "I was the one who was completely shrouded in the fireball while you were hiding behind me!"

"Just go!" Mort ordered, dragging me away, just as the lightheaded Sealy began to sit up and feel around for her fallen weapon. As Mort and I ran for the shower-room exit, we could hear the enraged scientist shouting into her walkie-talkie, as the flames of various solvents and cleaners grew higher all around her.

"All *Ink Retention* operatives, this is *Sugar Bomb*! Break out the hardware! *Dead Man Walking* is running, repeat, *Dead Man Walking* is running! Shoot to wound, but as painfully as possible!"

"I confess that I'm glad she's still alive," I admitted as we ran through the shower room.

"Run, Bucky!" Mort growled, leading by example.

"Oh, crap!" I realized, skidding to a halt. "I forgot my castrating knife!"

"Bucky, *no!*" Mort hollered, but it was too late. I was already running back through the unfinished room toward the pool, and, unfortunately, my situational awareness wasn't optimal. As I neared the door, my foot snagged on a sneaky power cable, and I found myself flying headfirst toward the doorway, my windmilling arms do little to slow my bird-like migration.

Actually, my clumsiness turned out to be a good thing, as Sealy was coming through the door just as I was going back out. I couldn't avoid a mid-air collision, and the top of my skull intersected her left eye, sending her glasses and submachine gun flying as she was knocked unconscious once more.

"Good greaseballs, not again!" I muttered, landing hard on top of her. The top of my red head was screaming from the force of impact, but I forced myself to roll away and try to revive the fallen scientist warrior.

"Holy hangnail," Mort breathed, having seen the entire bit of stunt-work. "Bucky, you're a *ninja!*"

"Come on, evil pretty lady," I urged Sealy, raising her into my lap and lightly slapping her unresponsive face. "The room's on fire. Wake up!"

"Are you crazy?" Mort demanded, running back to me. "Leave her! Let's go!"

"I don't have a whole lot of credos to live by," I informed

him. "But one of them is to get through life without killing anybody, even after they repeatedly try to kill me."

"That is a terrible credo," Mort snapped. "It's even worse than the bad action movie credo: *'If you finance it ... they will come.'*"

"Just help me pick her up," I shot back, struggling to raise the scientist's deadweight from the floor.

Although still grumbling, Mort obligingly helped me to pick up Sealy's limp form, and heaved her over his shoulder. We were about to make a run for it again, when a strange glint of light caught my eye from the pool we had just exited. The small, white object was hard to make out in the midst of the flames, but it was clear to me what it was. It was my castrating knife.

"Bucky...." Mort cautioned me. "Don't do it."

Before I could reply, Dr Archie Aptrick had appeared from the lockers at the far end of the shower room, also wearing a white lab coat, but with a Russian AK47 assault rifle held tightly against his shoulder. Mort and I both hit the deck as the weapon began to spray, the bullets tearing up the doorway above us.

"Get ready for the next clash of continents, Bucky!" Archie was whooping, charging through the long room and firing as he came. Mort and I both scrambled out of the doorway and onto the pool deck, unfortunately dropping the still-unconscious Sealy to the hard floor, the back of her head smacking against the edge of the pool.

"Okay, I'm pretty sure I heard an occipital fracture that time," Mort cringed.

"Yeah," I said, snatching Sealy's fallen MP5 from the floor and tossing it to Mort as we began running for the next exit on the other side of the pool. "She's gonna have cognitive issues later on."

"What am I supposed to do with this?" Mort asked,

looking blankly at the weapon in his hands. It was the wisest question I had ever heard him ask.

"Sorry, the toss was action movie instinct," I apologised. "Just slowly set it on the floor, and we'll all probably be a lot better off."

"Fair enough," Mort agreed, failing to follow my directions precisely as he carelessly tossed the automatic weapon back into the pool, right into a spreading pool of burning butane.

"Oh, that's not good," I said.

"I believed you!" Mort screamed. "*I trusted you!*"

"Get down!" I roared, tackling him to the floor just as the bullets began to go off in the centre of the inferno, spraying the room in every direction.

Archie came into the room at about the same time, hosing down the pool with his Kalashnikov without even looking to see where we were. However, one of the MP5's bullets was more discerning than the others, and almost instantly found its way into Archie's left kneecap. He fell to the ground in a barrage of girlish shrieks, clutching his injured leg.

"Patella!" he wailed from the floor. "*Patella!*"

"Okay, I think it's empty," Mort decided, lunging to his feet again. "Move, Bucky!"

"Not without my castrating knife!" I insisted, vaulting back down into the pool's deep end and charging through the flames.

"Why am I the rational one all of a sudden?" Mort demanded. "Bucky, leave it!"

"Never!" I yelled back at him, springing over the sizzling wood of the chair I had been tied to. "We had to buy a New Holland bidirectional tractor to get that thing!"

Although still in agony, Archie managed to seize his

automatic weapon and open fire on me as I ran, causing various things to explode in my wake.

"Hey, ladies and gentlemen," I muttered as I ran, able to blot out the panic better by pointlessly narrating. "Remember that 'Safety First' motto from the early 1990s? It's over. Welcome back to *The Death is Bad Show*, with your host, Bucky Laroo...."

With bullets pattering all around me, and contents-under-pressure canisters breaching with deafening roars in the intense heat, I somersaulted over one of the fallen steel tables, snatching my knife from the flames as I passed over it, and then made the best running long jump of my life as I charged back toward Mort, clearing the rim of the pool at the five-foot marker. Archie ran out of bullets, and was trying to reload his rifle, but was finding it difficult to do while still clinging to his injured kneecap with both hands and moaning, "Pa-tell-a!"

Mort could only stare at me from the far exit as I irritably strode back to Archie through the flames, and gave him a right-handed haymaker across the jaw just to shut him up. His body slumped down alongside Sealy's, and I kicked his empty rifle into the fire.

"How did you do that?" Mort called out, aghast. "One punch? Are you kidding me?"

"I've literally been punching killer cows since I was five," I snapped. "And their skulls are a lot harder than people skulls. Come on, Mort. Now we've got two bodies to pack out of here. Fireman's carry, let's go!"

Obviously uncomfortable with the plan, Mort nonetheless rejoined me, and heaved Archie's body over his broad shoulders, pausing to admire the way that the flames reflected off his sweaty, muscular torso. I picked up the lighter Sealy, and we made our way back toward the convention hall, charging past other rooms and hallways which were beginning to combust with unsettling speed, considering that the building was intended to be a casino hotel with windows that didn't open. Flaming beams were already toppling all around us, and the smoke was getting darker by the second.

"Bucky, dramatically-flaming property damage is no fun in real life!" Mort shouted at me, serpentining around the burning rubble. "I hate real life!"

I could also hear Argo and Gapps yelling at each other and into their walkie-talkie's, but I couldn't tell where they were. I didn't have time to think about it. The main lobby was directly ahead of us on the other side of glass doors, no more than a hundred feet away on the far end of the main casino floor.

"*Laroo!*" I heard Argo screech from behind us. "Where's that skull?"

"Bucky will die before he tells you!" Mort defiantly hollered back as the newly-installed crystal chandeliers began dropping from the ceiling like strafing bombs. "Just surrender now!"

"I never said that," I snapped, the smoke beginning to make my throat and eyes burn. "Dude, it's just a dead dinosaur."

"No it's not," Mort reminded me. "Aquatic reptile."

We shoulder-slammed the glass doors and staggered into the main lobby, which was largely completed, and refreshingly smoke-free due to the layer of glass separating it from the rest of the building. However, we didn't have time to appreciate the sudden burst of cooler fresh air. As soon as we were through the doors, we collided with the massive frame of one last creepy figure wearing a cloak. Suddenly thrown off-balance by the brick-wall of a cult member who stood before us, Mort and I stumbled back and fell to the floor, Sealy and Archie landing on top of us.

The two unconscious scientists were promptly jolted back to the land of the living, as evidenced by Archie's immediate return to moaning, "Patella...."

"Oh, right," Mort coughed, the wind knocked from his lungs by the force of impact. "There were five suburbans, weren't there?"

"Yeah," I coughed in turn. "There were five."

"Oog...." the cloaked giant gurgled, covering us with the tiny US .45-ACP Liberator pistol in his hand. "No move!"

"Good boy, Packy," Sealy chuckled as she slowly climbed off me and helped Archie to his feet.

Packy lowered his hood to reveal the face of a somewhat donkey-featured thug with a shaven head and a blank stare. A bit of drool was hanging from the corner of his lips, which seemed to be twisted into a perpetual sneer of overcompensated confusion.

"Bucky, that is the biggest cult member I have ever seen," Mort reluctantly informed me. "And I've been in a lot of cults."

"Org!" Packy said threateningly, taking a heavy step toward us that made the glass doors reverberate.

"Don't move, Bucky!" Argo ordered as he and Gapps rushed in from behind us, also clad in white lab coats, and heavily armed with automatic rifles that are illegal to even mention by name in Canada.

"Okay, you got us," I freely confessed. "Can I suggest a momentary truce, at least until we're out of the burning building?"

"I could live with that," Mort and Archie whimpered in unison.

"Silence, Bucky!" Argo snapped. "You'd like that, wouldn't you? But guess what. You've been just enough trouble to edge a scientist beyond the point of collected reason for the first time in recordable history! Maybe I'll never find the skull if I leave you here, but I am officially cheesed-off enough to not care anymore! I am *cheesed!* Packy, make sure they don't leave."

"Boom them?" Packy grunted inquisitively.

"No, no, Packy-Poo," Sealy admonished the hulk, standing on her tiptoes in order to scratch him behind the ear. "If you shoot them, they won't suffer a horrible lingering death in the flames. And I think we owe them that."

"Okay, I want you to be straight with me, homicidal nerds," Mort requested. "Is there any form of amusing Hollywood anecdote that I could share to make you change your minds? For example, a couple of years ago I was coming back from a botched audition for Danny Trejo's hit action-drama, *Arkansas Toothpick*, and I happened to be sharing a taxi with Katie Holmes' dietician. Before you know it, he's telling me that if Katie doesn't secretly have at least three jelly doughnuts between the hours of four and six a.m., Tom usually wakes up with–"

"I seriously hope that safety is close enough for me to hear your dying screams from," Sealy interrupted.

"I'm going to miss the opportunity of having you as a sister-in-law," I muttered, glaring at her.

"Why?" Sealy said with renewed excitement. "Did Corky say something about that? What did he say?"

"Dr Kent," Argo warned her. "We talked about this, remember?"

"Sorry," Sealy said sheepishly.

"Our deepest regrets, Max-Ram," Argo called out, as he and his cohorts began backing toward the exit, still covering us with their machine guns. "Nobody in Hollywood will ever kill Canadians as well as you did. The arterial spray looked so real.... Honestly, I've always wondered if those rumours about live ammo and casting Canadian drifters had some kind of validity. Bucky, good riddance, and Amnyed's eternal curse upon you. And Packy ... your behaviour at last year's Christmas party has made the decision to leave you here a lot easier on all of us, so ... thanks."

"No long hugs," Packy glumly reminded himself. "Makes sober scientists uncomfortable."

"I should say so!" Sealy snapped as the four of them turned the corner, leading to the foyer exit. Mort and I were now alone with a man who probably weighed more than the two of us and a bookshelf combined. Packy smiled widely, showing off the three teeth that were left in his mouth as he tossed away his Liberator. Clearly, this was a man who didn't need a gun.

"Think about this, Packy," I urged him. "Look at what they're making you do."

"Doctor!" Packy snapped, highly offended by my casual address.

"He's a scientist, too?" Mort said incredulously.

"Particle physicist," Packy clarified. "Uk."

"Okay, Dr Packy," I said reasonably. "Don't you see that you're letting them use you for their own ends? They left you here to die. You know what they think? You're an asset. An expendable asset. Is that all you are? What do *you* think you are?"

Packy had been slowly advancing on us, but now his feet were still, and I thought I detected a glint of hesitation in his bleary eyes.

"Cowboy words make Packy's heart hurt," he admitted, scratching the top of his bald head.

"Exactly," I said with an understanding nod. "It hurts to be used, doesn't it? So why don't we show them that you're a man who won't be walked on? Why don't we all walk out of here?"

It was a valid suggestion. Smoke was coming in under the glass doors, and the fire from the casino was working its way through the drywall. The lobby would be engulfed in minutes.

Packy's fledgeling sense of self-worth was obviously grappling against his long-ingrained sense of dog-like obedience, and it was making him a bit panicky. He wasn't accustomed to such inner turmoil.

"But-but...!" he sputtered. "But Brethren promise Packy chocolate if Packy break cowboy and fat man with nice hair. Packy thoughts swimming weirdly...."

"It's not fat!" Mort protested. "It's ... slightly hypotensive muscle tone."

"Packy want Packy's chocolate!" Packy wailed, beginning to cry.

"Think about the time, Doctor," I reminded him. "By the time you, uh, break us, this whole building's going to be burned to the ground with you in it. You're going to die here, and for what?"

"Packy's heart and brain all jumbled," Packy whimpered. "Packy want chocolate ... but Packy want respect, too!"

"You can have both," I promised. "Get us out of here, and the chocolate's on us. We'll clean out the nearest gas station. You'll have Milk Duds out the wazoo."

"Milk Duds?" Packy exploded, instantly incensed. "*Milk Duds?*"

"Why is he saying that so loudly and without smiling?" I nervously asked Mort.

"*Packy hate Milk Duds!*" the gargantuan scientist bellowed.

"Hey, that was going to be my first guess!" Mort said, delighted at having been right.

"Mort," I growled.

"Okay," Mort confessed. "It was my second guess...."

"Cowboy!" Packy seethed, pointing an accusing forefinger the size of a corn dog at me. "Cowboy pretend to care, but then offer Packy sticky caramels that stick in teeth!"

"Hey, millions of people around the world love the creamy chewiness of Milk Duds," Mort said defensively.

"Packy, listen...." I said placatingly.

"Packy kill!"

"Okay, this time that was definitely my first guess," Mort remarked.

"Fine, let's get on with it," I sighed, leaping in the air to punch Packy in the face. However, I had underestimated his height, and my fist glanced harmlessly off his shoulder.

"Die, cowboy!" Packy rasped, his massive fist whistling over my head as I danced around him, wisely remembering my days as a rodeo clown at the Coyote Yelp No Bull Buck-o-Rama. Giving a better calculated leap from behind him, I landed hard on his back and held on for dear life, hammering my puny fist onto his bare scalp.

"You're doing great, Bucky," Mort encouraged me from ten feet away. "Punch things!"

"You punch things!" I snapped as Packy frantically backpedalled and began slamming me into the nearest wall.

"Yes! Punch things!" Mort rasped, his voice dropping into a resonantly ominous gurgle. *"And I do declare ... I shall pun—"*

"Just shut up and hit him!" I screamed.

"Alright, alright," Mort muttered, running up and punching Packy in the nose. "Talk about ruining an intro."

I vaulted off Packy's shoulders as he staggered back, his hands clutching his nose. I landed lightly on the ground in front of him, rolling away from his stomping feet.

"It's just like rodeo clowning, Mort," I called out. "Keep

your feet moving! He's just like a bull, except slower and stupider, so this should be a piece of ca–"

I was cut off as Packy's left fist found Mort's chin, sending my celebrity friend across the room.

"Wow," I couldn't help marvelling as Mort bounced across the floor like a flat rock on water. "Just think of how ironic it would have been if he had hit me just then...."

"Packy hate obvious dramatic irony!" Packy declared, grabbing me by the throat with his right hand and slamming me to the wall once more. My feet were dangling about eight inches above the floor, where Packy's right foot was pressing down on Mort's head.

"Yeah, it's so overused for comedic effect," I gurgled in agreement. "Mort, you've starred in forty-nine action movies and one buddy cop movie with a monkey! Do something!"

"Any suggestions?" Mort said, his cheeks squished into the floorboards.

"Give him the tracheotomy pinch from *Operation: Preemptive Commonwealth*!"

"Stunt man," Mort replied from beneath Packy's right cleat.

"The rosewood forceps cardioectomy from *The Maple Leaf Bleeds*?"

"CGI and three stunt men," Mort admitted.

"Oh, for the love of cow cud, just punch his shins," I growled, managing to wrap both of my hands around one of Packy's pinky fingers and bending it back savagely. Packy let out a piercing screech, and then began hopping madly on one foot as Mort obligingly drove a fist into the giant's shin bone.

"No fair!" Packy sobbed, promptly throwing in the towel and charging toward the exit. "Packy calling his gramma!"

"That was *so* not a memorable climax," Mort was muttering as we shakily rose to our feet and stumbled toward the exit, just as the first flames began to burn through the walls all around us.

"Yeah, in reality it's the simple things that usually work," I informed him.

We turned the corner into the final room between us and freedom, only to discover that the entire foyer was engulfed in flames.

"Crap, they torched it!" Mort realized. "Scientists are evil!"

"No other option, buddy," I said. "See ya on the other side!"

Taking a deep breath, we charged straight through the fire and shoulder-slammed the heavy doors on the far side, which might as well have been made out of Packy himself. The only exit from our burning prison had been chained shut by Packy on his way out.

"Packy!" I shouted, beating on the doors. "You open this door, or I'll tell your gramma that you've been eating chocolate without brushing your teeth!"

Apparently, Packy couldn't hear me.

"Well, this is it, Bucky," Mort said morosely, slumping down beside the doorframe. "It's been an honour riding with you, cowboy. See ya on the metaphorical other side...."

"No, just wait a second," I advised him. "I've been in a lot of similar situations, and something usually shows up at the last possible second to resc–"

Mort and I both narrowly escaped flattening as Corky and Sassy's Bucky-Paver tour bus plowed through the doors between us at roughly seventy kilometres per hour, skidding sideways and slamming to a halt in the midst of the fiery room.

"*All aboard, Bucky!*" Sassy roared from behind the steering wheel, cranking the door open. "The cavalry's here!"

"How did you get here?" Mort blurted, scrambling inside.

"I called them on Shania Twain's sat-phone after I hit you in the head with a tackle box yesterday," I explained, following him inside and slamming the door. "Then I met up with them before I went to sleep last night and gave them the skull and egg and my fiddle for safekeeping, and in case we died. Sorry for not telling you. It was for your protection."

"How did you call them without the scientists knowing about it?" Mort demanded. "They knew when you called Betty-Sue, and we had the only other secure line with us!"

"No we didn't," I corrected him. "I called their other unregistered sat-phone. The one that Corky stole from Avril Lavigne."

See what I mean? Contingency plan. Never leave home without one.

"We followed you and called that Mudford guy, like you said," Corky confirmed as Sassy slammed the bus into reverse. "He's bringing the thunder right now, but we saw the fire and figured we couldn't wait."

"Plus, I've always wanted to drive a bus into a building," Sassy added. "Everybody hang on!"

"Let's blow this chili stand!" Corky cheered. However, before the words were even out of his mouth, he spotted a small pale object lying on the floor by the lobby entrance. Whatever it was, Mort and I had leapt right over it without noticing, and it was half-buried beneath a flaming section of rafter which had fallen from the buckling ceiling. Corky's keen eyes bulged in horror as recognition set in. Before Sassy could stop him, he had slammed the gearshift back into park, and pocketed the keys.

"What?" I asked.

"Never touch my keys, clown shoes," Sassy snarled,

ignoring the fact that Corky was the sole registered owner of the tour bus.

"That's Sealy!" Corky cried, immediately wrenching the doors open and diving back into the flames. "What the heck is she doing here? Those diabolical lab coats left her for dead!"

I opened my mouth to yell out that she was already dead, or possibly still alive but pure evil, but a sudden eruption of automatic gunfire silenced me. One of the side windows was instantly shattered, and the sound of a multitude of bullets striking the metal frame filled the bus a second later.

"*Holy Himalayan holy man!*" Sassy squawked, diving out of her seat as Mort and I hit the floor. We all pressed ourselves as flat as we could onto the carpet, as the side windows continued to detonate all around us.

"Okay, I really don't think it was necessary for you to *take the keys, Corky!*" I exploded. "We would have waited for you!"

"They're shooting at us! They're shooting at us!" Mort kept squalling. "And we're on fire! We're going to get iced and roasted all on the same freakin' day! Do something, Bucky! I'm too significant to die!"

"I've always wanted to have a real cowboy barbecue!" Argo's belligerent voice whooped at us from outside the bashed-open doors, carrying over the incessant roar of gunfire. "Char-grilled, baby!"

"Oh, I *know* you didn't just start shooting up my bus," Sassy was muttering, grabbing the Bucky-Blaster from its special scabbard on the back of the driver's seat and earring back both hammers. "*Austin la visa, baby!*"

"I don't think that's quite right," I commented as Sassy blew out her own rear window with both barrels of 10-gauge, sending Argo and Gapps scrambling for cover. My mind made a halfhearted suggestion about telling her that killing people made Jesus sad, but the more dominant part of my mind decided that Mort was right. Jesus would probably understand extenuating circumstances, and I was pretty sure that this qualified.

From where I lay, I could still glimpse the open doorway, and, in spite of the smoke that was now rolling through it, I could see my valiant older brother rushing to Sealy's side.

"Corky, it's too late!" I shouted after him. "We've got to get out of here before the roof comes down!"

"That's my girlfriend we're talking about!" Corky yelled back, seizing the heavy boards and flipping them away as if they were made of straw.

"Uh, yeah, about that...." I hesitantly called out, cringing at having to be the one who broke the news to him. "Your girlfriend's not exactly what you wanna bring home to Gramps."

"You're just saying that because that's what Gramps said about all my girlfriends!" Corky hollered, scooping up the fallen maiden and carrying her like a superhero back to the bus. A second later, they were both on the floor beside me and Mort, and Sassy slammed the doors.

"*Go go go go go!*" everybody in the bus who was not unconscious shouted at Sassy.

"We can't go," she said with a sudden demeanor of calm. "We can't get up enough speed backing out of here. This is a bus, okay? It doesn't exactly go zero to sixty in under ten. They'll pick us off with heavy artillery before we get six feet."

"Okay, *now* can I say goodbye?" Mort requested. "There's no way out of this one."

"Oh, don't be too sure," Sassy said, her eyes narrowing with grim intensity. "I may have lied to you guys a little before."

"What?" I demanded.

"I said I've always wanted to drive a bus into a building," Sassy said, snatching the keys from Corky's hand and clambering into the driver's seat. "Actually, I've always wanted to drive a bus right through one. Might wanna hang onto something."

I would like to chronicle the events of the next thirty seconds or so for you, but I think I must have either repressed the memory or just blacked out at some point from the sheer terror of it, because the next thing I recall is the bus flying down the mountain road, more than a kilometre from the remote casino that would never see its grand opening. The empty window frames were doing a good job of sucking the last of the smoke outside, and the fact that the entire windshield was now missing as well allowed a very refreshing cross-breeze to blow through the length of the long vehicle, which is possibly what finally revived me. Sassy was laughing harder than I had ever seen her laugh before, and the rest of us were huddled on the floor with our thumbs in our mouths, including Sealy who must have regained consciousness right about the time that I was losing it.

"*Never ... do that ... again!*" Mort quavered, shaking like a practising Quaker.

"Listen to Mort," I advised my sister. "And I'm not going to say that very often."

"Well, now what?" Corky asked, as Sealy trembled in his arms. "We've got the skull, but it's too late to get on Megiddo's show tonight. It's already airing, it's prerecorded, and we're at least two hours from Kelowna."

"But we're less than an hour from Kamloops," I realized, sitting up a little straighter and seeing a ramshackle road posting flash past. It said that Kamloops was only eighty kilometres away. "We don't need Megiddo's show. All we need is him."

Mort and I turned to stare at each other, our faces lighting up with sudden revelation.

"And we know where he's going to be tonight," Mort finished my thought. "Assuming, of course, that he didn't go to the barn and get blown up."

"No," Sealy sighed. "We were scanning the transmissions from the barn, so we knew you contacted him. We just anonymously sent him some documentable proof that you were a homicidal lunatic, and advised him to stay away. He's fine."

"We?" Corky said, confused. "What do you mean, we?"

"Cops ahoy, buddy-boy!" Sassy whooped back at me, pointing at the blue and red strobes of the advancing police cruisers on the road ahead of us.

"Oh," Sealy said miserably. "I guess that's for me. Sheesh.... Thanks for saving me again, Corky, but I think this is where I get off."

"What are you talking about?" Corky asked, looking sharply at her.

Sealy just smiled bravely as she gave him a kiss on the cheek, and then gently squeezed his hand.

"Ask your idiot brother."

A COWBOY TAKES
THE STAGE
◇◇◇◇◇◇◇◇◇◇◇◇◇◇

AND SO IT WAS that justice was wrought upon the Galapagos Brethren. In spite of all their scientific knowledge and special-ops training, the vengeful scientists had a hard time explaining to the Royal Canadian Mounted Police why they had been chasing a shot-up bus down the road in black Suburbans loaded to the roof with unregistered automatic weapons, land mines, bulletproof lab coats, fake Swedish passports, and blood-signed statements of their intent to murder me. Also, their belligerent insistences that Lake Okanagan needed to be nuked as soon as possible for the good of the world didn't help matters much. It's common knowledge that every Mountie in Canada loves the legend of the Ogopogo, regardless of whether or not they actually believe in the dang thing.

"We're innocent!" Argo was squawking as the hefty Sergeant Mudford slammed him up against the side of a police cruiser and handcuffed him. "All we're trying to do is protect the innocence and comfort of the world from the threat of Impossible Lies! Do you have any idea how much it costs to make those museum display plaques? Do *you* want to pay for the new ones? We're the heroes here! *Cowboys don't get to change the world!*"

"Oh yeah?" Mudford growled. "If you're such a hero, then what are you doing with Shania Twain's stolen satellite phone? We've been looking for that thing for years! Better duck, Doc, cuz the book is getting thrown at you!"

"Huh," Sassy remarked, watching the drama from the side of the road with her hands in her denim overall pockets. "That worked out better than I expected. *Heh heh!*"

Dr Kay Argo and Dr Theo Gapps were blubbering even louder than the injured Dr Archie Aptrick as they were led to their respective police cars in handcuffs. The only one who took imminent incarceration in stride was Dr Sealy Kent, who remained prim and dignified as she stepped into the back of an RCMP crew-cab pickup, wisely choosing to remain silent while allowing Corky to do all the blubbering that he wanted. (Dr Patrick "Packy" Sedak evaded capture in one of the black Suburbans and was never seen again, although some have attributed a nearby convenience store robbery to him. The break-in occurred later that night, and the only thing stolen was the candy-bar rack and the complete box set of *Gaining Self-Confidence to Establish Self-Worth in the Modern Workplace, with Liev Schreiber* motivational CDs. I wish him well.)

After the wailing and gnashing of the scientists was finally muffled by car windows that didn't open, Sergeant Mudford took me aside to speak privately.

"Corky and Sassy told me about the skull," he whispered, glancing about to ensure that we weren't being eavesdropped on. "I always knew there was something in that lake! And, if I know Bucky Laroo, you're the only one hapless and indestructible enough to prove it to the world. Y'all get outta here now, and get that thing wherever it needs to go. I'll just fudge over the paperwork. But I want my picture taken with the skull when this is over. My little girl will love it."

"I appreciate your helpfulness, if not your overall sense of ethical propriety," I replied, shaking his hand gratefully. "By the way, you might have heard something about me being that guy who's putting bombs in all the pipelines around Dawson Creek...."

"I didn't hear about that," Mudford said, looking a bit suspicious. "Should I have?"

"Ha ha, no, of course not," I laughed weakly. "I absolutely detest Dawson Creek and all the people I've met there. Why would I ever go anywhere near– Okay, that came out wrong, but it's not me. I promise."

"Good enough," Mudford shrugged with an apathy that seemed to be disturbingly commonplace to him. "Get on your way now, and ride hard, cowboy. I'll let the windshield violation slide until people stop trying to kill you."

It was nearly 7:30 p.m., and the sun was getting lower on the western horizon when I followed my family and Mort back into our massacred bus, and Sassy asked, "Okay, where to now?"

"Kamloops," Mort and I said in unison.

"What the heck is in Kamloops?" Sassy demanded as she began to drive once more, leaving Corky to pout in the kitchenette area. "Deserts and ginseng. That's it. It's like the water-scalded booboo of British Columbia."

"I like Kamloops," Corky managed to say in the city's defence, wiping the last of his tears. "It's got a go-kart track and a regional BC Ambulance Service dispatch centre. I have very fond memories of both."

I decided not to pursue the question of when he had been in either location, instead choosing to inform my siblings that Megiddo was taking his family to the city that night.

"He's going to a concert," I explained grimly. "And

we're going to crash it. Then we can get the skull in front of thousands of people and TV cameras. It's *The Fighting Mackenzies*, so some station's got to be offering live coverage."

"Ronnie and Cherie are in Kamloops?" Corky said in disgust. "Okay, let's do it. I don't even care if we get arrested and the skull gets intercepted. As long as we get to disrupt their concert. Just like they did to ours when they opened for us in Edmonton."

"That was six years ago," I pointed out. "And it was a justifiable interruption. A fourteen-month-old baby had wandered off in the crowd, and Ronnie was asking everyone to look for it."

"Well, he could have at least waited until intermission," Sassy said bitterly. "Seriously, how far is a fourteen-month-old going to go in an arena that big? Most of them can barely walk at that age, especially one that was so prone to airway occlusions if left unmonitored for any amount of time."

"Good logic," I said, trying to tune them out and instruct them at the same time. "The only problem is that I'm not sure where the concert is. Sassy, turn on the radio and see if they're talking about–"

"Arid Acres Coliseum," Corky said promptly. "It's the only place big enough for a group as supposedly 'big-time' as those two inbred hillbillies. All the big concerts and conventions are there."

"Delicately put, as always," I acknowledged. "Look, I can't ask you guys to go in with me. I'm going to get on that stage no matter what, which means the security guards will probably arrest me for assault if I have to fight my way past them. But this is bigger than me. I love you all, either way."

"Darn tootin,' we're coming with you," Sassy exclaimed. "We'll get you to the stage, baby bro."

"We're celebrities," Mort reminded me. "We get arrested for assault all the time, but it never sticks."

"Anyway, we'll do it during intermission, when the security around the stage will be lighter," Corky decided. "See? I still have integrity, even if Ronnie Mackenzie doesn't."

"Why would we wait for intermission?" I said. "The cameras might not even be on then, and lots of the audience will be hitting the concessions. We need to maximize our initial coverage, okay?"

The three of them turned to stare at me as if I was a brainless amoebae, the bus veering dangerously across the highway due to Sassy's prolonged unblinking participation.

"It's The Law of the Spotlight, Bucky," Mort finally explained. "It's the one last thing that's sacred in the celebrity community. When it comes to other celebrities, you can take their spouse, their dignity, and even their life, and Hollywood will forgive you. Hollywood forgives almost everything: Adultery, impaired driving, drug abuse, child-like tantrums, statutory rape, and even regular rape with thirty-plus subsequent years on the lam in countries without US extradition policies. It doesn't matter what you've done. Once you win that Oscar, packed auditoriums will give you a standing ovation, even if you aren't allowed in the country to receive it. It's a beautiful world of grace, Bucky, but there is still one thing that is tantamount to the unforgivable. You *never* touch another celebrity's microphone!"

"*My spotlight and I are one,*" Corky and Sassy recited in unison, apparently from some ancient celebrity mantra. "*Let no man rend us asunder.*"

"Exactly," Mort agreed, peeling off the remains of his shredded sweatshirt and pulling on the dark blue sweater that Corky had given him. "It's intermission or nothing."

"I may abhor the ground that Cherie Mackenzie treads upon," Sassy stated, "but the Law is bigger than all of us."

"Whatever," I said, rolling my eyes. "Intermission it is. I'm just glad we'll only be dealing with unarmed security guards. I don't know if I could handle anymore evil atheists."

"You know, Bucky," Mort said in a counselling tone, "you really shouldn't keep referring to the lab coats as evil atheists."

"They are evil atheists," I pointed out. "Well, they're evil atheists and one evil theistic evolutionist."

"I know," Mort said patiently. "Trust me, I know a lot of atheists, and I have never met any as venom-spewing, baby-eating evil as those guys. But you have to think about the future, man, even in casual references."

"You mean a future where we live together in peace with all mankind, regardless of belief?" I replied. "That's a very good point, Mort."

"No, no," Mort corrected me, rolling his eyes. "I just meant that you have to think about the future in regard to selling the book or movie rights. This is a big story, but you'll never get a publisher to print a true story with a so-called protagonist who consistently identifies his antagonists as evil atheists, or even regular atheists. The liberal media isn't going to appreciate that kind of lumping. They're all pretty sure that the undeniable, unfathomable, unadulterated evil of Stalin and Madelyn Murray O'Hair was some kind of fluke."

"I wouldn't worry about it," I said dismissively. "I'm sure plenty of memoirs and non-fiction works have been published wherein atheist protagonists rightfully refer to their monotheistic antagonists as evil Christians. Every faith has its dark and misguided extremities. I'm at peace with it."

"Hey, I'm just saying that you shouldn't compromise any future book deals by what you say now."

"Good advice," I admitted. "Of course, if I ever was loony enough to write more memoirs, I would be conscience-bound to record that you just referred to a group of atheists as venom-spewing baby-eaters. Is that problematic?"

"Crap," Mort muttered. "You and your family's stupid photographic memory."

"Relax, Mort," I soothed him. "I'm sure that book publishers and reading audiences are sophisticated enough to understand that I'm only referring to this select offshoot of the atheist faith as evil, rather than their entire global congregation."

"Oh, sure," Mort scoffed. "Like that sentence wasn't contrived as some kind of potential placation."

"Ah, whattaya gonna do?" I said with a shrug. "People say all kinds of weird crap in real life."

The radio had announced that the concert would begin at 8:00, and it was nearly 8:15 when we arrived at the Arid Acres Coliseum, stealthily bypassing the overflowing main parking area and pulling into the fenced rear village where the staff and performers' vehicles were located. I thought it was odd that there were no guards at the gate, but I didn't have time to think about that. We had to figure out a way to get backstage.

Fortunately, *Lost Cause Kin* had played a jamboree at the centre a few years earlier, and Sassy remembered a large maintenance closet near the northeast exit, one that she and Junior had secretly used when they wanted to set fire to small objects in peace. She said it was out of the way of the main routes to the stage, and was big enough for all of us to hide in until intermission.

"Won't the building be locked?" I asked.

"Oh, he's so innocent," Corky laughed. "We're going to

need a butter knife, a hairpin, a hair-curler, hair spray, and a DeWalt jigsaw. We'll be inside in no time."

"You know, I am trying to get through this preposterously sequenced misadventure with some sense of ethical high-ground," I informed them. "It's pretty much the only thing I've– Okay, I deliberately crashed a helicopter and left the scene without calling medical aid for the pilot, but I still think I'm clinging to some form of morality."

"Relax," Sassy said, parking in the lengthening shadows near the northeast exit. "It's not a crime if you're only bringing stuff in. We leave the hair spray in the hallway when we leave, and, technically, we're just delivery dudes dropping off cosmetics. Oh, by the way, I forgot to tell you. I think that egg started hatching four hours ago. Totally forgot."

"Oh, perfect," I groaned. "I thought this kind of bad timing only happened in the movies."

"No, that's not true, Bucky," Sassy assured me. "Sometimes it happens in poorly-structured novels, too."

I rushed over to the new baler twine box on the dining table, but only the Ogopogo skull was in it. The big blue egg was gone.

"Where is it?" I demanded.

"In the toilet," Sassy said airily, scanning the area around our bus with a pair of binoculars. "Don't worry. It's broken."

My first instinct was to rush to the tiny bathroom in the rear of the bus, but I had to stop myself for a moment and clarify, "You made a sixteen hour trip down here, non-stop, without a working toilet?"

"Yeah, but the kitchen sink works," Sassy explained.

"What does that mean?" I asked.

"What does what mean?" Sassy replied impatiently.

"Nothing."

I ran back to the bathroom, but the toilet bowl only contained the fragmented remains of the egg's shell. The baby Ogopogo was nowhere to be seen.

"*Somebody find the dinosaur!*" I shouted.

"Corky, baby-ghanoush lost the Pogo," Sassy translated wearily, beginning to crawl down the length of the bus on her hands and knees. "I'm on it. You guys go wait for me in the closet."

"No time to worry about more dead dinosaurs, Bucky," Mort advised me, scooping up the twine box. "Let's do this."

"There's something really slippery under this sink!" Sassy reported, crawling into the cupboards beneath it.

"Is it moving under its own power?" I inquired.

"I'm not sure," Sassy admitted, poking at the darkened mass with a broom handle. "Do we have a large box of table salt?"

"I've got the security cameras timed out," Corky announced. "Bucky and Max-Ram, get ready to move."

"Just find the dinosaur," I sighed, rubbing my twitching eye.

"Hey, Corky?" Sassy's muffled voice called out from the living area. "If I can smell bitter almonds wafting out from under the futon, is that bad?"

"Wafting or reeking?" Corky asked, apparently needing specifics as he quickly stuffed his belt with his *MacGuyver*-esque lock-pick kit.

"Just keep moving," Mort said urgently, grabbing me and Corky and leading us to the front of the bus. "You guys wouldn't happen to have any amyl nitrite on you, would you?"

"Like we have time for you to relapse right now," I said as Corky led the dash across the parking lot. "Wait a second.... Hey, Corky, those security cameras aren't moving!"

"That's why they were so easy to time out," Corky said evenly. "Pass me that jigsaw."

Two minutes later, we were inside the Coliseum, and we weren't facing scores of security guards, contrary to my best-case anticipation. The rising staircase ahead of us was empty, as was the long hallway at the top of it. We could hear the cheers and shrieks of the five thousand-plus fans in the main arena, but no music was playing yet. That was also odd. The concert was supposed to have started twenty minutes earlier.

"There's the closet," Corky said, pointing at a door on the left side of the hall, about halfway down. "You can still see the scorch marks on the bottom."

We ran down the hallway and slipped into the darkened room, closing the door behind us. I felt around for a light switch, but couldn't find one.

"Where's the light?" I demanded. "I can't see a thing."

"That doesn't mean you have to whimper and whine about it," Corky snapped.

"I'm not whining," I replied.

"Yes, you are," Corky assured me. "I can hear you right now. Look, if you're going to whine with fear, just bite down on a roll of paper towels and press your tongue hard against the roof of your mouth. That's how I got through the infected Lizzy Caplan explosion scene in *Cloverfield*. Man, that movie was awesome. We need to rent that one when we get back home."

"I hated the open ending," Mort pointed out. "I mean, did they kill the monster or what? I always made sure I killed everyone and everything in my movies, just to give my audience a horrifically desensitized sense of closure."

"I always appreciated that, Max-Ram, and I consider myself a better person as a result of it," Corky noted. "Bucky, seriously, if you don't cut out that whining, I'm going to strangle you with your own tongue and dig out your eyes with a salad fork!"

"I'm not whining!"

"Unintelligibly mumbling?"

"Corky, I'm not making noise."

"Hey, he's right," Mort realized. "I can still hear it when he's talking. What is that?"

"I can hear it, too," I said. "Somebody find a light."

After a few more moments of fumbling in the dark, Corky finally found the light switch. However, when he clicked it on, we realized that the situation at Arid Acres Coliseum was much more complex than we had imagined.

They bodies of more than a dozen staffers, musicians, and security personnel were heaped in the middle of the small room, every one of them with the feathered tag of a tranquillizer dart sticking out of some part of their anatomy. Beyond the pile were the only other conscious people in the room, but they were in no condition to talk. Sibling dynamos Ronnie and Cherie Mackenzie were sitting back-to-back on the floor, swathed with more rope than I had seen in a very long time. It was they who had been making the whining sounds, desperately trying to call out to us through the large shammy sponge that each one had stuffed into their mouths.

"What the cow?" I said.

Before we could do anything, we heard the distinctive sound of the room's only door being locked, followed by an oddly-familiar feminine cackling.

"Nice try, Bucky," the voice sneered. "You came so close. But some things are bigger than all of us. Enjoy your stay with us."

"*Amber?*" Mort said, horrified.

"Hello, Max-Ram," she laughed back at him. "And that completes the party."

"Amber?" Corky said in confusion. "Who the heck is Amber?"

"Irrelevant," Mort shot back, not very convincingly. "Amber, open this door, right now!"

Amber did not directly reply, but we could hear her receding footsteps and continuing laughter as she strode down the hall. I rammed the door with my shoulder, but only succeeded in hurting myself.

"Okay, that really hurt," I admitted, rubbing my numb shoulder. "We need Sassy over here, pronto. Corky, call her cell."

"Yeah, I'm on it," Corky said, dialling the sat-phone he had stolen from Avril Lavigne. A moment later, Sassy's maniacally-laughing *Predator* ring-tone came from his other pocket.

"You have all the phones?" I said in disgust.

"Sorry, Bucky," my brother said sheepishly. "I like to be reachable."

"Oh, for the love of giblets," I muttered, shaking my head.

"'an 'oo un'eye 'ee?" Ronnie Mackenzie requested, butting in at the most inopportune time once again.

"'eeze?" his twin sister added politely.

"Shut up, Ronnie!" Corky snapped. "We're a little busy at the moment, okay?"

"Okay, Mort," I decided. "It's time for your resources to start pulling their weight. Call somebody to come and get us."

"Why don't we just call the cops?" he asked.

"Because we're breaking and entering," I snapped.

"Well, that's debatable," Corky commented.

"No it's not!" I stated. "But they'd never let us near that stage. Come on, Mort, it doesn't even have to be a friend.

Just call anyone, convince them that you're you, and then offer them money to get us out of here."

"Nobody's going to do that, Bucky," he ventured, looking a bit green.

"Look, Mort, I know you've never actually had friends, and most of your influence is gone, but all we need is someone who knows your name and likes money. That shouldn't be too hard to find. Call 411 and ask for a Bob Smith in Kamloops. One of them has to know you."

"*I don't have money!*" Mort blurted, his eyes filling with tears at the admission.

"What?" I said.

"Please don't hate me, Bucky," Mort begged. "I didn't tell you, because I wanted to help you on this crazy, wacky, life-defining quest. I have no money. None."

"You're *broke?*" I exploded. "How is that possible? You had 9 billion dollars banked, and 1.5 billion tied into real estate!"

"And 3.8 billion in unseized elephant tusks and Scandinavian whaling ventures," Mort concluded.

"How exactly do you manage to lose more than 14 billion dollars in three years?" I demanded.

"It's complicated, Bucky. I happened to be looking for a good investment opportunity a couple years ago when I got an email from this very wealthy deposed prince of Nigeria. He needed my help in keeping his nation's wealth out of the hands of the unscrupulous rebel leaders who had overthrown his family. All I had to do was open up my banking information to him for a guaranteed 65% cut."

"And you did it," I said, disgusted.

"Yeah," Mort nodded. "So that netted me an extra 8 billion dollars overnight. But then I went to Vegas to celebrate, and I woke up four days later with a stripper who was wearing one of those cherry pop-rings on her left hand.

I was married just long enough to realize that drafting and signing a pre-nup when you're blackout drunk, and she isn't, is a really bad idea. What little money I had left got sucked up into monthly payments to Ashton Kutcher over the past year."

"What?" I said.

"Nothing," Mort said sharply. "Forget that last part."

"So, let me see if I've got this right," I said, speaking as slowly as I could in order to prevent myself from blowing my stack. "Somewhere in this world there is a Las Vegas stripper who just walked away with 22.3 billion dollars?"

"Pretty much," Mort said miserably. "Then she dyed her hair and changed her name from Amber Ruby Diamond to Britt 2.0. She's actually been doing quite well for herself ever since."

Corky and I both stared at him.

"You have got to be kidding me," I finally said, feeling a twitch beginning to develop in my other eye.

"Why does anything about me surprise you anymore, Bucky?" Mort wanted to know.

"That's the best question I've heard in years," I snarled.

"Thank you."

"So that's why Sting's dating her?" I guessed. "As revenge for the girlfriend you stole from him?"

"You know, I actually hadn't thought of that," Mort admitted. "But it makes sense, now that you mention it."

"And when we tried to buy him off on the walkie-talkie," I continued, feeling numb, "and he said that your money was peanuts...?"

"...he was being literal, not metaphorical," Mort sighed. "The only thing I got out of the divorce was our half-acre peanut farm in Plains, Georgia. And it's bombing something awful, Bucky. It's like Incident II, only metaphorical."

"What?"

"Nothing."

"So Britt 2.0 is *here?*" Corky asked with a mix of horror and star-struck delight. "But why would she lock us in here? She grew up as a sweet farmgirl in rural Wyoming before getting her big break into–"

"Please don't try to justify her using that surprisingly common argument," I snapped, finally going to the far end of the room to pull the sponge gags out of Ronnie and Cherie's mouths. "And I don't think we should even believe her biographies anymore. I don't care how rebellious she might have been growing up, no Wyoming farmgirl in history has ever ended up twirling around a pole in Las Vegas."

"True, " Mort agreed. "That's more of a Polish illegal immigrant thing. Rebelling on a Wyoming farm usually means running away to your boyfriend's cattle ranch in Montana."

"Thanks, Bucky," Ronnie gagged as the shammy was removed from his mouth. "Corky, what are you doing here with Max-Ram Target? What's going on?"

"What happened?" I asked, ignoring the understandable line of questioning. "Did you see Britt 2.0 here?"

"She showed up while we were setting up a couple hours ago," Cherie explained, gasping in the unspongy air. "She said she was a big fan, and wanted to wish us luck on the show. Next thing I know, *Sweet Conformity*'s taken out all our roadies and building security with tranq guns, and we're getting herded in here. She said she'd let us live if we agreed to tell the press that we had called in sick and she had agreed to take over. Then she said something about our music not being loud enough to drown out the inevitable, whatever that means."

"Told you she was evil," Mort reminded me. "Even by pop star standards. How do you think she knew we'd be here? She has enough connections to monitor The Establishment's communications! The Galapagos Brethren led her straight to us."

"Which means that she knows everything," I ventured. "She knows what we're doing here, and she probably knows about the skull."

"Can you untie me, please?" Ronnie requested. "My hands are swelling. I depend on my hands for my livelihood."

"Please, Ron-boy," Corky scoffed. "I've heard you play guitar. Trust me, we're doing you a favour leaving you tied."

"Come on, Corky, be a sport," Cherie urged him, making an effort at smiling sweetly. "Sure, we've had our differences over the years, but you must have known that it was all a ruse to mask my flaming desire for you. Did I ever tell you that?"

"Nice try, sweetheart," Corky said coldly, his newfound devotion to Sealy making him a lot harder to manipulate. "If I had a nickel for every time a beautiful woman tied up in a closet said that to me, I'd have at least twenty-five cents more than Max-Ram."

"That's hurtful," Mort cringed.

"Why exactly have you been talking to tied-up women in closets on at least five occasions?" I asked, looking suspiciously at my brother. "Actually, don't answer that. Let's get out of here. It's just a wooden door, and we've got three able-bodied men here, plus Ronnie."

"Hey!" Ronnie protested.

"I wish our baby brother Plucky was here," Cherie sighed. "Plucky always knows what to do. He's my hero."

"Corky, learn from this woman!" I couldn't help instructing.

It was at that moment that the concert started, the

muffled chords of the opening number penetrating the walls of our confined prison. But it wasn't *The Fighting Mackenzies'* signature tune, *The Old Cookie Jar Song*, that we were hearing. It was Britt 2.0's hit single, *Sandpaper Me Softly*, and the hyperventilating crowd definitely didn't seem to mind the abrupt change of program and musical genre. Everybody loves a superstar cameo.

"Can you believe this?" Cherie demanded. "She's hijacking! What's going on here?"

"This is her plan?" I had to ask. "She figured out where we were going, and then she just locks us in here and steals a *Fighting Mackenzies* concert?"

"After telling her beloved Sting Ripblood where we are," Mort guessed miserably. "The blaring music will muffle the gunshots."

"What are you talking about?" Ronnie whined.

"Sting Ripblood wants to kill me," Mort sighed.

"Really?" Cherie asked skeptically. "Jeepers, it was just a horse...."

"Well, he might be after me, too," I pointed out. "The Scientific Establishment leaked a story about me being the EnCana Bomber."

"But why?" Ronnie gasped, appalled. "You're one of the sweetest people we've ever met, Bucky."

"You really are," Cherie kindly agreed. "Why would anyone try to frame you as an eco-terrorist?"

"I found a living dinosaur," I said.

"*Die, Bucky!*" Ronnie shouted, sweeping my legs out from under me with a sudden karate kick. As soon as I hit the floor, his legs were wrapped around my throat, choking me.

"Git'im, Ronnie!" Cherie cheered with deranged glee. "Give him that nutcracker neck-snap Chuck Norris taught you!"

"Okay, everybody calm down," Corky said in a bored voice, calmly helping Mort pull me away from my new attackers. "It wasn't a dinosaur. It was an aquatic reptile that coexisted with the dinosaurs."

"Wow," Cherie said, as if awakening from a trance. "That is so weird. Just hearing the words 'living dinosaur' triggered such an irrational response from us. I am so sorry, Bucky. We've known you for five years!"

"Yeah, sorry, dude," Ronnie apologised.

"You really get used to this?" Mort asked me.

"Years ago." I nodded. "Seriously, feel my pulse. It's normal. Corky, this has been a delightful little detour, but why don't you go ahead and call someone? Call Avril Lavigne and tell her you'll give her back her sat-phone if she lets us out of here."

"Anything's worth a shot," Corky admitted, dialling the phone. He held it to his ear for nearly forty seconds before pocketing it again, and stating, "Well, that didn't work."

"Did you get her voice mail?" I asked.

"No, the battery's dead," Corky explained.

"Of course it is," I said. "And Sassy's cell phone is password protected just in case Shania Twain ever tries to retaliate."

"Okay, now can you untie us?" Cherie asked. "I can't feel my backside anymore."

"Silence, you vixen," Corky snapped. "We're trying to think. And you just tried to kill Bucky."

For the next hour or so, there wasn't much to do but sit back and listen to Britt 2.0's undeniably catchy, if generally uninspired, lyrics drift through the immovable door, meshing nicely with the snoring of the guards and backup vocalists on the floor. There wasn't much space to move around, and the air was beginning to smell like a compost heap on a humid day.

And then we heard the footsteps approaching. Britt 2.0 was still singing, so we could only guess that Sting had arrived, and we were all about to die. The footsteps stopped directly outside the door, and we heard a gun hammer being cocked back.

"Corky?" a voice that was definitely not Sting Ripblood's called out.

"*Sassy!*" Corky and I blurted, rushing to the door.

"Britt 2.0 is here, and she's pure evil, and she locked us in!" Mort explained in a rush. "And Sting Ripblood could be here any second. You've got to get us out of here."

"Please, Sassy!" Cherie begged.

"Is that you, Mackenzie?" Sassy's voice growled. "Why don't you just wander off and find a fourteen-month-old baby?"

"Give it a rest, Sassy," I snapped. "Open the door!"

"I can't open this," Sassy protested. "There's a vending machine welded across the doorframe!"

"Are you serious?" Corky said incredulously.

"Nope," Sassy chuckled. "Ha! Key's just broke off in the lock, ya bunch of pansies. Hang on, I'll Bucky-Blast it."

"You brought a shotgun?" I cringed. "Great. This just went from misdemeanour B&E to armed invasion."

"Relax, I hid it in my guitar case," Sassy soothed me. "Everybody hug the left wall. I'm going to take out the doorknob at an upward angle."

"Wait a second!" I shouted. "Was that your left or our left?"

"What difference could that possibly make?" Sassy scoffed. "*Fire in the hole!*"

"Floor!" I blurted. Mort, Corky, and I all bit the linoleum as the shotgun bellowed and buckshot pellets tore through the doorjamb and into the wall, passing neatly through the area where my face had been a second earlier. I cringed as I slowly stood and reached for the door.

"Oh, I almost forgot," Sassy said. "Double tap. Always double tap."

I didn't drop quite fast enough that time, and three pellets tore into my left shoulder as I collapsed, howling in pain. But the job was done. Sassy gave the door one hard boot, and it swung open.

"And that's the way you do it," she said proudly, shouldering her 10-gauge.

"*You just shot me, El Mariachi!*" I roared, clutching my bleeding shoulder.

"That's quite alright, Bucky," Sassy consoled me. "The whole thing is already distant history to me. Don't let the past be your bog."

"Where's the Pogo?" Corky asked.

"Oh, right, I totally forgot about that," Sassy admitted. "I just came in here because I got bored."

"Where's the dinosaur?" I demanded, seizing her collar to help her focus.

"Aquatic reptile," she corrected me.

"*Where is it?*"

"I couldn't find it," Sassy shrugged insolently. "Anyway, what business is it of yours? I brought that egg up out of the bottom of the lake. That is the very definition of salvage rights, buddy-boy. Look it up."

"And I'm the one who made that egg an orphan in the first place, so it's my responsibility!" I barked, angrily grabbing a towel from the linen rack and tying it around my shoulder. "It's on me, Sassy! No one else."

"Whoa," Mort said, impressed. "Goosebumps, baby."

"*I don't care how dramatic I'm unintentionally sounding!*" I blew up. "I'm sick of your incompetence, all of you! I'm sick of your selfishness, and I'm sick of your maddening ability to distract yourselves with matters of pop-cultural significance at the drop of a gnat! In the past two days, I have been shot at with grenades, chased by a helicopter, interrogated by scientists, shot at by scientists, stepped on a bomb, fallen over a waterfall onto a grizzly bear, had a fish hook stuck in my face, and now I've been shot! *I want my boring back!* You are all going to shut up and help me get this over with so that I can go home to my wife and never leave Coyote Yelp Pass, ever again! Mort, Corky, you're with me. We take that stage no matter what, even if Corky has to spontaneously seduce Mort's ex-wife."

"I'm on it," Corky quipped.

"Hey!" Mort protested.

"Sassy, get your butt back into that bus," I ordered. "Tear it apart until you find that Pogo, and keep it safe. Nobody comes near it except us. *Do you understand me, soldier?*"

"Yes, Bucky," Sassy whined.

"Are you sure you're up for this, Bucky?" Mort asked. "You're bleeding, man."

"I ain't got time to bleed," I snarled, secretly relishing the long-awaited opportunity to steal Jesse Ventura's awesome line from *Predator*. "Let's do this!"

My siblings and Mort all roared in agreement, and we charged out into the hallway, slamming the door behind us and leaving the Mackenzies tied up in the closet.

"I think they forgot us, Ronnie," I faintly heard Cherie remark.

"Yes, we did!" Sassy yelled back as she ran toward the parking lot, reloading her shotgun.

Corky was the only one who knew his way around, so he led the way through the various backstage hallways until we arrived at the final row of doors leading to the stage area. The music was deafening, but we couldn't see anyone guarding the way. Peaking around the corner of the hallway, we could see the hanging backdrop behind the stage, but no movement. Britt 2.0 and her entire army of dancing minions were still busy performing.

"It's clear," Corky said. "There's only twelve *Sweet Conformity* dancers, right? They can't spare anyone to act as a rearguard."

"Why would they need one?" Mort reminded him. "Everyone they're concerned about is tied up or tranquillized in the closet. So they're letting their guard down. We need to exploit that, somehow."

"But Britt 2.0's still got the stage," I sighed, nervously clutching the twine box. "And twelve goons watching her back. We've got to stay out of sight until she leaves the stage."

As I was speaking, the song and music ended, and we heard Britt 2.0 jubilantly addressing the adoring hordes.

"Thank you, Canada!" she cheered. "Kamloops, I love you!"

Reassured of Britt 2.0's affections, the crowd erupted once more.

"It's been so great being here," Britt 2.0 gushed. "I want to thank *The Fighting Mackenzies* for thinking of me on such short notice, and we wish them both a speedy recovery from their sudden onset lunar-photo lupinomorphosis."

"Hey, that's *my* pseudo-scientific term!" Mort angrily pointed out. "She stole that from my forty-first movie, *A Wimpy Canadian Werewolf in Texas*."

"Quiet!" I growled.

"This must be it!" Corky hissed. "Intermission!"

"We're going to take a short break," Britt 2.0's voice announced, confirming Corky's guess. "But, when we come back, *Sweet Conformity* and I are going to blow the roof off this place! And don't forget that we've got an upcoming special guest appearance by none other than my true love...."

Pause for ecstatic applause....

"That's right, Kamloops!" Britt 2.0 whooped. "Sting Ripblood is taking time out of his shooting schedule to perform my new duet with me tonight!"

"Oh, give me a break," Mort groaned. "He sings, too?"

"I guess 22.3 billion dollars gets you the best possible boyfriend on the market," I said with a deliberate amount of snark.

"What doesn't this guy do?" Mort demanded.

"I read that he can't curl his tongue," Corky reported.

"That doesn't help me," Mort snapped. "Neither can I!"

"Oh, and one more thing," Britt 2.0 was announcing, as if she had just remembered an important detail. "Sting said to let you all know that he's coming straight here from shooting one of the grittiest fight scenes in our upcoming action-drama, *Compound Fracture IV: Greenstick Pinch*, so don't be alarmed if he looks like he's covered from head to toe in quarts of blood. *Heh heh!*"

"I'll say this for her," Corky remarked. "She covers her bases well."

"Sting's not here yet," I realized. "He can't be, or we'd be dead already. She's waiting for him to show up."

"This was their backup plan," Mort guessed. "They didn't know if we'd be going for Megiddo himself, or just for Kelowna. Sting was probably searching for us in Kelowna, because they didn't know we'd be coming here until she told him. Jeepers, this woman isn't just evil, she's *tactical!*"

"Crap, they're coming," Corky said, pushing us down the hall. "Hide!"

We took the nearest door, which turned out to be a mistake. We stumbled into a room full of red roses, powdering stations, and racks of scanty lace costumes. And the room wasn't void of humanity, either. Setting out bottles of eyeliner in neat rows on the counter was none other than MC Morlock, who was apparently a stand-in makeup artist now that Britt 2.0 was operating on a minimal staff. His eyes widened as he realized who had just barged in on him, his crimson-and-purple dreadlocks quivering.

"Horseman of the northern sun!" he exclaimed, thereby confirming that Britt 2.0 was aware of everything. Before I could attempt to reason with the gothic goon, he had seized a bottle of hair spray and a cigarette lighter, and began frantically thumbing the igniter.

"*Die, Bucky!*" he rasped.

We all tried to duck, but only a mist of hair spray enveloped us. The flicking lighter was refusing to spark, leaving the mist of hair product and butane unignited.

"*Reality!*" Corky blurted, charging through the haze of spray and dropping MC Morlock out cold with two left hooks and a right uppercut.

"Holy waffles, this is Britt 2.0's dressing room!" Mort screamed in a whisper. "We've got to get out of here!"

"Too late," I muttered, hearing synchronized footfalls approaching the door like Germans in the streets of Paris. I made a dive for MC Morlock's body, snatching him up and dragging his limp body into the world's tiniest bathroom. Corky and Mort crammed in after me, and we could barely get the door shut behind us. Once it finally did click into place, we couldn't move at all, packed like a can of sardines, and smelling similar to one.

"Go make sure our guests are behaving," Britt 2.0 was ordering as she strode into the dressing room. "Sting should be here to murder them any minute."

"*Yes, Britt 2.0,*" all twelve dancers droned in hypnotic unison. "*It shall be done.*"

"Backup dancers," Mort muttered in disgust. "The

brainless puppets of all evil pop stars. Seriously, getting a GED isn't that hard, and a few computer courses...."

"Shut ... up!" I said through gritted teeth.

"And where the heck is MC Morlock?" Britt 2.0's voice demanded. "I swear I'm sending Sting after him next."

"*Your will is perfect, Britt 2.0,*" the twelve replied.

"Jeepers, and I thought this dude was creepy," Corky whispered, shuddering involuntarily. "And they're going to know that we're gone in about two minutes."

The synchronized footsteps withdrew to the hallway, and we heard the dressing room door close, followed by the sound of Britt 2.0 dialling the house phone.

"Pick it up!" Corky hissed, pointing frantically at the phone on the wall which was already being mashed into my ear in the tight confines. I slowly lifted it to my ear and covered the mouthpiece. I could hear ringing, and then someone on the other end picked up.

"Hey, baby, how far out are you?" Britt 2.0 cooed sweetly.

"Twenty minutes," Sting's voice replied, slightly muffled by the rotor sounds of the new helicopter he had apparently acquired. "Everything under control?"

"Just like I said it would be," Britt 2.0 cackled. "They walked right in. You'll find them in the utility closet by the northeast exit, with *The Fighting Mackenzies*. Oh, and get this. We were all worried about having to watch the audience, but the fools just tried sneaking in from backstage!"

"Ah, of course," Sting said knowingly. "Intermission."

"So predictable, these good guys," Britt 2.0 laughed. "That's what a sense of morality gets you when you mess with pop stars! *Bwa ha ha!* Soon Bucky Laroo will be dead, and Max-Ram Target vanquished, never knowing that his name was at the top of that precious list. And guess who will move up when that happens?"

"What?" Mort whispered, his ear pressed close enough to mine to overhear the conversation. "So it's not a hit list."

"Quiet," I growled.

"What about the skull?" Sting asked.

"Bird in a cage, baby," Britt 2.0 assured him. "The carrot in cowboy boots had the box right in his hands. All you have to do is open the door and let Dr Heckler and Mr Koch do all the talking. Ha! You do have the G36 I gave you for Christmas, right?"

"Never leave the US of A without it," Sting replied.

"We're so set for the big time now," Britt 2.0 gloated. "When Max-Ram dies, all of Hollywood will be ours, and I will transcend the noxious mire of the pop music bog with my new crossover movie career! And killing Bucky Laroo will put even The Establishment in our pocket. The world of entertainment, and the world of science, all at our beck and call.... Glorious."

"It is looking like a good day to be Sting Ripblood and Britt 2.0," Sting admitted, momentarily lapsing from his guarded nature. "It seems so long ago that you started down this path, and all because Beyoncé Knowles told you that you didn't have a chance of crossing over."

"We'll show her yet!" Britt 2.0 chided him. "Oh, it's so fun to be the secret bad guys, like all pop stars! And to think that, only two years ago, you were still clinging to your ridiculous concepts of nobility and honour. You should have met me a long time ago."

"Hey," Sting could not help protesting, "it's not ridiculous to fight with hono–"

"Whatever," Britt 2.0 snorted. "You're still using that conscience, babe, and we talked about that. Letting things get personal, opening the door for emotion, '*We have to tell Karl that his brother is dead,*' yada, yada, yada.... Just remember why we're doing this. This is business, Sting.

With Max-Ram gone, that contract is a shoo-in, and you and I will reign as king and queen of all Hollywood!"

"Fine," Sting sighed. "Just give me twenty minutes and it'll all be over. What about Ronnie and Cherie?"

"Are you crazy?" Britt 2.0 snapped. "I love *The Fighting Mackenzies*! Leave them alone. We'll just buy them off."

"Good point," Sting agreed. "There's truly no greater twin brother and sister country-western duo in all of Canada."

Outraged by what he was overhearing, Corky grabbed the phone from my hand and opened his mouth to yell into it. Fortunately, Mort was able to clamp a hand over his mouth before our position was given away. I wrested the phone back from my brother and covered the mouthpiece again.

"I still have doubts about this plan," Sting was reluctantly confessing. "The whole purpose of this contract was to find a star who could do the job with honour. Not to mention that doublecrossing The Establishment is dangerous. If they figure out that we were the ones who ratted out their hitman to the cops...."

"You know that had to be done," Britt 2.0 said icily. "If P.L. Townes had gotten to Bucky before us, Max-Ram could have been taken out in the crossfire, or rescued, which is even worse. For the sake of control, they both die by our hand, or nobody's. You need to be strong, baby. We're so close, you can't falter now. Are you sure the presenter will show up here?"

"He's been anonymously notified that it all ends there tonight," Sting affirmed.

"Excellent!" Britt 2.0 crowed. "But you need to hurry. We need to clean up the slaughterhouse to create the illusion of honour. Oh yeah, and one more thing. After the cowboy is turned into plant food, we must discuss MC Morlock."

"What?" Sting said. "He's your most loyal minion."

"I know, but he's failed me for the last time," Britt 2.0 grumbled. "I'm stuck here doing my makeup on my own! If I smudge my Lash-Blast, it's over for him."

The phone clicked in my ear as the villainous pop princess hung up. I gently replaced the receiver, and twisted around to look in confusion at Corky and Mort.

"Presenter?" I whispered. "What's she talking about?"

"I don't know," Mort replied. "But it has to be about that contract, whatever it is. Sting's going to try to get it tonight. There must be some kind of deadline."

"MORLOCK!" Britt 2.0 bellowed, which would have made us all jump if the friction from the walls had been removed from our compressed bodies. "Wherever you are, show your Goth face in five seconds, or you're going to meet the mother who died giving birth to you!"

"That is cold," Mort winced.

"Last warning!" Britt 2.0 continued. "5...! 4...! 3...!"

Before she could finish her countdown to disaster, the dressing room door burst open and a single dancer lunged inside, so panicked that he couldn't even wait for the others to catch up and make the announcement in unison.

"Britt 2.0!" he whimpered. "Max-Ram Target and the Prophesied One have escaped! We must get you back onstage before they claim your microphone!"

"*Impossible!*" Britt 2.0 exploded. "Fan out! Search every room! *Find them!*"

"Yes, Britt 2.0! It will be done!"

"And set a guard in the sound booth," Britt 2.0 added. "Claiming a microphone will do them no good if they can't turn it on."

"Your words are wise and filled with power, O Most Magnifice–"

"Just go, you butt-smooching minion!" Britt 2.0
screamed.

"Yes, Britt 2.0!" the minion whined, his footsteps
pattering into the distance.

"Sweet Buddha," Britt 2.0 was muttering as she stormed
out of the room, "I hate working with puppets. And I freakin'
hate Canada!"

As soon as we heard the door close behind her, I opened
the bathroom door, and we all fell out on top of MC Morlock,
who was still unconscious.

"Well, that was fun," I remarked, standing and dusting
myself off, a rather futile gesture considering the layers of
soot and dried mud I was still covered with from the past two
days. "You know, before I started having these adventures, I
had no idea that evil people were so self-aware."

Mort snorted. "Welcome to Hollywood."

Corky was busy binding MC Morlock with his own
five-foot-long dreadlocks as he said, "Okay, we have to get
to that sound booth before they do. If they get there first,
we can't get a word out. And don't even think about getting
on the jumbo-tron."

He heaved MC Morlock back into the bathroom, and
I cracked open the door to the hallway. There was a lot of
clamour, but I could see no one.

"It's clear," I reported. "But we'll never get to the sound
booth and back to the stage in time."

"We'll split up," Mort decided, snatching the box from
my hands. "You two go take care of the sound booth, and
I'll get on stage. Once the crowd recognizes me, it should
be a done deal."

"Be careful, Mort," I grudgingly warned him.

"You too, Bucky," he replied with a smile. "Go!"

We parted ways as we left the dressing room, and Corky
led me in a charge up the flight of stairs to the overlooking

sound booth above the stage. We could see the lit-up control console inside, and the viewing window beyond it, but a lone smirking dancer had filled the doorway before we could gain entrance. With bare feet, grey sweat-pants, and a sleeveless white muscle shirt that actually earned its name quite well, he blocked our way with his toned form, daring us to advance farther.

"Gotta get past me first, cowboys," he sneered, assuming a threatening waltz position. "You think you stand a chance against a mean-streets raised bus-station dancer who never finished high school?"

"Let's knock the hip out of his hop, bro," I growled. "Do you have those rolls of Loonies?"

"No, don't!" Corky said sharply. "Hold your ground, Bucky. Don't move."

"What?" I said, not accustomed to hearing my brother advise against a rumble opportunity.

"Do not attack!" Corky snapped. "I am not kidding here!"

Before I could argue, the music had started again, followed immediately by renewed cheering and applause. Intermission was over.

"You're too late," the dancer gloated. "Oh, and, by the way, I hardwired the music console to only accept a password or remote command from Britt 2.0. You can't stop this concert now."

"Corky, come on," I urged my steadfast brother. "We can figure out a way to kill the music, let's just take this punk down."

"Just look at him, Bucky!" Corky warned me. "Look at the whole crew. They're ... they're...."

"They're what?" I demanded.

"Now I can't remember," Corky admitted. "I want to say East Indian, for some reason."

"We're Puerto Rican, you idiot," the young dancer snarled. "Everyone in *Sweet Conformity* is Puerto Rican-Canadian. Well, Simeon is technically Jewish, but he wants us to keep that on the down-low for the time being."

"What does that have to do with anything?" I asked.

"Are you kidding?" Corky said, glancing skeptically at me. "If they were white, we could just wade in swinging, or even if they were predominantly white with a smattering of other ethnicities thrown in for colour, like the gangs in the movies or *Star Trek*. But two white Protestant rednecks cannot just attack a lone Puerto Rican, no matter how scary his tattoos are. For the record, I think there's established guidelines about rednecks attacking Jews, too."

"Ah, that old chestnut," I said knowingly.

"Hey, I didn't write the rules," the dancer said with a shrug, drawing a tranquillizer pistol from the drawstring of his sweats. "Let's take a walk, carrot-top cowpoke. Sting Ripblood is waiting."

He took a confident step toward us, but was immediately intercepted by the flying sandbag that Mort had hurled at his face from the end of the hall, and knocked flat. Corky lunged forward and snatched up the fallen tranq pistol.

"Are you okay, Bucky?" Mort said, jogging toward us.

"Oh perfect," Corky muttered. "Three white guys take out a Puerto Rican with a sandbag. Tell me that's not a headline."

"Why aren't you on stage?" I asked. "They're starting!"

"They beat me there," Mort said hurriedly. "But Britt 2.0 isn't there yet. It's just the opening dance number. We've still got time, but we've got to go now!"

"But they'll never let us reach the microphone," Corky protested. "They've taken the stage."

"No, think about it," I said. "This is *Sweet Conformity*. They've made their name as the ultimate synchronized dancers, and they'd never give that up in public. All we have to do is outmaneuvre them to the mike. If they want to focus on stopping us, they'll have to break conformity. And that's unthinkable."

"That sounds insane," Corky pointed out, but then began to smile. "On the other hand, I've never had the right to call myself anything else!"

"Let's do this!" Mort roared, picking up the twine box and leading our enthused charge backstage.

The cheering and music were louder than ever as we rushed up the backstairs to the stage and came around the backdrop. However, we were stopped in our tracks by the sight that greeted us.

The other eleven members of *Sweet Conformity* were dancing full-tilt in three spaced rows, dressed in similar sweats and muscle shirts as the one we had sandbagged, but that was not all they had. Each dancer held not one but *two* single-edged swords, making their dance the most awing and lethal thing I had ever seen. With each synchronized leap, twirl, and pose, the points of their respective swords would come within a few centimetres of each other, but they were so disciplined and coordinated that not one clinked against the tip of another.

We could see a lone microphone stand perched on the far edge of the stage. But getting to it would be like navigating through a running lawn mower.

"Hmm, sharp things," Mort mused. "Nice touch."

"Welcome back, Kamloops!" Britt 2.0's voice exclaimed from over the PA system. "Just a reminder from the fire marshal, requesting that you all remain in your seats for the duration of *Sweet Conformity*'s non-traditional Japanese *katana* dance ... which they are performing for no reason in particular. For legal reasons, we would also like to remind you of the injury/fatality waivers which every one of you was legally required to sign prior to entering the auditorium. It's been a great night here at the Coliseum, and it would be a shame if anyone got *turned into mincemeat for ignoring the rules!*"

"How much do you want to bet that our forged signatures will be found on waivers after we're dead?" I asked dryly. "Dang, Britt 2.0 is good at being bad...."

"So they can just hack us to pieces on live television, and it's all our fault?" Corky cringed.

Mort didn't say anything for a long moment. He just stared with a face of stone at the deadly dance crew defying gravity in front of us. His lips were silently moving as he counted beats.

"Mort?" I said.

"Relax, Bucky," he said with a calmer voice than I had ever heard him use. "I've got this. My time in your barn loft has honed my body and mind in ways that you cannot imagine, and it's time to let that new cat out of the bag. It's all about timing with the music. And nobody has more predictable rhythms than Britt 2.0."

Without another word, he charged headlong into the mass of whirling steel and white wife-beaters. Almost instantly, blood was drawn.

"*Mort!*" I squawked. "Get out of there!"

"Crap, he'll never make it!" Corky panicked, drawing out his castrating knife. "I'm going to try to cut the power to the music."

"Like this?" Britt 2.0 growled, appearing behind us and pressing a single remote-control button. The music was silenced in an instant, but *Sweet Conformity* kept dancing faster than ever, with Mort frantically trying to keep up. The roaring of the multitude had ceased as well, as they became too enraptured by the lightning fast game of eleven-on-one Whack-a-Mole being grimly played out on the stage.

Apparently, they assumed that the blonde intruder in the blue cardigan was just a part of the act, in spite of the fact that he had already been nicked by the tanto-point blades at least three times.

"Har har!" Britt 2.0 chortled, strutting back and forth in her typical lace-doily outfit. "You fools! Do you really think I'd let MC Morlock program my army of Jonas Brothers lookalike zombies without a default setting? You can't stop them until the music stops them. And, without music, they'll dance Max-Ram Target right into the floor varnish. He'll be alive, of course. Sting gets to kill him. Nobody else. But the condition he's in when he dies is all up to you. Give me the skull."

"Call them off!" I shouted at her. "He was your husband, for Pete's sake!"

"Thank you, Mr Cowboy, I'll take it under advisement," Britt 2.0 said dryly, smashing the remote to the floor.

"Bucky, I think this was a bad idea!" Mort's voice called back to us, breathing raggedly as he frantically performed gymnastics for dear life. "I'd like to come out now."

"Why, you evil, sexy little...." Corky snarled, raising the tranquillizer pistol and stepping toward Britt 2.0. However, before he had taken two steps, the perpetually black-clad Sting Ripblood appeared around the corner, aiming his aforementioned HK-G36 assault rifle at us.

"Pull the e-brake, cowboy," he cautioned Corky. Corky lowered his tranq gun and froze.

"Now remember what I told you, sweetie," Britt 2.0 chided Sting, stepping over and kissing his cheek. "No more fighting with honour. Murder them quietly in the hallway. Now, if you'll excuse me, it seems that I've got an a cappella number about to start. Gotta be adaptable, right?"

She began to walk primly toward the stage, where Mort was now rolling about on the floor, trying to avoid feet as much as swords. The audience must have thought that this was a comedy piece, because they were now laughing hysterically at the onstage antics, apparently unable to see all the blood that was leaking from Mort's writhing form. It truly seemed that all was lost.

Fortunately, I had all but given up on believing that such a grim outcome would ever be the case.

"*Ah-ha!*" Sassy exclaimed, bounding out from behind a curtain and jabbing a Shocking Silly, Ver.II into Britt 2.0's neck. "Jolly good, and tally-ho, and cheerio, and other assorted triumphant Britishisms!"

"*Blaagh!*" Britt 2.0 squalled as a few hundred volts of low-amp electricity jolted into her jugular vein. She immediately dropped to the floor and lay still.

"What the...?" Sting blurted, just as Corky and I tackled him to the floor, sending his machine gun flying.

"Flank him, Bucky!" Corky hollered, pinning Sting's arms to his sides. "Branding position!"

I seized the crazed action star by his belt and vest, lifting him in the air and slamming him to the ground like a calf on Branding Day.

"Impossible!" Sting cried out, writhing futilely as Corky knelt by his head and I knelt at his feet, stretching him out between us. "You can't defeat me! Cowboy's don't get to change the world!"

"Oh yeah?" I snarled, holding fast to his right shoe and driving my left cowboy boot behind his left knee. "*Neither do actors!*"

Sting's face paled as the truth of the horrifying statement sank in, but then he freaked out and began thrashing wildly.

"Sassy, hit him with the tranq gun!" Corky shouted, kneeling on Sting's head and hanging onto his wrists.

Sassy was already on the move, scooping up the tranq

Lane Bristow

pistol as she dashed toward us. Then she dove straight at Sting with an arcing left hook, smashing the dart pistol across his face.

"I think Corky meant that you should shoot him with the tranq gun," I pointed out, as Sting went limp, momentarily stunned.

"Now it's up to you, Bucky!" Sassy declared, unslinging my fiddle from her back and drawing the bow from her belt. "You're the only one who can save Max-Ram Target."

"How?" I cringed. "That's *Sweet Conformity*. They're unstoppable."

"It's your spotlight now, baby brother," Sassy said, handing me my instrument. "Square dance them away!"

"No...." Britt 2.0 moaned from the floor, groggily trying to rise. "You wouldn't!"

"Okay, I'm bleeding profusely now," Mort interjected from the stage.

"Go, Bucky!" Sassy urged me, grabbing Sting's legs as he began weakly struggling again. "It's the only thing no dancer can resist, and you're the only one who can do it!"

"No, I can't!" I protested. "I only know *The Orange Blossom Special*."

"And he's terrible at it," Corky added.

"And I'm terrible at it," I agreed.

"Don't think it, son!" Sassy insisted. "Feel it. Just let out a 'yee-haw!' and let the music take it from there. That's how I learned to play the oboe."

"You learned to play what?" I said.

"I think a *katana* just nicked my spleen," Mort called out. "Little help here, please!"

Sting was trying to rise again, but Sassy and Corky were holding him fast.

"Do it, Bucky," Corky finally conceded. "We'll take care of this rabble."

"Oh, crap...." I sighed, lunging to my feet and charging onto the stage, tucking my fiddle under my chin on the fly.

Please, Jesus ... if I'm going to die, let it be bad enough to warrant a closed-casket funeral....

Every sword was immediately turned on me as *Sweet Conformity* instinctively adapted their synchronization toward their newest victim. It was clear that Britt 2.0's instructions about taking Mort alive did not apply to me in any way.

Oh well.

"*Yeeeeeeeee-haw!*" I whooped, sawing furiously on the fiddle.

The music was passable, and the effect undeniable. Every dancer immediately held their swords vertical, joined arms with the man nearest to them, and began square-dancing their cares away. It was incredible. By the simple act of forming pairs, their curse of perpetually-perfect synchronization was broken for all time.

Mort was still moving weakly on the stage floor, and the dancers' feet were away from his prone form for the moment. But it's not just the music that makes a great square dance. You've got to call it, and that part was on me, too. I barely had time to think as I kept sawing that fiddle and then began spouting lyrics faster than I could even think of them.

> *"Raise your swords up o'er your heads,*
> *Or you'll put out an eye!*
> *Hold them aloft, just like He-Man,*
> *Let out a Greyskull cry!*

> *Skip to the left! Skip to the right!*
> *Skip back ten steps or more!*
> *Cram real tight against the walls,*
> *Let Max-Ram off the floor!"*

The dancers had no choice but to clear the dance floor as per my directions. However, most of them still had a crazed look in their eyes, and I knew that I had to keep playing to keep them in check.

"'*Step back! Step back!*'" I kept calling out, trying to keep the dancing henchmen against the far wall, away from Mort. "Move, Mort, dang it! '*Step back! Step back...!*'"

Mort was barely able to raise his head from the floor, but I suddenly noticed that he wasn't the only one on the stage floor. Still quivering from the residual currents of her recent cattle-prodding, Britt 2.0 was nevertheless dragging herself across the polished floor, an unshakeable light of determination in her evil eyes.

She was heading straight for the microphone.

"No...." Mort moaned, forcing himself to crawl after her, in spite of the brutal pounding he had just taken.

The audience was completely silent by that point, no doubt trying to figure out exactly what the heck they were looking at. *Sweet Conformity* was lined up against the far wall, skipping in time to my repetitive calls like a skipping record, and Max-Ram Target was in a slow-motion race across the floor with Britt 2.0.

"Oh, come on!" I shouted, still sawing frantically on the fiddle. "Like we really have time for the dramatic slow race! *Move, Mort!*"

I couldn't even stop playing, for fear of the still-armed dancers reverting to their default setting, and no one else was in a position to intervene, either. Corky and Sassy were still trying to keep Sting Ripblood under control, an effort that had sent the three of them rolling out from under the backdrop and across the stage in a tangle of flailing fists and cowboy boots.

"Hold still, little doggie!" Sassy was growling, finally managing to raise the pistol in her fist and fire a tranq dart into Sting's left calf. His leg began going numb, but he was still thrashing madly.

"You know our laws, Max-Ram," Britt 2.0 wheezed, slowly gathering strength as she crawled across the floor. "Once I touch that mike, this has all been for nothing."

"Go, Mort!" I shouted. "'*Step back! Step back...!*'"

"Give it up, babe," Britt 2.0 was jeering. "You can't stop the pop-cultural desensitization of North America, and you can't stop the will of The Establishment, and you can't stop this concert!"

"I promised Bucky...." Mort whispered, pulling himself forward with his forearms.

"Cowboys don't get to change the world, Max-Ram," Britt 2.0 hoarsely reminded him, managing to shakily rise to her hands and knees, no more than ten feet from the mike. "And guys like you don't get theatrical comebacks. Best case scenario, you'll be making independent ensemble dramas with Ray Liotta and Forest Whitaker forever!"

"*Never!*" Mort croaked.

They were both nearing the base of the microphone stand, but both were also nearing the end of their strength.

"Face reality, Max-Ram," Britt 2.0 muttered, pulling herself hand-over-hand up the tall pole, the microphone within inches of her hand. "The day of the 80s action hunk is over. The day of the pop star and flashy CGI is at hand."

"*Yaah!*" Mort roared, scrambling to his feet and diving for the microphone. He collided with his ex-wife, and the two of them toppled to the floor, the mike underneath them.

There was a brief struggle, and then a lone hand arose from the pileup, the squelching microphone in its grasp.

A hand with red nail polish.

"Oh...." I said, my fiddling beginning to trail off in defeat. "Fish poop in a bowl."

Sometimes, it can be a real burden being determined to go through life without using real curse words.

Britt 2.0 was smirking down at Mort as she rose to her knees, the microphone triumphantly held aloft. Then she brought it to her lips, and addressed the stunned audience.

"Welcome back, Kamloops!" she said teasingly. "Who here is ready to rock out like it's ninetee–"

She was silenced in an instant as Mort's bloody right hand shot up and clamped over the microphone, his eyes dark and menacing. The audience's horrified gasp was almost as loud as their cheering had been a few moments earlier, creating a noticeable amount of suction that dragged a few pieces of loose sheet music across the stage. I was just as shocked, the fiddle bow dropping from my fingers as I lost my concentration. The sudden absence of music meant that *Sweet Conformity* was now free to finish hacking us all to bits, but even they had stopped dancing, their mouths hanging open and their swords clattering to the floor. Silence and stillness filled the auditorium for fifteen endless seconds, a silence that was only broken when Sassy finally blurted, "Holy crap, he's Kanye Westing her!"

Mort sat up determinedly, and wrenched the microphone out of Britt 2.0's trembling hand, in defiance of all celebrity laws. Britt 2.0 could only push herself back in awe, staring at the ultimate day-seizing man's man whom she had let get away.

It took Mort another few moments to rise shakily to his feet, the final tattered remnants of his third borrowed shirt fluttering to the floor.

"Everybody in this auditorium," he instructed hoarsely, "just shut the crap up, and listen. My name is has-been Hollywood action hunk Max-Ram Firewall Target. I am here tonight on behalf of my oldest and truest friend, Bucky Laroo, a good cowboy, with no middle name that I am aware of, who has discovered a living dinosaur.... Well, actually he discovered a living prehistoric aquatic reptile that coexisted with the dinosaurs, and he accidentally killed it, but ... whatever. A lot of really smart people have been trying to kill him for even making the discovery, but I'm here to tell all of you, and everyone watching from across Canada and beyond, that it all ends right now. Anybody who tries to kill Bucky Laroo from this point on will answer to me. Bucky?"

"I love you, Max-Ram," Britt 2.0 gasped in sudden revelation.

"We'll talk later," Mort assured her. "Bucky?"

I awkwardly stepped toward my celebrity friend, who graciously handed me the microphone.

"Dr Harmon Megiddo," I said clearly, still quivering with adrenaline. "If you're in the audience, there's something you, and everyone in the world, needs to see."

From several rows back on the arena floor, a portly man with a large dark beard and larger spectacles stood up, and cautiously began walking down the aisle toward the stage.

I turned to retrieve the twine box, only to find it already being presented to me, and by Sting Ripblood, no less. With a look of honourable, if weary, defeat in his shiny black eyes, he placed the box in my hands, turned away, and limped off the stage. We all watched him walk away. It was impossible not to. The guy was just too cool, and the limp from his tranquillized left leg somehow made him look even cooler.

Mort was helping Dr Megiddo onto the stage by the time I returned to the microphone with the box. I shook the hand of the stone-faced scientist, and placed the box in his hands.

"That's it," I said, glad to be rid of the thing. "That should answer any questions you may ha–"

"*Horseman!*" a demented scream cut in from behind us.

"*What the crap?*" I heard Corky blurt.

I spun around to see MC Morlock charging full-tilt across the stage, his skinny arms managing to support the two hundred pound anvil that he carried above his head, his chewed-off dreadlocks snapping in the wind behind him.

"My own hair cannot keep me shackled!" he shouted as he bore down on us. "*This one's for you, Mom!*"

"Bucky, look out!" Mort roared, his years of action movie theatrics finally paying off as he executed a perfect Max-Ram Lateral Corkscrew Power Dive®, knocking me and Dr Megiddo out of harm's way. However, the box was dropped in the process, and the anvil was flung mightily upon it a second later, reducing the much-debated skull to ground powder in an instant.

"Are you *crazy?!*" I exploded at MC Morlock.

"I'm Goth," he replied evenly. "What was your first clue?"

He never got a chance to say anything else, as Corky had snatched up the tranq pistol and rapidly fired all fourteen darts into the crazed choreographer's back.

"I'm running away from the light!" MC Morlock proclaimed with a great amount of pride as he pitched forward onto his face and began to snore.

"*Dang*, that guy's creepy!" Corky muttered, shaking his head in disbelief as he lowered the empty dart gun.

Mort and Britt 2.0 were helping Dr Megiddo to his feet, but all I could see was my precious cardboard box and the two hundred pound piece of metal sitting on top of it.

"No, no, no, no, *no!*" I said despairingly, falling to my knees beside the flattened box and heaving the anvil off it. It was to no avail. The Ogopogo skull was nothing but a pile of drifting white dust.

I'm not ashamed to say it. I wanted to cry. I'm a little bit ashamed to say that I actually did start to cry as I knelt on that stage in front of a national audience, but I have to tell you what happened, whether I'm proud of it or not.

"It's okay, Bucky," a kind voice said, as a kind hand was rested kindly on my shoulder. Perhaps it was all the kindness, and the distraction of my own blubbering, that kept me from recognizing that the person standing over me was my sister until I looked up at her, but Sassy just smiled.

"It's okay, little red," she said. "I did what you said. I've got this."

It was only as she stepped toward the microphone that I noticed my fiddle case was in her hands.

"Attention, world!" she cried out, holding my fiddle case aloft and flipping open the lid. "I give you the living past ... in the present!"

There was a long pause as the audience only reacted with confused murmuring, not sure of what they were supposed to be looking at. Noticing this, Sassy lowered the fiddle case and looked inside. After a few moments, she began biting her lip.

"Okay, in retrospect, a few air holes might have been a good idea," Sassy dutifully admitted. "But it was alive five minutes ago, I swear. Ladies and gentlemen, I give you the very recently deceased past ... in the pres–!"

"No!" I blurted, snatching the case from her hands and gingerly lifting the limp hatchling from it. I set its slippery body supine on the floor, and frantically began performing CPR, encircling my hands around the small rib-cage and compressing the area over where I figured its heart would be with my thumbs. "Come on, wake up, you stupid lizard! You're not going extinct again!"

"I'll help you, Bucky!" Corky declared, dropping to his knees beside me and producing a CPR pocket mask from his denim jacket. "Boy, it's a good thing I never leave the house without this thing. Is two-person CPR still at a rate of 15 compressions and 2 ventilations for infants, or is the provincial standard 10 and 1 across the board now?"

"Just kiss the dinosaur!" I shouted.

"Fine," Corky said. "Ignore the established guidelines clinically proven to increase the likelihood of ROSC."

"Kiss it!" I rasped, quietly singing *Another One Bites The Dust* through clenched teeth in order to properly time my compressions, assuming that dinosaur rates were the same as human.

"You're supposed to sing *Staying Alive* by the *Bee Gees*, you freak," Sassy reminded me.

"Only because it's less disturbing to bystanders," I snapped. *"Another One Bites The Dust* has a more distinctive beat."

"Touché," Sassy admitted.

"Bucky, it's dead," Mort squeamishly pointed out, staring down at the small creature's loosely flopping flippers.

"Everyone who's ever had CPR was dead!" I snarled, still delivering timed compressions with both thumbs. "Death is inconclusive."

"Here, allow me," Sassy volunteered. Without another word of warning, she produced the Shocking Silly, Ver.II from her pocket and jabbed it into the Pogo's chest.

The electrical jolt passed through the dragon's body and into me and Corky, sending all three of us several feet across the floor. I felt as if my brain had been doused with gasoline and set on fire.

"Clear!" Sassy announced, the palm-sized cattle prod already back in her pocket.

For a long time, I could only lie numbly on the floor, staring at the ceiling and listening to the Seven Dwarves whistling cheerful show tunes within my shorting cerebellum. When I was finally able to move again, I lolled my head to one side, and found myself staring into the green eyes of a curious little blue sea serpent, a micro-sized spitting image of its mother.

"*Meh*," it said to me, craning its neck forward and sniffing my face. "*Meh. Boof.*"

"You're the Ogopogo," I said in a daze.

"*Meh, meh!*" the Pogo replied, waddling toward me, still trying to figure out how its flippers worked.

A minute later, I was standing in front of the microphone with the hatchling in my arms. I didn't have to say anything. I just stood there listening to the rippling murmurs of shock and awe working their way through the crowd.

"Hi," I finally said. "I'm Bucky Laroo."

OF PROTEIN AND
PLESIOSAURS
◇◇◇◇◇◇◇◇◇◇◇◇◇◇◇◇◇◇◇◇◇◇◇

I N A WAY, I guess it was the beginning of the end as I stood there on that stage, but it was a pretty drawn out ending, and more and more reporters and camera crews seemed to be pouring into the Coliseum every second. Some police began showing up, too, prompting Britt 2.0 and *Sweet Conformity* to make a discreet exit, leaving MC Morlock to face the music on their behalf. Once everyone was assembled, the grilling began in earnest.

First, Dr Megiddo looked the creature over thoroughly, and pronounced that it truly was a plesiosaurus. Then I had to tell the entire story of how I had found and killed its mother, leaving out enough details to prevent Corky and Sassy from going to jail. Then a bunch of women came to the stage for Mort's autograph, while simultaneously offering to bandage his multitude of lacerations. After that, there was a lot of questions about the Ogopogo, some curious and fascinated, and some downright hostile. I remember one professor in the third row from a university that I don't feel like endorsing right now, who refused to accept that plesiosaurs had been living with humans all along. Finally, unable to deny the obvious any further, she stood up and announced, "Well, ladies and gentlemen of the press, I would like to go on the record and state that I am now a believer ... in localized interdimensional rips in the space-time continuum, which, by means of a mechanism not yet discovered, have allowed beings from the past to enter our modern world!"

"What in tarnation would cause something like that, lab coat?" Sassy demanded as the crowd gasped in horror.

"Beats me," the professor replied. "Aliens, maybe. Honestly, Bucky, I would be interested to know what your theory is."

"Mine's pretty basic," I said, figuring I might as well get it out in the open. "Hi, my name is Bucky, and I'm a young-earth Creationismist."

"*Hi, Bucky*," the portion of the crowd that wasn't glaring at me replied.

Possibly I should have stopped there, but, for some reason, I kept going.

"I'm also anti-choice, I believe sexual orientation is a myth, and I don't think women should be allowed to wear shoes until age twenty-one. I'm pro-meat, pro-fur, pro-leather, and I believe that ninety percent of reality television shows are scripted and reenacted. Seriously, folks, how do you think they get crane shots on *Mantracker*?"

Suck it up and cinch it up.

"Bucky," the professor in the audience said patiently, "putting aside all of my boiling rage for the moment, we've been over this. For years, we've been over this. God is something you're free to believe in, but you can't show Him to us. I can show you science. Right here and now, I could recreate the Miller Experiment. I could create amino acids, the building blocks of life, in a test-tube, and show them to you. At the end of the day, how does your King James Bible compete with that?"

I really didn't know what to say. I wasn't a preacher, and I sure as heck wasn't a scientist. The whole auditorium was silent, though, as if expecting the answer of one or the other to come out of my mouth. But I couldn't think of a single word.

As it turned out, it was Sassy to the rescue again.

"I'm all over this, Bucky," she announced, snatching the microphone away from me, emboldened both by Mort's example and by the fact that I would never be a celebrity in her mind. "Okay, bunson burn lady, and everyone else, my name is Sassy Laroo, and I graduated high school with honours in metal shop. And, from what I recall of my science classes, the Miller Experiment didn't *quite* answer all the pertinent questions I had about life formation. Allow me to expound.

"In 1953, a graduate student named Stanley Miller designed a spark chamber for an experiment on the formation of life from basic elements and compounds, including methane, ammonia, water vapour, and hydrogen as a re-creation of a primitive atmosphere. It is perhaps interesting to note that oxygen was not present in the chamber, as it would have oxidized the other components too quickly.

"Instantly, we can see that this experiment cannot be an accurate re-creation of prehistoric atmospheric conditions, as the ozone layer, which is made of oxygen, blocks the ultraviolet radiation which would otherwise destroy the ammonia. Since amino acids cannot form without ammonia, the entire experiment was proceeding on a flawed reducing atmosphere assumption. Furthermore, fossil evidence, such as amber bubbles, indicates that in the past our atmosphere had fifty percent or more oxygen than it currently does, so it was most likely present when that first unicellular life form on the bottom of the sea was trying to get off the starting blocks.

"Miller's experiment also included a trap beneath the chamber to collect and protect the newly-formed amino acids, as continued exposure to the sparking gases would have destroyed them. This is another problem for the evolution of primordial soup, as energy is required to form an amino acid, but will also subsequently destroy them if they are not protected, and the bottom of the ocean has no such defensive mechanism that I, or anyone else, is aware of.

"The amino acids created by the experiment formed only 2% of the disgusting red goo that was collected in the trap. The remainder of the booger box was 85% tar and 13% carboxylic acid, both of which are obviously toxic. Having the building blocks of life appearing in a mixture that is 98% toxic does not make our first living cell's chances of survival anymore promising. Being in the ocean isn't going to help matters, either, since the formation of proteins from amino acids in a closed system results in an equilibrium reaction that yields water. As the water concentration increases, the reaction reverses, and the protein disintegrates. We see similar occurrences in the process of hydrolosis, wherein nucleotides are driven apart as they release energy in the water. An incredible amount of energy would be required to forge chemical bonds under optimal conditions, and water really is one of the furthest things from optimal that I can think of.

"Anyway, Miller's Experiment created two types of amino acids out of the twenty known varieties. That, in and of itself, is not problematic. But the fact that a 50/50 of mirror-image amino acids were created, as also occurs in other natural processes, is very problematic.

"These opposite amino acids, informally referred to as left-handed and right-handed, combine easily in natural environments if they come into contact with each other.

However, the links of amino acids which form proteins in life forms contain only the left-handed varieties. When you consider the fact that the number of amino acids in a protein chain ranges anywhere from 100 to nearly 27,000, for an average of 400, it becomes clear that the formation of a single protein by way of natural processes is delving far beyond the realm of long odds. In fact, biochemists have calculated the odds of an all left-handed chain forming, without incorporating a single readily-available right-handed amino acid into the mix, at approximately 1 in 4x10 to the 121st power. It should be noted that the bonding of a single right-handed amino acid renders the entire chain inactive.

"To further complicate matters, proteins are symbiotic with DNA, as it has been repeatedly demonstrated that neither one can exist without the coding and direction of the other. Unless the scaffolding theory has come up with something conclusive for once, the problem here is that the structural units of DNA chains are three-portion chemical compounds known as nucleotides, which consist of a heteracyclic base, one or more phosphate groups, and a sugar. Much like the mirror-image amino acid problem, sugars combine so readily with amino acids that the two compounds effectively cancel each other out, making them incapable of continued protein or DNA formation. This means that fully interdependent chromosomes had to form without ever coming into contact with their respective component parts.

"Oh, and, just for the record, sugars also occur naturally in left-handed and right-handed varieties. Only the right-handed ones are found in life forms. Again, we just might be going beyond long odds.

"In order for nucleotides to bond in the first place, they require two things: A heck of a lot of energy, and the combined workings of at least one hundred protein enzymes. So the nucleotide links can only be bonded into DNA by enzymes which cannot form without the coding of DNA. And we haven't even got to protein function yet, which needs to be determined before life can start.

"As a new protein is created within a fully-formed cell, it folds itself in less than a second over the course of its short journey to link up with the other proteins, and this folding determines the function. Along the way, specific chaperone proteins direct the folding of the newbies. On an interesting side note, the formation of chaperone proteins is supervised by, you guessed it, other chaperone proteins.

"So the bottom line is that our first protein forming on the bottom of the ocean could not even fold without the help of hundreds of other proteins at the very least, and the folding is critically precise. Chemically identical proteins can be properly folded into healthy functions, or misfolded into deadly diseases.

"Assuming, just for a moment, that our first few hundred proteins manage to form, fold, and avoid contact with the concurrently forming nucleotides, all by random chance in the exact same location at the bottom of a Godless ocean, life still can't get traction quite yet. Not only does the protein have to make the battleship, it also has to navigate it to precisely the right docking area in the interconnected chain of preexisting proteins. There are literally billions of wrong destinations, even in our only partially-formed cell, but there may be only a single correct one, and improper connection of proteins can cause disease.

"In 1999, the Nobel Prize for Medicine went to Dr Guenter Blobel for his discovery of amino acid address tags which direct proteins to their correct position within the chromosome. Let's just add that little formation into our calculation of random chance odds, shall we?

"Apparently, the odds can't be too long yet, because

Biology classes in our university-level educational centres are the first ones to inform us that evolution is a fact. So they have obviously also factored in the odds of proteins not only forming, but also regulating their own formation. You see, every living cell needs an on/off switch to prevent the forming proteins from continuing to form until the cell literally bursts from overfill. These controlling mechanisms are known as regulatory DNA sequences, which can only operate interdependently with specialized proteins. Regulatory proteins fold perfectly to attach to the regulatory DNA segment, and together they form the on/off switch. Again, we're seeing that protein production is only possible with the combined workings of preexisting proteins and DNA, both of which need to be fully formed on the bottom of the ocean before the primordial soup can come to life. And, again, I'm sure that the scaffolding theory has rendered moot everything that I'm saying.

"Speaking of fully formed, it has been calculated that the odds of a single DNA strand forming by chance is somewhere in the neighbourhood of 1 in 10 to the $119,000^{th}$ power. To put this number into perspective, the diameter of the visible universe in inches is only 10 to the 28th power. And, if you really want to have fun measuring something in inches, try measuring the less-than two tablespoons of DNA found in a 50 trillion cell human body if all the chromosomes were laid end-to-end. I'll give you a hint. It's 17,067,825,747,224,146.98 inches, or roughly 550,000 return trips to the moon, assuming a surface-to-surface distance.

"But I digress. Let's stick with protein evolution for now as the Biology class textbooks always seem to, ignoring the formation of DNA altogether.

"We're going to skip ahead to a time when random chance has defied the odds and created a complete protein, which, by association, means a complete chromosome count within a complete unicellular life form. Based on what we know about minimum life requirements for the simplest of life functions, we can assume that this cell has at least 250 perfectly placed and folded proteins. We will further assume that, like all known life forms, it contains the enzyme Cytochrome C and its 38 invariant amino acids. And we'll frost the cake with an active genome count of 20,000, putting it in the same genome ranges as cnidarians, widely considered to be among the most primitive of all life forms, and humans.

"Once all of these basic factors, and various others, come together by random freaking chance, our protein is more or less considered to be alive in the technical sense, and is therefore ready to start evolving. Now we're cooking with gas and burning vegetable shortening and a glass of water. All we have to do to get started is completely reorganize the various links of amino acids, called side chains, in a single protein. Once that's done, evolution is off and running.

"Protein side chains occur in hydrophobic and hydrophillic varieties ... much like dogs, except that you don't have to shoot hydrophobic side chains in the head with a .375 Magnum before they bite you and give you rabies. Because hydrophobic side chains are oily, and thus repelled by water, they are usually found in the core of the protein, unless the protein is located in an equally hydrophobic environment, such as a cell membrane. Hydrophillic side chains are generally located on the outside of the protein, with similar exceptions. The basic shape of the protein is largely dependent on the arrangement, or sequence, of these different chains. In order for the shape of the protein to change, let alone evolve, the chain must be completely reorganized, which would destroy the protein. Even without altering the sequence, the occurrence of too many hydrophobic chains on the outside of a protein can cause the surface to become sticky. This can lead to proteins sticking together, which, in turn, can cause disease. As an example, sickle cell disease, which is also called sickle cell anaemia and is another celebrated proof of evolution in action, occurs through a mutation of haemoglobin which replaces a single hydrophillic side chain with a hydrophobic one, leading to eventual cell disruption and subsequent vaso-occlusive crisis. Again, we are only left with detriment to the existing protein, to say nothing of its respective life form, with no increase in genetic information. So, in order for evolution to take place, the protein sequence would have to be completely altered in such a way as to create a new and, more importantly, viable and undiseased protein, and now I think we've gone from long odds to genuine mathematical impossibility.

"By the way, I did bring a camera, and you can all get your photo taken with baby Pogo here for five bucks. Any questions...? Okay, nice meeting you all. Bucky?"

She then handed the microphone back to me and walked off the stage, leaving the audience in awkward silence. I had nothing left to say. I traded Dr Megiddo the microphone in exchange for the baby Pogo, and hurried to catch up with my sister, with Corky and Mort close behind me.

"Sassy!" I called out in awe, as we ran out into the darkness of the back parking lot.

"What's up, baby bro?" she said mildly, popping a stick of chewing gum into her mouth.

"That was ... really breathlessly long," I said.

Sassy just shrugged. "I've always had a photogenic memory, Bucky."

"Yeah, great speech, Sassy," Junior agreed.

"Thanks, babe," Sassy acknowledged, then had to do a

double-take. "Wh-what? *Junior?* Snookum crackers! Where did you come from?"

"I came from the pits of an empty and anguished soul," Junior Van Der Snoot dramatically replied, apparently having followed us out from the auditorium. "Sassy Laroo, I love you more than anything, and I'm not waiting anymore. I've got a chartered plane to Vegas and a Barry Manilow impersonator on standby. Let's do it, Sassy. Let's get married, tonight!"

"Sweetness!" Sassy roared, bouncing up and down, and then pouncing on Junior. "My dream wedding! You figured it out, what I couldn't figure out all these years! Yes, let's do it!"

"How did you know we were here?" I asked.

"Oh, that," Junior casually admitted. "Actually, I came to ask Cherie Mackenzie out on a real date, since that drunken fling we had a couple weeks ago doesn't really count. But then I saw Sassy locked in mortal combat with Sting Ripblood, and I just knew she was the only woman for me, and I had to get her back."

"Wait a second," Sassy said, stopping to look at all the facts. "You had a plane and a Barry Manilow preacher on standby without even knowing that I was here? What did you say about Cherie Mackenzie a second ago?"

"I don't recall," Junior replied.

"I do," I piped up.

"Silence, Bucky," Sassy said grimly. Then she abruptly reverted to giddy, and exclaimed, "Well, destiny doesn't slap you in the face harder than this! *Whoohoo!* Dream wedding, here I come! So long, Bucky and Corky and fat remnants of Max-Ram Target! I'll bring you back a snowglobe! Junior, do you have a pen and napkin? I need to take this newfound sense of overflowing jubilation and write a song with it!"

After only a brief farewell, the happy couple hopped

onto Junior's bicycle and rode off into the night, with Sassy calling back her request for us to not eat the Pogo until she got back, as she was quite curious about how it would taste by then. Corky and I readily agreed to this. It seemed like the least that we could do for our sister on her wedding day.

No sooner had the wedding bike disappeared into the darkness than a second figure emerged from it, this one lacking all of the confidence and joy that Junior had exuded. It was Sting Ripblood, stumbling toward us with a half-empty bottle of tequila in his hand. We watched him nervously as he approached, trying to ascertain whether or not the man was still armed.

"Do you have any idea," he slowly asked, stopping in front of us, "how many traitorous, heartbreaking wiseguys never managed to turn State's evidence against Boston's Irish crime syndicates because of me? Do you know how many?"

"No," Corky replied for all of us.

"All of them!" Sting barked. "I stopped all of them! Tommy-Gun O'Flannagan would have been in the big house six years ago if not for me. But one stupid cowboy and Max-Ram Target can get to the stage, and I can't do a thing about it. And now Britt 2.0 says she's leaving me because I'm not half the man that Max-Ram Target is!"

"She said that?" Mort said, suddenly intrigued.

"Stole 22.3 billion and tried to kill us all," I quipped, hoping the quick reminder was blunt enough to remove any rekindled romantic ideas from his head.

"Yes, she said that," Sting muttered. "With scorn and disdain for me, and sincere adoration for you."

He was tossing away his bottle as he spoke, and then pulled the G36 out from under his shiny black trenchcoat.

"Whoa, horsey!" Corky and I roared, holding our hands

out pleadingly. However, all Sting did was toss the weapon onto the pavement.

"I'm no longer worthy to carry an unlicensed firearm in Canada," he said morosely. "Do you have a Samurai sword on the bus that I can borrow for just a couple of seconds?"

"No," Corky said, gesturing toward the Bucky-Paver. "But I can make you a cup of hot chocolate with extra marshmallows. The big pink ones."

"That would be really nice," Sting said tearfully, pausing to pet the Pogo in my arms on the head. "Hey there, little guy."

"*Meh*," Pogo replied, nuzzling Sting's hand.

"Are you just going to leave that machine gun lying in the parking lot?" I asked.

"Silence, Bucky!" the others admonished me, already boarding the bus, while visions of marshmallows danced in their heads.

"I will gladly be silent," I assured them. "Can you take me to a hospital, please? I've been getting lead poisoning in my shoulder for a couple of hours now."

Mort and Sting wanted to get away from the crowds of fans and reporters and scientists, so Corky agreed to my request. Sting dismissively left his new helicopter in the parking lot as we got in the bus and drove away, enjoying the cool breeze from the shot-out windows. And Corky reluctantly loaned Mort yet another one of his shirts.

At the hospital, Mort and I were treated for our respective *katana*, fishhook, and shotgun injuries, with Sting keeping a respectful vigil by our sides. Meanwhile, Corky sweet-talked some raw fish off the hospital's cafeteria staff. When the rest of us returned to the parking lot, he had minced the slab of salmon up with his castrating knife, and was sitting on the hood of an ambulance, feeding the smelly mess to our baby dinosaur from a plastic sandwich bag. The Pogo was gratefully gulping it down.

"Small bites," I couldn't help warning the small creature. "Itty-bitty bites. And we should probably keep it out of sight for a while."

"I really need that hot chocolate now," Sting reminded us, still a bit morose.

"So?" Mort asked him as we boarded the bus once more. "Are you going to tell us why exactly you were trying to kill us? Honestly, I can't believe I forgot to ask you that until now. We know it had something to do with a list and a contract."

"I can't bear to even say the words," Sting admitted, gesturing toward the end of the bus as I clicked on the lights. "But I'm sure he'll tell you."

The rest of us were quite startled to realize that, in our absence, the bus had been boarded by an imposingly muscular bald man in his fifties, wearing a dark three-piece suit that probably cost more than the bus itself. He was sitting calmly at the kitchenette dining table, drinking from a glass of Corky's vintage reserve-label chocolate milk.

"Hey, Max-Ram," he said mildly. "Just the man I've been looking for."

"*Bruce Willis?*" I blurted, my heart nearly stopping as I recognized the Hollywood action hunk that Mort and Sting could only dream of being.

"You can call me that, Bucky," he agreed. "However, for certain unspecified reasons of legal security, I am going to state for the record that I may just be a character who looks and sounds exactly like Bruce Willis, and has all of his nuances and mannerisms, including left-handedness."

"Bruce Willis is left-handed?" I whispered to Corky.

"Gun hands don't lie, Bucky," he assured me, still preoccupied with making Sting's hot chocolate. Apparently, he had grown accustomed to superstars stopping by his bus uninvited a long time ago. "Just like Morgan Freeman and Angelina Jolie."

"What are you doing here, Da– uh, I mean, Bruce Willis?" Mort asked, looking a bit pale in the presence of one of his greatest heroes.

"'Da–?'" Bruce Willis queried, raising an eyebrow.

"Dunn," Mort explained awkwardly. "David Dunn, your character in *Unbreakable*. I always associate you with him."

"That movie was so awesome," Corky remarked. "I don't care what the critics say, it kicked the crap out of *The Sixth Sense*."

"It really did, didn't it?" Sting agreed, before launching into a passable Samuel L. Jackson impression. "'*You know why, David...? Because of the kids!*'"

"'*They called me Mr Glass!*'" Corky, Mort, and I gleefully joined in the memorable line from M. Night Shyamalan's overlooked 2000 classic.

"It gives me goosebumps every time," I confessed, shaking my head admiringly.

Bruce Willis just stared at us, and then asked, "Are you finished?"

"Sorry, Bruce Willis," I apologised on behalf of the group. "Historically, we're an easily sidetracked bunch."

"Well, well, Sting," Bruce Willis commented, smiling inscrutably at his cowering protege. "Word gets around in the Hollywood circles, and I hear that you've been snooping around like a regular little Nancy Drew for the past year, so I assume you know why I'm here."

"Please call me The Hardy Boys, not Nancy Drew," Sting requested, cringing.

"I'll call you The Bobbsey Twins the next time you stick your nose where it doesn't belong," Bruce Willis snapped. "What happened to you, man? You used to be all about honour. But a helicopter ambush and a grenade launcher? How'd you come to that?"

"I've been dating a pop star," Sting said miserably.

"Ah, of course," Bruce Willis said understandingly. "Well, shame on you anyway. Even if you had defeated Max-Ram, you wouldn't be worthy of the contract. You have brought dishonour to all action hunks. And now that Max-Ram has defeated you, I'd say the matter is settled."

"*No!*" Sting could not help crying out in horror.

"Actually," I had to point out, "it was kind of me and Corky and Sassy who defea–"

"*Bucky, shut up!*" Mort said with a lot more severity than usual. "Please continue, Bruce Willis."

"You seriously have no idea what's going on?" Bruce Willis clarified, slowly standing and straightening his suit. "You were just defending this Canadian out of loyalty and friendship?"

"Of course," Mort said proudly. "Bucky's my best friend. Well, actually he's my only friend, but I'm working on that."

"Then your ignorance makes you all the more worthy," Bruce Willis applauded him. "It proves that you accomplished this task with purity of heart."

"I did?" Mort said. "What task? What?"

"Back in the early 90s," Bruce Willis explained, "some of the leading action stars and filmmakers began a secret experiment, in order to renew and revitalize the brawny action hero genre of the 80s. They were looking for the next great action star. Various unknown musclemen and martial artists were selected from around the world, and vetted against one another in feats of strength and combat skills, although fights to the death were considered acceptable as well, if they were honourable and kept discreet enough.

However, this experiment was ultimately considered to be the greatest Hollywood blunder of the decade."

"*Hudson Hawk*?" Sting quipped bitterly, slumped in the driver's seat as he nursed his shattered ego.

Bruce Willis glared at him. "No. Worse than that."

"What was worse than that?" Mort asked, quite confused.

Bruce Willis had to give a slight shudder before replying, "Jeff Speakman."

"Holy cow cud," I winced.

"Yeah," Bruce Willis glumly agreed. "That's what we get for letting George Lucas chair a search committee. Action cinema was this close to never recovering, and then John Woo and Michael Bay came swinging in to finish it off while it was already down."

"Travesty...." Mort whispered, blinking away tears.

"It has been kind of a dark decade for action movies, hasn't it?" I recalled. "Did you know that Tobey Maguire was the highest-paid action star of the last decade? And then we've got Adrien Grenier playing an action star on HBO's *Entourage*, and people are actually supposed to believe it? What's the world coming to?"

"Man, that show stinks," Corky remarked.

"It really, really does," Sting emphatically agreed. "Just when you thought that *Fastlane* with Peter Facinelli was the bottom of the barrel...."

"No kidding," Bruce Willis grunted. "It's taken fifteen years for the world to start missing the classic action of the 80s: Gritty, raw, old-school stuff. Not just a bunch of slow-mo and wire stunts and skinny pretty-boys with great hair who actually win in fistfights. *Get real!* Pretty-boys get their puckered byoo-toxes handed to them in a box in the real world. But the times are changing, and, with classic action hunks like you and Sting and Mark Wahlberg making the rounds, we knew that it was time to make our move. You're the children who lived the action of the 80s. You're the only ones who can bring it back. Or, at least, one of you can. And, call me crazy, but I'd say the one of you who *wasn't* trying to murder his primary competition is the one who deserves it most. And this was a secondary consideration, but we also figured that it would be wisest to give the prize to the man whose films have generated a quarter of a trillion dollars globally. Our bottom line does have to factor in somewhere."

"It's not fair!" Sting moaned, now weeping openly. But the numbers didn't lie. Thus far, his films had generated less than an eighth of a trillion dollars, including merchandising.

"Max-Ram Target," Bruce Willis announced, producing a brown scroll from his suit jacket and unrolling it, "on behalf of all 80s action hunks, and the combined wisdom of Hollywood, it is my great pleasure to award you ... The McTiernan Contract!"

"Who writes scrolls on papyrus anymore?" I had to ask under my breath. "Actually, who writes scrolls at all?"

Mort looked stunned as he accepted the scroll, and gasped aloud as he began reading it.

"Is this...?"

"Yes, it is!" Bruce Willis proclaimed. "This one-of-a-kind contract entitles you to star in fifty major Hollywood action films of the quality that only the great American director John McTiernan could previously have hoped to achieve. In addition, you will receive this cheque for 500 million dollars, all the martial art and combat training you want, and extensive subliminal advertising venues within Subway and McDonald's commercials to ensure that each film is eagerly anticipated by every known weight demographic, thereby ensuring that each and every one of your movies is a blockbuster hit!"

"Holy beet roots!" Mort blurted.

"It's just not fair!" Sting wailed.

"Hot chocolate?" Corky offered, handing our distraught guest a steaming mug.

"Subliminal what?" I had to ask.

"Silence, Bucky," Bruce Willis replied, putting his hands on Mort's trembling shoulders. "The movies need you, Max-Ram. They need you to bring back the lost days, when actors were actors, and action hunks were action hunks. Now everybody has this crazy idea that the two are somehow connected. We need to nip this disgusting trend in the bud. And only you can do it. It's you, Max-Ram. It's your time. Your destiny. Visionary directors, talented actors.... It has to stop. Fulfill your destiny, and bring back the glory days of the 80s. Take the brains out of the bullets, Max-Ram. Put bullets back into the brains."

"Holy hole!" Mort squawked. "Bucky, did you hear that? A contract named in honour of the great John McTiernan! His films have influenced so many parts of my life, in so many subtle ways!"

"Well, if you look back carefully over even recent events," I noted, "you'll probably find that he's subtly influenced almost all of us."

"I'm back!" Mort yammered, beginning to bounce up and down on his toes. "I haven't been this elated since the day I first realized that my dashing Hollywood smile could bring me even more profit and notoriety if I used it to smuggle drugs through airports in my incomparably deep facial dimples! This is the greatest day of my life! I'm back!"

"Great," I said, somewhat less enthusiastic. "You're back."

"You did what with your dimples?" Bruce Willis asked, cringing.

"I'm back!" Mort hollered once again, running to the open door and holding his scroll aloft for the entire empty parking lot to drink in. "Forget fulfilment in literary legacy! Forget meaningful contribution to society! *I'm Max-Ram Target!* Do you hear me, world? *'Max-Ram's back! All right!'*"

He did a Max-Ram Lateral Corkscrew Power Dive® out of the bus and dashed madly across the parking lot, whooping and cheering. The rest of us followed him outside and watched his victory dance.

"Huh," Bruce Willis said. "He seems pleased."

"Is there a runner-up prize?" Sting asked meekly.

"Yeah," Bruce Willis said wryly. "Corky, give him another marshmallow."

"I'm on it," Corky quipped, ducking back into the bus.

"*The McTiernan Contract is mine!*" Mort screamed to the skies. "All of it! Mine, all mine! *Read it and weep, Christian Bale!*"

It was about that time that Bruce Willis finally noticed the Pogo wriggling in my arms, and inquired, "Is that a live dinosaur you're holding?"

"No it's not," I replied, watching Mort burn off his overflowing excitement by dropping down to do fifty pushups in less than a minute. "Technically, it's a live aquatic reptile that coexisted with the dinosaurs."

"Ain't that something...." Bruce Willis mused. "I had no idea Canada could be this much fun."

"Oh, it's a hoot," I assured him.

When Mort finally sprang back to his feet, he had to wipe away a few more joyful tears before stating, "Wow, I can't believe this. Thank you, Bruce Willis! I swear that I'll never take my fame and career for granted again. I'm going to make Hollywood into the 1980s all over! The days of Dolph are here again!"

"Dang right, they are!" Bruce Willis cheered, but then paused to consider what had just been said. "Wait.... The days of what?"

"Action hunks will be action hunks once more!" Mort ranted, ignoring the question. "No more will we see this horrid trend of admittedly-talented pretty-boys briefly beefing up and stealing all the good action roles. We are going to monopolize every action movie from now on. Leave the acting to them. Leave the action to us!"

"Right on!" Bruce Willis roared, high-fiving Mort.

"Testify, Max-Ram!" Corky crowed. "*Yippee-Kai-Yay!* That's a celebratory cowboy expression, Bruce Willis, just in case you're unfamiliar with it. I notice you haven't taken too many cowboy roles."

"We'll talk later," Bruce Willis confided to him.

"Gotcha," Corky nodded, with an understanding wink.

"I will introduce great action movies to a whole new generation!" Mort continued ranting. "But that's not all I'm going to do. It's not just enough to mimic what once was. I'm going to restore the glory of the 80s and make them even *better!*"

"Really?" Bruce Willis said keenly.

"How is that even possible?" Corky asked.

"By achieving my lifelong unfulfilled dream," Mort gloated. "Get ready to have your minds blown.... I'm going to combine action cinema with stirring Broadway-style musical theatre!"

There was a prolonged moment of stunned silence before I had to admit, "Huh.... I didn't see that coming."

"Ooh, boy...." Bruce Willis said, suddenly uneasy. "Maybe this was a bad idea."

"Can it, yesterday's news, I'm notarized!" Mort said harshly, holding up his contract. Then he composed himself and added, "Not that I'm ungrateful, of course. As soon as I get back to Hollywood, you and me are getting to work on our first screenplay! Did you do any of your own lyric work on *Respect Yourself*? Boy oh boy, I hope so, because that is exactly the epic quality we're going to need."

"I can't do that!" Bruce Willis cringed.

"Well, not all by yourself," Mort conceded. "Is Bobby Vinton still alive? If he is, get his people on the phone."

After breaking out more of Corky's chocolate milk and toasting Mort's upcoming film ventures, a slightly subdued Bruce Willis drove off in one of the Batmobiles, and Sting Ripblood pulled himself together long enough to honourably cede victory to Mort. Then he surprised us all by announcing that he was going back to the set of *Compound Fracture IV: Greenstick Pinch*, where he intended to cancel all plans for the fifth installment in the series. The completion of the fourth film would officially mark the end of the classic franchise, leaving the road paved and wide open for Mort's triumphant return to Hollywood. Clearly moved by this, Mort gave Sting an emotional farewell before his defeated nominee walked off into the darkness, heading back to his helicopter.

It was a peaceful night after that. We decided to get out of town before more scientists and reporters caught up with us. Mort drove the bus back toward Buffalo Borborygmus Pass, where we hoped to salvage what was left of my truck, while Corky filled the kitchen sink with water, and let the Pogo splash around happily in it. I plugged Avril Lavigne's stolen sat-phone into its charger, and called Betty-Sue to let her know that the ordeal was over. She picked up on the first ring.

"You don't think women should be allowed to wear shoes?" she inquired skeptically, without even a greeting.

"You hate every pair of shoes you own," I reminded her, smiling at the very sound of her voice. I loved her angry voice just as much as I loved her husky manipulative voice.

"*Touché*," she chuckled. "So ... it's over?"

"It's over," I assured her. "The international media's in a feeding frenzy by now."

"Pogo and you are on every channel," Betty-Sue informed me.

"Really?" I said, impressed. "Both of them?"

"Both of them," she assured me. "The cops just left. I guess they believed me once we started watching the concert. And they called that Mudford guy, too. He vouched for you."

"What about the bomb stuff?"

"Do you remember that beaver dam that was flooding the 75-acre field?"

"Yes."

"Well, your memory's the only place you're going to be seeing it now. Ha!"

"I love you so much when you blow up aquatic rodents," I stated.

"I love me, too. And I love you. What are we going to do with the dinosaur?"

"I don't know," I said honestly. "And I don't intend to know until I wake up tomorrow. Maybe I'll give it to Megiddo, or maybe we'll just go back to the cave and let it go. What do you think?"

"Maybe Sassy's right," Betty-Sue laughed. "We should just eat it."

"We just got out of trouble," I reminded her. "Let's stay there."

After we had located my thankfully-unlooted truck and

hitched it to the back of the bus, it was well past midnight, and none of us felt like getting a hotel. Instead, we drove the bus back to the remoteness of the old abandoned barnyard, parked about sixty feet away from the barn, climbed up onto the roof, and Corky fired his old spud gun at the front door until the barn exploded. As he put it, "No sense wasting a perfectly good armed incendiary device, Bucky. Grab some spuds."

The blast was better than any of Sassy's homemade fireworks, and the subsequent blaze was better than any bonfire. Corky, Mort, and I sat in peace on the roof of that battered bus, basking in the glow of the inferno and each other's company. When the fire began to die down, we lay back on the roof and watched the stars.

"I wonder how many more people hate you now, Bucky," Corky pondered. "Lots, I bet. As long as I've known you, people have hated it when you're right. Heck, I had a hard enough time not hating you when you were up on that stage, and I've always believed that the universe is only 187 years old. I can't even imagine what the 20 billion year folks are feeling right about now."

"True enough," I said acceptantly. "I suppose I should be all riled up by the injustice of it, huh?"

"Nah," Mort decided. "I grew up in the movies, Bucky. Trust me, I know what injustice is. Injustice is that Arnold Schwarzenegger and Sylvester Stallone never did a movie together. Injustice is that Jackie Chan and Jet Li did do a movie together, and it was terrible. But the world hating cowboys for disrupting the established order.... That's just hard inevitability. If what you really believe is true, no matter how unpopular it might be, then people can only hide from it for so long. Eventually ... the world's just gotta suck it up and cinch it up."

"Wow," I said. "Thanks, Mort."

"No problem, Bucky," Mort said mildly. "And, of course, if it turns out that the entire King Jimmy is literally true, and the Antichrist is one day going to be celebrated as a god by a doomed and deluded public, thereby allowing him to rule and ruin the world ... you'll be able to think of the pivotal role you played in aiding his ascension simply by forcing people to question atheism."

I cringed so hard my face nearly got stuck in it.

"Thanks, Mort."

"Don't mention it."

"I miss Sealy," Corky admitted after a few more contemplative minutes. "Sure, I know she tried to kill you, Bucky, but lots of the girls I've dated have told me how much they wanted to kill you. A few even tried. But I've never met another girl who was so perfect for me. We were like PB and J. Or Ving Rhames and direct-to-DVD prison fight-club movies."

"Sorry, bro," I sighed. "Maybe the next beautiful girl who tries to kill me will be the one for you."

"I thought she was the one," Corky said regretfully. "Remember the night we met her? Just like this. Love at first sight, Bucky. You only get that once in life."

"Yeah, that's exactly how it was with me and Rumor," Mort said empathetically. "One look in each other's eyes, and we were gone...."

We lay in silence for a few more minutes, listening to the creaking of the few remaining barn uprights, engulfed in flame.

"Mort?" I said.

"Yo?"

"Who's Rumor?"

Mort was silent for another twenty seconds before replying, "Nobody."

"Mort ... Bruce Willis has a daughter who is a lovely and talented young film actress named Rumor Willis."

"So?" Mort asked, trying to sound casual.

"So when I found you in the barn, you were wearing a wedding ring, and, when asked about it, I thought you said, 'Rumours, Bucky. Nothing more.' But that was actually 'Rumor's, Bucky,' with an apostrophe and an American spelling, wasn't it?"

"There's a Canadian spelling?"

"Mort, are you married to Rumor Willis?"

"I have no comment on that."

I was obviously intrigued, particularly considering the fact that Rumor's stepfather, Hollywood pretty-boy Ashton Kutcher, seemed to be blackmailing Mort about something, but I was too tired to pursue the subject.

"Fine, keep your secrets," I said, as my eyes closed for the final time that night.

THE DAYS OF DOLPH
◇◇◇◇◇◇◇◇◇◇◇◇◇◇◇◇◇◇◇◇◇◇◇◇◇◇◇◇◇◇◇◇◇

I'M REALLY GLAD THAT I got a good sleep that night, because the next day was Tuesday, July 13th, 2010, and it was a pretty miserable day for me. No, the barn we had blown up didn't start a wildfire, at least not while we were there, but there were other sinister forces at work that day, forces that apparently never slept and never knew when to quit.

I had barely slept for the past three days, and neither had Corky and Mort, which is probably why we were still asleep on the roof of the bus when Corky's sat-phone started ringing at two o'clock in the afternoon. I was still half asleep as I heard him fumbling around for the jangling device.

"*Potpourri and Lentil, Incorporated*," he mumbled into the phone, apparently still groggy enough to forget that people who called him on official *Lost Cause Kin* business were unlikely to call the phone that he had stolen from Avril Lavigne. "Betty who...? I'm sorry, ma'am, you'll have to be more specific than that.... Oh, right, the one who married Bucky.... Yeah, hang on." He reached across Mort's snoring body to rap the phone against my head. "Buck-keister, Betty-Sue's been kidnapped by a bunch of guys in lab coats and Sting Ripblood. She wants to talk to you."

Equally groggy, I accepted the phone and croaked, "Hey, baby, it worked. I love you, too."

"Uh, Bucky?" Betty-Sue replied. "Little problem here."

"Yeah, I'll put out more salt for the cows as soon as I get back. Early tomorrow morning, if we don't make any stops. Then it's back to ranching like usual."

"Are you awake?" Betty-Sue demanded. "Sting Ripblood and a bunch of scientists are holding guns to my head! They landed a Concorde jet in the bale yard. I think one of Smoky's kittens got sucked into the intake manifold, and I have no idea where Gramps is."

"No, *you're* awesome," I murmured sleepily. "There's a baby Pogo in the bus. We cut open Corky's waterbed so it could swim around. I don't know how we're going to move the bus without getting soaked."

"You're still asleep, aren't you?" Betty-Sue growled. "Bucky! Six of the cows have pinkeye and there's mutant Venus flytraps in the east barley field."

"We're on the way!" I blurted, jolting awake and giving Corky a wake-up boot. "Corky, give me the keys. We'll pick up some penicillin and weed-eater on the road."

"Bug off, you rooster!" Corky snarled, pulling his black cowboy hat over his face and refusing to open his eyes.

"Betty-Sue, listen carefully," I instructed. "Forget everything you ever learned in B-movies. If any of the flytraps look big enough to swallow a human, just give them both rounds of 12-gauge from Gramps' shotgun right at the roots. Don't waste your shots on the jaws like Steve McQueen always did in his 50s classic, *The Vines of Wrath*. That just makes them mad."

"Cute advice, Bucky," Betty-Sue said dryly. "Think I should use the slugs or the double-ought?"

"Anything but the birdshot. Hey, was I still asleep, or

did you say something about Sting Ripblood and lab coats and guns pointed at your head?"

"Laroo...." Sting Ripblood's voice snarled over the line.

"Oh," I said, feeling my heart dropping into my colon. "Hi, Sting. I thought you learned your lesson and went back to Affluenceville. Did I misread that situation?"

"No, Bucky," Sting gloated. "You read exactly what I wanted you to read from the situation. Because, unlike Max-Ram Target, I can actually act when there's something at stake. And, when there's a contract in the wind entitling the bearer to fifty pictures of a quality reminiscent of the great John McTiernan, I can act my ever-loving giblets out. Yeah, you read it right, cowboy. And then you relaxed, while I was flying as the crow flies, except a lot faster, straight to Cattle Poke Ranch. Sure, your ol' Gramps put up a bit of a fuss with that 12-gauge side-by-side, but that's why it pays to have backup."

"What did you do to Gramps?" I demanded. "What did you do to my wife? *Sting!*"

"Don't let him hurt me!" Mort yelped instinctively, jerking awake.

"Shut up, Mort!" I barked. "Sting, if my wife has one scratch on her when I get there, you are gonna ... peel the paper wrapper off her Bandaid, because it always rips when I do it! *And then you're going to die!*"

"Ooh, so dramatic," Sting chuckled. "Big man, Bucky? Pathetic.... Do you really think you stand a chance against us, Mr Cowboy?"

"I'm warming up to the idea," I growled. "And quit stealing lines from *Die Hard*!"

"You sock it to 'im, baby bro," Corky mumbled from under his hat, holding up a supportive Black Panther fist.

"Bucky, what's wrong?" Mort asked, sitting up.

"Listen to me, you dirtbag," I threatened Sting. "I don't

care how lethal you are, and I don't care what kind of backup you have– Wait a second.... What kind of backup did you say you had?"

"The kind who want something from you," a second familiar voice replied, "as bad as Sting Ripblood wants something from Max-Ram Target."

"Argo?" I said. "Is that you?"

"Bouncin' with my whole crew," the evil scientist laughed. "Hello, Bucky. We want that Impossible Lie Baby, and we want it shish-kebobed on a platter."

"Seriously?" I said in disgust, holding the phone out so that Mort could listen in. "That's what this is about? Pogo is on the cover of every newspaper and the top story of every morning news show on the planet by now. Just give up, and start researching dimensional vortexes to protect your stupid theory."

"*That's not how it works, saddle sore!*" Argo roared. "We haven't actually defended the theory since 1963, and we don't intend to start now! My job is to make sure that it's never challenged in the first place. Challengers end up where Amelia Earhart ended up after she claimed to have spotted a pod of kronosaurs in the mid-Altantic."

"Amelia did what?" I asked.

"Look," Argo said, trying to remain calm, "try to understand the accountability-free hope that you're destroying, Bucky. Evolution gives me the strength to go on. When I look at my grandchildren playing in the yard, I can't help but be inspired by the thought that, millions of years after they're dead and rotted away to dust, our species has the potential to ascend into a more enlightened consciousness form, assuming that we don't destroy the planet through greenhouse gas emissions, which is every bit as real a problem as Al Gore claims it is and in no way a cleverly-veiled fear-exploitative plot for the unification of governments into a global superpower. *Heh heh!*"

"I can see how that would bring a tear to the eye," I growled.

"Max-Ram, is that your shallow mouth-breathing I hear?" Sting's conferenced voice demanded.

"I'm here, Sting ... ol' buddy," Mort swallowed nervously.

"'Ol' buddy?'" Sting said mockingly. "I thought I was yesterday's news."

"No, no," Mort quickly assured him. "I called Bruce Willis yesterday's news, although it may have just been a character who looks exactly like him. I would never do that to you, Sting."

"Bruce Willis will never be yesterday's news!" Betty-Sue's voice cut in indignantly.

"Betty-Sue!" I shouted. "Can you hear me? Are you okay?"

"I'm fine, Bucky. And some hot librarian chick just told me that Gramps is fine, too. She says they just stuffed him in the empty pickle barrel down in the cella–"

"*SILENCE!*" Sting bellowed, loud enough to even make Corky jump and sit up.

"I'm up! I'm quiet!" he squawked.

"Sting, we can work this out," Mort said, doing his best to assume a reasonable tone. "We'll bring you the Pogo, you let Betty-Sue go, and I promise I'll consider giving you the contract."

"Yeah, that was brilliant," I said irritably.

"Fine," Mort sighed. "The contract's yours, Sting. Just let the cowboys go."

"Ha!" Sting scoffed. "You wish it was that easy, don't you? What you fail to comprehend is that I can't be bought, charmed, swindled, or placated. I don't care about this bunch of pant-crapping nerds—"

"Hey!" I heard Gapps protest in the background.

"—and I don't care about the 640 million dollars in negotiable bearer bonds that they're paying me for my cooperation. Heck, I don't even care about you running over my two-time Olympic Dressage gold-medalist with a back-hoe. I want that contract, but I can't just take it. I need to pry it from your bloodstained death-grip after honourably defeating you."

"*You're insane!*" I exploded. "All actors are insane! *Give me back my wife!*"

"First things first," Argo snapped back. "First you bring us the Impossible Lie, and the contract. Then you release a public apology to the press, claiming that your little monster was just an animatronic facsimile made by an advanced robotics company, recently franchising out of Japan. Then you get your wife back. Tick-tock, Bucky."

"Fine, you banana-chugging freaks," I snarled. "Talk to me."

"Listen up good, Bucky," Sting instructed, "because I'm only going to say this once."

"That's needlessly unreasonable," I had to point out.

"Okay, you're right," Sting admitted. "Sorry. I got most of my drop-instruction training from movie villains, and you know what a bunch of witless wonders Hollywood action screenwriters are. Bunch of sniffling, line-running, sweaty-pitted—"

"Yeah, I get it," I interrupted. "What do you want me to do?"

"Your wife and grandfather are being held in separate locations, so don't think about storming any trenches. You rescue one, the other gets smoked. Got it?"

"Fine," I agreed.

"Bring the Pogo and my contract and Max-Ram Target to Gramps' cabin in four hours," Sting said. "You'll get further instructions from there."

"Four hours?" I said incredulously.

"Yes, four hours," Sting clarified reasonably. "Or your wife becomes part of the muskeg. Be there, cowboy."

Then he hung up.

"Four hours to drive across the length of British Columbia?" Corky said. "That could take sixteen hours, even speeding."

"I know," I muttered. "Crap! We need a flight, but we'll never find something direct to Coyote Yelp Pass. And even if we can get a direct flight to Affluenceville leaving right away, and then hire a chopper, what are the odds of us making it back to Cattle Poke in four–"

I was interrupted by the phone in my hand as it began to ring again.

"Hello?" I squawked, answering it. "Betty-Sue?"

"Sorry, were you saying something?" Sting's voice inquired.

"What?" I said. "No."

"Oh, it sounded like you were protesting about something just as I hung up, like the ransomed person always does in the action movies. I didn't want to be rude."

"No, I wasn't saying anything," I assured him.

"Okay, sorry to waste your time," Sting apologised. "But, as long as I've got you on the line, was there anything else you needed clarification on?"

"No, you've been very clear thus far."

"Alright," Sting said, relieved to have that cleared up. "See you in four hours."

He hung up again.

"See what I mean?" Mort marvelled. "I'm sending

transcripts of these calls to the action screenwriters' union."

"Get in the bus," I ordered, swinging down through one of the shot-out side windows from the roof.

"That whole call was so awesome, Bucky," Mort couldn't help gushing as he and Corky clambered down after me. "'*Tick-tock, Bucky.*' And when you yelled '*Give me back my wife...!*' Perfect delivery, dude."

"*Somebody just drive the bus!*" I roared, again with perfect delivery. "Corky, how far to Kamloops?"

"Forty minutes," he estimated, jamming the key into the ignition and gunning the engine.

"Head for the airport," I said as we rolled out of the barnyard. "It's our only shot."

As we shot down the road, I tried to call Sassy to make sure she was okay, but only got her cell phone's voice mail. With no time to worry about interrupting the first day of her honeymoon, I left her a detailed message about what was going on, and urged her to be careful. Then I called Sergeant Mudford to figure out exactly how the scientists he had arrested were currently bunkering down at my ranch. He stated that Sting Ripblood had posted their bail shortly after midnight, and was aghast to learn that the certified celebrity custody which the Galapagos Brethren had been released into was now untrustworthy as well.

"Are you telling me that The Scientific Establishment is using Hollywood as pawns to further their own agenda?" Mudford gasped. "Has that ever been done before?"

"I'm going to say no, just to save time," I replied. "Sarge, they're at my ranch right now, and they've got my wife!"

"Oh," the sergeant said. "So I suppose that this parliamentary release request Sting gave me, signed with Prime Minister Stephen Harper's own red pencil crayon is probably bogus, too, huh?"

"Just get some cops to Coyote Yelp Pass, please," I sighed. "I've got to get my wife back."

"Wait for us, Bucky. This could be dangerous."

"There's no time," I said. "I've got less than four hours."

"I'm getting a team on a chopper right now!" Mudford declared. "To heck with delegated areas of operation! Nobody makes the RCMP look like a bunch of doofuses more than once in a twenty-four hour period!"

As soon as he had hung up, I was dialling 411 to get the number for the Kamloops Airport. When the operator connected me to the airline registrar, I told her that we needed an immediate flight to Coyote Yelp Pass. Of course, she informed me that such a request was impossible. Then she asked me where Coyote Yelp Pass was, as it wasn't coming up on her computer.

"Listen to me," I said. "We don't have time for anything but a direct flight, leaving within the hour. It's an emergency."

"Oh, I'm so glad you used the word 'emergency,'" the registrar said sarcastically. "Otherwise, I might have hesitated to order a complete tower redirection and rescheduling of every incoming and outbound flight at this airport for your personal convenience."

"*Your mother wasn't insistent enough upon a high-fibre diet when you were in grade school!*" I yelled as I hung up. "Corky! How long?"

"Ten minutes," my brother reported as we entered the city limits at well over the posted limit. "If we don't get pulled over, that is." Sticking his head out the window, he hollered, "*Get off the crosswalk, you stupid eight-year-olds! Can't you see I'm driving here?*"

"Okay, I'm panicking, too," I readily confessed. "But this is the point where my voice of reason says, 'Slow down.'"

419

"Relax," Corky soothed me as we careened around the corner of the playground on the inside tires, various farm implements flying out of my truck box as it whipped around behind us. "We'll be out of this school zone in twenty seconds. Fifteen if I really floor it."

"How does this happen?" I wondered, slumping into one of the cushioned seats. "All I wanted was to take my wife on her dream honeymoon. I was just being a good husband!"

"Don't beat yourself up, baby bro," Corky consoled me, running over a stop sign. "It's like Gramps used to say every Taco Night: 'Get sour cream in the salsa, boy, but never get salsa in the sour cream.' Heck, remember how mad he'd get if that sour cream tub had a speck of tomato sauce in it at the end of the meal?"

"Okay," I said with a nod. "That's ... not helpful at all."

"He means that double standards are a fact of life, Bucky," Mort translated, stroking the contented Pogo on his lap. "And, as such, your predicament is not one that should have caught you off-guard. If there's one thing that we've learned from teen-oriented Disney movies, it's that when you follow your dreams and become an overnight sensation, you will eventually forget to attend a minor community event that means a lot to your friends back home. Then they'll take it personally to a highly unreasonable degree, and you'll have to make an apology speech that features the words, 'I know I've been a total jerk,' even though all you were doing was living the dream that these same so-called friends originally encouraged you to follow. You should have seen this coming."

"Why do we even watch these movies?" I had to ask.

"I've been asking myself that a lot, lately," Mort admitted. "They're all such a bunch of stupid, whiny, sexy.... Blagh!

This is why the world needs this contract. We need the days of Dolph back."

"The days of what?" I asked, still not knowing what time period that referred to.

"Dolph Lundgren, Bucky," Mort confided. "The underappreciated man who epitomized 80s action. The Swedish Slab."

"I don't think that's his real nickname," I said.

"No, it's probably not. But, believe it or not, his Ivan Drago character in *Rocky IV* was my primary inspiration for becoming an action hunk."

"Wow. I didn't know that."

"Being a blonde action hunk is an uphill struggle, Bucky. We all need success stories to aspire to."

I had the Pogo in my arms as we parked the bus illegally in front of the airport terminal and rushed inside, ignoring the multitude of stares and protests. Very rudely, I admit, we jostled our way to the front of the nearest *Can-a-Jet* lineup, and asked for a flight of any kind, commercial or cargo.

"Sir, I'm sorry," the patient lady replied. "But we have no seats available at the moment, and our next open flight to Affluenceville doesn't leave for two hours. I'm going to have to ask you to return to the back of the line."

"Lady, can't you make something happen?" I begged. "I'm holding a living dinosaur! Doesn't the airline have contingencies for this kind of thing?"

"No, sir," she replied, even though she was having a hard time taking her eyes off the wriggling plesiosaurus in my arms. "We have no dinosaur policies. It was suggested at one time, but The Scientific Establishment cracked down on the idea pretty hard. And the only plane leaving within the hour is a cargo carrier. They're already on the tarmac, loading up with food and medical supplies to deliver to refugees in a war-torn–"

"My name is Hollywood action hunk Max-Ram Target!" Mort announced, pushing past me and holding The McTiernan Contract in the lady's face. "And I need that plane!"

The mind-blowing power and authority in his voice made everyone tremble, including me. The lady behind the counter promptly snapped to attention and hit the emergency intercom.

"Terminal to Tower, this is Debbie!" she blurted, her voice echoing to every traveller and employee in the airport. "I am declaring a *Code Suri Cruise* celebrity emergency! Hold all patterns, ground all outgoing, clear all runways, and begin immediate offloading of Red Cross Flight 911. Security, we need a diplomatic escort to Gate Six. We've got a tour bus and pickup truck to load up!"

"Tower to terminal," the PA immediately garbled back. "Copy that, Debbie. Attention, all airport staff: *Flip the switch!*"

"Thanks, Debbie," I called out as Corky and Mort rushed me back to the bus. By the time we had arrived, security vehicles were flanking it, their lights flashing, and the drivers waving frantically for us to follow them. The convoy took off to the restricted area, through an automated gate and onto the tarmac, where the protesting Red Cross workers were being forcibly dragged off their plane. Some people think that everything they do is so important.

"Wow," Mort remarked. "If I could have worked this newfound confidence into my acting, I never would have needed this contract."

"We share your joy, Mort," I congratulated him as Corky gunned the bus's engine and raced up the plane's rear loading ramp, flattening a few remaining boxes of freeze-dried emergency rations.

"It's a good day to die, Mr Pilot Man!" Corky shouted

to the cockpit through the shattered windshield. "Spread your wings and fly! And if you don't know where we're going, call Bert Bodine, our local bush pilot. I think he has the exact coordinates written down on an old newspaper somewhere."

"Who are you?" the pilot and copilot demanded in unison.

"*Fly the plane!*" Mort thundered once more, again causing everyone in hearing distance to tremble.

"Yes, Mr Max-Ram Target, sir!" the pilot whined, raising the cargo ramp behind my truck's tailgate and starting the engine without even waiting for the remaining cargo workers to clear the area.

Minutes later, we were in the air and northbound.

"Okay, here's the plan," Corky announced, fishing my 30-30 from the back of my truck and tossing me the box of ammunition. "We go in, we shoot everyone who we think might be evil, and then we take the supersonic jet that's parked in our bale yard to a non-extradition country. I want to say Portugal, but we might need to look that up."

"We're not killing anyone, and we're not going to Portugal," I snapped, snatching my rifle from him and beginning to thumb shells into it. "We go in armed, and we make the trade. If they're smart, they'll think twice about open combat with even odds, and then they'll leave. But we're not shooting anybody. I'm keeping Jesus happy today."

"We've been over this, Bucky," Mort said, rolling his eyes. "I'm sure that Jesus would agree with me that human value is a very fluid concept."

"No it's not!"

"Yes, it is," Mort said. "I cite a case from 2003, when the Irish Parliament passed legislation stating that anyone who blew over 0.24 on a breathalyser test no longer fit the legal definition of a human being. Something about the DNA pickling beyond recognition. The problem was that the legislative assembly deadlocked for the next week and a half, trying to decide whether to label drunks as 'sub-humans' or 'para-humans,' not realizing that, in the meantime, they had created a new and completely unprotected species. So, yes, for about ten days it was completely legal to shoot and kill bleary Irish eyes, whether they were smiling or not. Needless to say, citing this became a very popular homicide defence in the following months, as hundreds of drunk Irish people get shot every single week."

"You know what, Mort?" I growled. "I don't.... Uh.... Alright, you got me. That actually sounds just a little bit stranger than fiction, so I'm going to believe you. But just this once."

"Really?" Mort said, surprised. "Why? Seriously, Bucky, the only reason that I can't admit to being a pathological liar is because I keep lying to myself about it. *No, I don't!*"

We touched down at the Coyote Yelp International Airstrip a little over an hour later, and Corky was backing the bus out of the plane before the ramp was all the way down. Then we raced through Coyote Yelp Pass, the water from the slashed waterbed up to our shins, much to the delight of the Pogo who gleefully slid up and down the aisle. Corky never slowed down until we were back at Cattle Poke Ranch, and only then because the bus was intercepted by the east wall of Gramps' cabin. About a third of the bus ended up inside the building, with the engine compartment stopping right about where the TV in the sitting room used to be.

"Why do you always do that?" I demanded.

Corky shrugged. "It's a rescue thing."

Before he had finished speaking, an M4 Carbine assault rifle with a really ominous-looking underslung KAC

Masterkey shotgun attachment had been shoved through the driver-side window, pressing against the side of Corky's temple.

"Don't move, patty waft," Sealy growled from behind the trigger.

"Whoa!" I cautioned her, holding out an empty hand. "We're doing what you said, Sealy. Just take it easy."

"We didn't say anything about driving a bus through the wall," Sealy snarled.

"It wasn't a rescue," I promised her. "It's just Corky. And he's an idiot."

"No, he's not!" Sealy shot back at me, choking back a sob.

"What?" Corky said.

"*Crap!*" Sealy screamed, as her heart finally overwhelmed her allegiances. Then she threw the machine gun at me, clambered into the bus through the missing windshield, and pressed her lips against Corky's. The horn blared through the cabin as her backside ended up resting against the steering wheel, as there wasn't quite enough room for her to sit fully on Corky's lap.

"What the helmsman?" I said.

"It's all about the entrance, Bucky," Mort informed me. "Even the action screenwriters figured that out a long time ago."

"I'm so sorry for going along with this, Corky!" Sealy whimpered, seizing him by the shoulders. "I can't do it! You had me from ... from the moment Bucky brutally pummelled me unconscious."

"The first time or the second time?" Corky asked.

"I said I was sorry!" I snapped.

"Silence, Bucky," Corky hushed me. "The grownups are talking."

"No they're not," Sealy asserted, kissing him passionately once more.

I had seen enough, and was actually getting a bit nauseated. With the machine gun in one hand, I grabbed Sealy by the collar of her lab coat, yanked her out of Corky's embrace, and slammed her against the opposite wall of the bus. Then I pressed the barrel of the underslung shotgun under her jaw, which had the added benefit of simultaneously jamming the M4 barrel into her right nostril. When it came to matters of my wife, I didn't have time to be a gentleman cowboy.

"Hey!" Corky protested, lunging out of his seat.

"Where's my wife, Doc?" I rasped, my voice quivering with rage.

"Chill out, Harrison Ford," Sealy quipped. "I'm on your side."

"You were planning to brand me less than twenty-four hours ago," I reminded her. "Forgive me if I'm not quite ready to trust you."

"Really?" Mort said, clearly surprised. "She's already won me over completely."

"Exactly, Bucky," Corky agreed. "Have a little faith in your own destiny."

"Okay, everybody here who doesn't know where my wife is ... be quiet."

"Fine, since you're that frazzled," Corky submitted. "But, for the record, I really don't appreciate you man-handling and gun-pointing my fianceé."

"Fianceé?" Sealy gasped.

"Okay, I seriously didn't see that one coming," I confessed.

"What can I say, Bucky?" Corky chuckled. "When you know, you just know."

"Yes, yes, yes!" Sealy tittered, beginning to tear up again.

"True love gets me every time," Mort sobbed, weeping freely.

"Oh my gosh, is that the dinosaur?" Sealy said breathlessly as she spotted the Pogo's tiny head peering at her from the kitchen sink. "It's ... adorable!"

"Meh, boof," Pogo replied.

"Okay, this is a combination machine gun and shotgun," I snapped. "Do I need a bazooka to get you to focus?"

"Let her go, boy."

I looked out the side windows into the living room. Gramps was standing there with his hands in his pockets and his shotgun tucked under his arm, staring disapprovingly at me.

"She's legit, Bucky," he promised me. "She gave me my gun as soon as she heard you coming down the driveway. She couldn't do it."

"And I let him out of the empty pickle barrel down in the cellar two minutes after they called you," Sealy told me. "I swear I did. They had already taken Betty-Sue away. I don't know where. She said you'd know."

"Put the gun down, Bucky," Gramps said. "I raised you not to shoot scientists on tour buses."

Gramps still ruled the roost of Cattle Poke Ranch. I handed the dual weapon over to Corky, then turned and slumped against the wall beside Sealy. Corky clicked on the safety and silently reached over to open the bus doors. Gramps slowly stepped inside, and put a hand on my shoulder. Nobody said anything, but Sealy was looking over at me.

"Where is she?" I asked quietly.

"She said the best place for you to rendezvous was some romantic lagoon," Sealy replied. "Sting took her there. She said it was your favourite spiritual place."

Corky, Gramps, and I exchanged sharp glances.

"Holy snakeskin," Corky breathed. "Bucky ... she took them into The Spirit Realm."

"No way she'd do that," I said.

"There is a way she'd do that," Gramps pointed out. "She'd do it for you, Bucky."

"Um, what's The Spirit Realm?" Sealy asked.

I wasn't moving or speaking, but my mind was racing. I couldn't just wait to see how this played out. This was about my wife.

"Bucky?" Mort said, raising an eyebrow. "What's a Spirit Realm?"

"I'm going to find her," I said, snatching up my 30-30 from the kitchenette table.

"I'm coming with you," Corky volunteered, handing the M4 Carbine over to Mort, and pulling his .375 Magnum Winchester out from under the futon. "I hate fancy guns."

"Thanks, bro," I said gratefully. "Gramps, I need you to stay here and hold the ranch and give the Pogo its five o'clock chum. And keep Mort safe, okay? He's just got another shot at being a movie star. The cops are on the way, but you can't let them go after us. It's too dangerous for outsiders."

"Keep me safe?" Mort clarified. "Bucky, you're not leaving me here."

"Yes, I am," I stated, stuffing a spare box of bullets into my jacket.

"You're going to hunt evil spirits with rifles?" Sealy inquired.

"They're not spirits," I corrected her, chambering my Trapper and easing the hammer down as we all exited the bus into the living room. "They're just evil."

"What?" Sealy demanded.

"Well, some would argue that they really–" Corky began.

"Corky, for Pete's sake, you were with me when we

figured out that they weren't really spirits!" I irritably reminded him.

"Okay, so maybe I just hate to kill a good ghost story," Corky shrugged, filling his pockets with bullets. "Screwing up life with reality is your specialty, baby bro. Just leave me out of it from now on."

"I'm leaving me out of it from now on," I assured him.

"I'm coming, too," Sealy decided, drawing an MP5 out from under her lab coat, and chambering it. At the distinctive sound of the bolt being drawn back, Gramps, Corky, and I all instinctively threw down, covering Sealy from three sides.

Sealy froze, and then cautiously ventured, "Uh, Corky...? True love, remember?"

"Sorry, my little Thundercat," Corky apologised, slowly lowering his rifle. "You were trying to kill us a few minutes ago."

"This is not working for me!" I snarled. "Sorry, Corky, but, as long as she's holding an automatic weapon, I'm having a hard time trusting your fianceé as far as I can spit! Actually, I don't trust her as far as I can drool while lying face-down in a pillow. And she's not going into the swamp. I watched her contaminate herself and Mort yesterday."

"What are you talking about?" Mort demanded. "I'm not contaminated!"

"Yeah, we're coming with you," Sealy insisted.

"Nobody's coming," I said flatly. "It's dangerous enough for me and Corky. The rest of you would just be–"

The front door was kicked open as I was speaking, and everybody in that room was tense enough as it was. In an instant, Gramps, Corky, Mort, Sealy, and I had weapons trained on the armed intruder, clamouring for her to drop her gun.

Her?

"Bucky?" Betty-Sue gasped, lowering an HK-G36 assault rifle that looked an awful lot like the one Sting Ripblood had been carrying.

"Betty-Sue!" I blurted, sprinting to her.

"Omigosh, you're safe!" she cried, pouncing on me with a flurry of kisses. Then she pushed me back and punched me hard across the jaw. "Don't *ever* make me risk my life for you again! That's your job, Hopalong. Got it?"

"Just the knowledge that you've lived to punch another day is incredible to me," I assured her, getting up off the floor. I moved in to kiss her again, but it was at that moment that Betty-Sue spotted Sealy with the MP5.

"Gun!" Betty-Sue roared, whipping the G36 into her shoulder again.

"Whoa, take it easy, Betty-Sue!" Corky protested, sliding in front of Sealy. "It's okay. We're engaged."

"*What?*" Betty-Sue demanded.

"It's a long story," Sealy said passively, lowering her sub gun.

"Actually, it's quite a short story," I corrected her, putting a cautionary hand on the barrel of my wife's assault rifle and lowering it to the floor. "Like, ridiculously short. How did you get away?"

"Well, they drove me up to the sacrificial grounds in the Hummer, and then followed me into the marshes like a bunch of sheep," Betty-Sue explained, still eyeing Sealy suspiciously. "Then they just pushed me down and stood around chortling and high-fiving each other for the next two and a half hours or so. It was scary, but I figured my only shot was to test the legends."

"What legends?" Sealy asked.

"They say the hostile mountain spirits only prey on those who are under the Curse of the Forbidden Fruit," Corky explained.

"Which is why only me and Corky could have gone in after them," I added. "And it's why they left Betty-Sue alone."

"What is that, some kind of Christian thing?" Sealy asked skeptically. "Guardian angels now, Bucky?"

"I wish," I snorted. "No, the legend is about literal forbidden fruit, not analogical. And it must have worked. Betty-Sue's the proof."

"It was freaky," Betty-Sue readily admitted, still looking a little shaken up by the ordeal. "But, yeah, it worked. I heard a twig snap off in the distance, so I just lay down on the muskeg and closed my eyes until all the blood-curdling screams were carried off into the distance. When I finally opened them again, I was alone in the marsh with a bunch of strewn assault rifles and shredded lab coats. Then I just came back in the Hummer. I left it at the end of the lane when I saw the bus. Thought you might need a covert rescue."

"Would somebody please explain to me what the spirits are?" Mort persisted.

"No," I assured him.

"Holy hubcaps," Sealy said, her face turning green. "Do you mean that all of my former friends, colleagues, and sinister coven brethren are ... dead?"

"Yup," Corky said confidently. "Ground mincemeat in the ground. Digging fish-bait from the chandelier. Getting bonked on the head by the bones Fido buried. Riding the pine elevator down to the root cellar. Wearing pennies for eyeglasses. All dressed up, and no chance to grow."

"That's enough, Corky," Betty-Sue admonished him.

"Are you sure?" Corky pressed. "I've got an entire *Pondering Mortality Journal* full of these: Can't call your mummy cuz you are your mummy. You're causing groundhog traffic jams. It's Christmas come early for the carpenter ants– Aak! *Gag!* Okay, I'm done!"

Satisfied, Betty-Sue released Corky's windpipe, then turned to put a consolatory hand on Sealy's shoulder, while keeping her other hand cautiously near the trigger.

"I'm sorry, Sealy," Betty-Sue said sadly. "Your friends may have been psychotic murderers, but nobody deserves to go out like ... like that."

"Like what?" Sealy sniffled, wiping her nose on her white sleeve.

"Like a wood-chipper would be more humane," Corky remarked.

"Corky!" Betty-Sue groaned.

"What?" my brother queried. "If she's going to be a cowboy's wife, she's got to learn to swallow the bitterness of reality."

I shook my head, troubled, but unable to keep myself from making a surprise announcement.

"No.... She doesn't have to accept anything. Because we're going to stop anything from happening."

"What?" Gramps said, biting his lip. "Boy, you'd better not be thinkin' 'bout–"

"We're already thinking it, Gramps," I stated. "Corky, you know what I'm talking about. The forbidden fruit isn't the only legend. And, if it's true, who's to say the others aren't, too?"

"Bucky...." Corky said, stunned. "Even by my standards, that's just being cruel. Don't give her false hope. It's just mean."

"False hope?" I said, loathing the very sound of the words. "We just proved to the world that Ogopogos and, by extension, dinosaurs exist. We just survived repeated assassination attempts by the deadliest nerds and celebrities ever assembled. Heck, I think Sassy might have even presented a biological sequencing mandate that mathematically disproves the theory that has been a global staple for more than a hundred years. I'd say it's time for a little hope, and not just the well-wishing kind. It's time to believe that impossible shouldn't exist in the English language. I'm going into that bog, and I'm going to bring back the action hunk and theistic evolutionist and unreasonable atheists who want to kill me."

"Yeah, call them unreasonable," Mort decided, liking the sound of that better. "That softens it."

"What's he talking about, Corky?" Sealy asked, staring unnervedly at me. "What legend?"

Corky stared at me, too, and then gave a slow nod.

"The Fattening Before the Feast Legend," he explained. "Old Donald Budgekins claims that he knew a rebellious young Knick-Knack Indian named Chipchuk who managed to escape from the hostile mountain spirits. After capturing him, they carried him unharmed into The Glen of No Return, bound him to a tree with vines and thistles, and then force fed him pinecones and maple sap for the next three weeks to fatten him up. When they left him to gather more sap on the fourth week, his fat pushed the tensile strength of the vines to their breaking point and he escaped."

"Wow," Sealy said.

"Yeah," Corky agreed. "Wow. Unfortunately, the legend also tells that he became addicted to maple syrup as a result of his ordeal and died of hyperglycemia two years later. They buried him in the one-room shanty he died in, because it was easier than getting him out of it. His hearse was an oversize-load flatbed with a pilot car."

"Do you think it's possible?" Sealy gasped.

"Sure," Corky said. "You just use a winch and some skids. How do you think we keep convincing Bucky that Gramps' cabin is sliding downhill in that glacial trench?"

"I knew it!" Betty-Slue said, pointing an accusing finger at him.

"Multiple April Fools!" Corky cheered.

"How many years have you been working on that one?" I had to ask, cringing. "Wait a sec.... Were you moving the whole cabin or just the woodshed next to it? I mean, there's a foundation under the cabin. And plumbing. And a basement. And a driveway and front porch leading to all of them."

"I don't skimp on my pranks, Bucky," Corky said, looking offended.

"I meant do you think it's possible that my friends are still alive," Sealy interjected.

"I don't know," I said honestly, shouldering my rifle. "But I'm finding out."

"And I'm right beside you, baby brother!" Corky declared, chambering his .375. "Because if there's one thing we've learned from the films of David Cronenberg, it's that.... Okay, actually that doesn't apply to this situation in any way. But I'm coming."

"Thanks, big brother," I smiled, putting a hand on his shoulder.

"Take this, too, boy," Gramps said gruffly, handing over his double-barrelled shotgun. "You'll need it more than me. Anyway, I kind of like the look of that G36. Heckler&Koch just can't go wrong, can they?"

"Have fun with it, Gramps," I said appreciatively, slinging the shotgun strap diagonally across my chest, and cramming a few extra buckshot shells into my jacket.

At the sound of a bolt-action being worked, we turned to see Betty-Sue standing next to us with her dad's old .22 rifle in her hands and a determined glint in her eyes.

"Count me in," she decided. "And don't try to stop me, Bucky."

"Wouldn't dream of it," I chuckled. "I've fought with you my whole life, sugar monkey. It'll be an honour to fight beside you for once. But are you sure you don't want the G36? It's got a bit more stopping power ... and the clip holds more than five rounds."

"It's not what you hit with, Bucky," Betty-Sue said darkly, licking her thumb and using it to wipe the dust from her rifle scope lense. "It's where you hit. And I can shoot the ugly off an ape with this thing."

"No, you can't," I felt obliged to remind her. "You're a terrible shot. You are possibly the worst shot I've ever met. For the record, I love you."

"Okay, I'm terrible," Betty-Sue admitted. "I'll just wait until they get really close and then shoot them in the eye."

"Attagirl!" Corky cheered. "Let's do this!"

"Yeah!" Mort whooped, trying to figure out where the safety on the M4 Carbine was.

"I don't know what we're doing, but ... yeah!" Sealy joined in, switching her MP5 to the 3-round burst setting.

"Hold it," I said, hating to kill the buzz. "You two still aren't going anywhere. It's too dangerous. You'll stay here with Gramps until we get back."

"What?" Mort protested. "Come on, man! This is the first time I've had a shot at a real-life climactic showdown with guns! I'm coming."

"No, you're not," I said. "Anyway, you had a climactic showdown with guns on the night that you saved my life. Remember? Sealy, if you need more details about that night, you can read about it in the chapter *Flaming Marshmallow* of my autobiography, *Last Stand at Coyote Yelp Pass: The Tragic Cowboy Memoirs of Bucky Laroo*."

"Wow," Corky said, impressed by my wife's silence. "Betty-Sue, you didn't tell him to shut up."

"I've acclimatised," Betty-Sue shrugged. "Anyway, it turns out that shameless plugging is one of the most unavoidable and effective forms of cheap marketing. And, for the record, I think everyone should read my husband's laugh-a-minute thrill-ride of an autobiography, *Last Stand at Coyote Yelp Pass: The Tragic Cowboy Memoirs of Bucky Laroo.*"

"Okay, we get it," Mort said irritably. "Yes, we all love *Last Stand at Coyote Yelp Pass: The Tragic Cowboy Memoirs of Bucky Laroo*, but I disagree that I've had a climactic showdown with guns. As I recall, evil pop-singing sensation Minnie Marshmallow was the only one who had guns. My role was thus limited to running and screaming. That's an extra's role, Bucky. An *extra!*"

"Mort, you've still got your contract," I reminded him. "And, now that we have Betty-Sue back, you get to keep it. What are you complaining about? Now you want real-life action?"

"I'm the textbook example of an overreacher, Bucky."

"You're staying here. Gramps, show them that new song you learned on the bagpipes."

"Gladly," Gramps quipped, going to his room with the Pogo in his arms.

"I'll wait for you, Corky," Sealy said softly. "And I mean that both romantically and literally, because I can't really leave. Only Sting knows how to fly the Concorde."

Corky had tears welling in his eyes as he confessed, "No woman's ever said those words to me before. And I mean that romantically and literally, as well."

"Oh, brother," Mort groaned, rolling his eyes. "Bucky, you're kidding me, right? You seriously just want me to stay here and listen to Gramps play the bagpipes while you go charging off to battle swamp monsters?"

"Hey, you've never heard *Safety Dance* by *Men Without Hats* until you've heard it on the bagpipes," I assured him.

"Bucky!"

"Fine, do something else. Start working on that

screenplay. With your action cliché awareness and Sealy's scientific background, maybe the two of you can come up with a smart, stylish thriller with plenty of crackling action.... And I really need to stop reading movie review blurbs on DVD jackets. *Let's go kick some hostile mountain spirit butt!*"

Corky and Betty-Sue roared their consent, and the three of us ignored Mort's whining pleas as we charged outside to the horse corral. Corky hitched the horse trailer to what was left of my truck while Betty-Sue and I began catching and saddling our noble steeds. Then we loaded Homestretch, Betty-Sue's paint mare Porkchop, and Corky's pinto gelding Jimmy-Boy III into the trailer, and drove off toward Banshee Screech Peak.

We parked the truck by the sacrificial grounds where Sassy and I had encountered The Sickle, and proceeded into the marshes on horseback. It wasn't too hard to find our way. Aside from Betty-Sue's directions, the trail of gun clips, human teeth, and pocket protectors was easy enough to follow for the next half kilometre, although the thick, sucking mud of the muskeg cost all of our horses at least one shoe. In spite of the arduous terrain, we kept going, urging our gallant mounts onward, mostly because of a sense of heroic urgency, but also because none of us really wanted to be in The Spirit Realm after dark. It had been sunny when we left Cattle Poke Ranch, but the perpetual low-hanging haze of Banshee Screech Peak was settling in more thickly by the minute, enveloping us in a really eery fog.

And, just as the story of Chipchuk had predicted, the trail led us straight to the weeping willows that shrouded The Glen of No Return, a lone island of trees in the midst of the vast ocean of muskeg.

"The Glen of No Return," Betty-Sue said reverently, as we reined our horses to a halt and stared at the heart of

The Spirit Realm, which we had only heard of in legend. "Mr Hayashi says that the weeping willows of this glen glisten with the tears of a thousand victims, and the chill wind blowing through the boughs carries their last dying screams."

"Yeah, I heard that, too," I acknowledged. "Actually, there were only two confirmed cases of Coyote Yelp Passians going missing in here in 1897 and 1932, but the early scribes thought a thousand was more legend-worthy."

"You know something, Bucky?" Corky said in annoyance. "Even when you're on your way to a climactic showdown with guns, you're still not a lot of fun."

"I was just going to say that," Sealy chimed in. "Man, we even think alike already."

"We sure do," Corky agreed. "Hey, what the...? Sealy! What are you doing here?"

"Mort!" I shouted, spotting him slinking through the foggy marsh behind Sealy, both of them armed with Sealy's illegal machine guns. "I told you to stay in the cabin. We're upwind of this place already!"

"Sealy, you need to go," Corky said anxiously, drawing his rifle from the saddle scabbard and carefully scanning the entire area. "How did you even get here?"

"I can only stand so much bagpiping," Sealy said dryly, shouldering her assault rifle. "So we stuffed Gramps into that empty pickle barrel down in the cellar and followed you in the Hummer. We're helping you, okay? Jeepers, what is the deal with this bog? It's all black, and it smells like a New Jersey oil refinery."

"*Get out of here!*" I shouted.

"No way, Bucky," Mort said grimly. "Anyway, I'm sure that anything you can take on with hunting rifles, we can handles with assault rifles and sub guns. Sure, I don't know how to load most of them, but the movies showed me how to shoot them. Remember my one-man-army science fiction epic, *Assault on Saskatchewan-5*? The lightest thing I packed in that was an M249 light machine gu–"

There was no twig-snap warning this time. The mud-covered hostile mountain spirit erupted from the bog like a dark chocolate volcano with glowing red eyes, no more than three feet behind Mort. With one powerful lunge, it snatched him up in its hideous talons and launched itself into the trees of the nearby glen, its lashing serpent of a tail splattering all of us with mud. Mort only had time to let out a short "*Blagh!*" and then he was gone. His MP5 splashed into the mud a couple of seconds later.

"The spirits got Mort!" I squawked, whipping out my Trapper and trying to get a shot off. It was useless. The spirit had evaporated into the trees as suddenly as it had emerged.

"Holy Swiss," Corky cursed involuntarily, crossing himself. "Saint Michael, hang in there for us, will ya?"

A twig snapped in response.

Instantly, Corky had sprang from Jimmy-Boy III's saddle. He dove through the air and tackled Sealy into the mud, sinking both of them out of sight just as a second pair of enormous glowing red eyes blasted out of the haze, passing directly over where Sealy had been standing. Betty-Sue and I both managed to fire one shot at the flying shadow, and mine found its mark in the phantom's neck, slamming it into the bog, with only its hairy hunchback visible. Corky surfaced from the mud with a gasp, just as the spirit began to rise up once more. My brother and I opened fire on it at point-blank range, emptying our rifles into its back and shoulders in less than five seconds. With one last bone-chilling scream, the spirit toppled into the bog and didn't move again.

"I got it!" Betty-Sue squealed, the .22 in her hands shaking from the pumping adrenaline.

Corky and I just stared at her, and then down at our own smoking rifles.

"Well, I was close," she grumbled.

"I'm sure you were," I encouraged her, thumbing more shells into the 30-30.

"What the helper elf was that?!" Sealy sputtered, popping out of the muskeg, every inch of her lithe body smeared with gobs of black mud and oil-slicked moss.

"That," I said, gingerly plucking Mort's fallen MP5 from the mud, "is what the superstitious locals call the hostile mountain spirits. Which is preposterous, really. They're just an indigenous variety of giant evil forest monkeys."

(See what I mean about first-person narrators holding back the truth in order to deliver last-minute plot twists? I could have told you from page one that giant evil monkeys roamed the slopes of Banshee Screech Peak by night, and, quite frankly, that would have made a considerably better opening line, something akin to "Call me Ishmael." But, no, my publishers at *Snazzy Spiffy Perfect Literary House* endlessly hounded and vaguely threatened me to keep that bit of useful information veiled from you for at least the first four hundred pages. The result is four hundred pages worth of awkward dialogue and a gloss-over style of prose that has possibly crippled this book. Don't blame me. Blame the literary experts who only want marketable formula.)

"*Giant monkeys?!*" Sealy screamed, scrambling to her feet and grabbing for her fallen M4 Carbine. "You mean like *Sasquatch?*"

"No, silly," Corky said airily, reloading his rifle. "Sasquatches are North American forest apes. These things have serpentine tails with which they wreak great mischief, so they're technically monkeys."

"Enough with the wreaking great mischief," Betty-Sue muttered. "Who came up with that expression, anyway?"

"You have Sasquatches living in your backyard?!" Sealy exploded. "And it never occurred to *any of you* that the rest of the world might want to know about it?"

"The world is looking for a forest ape," Corky said, staring at her as if the answer should have been obvious. "Nobody said word one about looking for giant evil forest monkeys. Are you telling me that the rest of the world doesn't know about these things?"

"Yes!" Sealy wailed. "The rest of the world has no clue about these things! How could you possibly not know that?"

"What are we supposed to be?" Corky remarked. "Mind-readers?"

"Who cares?" I snarled, chambering my rifle and wheeling Homestretch around to face the glen. "They've got Mort now! Corky, get your fianceé back to the Hummer. She'll be safe there."

"Oh no you don't," Sealy asserted. "You're not leaving me alone with Sasquatches running around. I hate Sasquatches! I always have."

"They're not Sasquatches," Betty-Sue said patiently. "Jeepers, lady, have you been listening to anything we've said?"

"Don't worry, Bucky," Corky assured me. "The layer of mud she's covered in will mask her scent, as well as her body's heat signature, just in case the monkeys utilize any form of infrared spectral visio–"

"Let's go!" I snapped, spurring Homestretch up onto the firmer ground of the glen, and then letting him run.

Betty-Sue put the spurs to Porkchop, while Corky pulled Sealy onto the back of Jimmy-Boy III's saddle, and we charged into the murky glen in search of our missing Hollywood action hunk, Max-Ram Target.

"Hang on!" Corky whooped to Sealy. "Let's hunt some funky monkey!"

The light was poor in the overshadowed haze of the glen, but the ground was solid. I was able to find and follow Mort's trail quite easily, one consisting mainly of monkey tracks, broken branches, fingernail scratches raked horizontally across tree trunks, and the occasional wrenched-out tuft of Mort's blonde hair.

"Where are they going?" Sealy shouted at me.

"How should I know?" I shot back. "Nobody goes in here. Nobody sane anyway."

"Oh, great," Sealy muttered. "The lair of the Sasquatch."

"That movie was awesome," Corky quipped.

"They're not Sasquatches," I reminded her once again. "How many times do we have to spell it out for you?"

"So what are they, smart guy?" Sealy demanded.

"Sascrunches," I replied.

"*What?*"

"We call them Sascrunches," I repeated more clearly, reining Homestretch expertly around a clump of pricker bushes.

"*That sounds exactly the same as Sasquatch!*" Sealy exploded. "How could you not know they were the same thing?"

"Because it's obvious," Corky explained. "They have tails. A forest ape wouldn't have–"

"So let me get this straight," Sealy protested. "If Sasquatches were the furthest thing from your mind, why in the world would you even think of the name Sascrunch?"

"Because," Corky expounded as Jimmy-Boy III sailed over a fallen log, "the first time we ran into one, it stepped on Sassy's toes and they made this really funny crunching sound."

"That was hysterical," I said, choking back a laugh in spite of the looming danger. "But you know what, Sealy? Sascrunch does sound a lot like Sasquatch, doesn't it? It's so crazy that we've never noticed that before...."

"So what gives you locals the free pass?" Sealy wanted to know.

"The ancient Knick-Knack Indians from this region called them the Seekers of Banana-Breath," I informed her. "Or *Bok-mok shmock-jock* in the Knick-Knack tongue. They warned the first settlers of Coyote Yelp Pass to leave their banana-munching ways behind them, and we've been a banana-free zone since 1826."

"There's been no bananas in this town since 1826?" Sealy said incredulously.

"Yeah, potassium deficiency is getting to be a bit of an epidemic around here," I admitted.

"Of course, we've had our close calls," Betty-Sue pointed out. "Old Mrs Quivercake is getting a bit daft, and she brought this jellied salad to last year's Harvest Potluck...."

"This is crazy!" Sealy insisted, hanging onto Corky's waist for dear life as we continued our blind charge through the foliage. "You're saying that those things attacked in force and carried off my fellow cult members because we eat bananas?"

"That's exactly what I'm saying!" I growled. "And they took Mort because you idiots threw banana smoothie on his face yesterday."

"Please tell me you're joking," Sealy groaned.

"Religious atheists consider banana consumption to be a holy communion with their primate ancestors," Corky said knowledgeably, not bothered by preaching to the choir. "And their banana ancestors, too, as humans have 76% of structural genes in common with bananas. You consider it communion; we consider it a grisly death sentence. To each their own, I guess. Topography and zoology sometimes make all the difference."

"And now you're just going to kill them?" Sealy whined. "They have to be an endangered species! Anyway, we share 98% of our structural genes with chimps, so these things are probably as close to human as an animal can be. Of course, we also share 98% of structural genes with mice, but that's probably not significant. My point is, shouldn't we at least attempt a non-lethal rescue, or even some form of negotiation?"

"Oh, you are going to *love* being a cowboy's wife," I said, rolling my eyes.

"Okay, I'll admit that their sudden appearance from under the mud was startling, but how bad can they really be? They're just animals."

"Well," I commented, "I'm not sure if the hell-forged spawn of Satan is the right term..."

"I never mentioned the hell-forged spawn of–"

"...but I will say that they're pure evil. Seriously, these are evil monkeys."

"He ain't kidding, pudding puff," Corky remarked. "Did you ever see that movie *The Relic*? The Kothoga monster's got nothing on Sascrunches. He only decapitated or transected his victims. Sascrunches make human coleslaw. They eat you from the toes up, avoiding all major organs and blood vessels until last. These are sick, sick monkeys, baby. They're like mosquitos crossed with komodo dragons crossed with something else really hairy and smelly."

"Bucky's toes?" Betty-Sue supplied.

"It's a medical condition!" I said defensively.

"Whatever you say, soupy socks," Corky snorted. "But this is the real deal, baby. Sascrunches are the most efficiently lethal creatures on the planet. They don't waste time with a bunch of stupid car chases and multi-angle explosions and Ben Affleck. They know just two things: Killing and eating, sometimes in that order."

"That was a bit of a reach," I commented.

"Not hardly, pard," Corky drawled. "You've seen it."

"No, I just meant that it seems like you really had to go out of your way to take a shot at Michael Bay there," I explained, swerving Homestretch around a moss-covered boulder. "He was totally off-topic."

"*Pearl Harbour* was unforgivable, Bucky," Corky growled. "We can't afford to let the world forget."

"Amen," Sealy concurred solemnly. "It was like a knee to the nuts of American history."

Betty-Sue and Porkchop had pulled into the lead of the column, but they suddenly halted, my wife's hand held in the air to command silence. Corky and I reined to a stop behind her.

"Do you guys hear that?" Betty-Sue said sharply "Is it just me, or is it getting ... whinier in here?"

We all listened attentively to the faint sounds of the air. Sure enough, the high-pitched tone we were hearing was unmistakable.

"That's Mort!" I whispered excitedly, as my celebrity friend's familiar incessant whining reached my ears.

"And Archie!" Sealy breathed, her ears recognizing another, higher-pitched whine. "I'd know that brown-nose suck-up sound anywhere."

"Everybody hold up," Corky hissed. "Dismount."

We tied the horses to the trees, and slunk toward the large gully ahead of us on foot, rifles clenched in sweaty hands. As the human whining and monkey shrieks grew louder, we dropped to our bellies and crawled silently to the edge of the trees, just before the ground began to slope downward. Below us was a wide valley nearly the size of a football field, with only a few trees scattered about. However, in the centre of the largest open space was a single enormous deciduous tree that was truly a sight to behold. Standing well over eighty feet high, with boughs that stretched out more than forty feet in every direction, it was an overshadowing presence to the entire valley. Its girth was nearly thirty feet around the base, and its roots, trunk, and branches were as twisted and evil as the monkeys who called them home.

And there were living human beings at the base of that massive tree, each one bound with ropes of vine and thistle to a high-thrust protruding root, their faces and clothing smeared with tree sap and peppered with coniferous needles. They were all but invisible from the thighs down, mostly due to a ground-hugging fog and the heaps of bleached bones that were piled up past their knees.

Unfortunately, getting to them would be a problem, because more than a dozen jubilant golden-haired Sascrunches with saucer-sized glowing red eyes were dancing around the base of the tree as well, sporadically leaping to swing from the mother tree's boughs by their hands and tails. Each one was more than seven feet tall when reared up on their smaller hind legs, with slender arms that were more than six feet long. Longest of all were their winding tails that coiled and snapped and lashed about like living bullwhips. Gramps had warned us repeatedly about Sascrunch tails. He had said that a good snap from one of those tails could split a prize pumpkin in half.

"Well, that ain't good," I remarked.

"I recognize the scientists and Sting and Max-Ram," Betty-Sue reported, squinting through the haze at the quivering mass of humanity lashed to the mother tree. "But, jeepers, who's the big guy in the middle?"

We all stared hard for a long moment, but it was Sealy who recognized the obese man first.

"*Vasil?*" she blurted, her jaw dropping.

"Holy cow cud, you're right," I realized. "Guys, that's The Sickle!"

"You said The Sickle was more of string-bean than you are," Corky pointed out.

"No, I never said that," I replied. "But he was a lot leaner last time I saw him."

"So it's true!" Sealy gasped. "The Sasquatches do fatten them up before eating them!"

As if to verify what she had just said, a lone Sascrunch began circling the base of the mother tree, awkwardly lumbering on its hind legs in order to hold the massive bowl it carried in both hands, fashioned crudely from a hollowed-out section of rotten log. It stopped by Argo first, who was shaking his head furiously, as if pleading for the torment to end. Ignoring this, the Sascrunch dug a long hand into the bowl and withdrew a fistful of gummy orange tree sap and pinecones, which were then crammed into Argo's mouth. Showing a great deal of simian intelligence, the monkey clamped its other hand over Argo's mouth and nose, forcing the scientist to chew rapidly and swallow before he was allowed to breathe again. Only after hearing the sickening "Gulp!" did the Sascrunch release Argo's face, and then moved on to force-feed Mort in a similar manner.

"*Ghlack!*" Mort gagged when his turn was over, his eyes bulging. "It's like inhaling jellied gasoline and fingernail clippings!"

"Be calm, Max-Ram," Sting advised him coolly. "As with all great action hunks, our minds are our greatest weapons. We'll think of a way out of this."

"You don't understand," Mort groaned. "It was a monkey movie that sank my career in the first place. This adventure was shaping up to be my big comeback, regardless of the contract. For the first time in my life, I've been living an action movie, right down to the letter: Machine guns, mad scientists, hot chicks, fist fights, car chases, bombs, monsters, crashing helicopters, Bruce Willis, people in cloaks ... and now freaking monkeys show up! I hate monkeys, man! It doesn't even matter if I get to star in a film adaptation of my own incredible true story now, because it's just going to be another stupid monkey movie!"

"You did a monkey movie?" Sting said, his face twisting with revulsion, although that might have just been the aftertaste of all the sap he had swallowed.

"Yeah, don't you remember?" Mort said. "I was a cop who got partnered with Orange Alps the Yodelling Orangutan.... Never mind. But that's why I stopped getting work. Hollywood never forgets monkey movies."

"I thought you couldn't get work after your elephant tusk smuggling scandal," Sting recalled. "And those comments in *US Weekly* about Natalie Portman's haircut."

"That was taken out of context!" Mort snapped.

I had seen enough. I lowered myself back from the valley rim, and we silently withdrew a few feet to plan our next step.

"Okay, that's really bad," I admitted, cringing. "That's a lot of monkeys."

"What do we do, Bucky?" Betty-Sue asked nervously, keeping a careful eye on the tree branches above us.

"Yeah, Bucky," Corky said. "What do we do?"

"Why am I suddenly in charge?" I demanded.

"So that every subsequent disaster-slash-fatality is on your conscience alone," Corky replied without missing a beat.

"Ah," I said understandingly. "I'm honestly surprised that I didn't think of that."

"Duh," Corky said with a smile.

"There's at least sixteen of them," I pointed out. "We can't just wade in swinging."

"Why not?" Corky inquired skeptically. "Monkeys aren't like Puerto Ricans or Jews. They're fair game."

"I'm not sure why, but the way you phrased that sounded really wrong," I had to state for the record. "Okay, let's think this through. We can't sneak up on them, because it's open terrain and they're swinging on every side of that big creepy mother tree. What we need is some kind of diversion, something to draw the evil monkeys away into the forest. Then we can go in and get Mort before they come back."

Corky could only stare at me in disgust.

"And you call yourself a cowboy," he said sourly.

"Hear me out," I insisted. "Remember 2005? The summer of Diabolical Jo?"

"Canadian serial killer?" Sealy inquired.

"Killer cow," Corky replied.

"Not just a killer cow," I corrected him. "The worst killer cow ever. She made Evil Sue look like ... like...."

"...an Italian military action?" Betty-Sue guessed.

"Is that an actual expression?" I had to ask. "It doesn't even sound current."

"Trust me, it's current," Corky assured us. "However, their food is incomparable."

"Hey, I love Italians," Sealy interceded. "You know what I hate? I hate it when people say '*Ciao*' like they're all sophisticated, but they don't speak a word of Italian."

"I thought *Ciao* was Lithuanian," Corky said blankly.

"Okay, shut up, seriously," I said, trying to keep our focus on matters of imminent death. "Anyway, Diabolical Jo's calf got sick, and Diabolical Jo wouldn't let us get close enough to treat it. You remember?"

"You want us to run the Diabolical Jo play?" Corky asked. "On Sascrunches?"

"What's the Diabolical Jo play?" Sealy wanted to know.

"Me and Sassy hid in a coulee downwind with the scour medication and throat tube," Corky recounted. "Then we got Bucky to skyline himself on a knoll above Diabolical Jo, with Homestretch waiting just out of sight beyond it. When Diabolical Jo went charging off to kill Bucky, we snagged her calf and jammed the pill down its throat."

"Bucky, that play didn't work," Betty-Sue recalled. "You told me that Diabolical Jo caught you before you could get to Homestretch, and she trampled you eleven times."

"True," I admitted. "Corky finally had to shoot her in the head with the .375 to get her to stop.... And, actually, that was the only part of the play I was planning on using."

The others paused for a moment, and then turned to stare at me, wondering if I was really saying what they thought I was saying.

"I *do* call myself a cowboy, thank you very much," I growled.

"If we get through this, I'm having your baby," Betty-Sue said, looking at me in awe.

"Fine, let's shoot something," I sighed, cocking my Trapper. "Do it for baby Rusty."

"Do you see this, world?" Corky cheered. "That's my baby brother you're looking at!"

With a unified battle cry, we lunged to our feet and charged down into the valley, our hail of bullets leading the way. Me and Corky were the first to drop a Sascrunch dead in its tracks with his .375 and my 30-30, and Sealy's M4 Carbine hosed down the vengeful second one that charged at my brother in retribution. Betty-Sue's .22s pelted into the dirt and trees all around us.

"*Die, monkeys!*" Sealy rasped, apparently putting her animal-rights vendetta on backburner for the time being.

"Bucky?" Mort gasped.

Startled by the deafening eruption of gunfire, the rest of the Sascrunches let out terrified howls and disappeared into the forest or up into the mother tree. However, I knew that they would be back soon.

"Go, Bucky!" Corky shouted, aiming high. "We'll cover the trees."

I ran to Mort's side, hurriedly thumbing more shells into my rifle along the way. Resting the weapon against the enormous root he was strapped to, I quickly unfolded my pocketknife and began sawing at the vines.

"Is that your castrating knife?" Mort asked squeamishly. "Seriously, I wanna know where that thing's been before I get nicked by it."

"Just pull!" I snapped.

"*Saaap....*" The Sickle moaned.

"You came to rescue us?" Kay Argo said, suddenly becoming choked with emotion. "Why would you do that?"

"Beats me," I replied as Mort tore his way to freedom. "It just seemed that leaving a bunch of scientists and action hunks to be turned into banana loaf was one of those things that would make Jesus sad. Hold still."

"I can't believe you did that," Argo marvelled as I hacked the vines around him. "No one's ever risked their life for me. Even my own crew wouldn't."

"Hey, I would have, Dr Argo!" Archie Aptrick insisted, but then thought the better of it. "Ah, heck, you're probably right. I wouldn't have. Survival of the fittest leaves absolutely zero tolerance for mercy. Actually, as a matter for further discussion, survival of the fittest really doesn't leave much leeway for animal rights, either, which is quite strange as evolutionists are leading emissaries of that particu–"

"Just *go!*" I shouted, freeing scientists left and right, swinging my castrating knife like a tiny machete.

No sooner had I cut through the last of the vines holding Sting Ripblood captive than a Sascrunch dropped down on me from the branches above with a devilish screech. Sting sprang into action as only the world's leading action hunk could, giving the giant monkey a flying high-kick to the jaw and a flurry of paralyser nerve strikes that dropped it onto its back with its limbs locked and twitching like a dying spider. Sealy's underslung Masterkey shotgun finished it off with a quick slug to the skull. Then she pulled a pair of golden 50-caliber Desert Eagle pistols from her belt and tossed them to Sting, who wasted no time in dispatching two more Sascrunches as they were dropping down upon us. With a single shot from each massive handgun, the coast was clear again.

"Oh, come on!" Mort protested, staring incredulously at the three dead monkeys heaped around Sting.

"*Run!*" I roared, hearing the hissing mutters of more Sascrunches rapidly descending from the overhanging branches. "We've got to get out from under this tree!"

My words came just a moment too late. As we charged out into the open, a single monkey tail whirled down on us like a lasso, snagging Mort by the throat. He was lifted as though weightless toward the branches above.

My Winchester came up spitting bullets as fast as I could work the lever. By pure luck, one of the wild rounds struck the prehensile tail, severing it and dropping Mort back to the ground. The injured Sascrunch dropped down after him, enraged by the loss of its primary weapon, and Mort tried to scramble to his feet to get away. Then Sting was on the move again, diving sideways through the air with a firing Desert

Eagle in each hand. All six of the heavy rounds were tightly grouped into the monkey's chest, dropping it dead before it could advance on Mort.

"I learned that one from you, Max-Ram!" Sting whooped, rolling to his feet and following the fleeing scientists, who were burdened by the weight of the barely-conscious Sickle. "The Max-Ram Lateral Corkscrew Power Dive®!"

"Yeah, but I could never hit anything while I was doing it," Mort replied glumly as we made our dash back toward the treeline.

Sealy was leading Sting and the scientists back toward the horses, while Corky and Betty-Sue covered their retreat. Another Sascrunch came charging in from one of the smaller trees to the west, and Betty-Sue scared the heck out of it with her .22 until Corky was able to intervene with his .375, dropping the charging monkey with one well-placed shot between the eyes.

"You're doing great, cranberry muffin," I called out, running toward Betty-Sue.

"Shut up!" she mumbled, slapping in a fresh clip and working the bolt.

Our ragtag group of cowboys, scientists, and action stars ran back up the slope, but the fast-moving Sascrunches were fanning out from the mother tree and bypassing our flanks, with the clear intention of encircling us and then closing in for the kill.

"Look out, Mort!" I yelped, pushing him out of the way as one of the larger Sascrunches charged at us. I emptied my Winchester into the evil primate as it closed in, but it still retained enough momentum to slam into me and Mort, and the three of us went rolling down the hill to the mother tree once more. The Sascrunch was good and dead by the time we landed in a heap at the bottom of the slope, but, unfortunately, it was lying on top of us and we couldn't move it.

"Okay, that's getting really heavy," Mort gasped breathlessly, after a few moments of futile struggling.

"*Bucky!*" Corky and Betty-Sue cried out in horror. They tried to run back to me, but the Sascrunches were closing in on them from all sides, and it was taking all of their combined firepower to hold the beasts at bay, along with Sting and Sealy. They had formed a protective ring around the unarmed scientists, but I didn't know how long they could keep it up.

I had my own problems to worry about. One of the Sascrunches had sniffed out me and Mort, and broke off from the main pack to charge down the hill toward us, roaring and drooling. My Winchester was lying in the dry grass beside me, just out of my reach. Gramps' shotgun was still on my back, but I couldn't pull it out. All I could manage to do was roll onto my side, draw my pocketknife, and frantically saw through the leather sling, the lone Sascrunch bearing down on us all the while.

"Bucky...." Mort gurgled as the giant monkey loomed over our protruding heads and shoulders. "Saw faster!"

The Sascrunch reached forward and wrapped its long, clammy fingers around my throat, pulling me out from under its dead counterpart, and toward its own gaping jaws. I could see its four peg-like tusks, each one more than five inches long. As I was dragged forward, I felt the leather strap finally bisecting under the blade of my knife, and the shotgun fell to the ground in my wake.

"Do it, Mort!" I croaked.

Mort did it. He snatched up the shotgun, eared back both hammers, and gave the Sascrunch both rounds of buckshot in the neck.

"I did it!" Mort squawked. "I did a heroic act with a gun!"

"Thanks," I wheezed, pocketing my knife and using my improved leverage to help Mort wriggle to freedom, shoving the dead monkey off his torso. Then I grabbed my rifle, and was prepared to run once more, but I caught a glimpse of something strange in the corner of my eye.

Mort was standing, but he wasn't running. When I turned toward him, I could see why.

She had arrived silently for one so large, a Sascrunch that towered at least two feet higher than the other Sascrunches' seven foot norm, with glowing red eyes that were closer to the size of dinner plates than saucers. Her silver fur bristled with the bulging monkey muscles that it concealed, and her tail was curiously trifurcated a few feet from the base into three whiplash ends, all of which seemed to move independently, giving her a total tail-reach diameter of more than twenty feet. And she didn't look happy to see us.

"Uh, Bucky?" Mort asked, his shotgun lowering involuntarily.

"Yes, Mort?" I replied, equally transfixed.

"Any other legends I might want to know about?"

"Yup," I replied. "The Legend of Big Mama's House."

"What?"

"She's the big cheese, Mort. The ... Queenscrunch."

"*Bucky!*" I heard Betty-Sue scream from behind us.

Mort and I both whipped our guns up as the Queenscrunch let out a spittle-laden roar, nearly blinding both of us with saliva. But we both managed to squeeze the trigger, and we both heard the sound of the hammers clicking down on empty chambers.

"*Craaaaaap!*" Mort rasped, breaking open the side-by-side.

Before we could even reach for spare shells, the

Queenscrunch backhanded us with a talon the size of a large snow shovel. We were swatted roughly thirty feet through the air, until our flight was intercepted by the merciful boughs of one of the weeping willows. That part actually wasn't so bad. The bad part was when the bough gave way beneath us, dropping us more than ten feet to the hard ground below. Both of our weapons and my cowboy hat were lying on the ground where our launch had commenced, and the Queenscrunch was lumbering toward us, drool spraying from her thick lips like a slimy lawn sprinkler and her crazed eyes widening to the size of small hubcaps.

"There's always gotta be slime," Mort moaned, clutching his bruised ribs. "Man, I hate monkeys...."

I was just as wracked with pain, but managed to roll onto my stomach and look up at the approaching lady of the tree. One of her tail-ends was curled over her back like a scorpion's stinger, but the other two were sliding over the ground on either side behind her, almost as if she was feeling for something with them. Apparently she was, because one tail-end found and wrapped around a large tree branch, and the other found the canon bone of a dead horse, its attached hoof clicking like a literal death rattle as the bone was likewise seized and raised up over her back.

My eyes widened as I realized what was happening, and I shakily stood to my feet.

"Mort," I quavered. "Watch out for her tail...."

"What?" Mort coughed, trying to rise.

"*Run!*" I roared. "*She's about to wreak great mischief!*"

We both dove out of the way in opposite directions, the branch and bone smashing down like mallets right where we had been standing as Mort was still corkscrewing sideways through the air.

I landed rolling, but all I could see were those hammering tail-ends, and more Sascrunches pouring into the valley of death. I caught a quick glimpse of Corky, Sting, and Sealy still hosing down every monkey in sight, two of whom seemed to be playing hacky-sack with a squalling Dr Argo.

"*Yaaah!*" Betty-Sue hollered, fighting her way through swarms of monkeys to engage the Queenscrunch's flanks at point-blank range with the old bolt-action .22. This time, she was too close to miss, but, unfortunately, that also meant that she was too close to be safe. The Queenscrunch flinched and cringed as the .22 rounds peppered her back and shoulder, but she didn't even look back as her third tail-end shot forward and wrapped around Betty-Sue's throat. My wife was lifted from the ground by the seemingly independent-controlled tail, while the other two continued to track every movement Mort and I made, trying to swat us like pesky bugs.

"Betty-Sue!" I squawked, pulling out my pocketknife once more. "Drop my wife, you monkey freak!"

I sidestepped the horse bone as it came crashing down again, and then leapt forward to slash my small blade across the Queenscrunch's face. The stinging cut made her grimace, but then she bunted me to the ground and took a swipe at me with her fearsome talon. I ducked under the large arm just in time, and the claws harmlessly passed through the base of a small tree behind me, felling it to the ground.

"*Allah Akbar!*" Mort shouted, snatching up the recently-deceased young tree and using it to pole-vault onto the Queenscrunch's shoulders, clamping a rather ineffective chokehold around her massive neck. The man may have rarely kept the same religion for more than a month at a time, but he knew when it was time to invoke a higher power.

Betty-Sue was hanging onto the tail-end around her neck with both hands, desperately trying to pull it loose, but it only seemed to be growing tighter. Her face was turning blue, and I was powerless to help her. I had only managed to rise to my hands and knees before the Queenscrunch grabbed me around the torso with both of her long hands, pinning my right arm to my side. I struggled in vain to get free as she raised me to her gaping jaws, licking her lips greedily.

Just when all seemed lost.... Ah, heck, I'm not going to build it up. It's already fairly obvious that I got rescued. Why are first-person narrators even expected to build up suspense? Seriously, it just makes us seem sneaky.

Anyway, I heard a roaring engine, and blinding headlights suddenly came bouncing down the hill, blinding the Queenscrunch. What might once have been a white honeymoon limo ran over at least three Sascrunches before it slammed into the mother tree a moment later, spraying clumps of mud in every direction. Although the windshield was smeared with muskeg, I caught a glimpse of a panicking young chauffeur behind the wheel. Then the skylight popped open, and Sassy and Junior clambered onto the roof, still dressed in their respective matrimonial attire. I really couldn't remember if I had ever seen Sassy wear a dress before, let alone an eggshell-white wedding gown. However, some things never change. My sister had two bandoleers strapped over her strapless shoulders, with her wedding bouquet in one hand and her10-gauge shotgun in the other. Junior was equally formal/combat ready, wearing a big-and-tall double-breasted black tuxedo, the effect of which was slightly lessened by the quiver of arrows on his back and the compound hunting bow in his ham-sized fist. However, his great-grandfather's old USMC Mameluke Sword on his hip added a rather distinguished touch.

Sassy's situational awareness was as keen as ever, and she had located the most pressing issue within a second of emerging from the limo. Her left hand instantly shot out in my direction, releasing her beloved 10-gauge and sending it spinning through the air toward me.

"Bucky!" she yelled. "Blast'er!"

I caught the Bucky-Blaster with one hand, eared back the hammers with my teeth, and squeezed the trigger just as the Queenscrunch bit down hard on the ends of the barrels.

The blast was muffled by her enormous mouth, but the effect of said blast was undiminished. For a long moment, the Queenscrunch's glowing eyes just kept getting wider and larger, while her body didn't move at all. Then her third tail-end finally relaxed, dropping Betty-Sue to the ground. A moment later, the queen of the Sascrunches collapsed to the forest floor, nearly landing on me and Mort.

"Alright!" Sassy crowed. "That's my baby brother!"

"Everybody in the limo!" Junior yelled, firing arrows at a rate and acuity-level that would have put Legolas the Woodland Elf to shame.

Sting was laying down cover fire with his Desert Eagles as Corky and Sealy herded the frazzled scientists into the back of the car. Sting was the last to dive in, and Corky slammed the door.

"Let's go, Bucky!" Sassy called out as she and Junior dropped back into the skylight. "This train ain't waiting!"

"Betty-Sue, go!" I barked, but she was already getting up and running for the front door of the limo. Mort and I snatched up our fallen rifles and my cowboy hat, and charged after her.

We were only fifteen feet from the stretched vehicle when Corky popped through the skylight and squawked, "Bucky, behind you!"

Betty-Sue already had her hand on the front passenger-side door, but her jaw-dropped as she saw what Corky was frantically pointing at. Mort and I both spun around, just as the now seriously cheesed-off Queenscrunch reared up behind us with her jaws gaping, obviously prepared to take both of our heads off in a single bite.

"*Holy spruce sap!*" Mort shrieked, as what was left of his hair began to stand on end.

A single sharp gunshot rang out, and the Queenscrunch crashed to the ground, shrouding Mort and I in a cloud of dust. And, just in case you think I'm trying to build suspense again, let me assure you that this time she was really dead. Honest, I wouldn't lie to you.

When the dust settled, Mort and I turned around to see Betty-Sue lowering her smoking .22, which she had been wise enough to rest across the roof of the limo.

"It's all about hitting the right spot," she said weakly, forcing a grin.

"Ladies and gentlemen, I give you secret agent Janis T. McKritch!" I announced as Mort and I scrambled after her into the front seat of the limo, slamming the door just in time for three enraged Sascrunches to slam into it. Frustrated, they began pounding their long hands against the hood and screeching like the banshees for which their mountain was named.

"Hey, Bucky," Sassy immediately called out, "have you been pocketing your brass? I've been brushing up on my hand-loads. I'm working on a chemical upgrade for regular gunpowder, patents pending. I call it *Megaton by Sassy*, and it's gonna–"

"No, I haven't been pocketing my brass!" I exploded, throwing her shotgun through the back window to her. "We're in a gunfight with swarms of man-eating monkeys!"

"Maybe if the monkeys had guns that would be a decent excuse," Sassy said in her stern librarian voice. "As is, I just consider it slacking off."

"*Would somebody just drive the bloody car?*" Argo

sputtered, recoiling as a Sascrunch began pounding a fist against the window beside him.

"Patience, son," Sassy advised, giving the panicked scientist a quick jolt from her Shocking Silly, Ver.II to calm him down.

"Actually, he raises a valid suggestion," I noted. "We should drive the car."

"Punch it!" Mort snapped at the petrified young driver, identified by his name-tag as Phil.

"Move the car, Phil," Sassy snarled over all of the panicked blubbering in the passenger compartment.

"Yes, ma'am, Mrs Van Der Snoot!" Phil whined, slamming the vehicle into reverse and hitting the gas. "Thank you for choosing Gold Bell Limos!"

The mud-caked limousine chugged about two feet backwards before the transmission apparently dropped through the engine housing, and the whole rig died. Again, I'm not trying to build any kind of key-turning suspense scene. That limo was flat-out dead. Silence filled the long car, broken only by the muffled sounds of the Sascrunches beating on the roof.

"Well," Junior said weakly, "in its defence, these things probably aren't built for plowing through several kilometres of mountain terrain, old-growth forest, and swamp. I sincerely give it props for getting us this far."

"Let me get this straight," I said through clenched teeth. "You made the admittedly noble decision to fly home early to rescue us, and then you decided that a chauffeured limo was your best rental option?"

"I'm not denying my wife at least some fragment of her honeymoon," Junior said, offended. "How callous do you think I am?"

I decided that hitting the divider button was wiser than words at that point. The tinted glass slid up, separating the compartment from the cab, and leaving me, Mort, Betty-Sue, and Phil in blissful silence.

"I think we're going to die," Betty-Sue remarked, leaning against my shoulder as we obligingly reloaded our rifles.

Through the spider-web crack in the windshield, I could see one of the Sascrunches jump up on the hood and begin to bounce on it, but most of the others had been distracted by the massive form of their fallen Alpha-female. They were slowly gathering around her, then tilting their heads back and howling at the sky. And then, one by one, they were turning their enraged red eyes back toward the limo.

"Yep," I agreed, pouring my extra shotgun shells into Mort's lap. "We're going to die."

"Bucky, I don't wanna die," Mort pointed out with some amount of urgency, hurriedly reloading Gramps' shotgun.

"Yeah, I'm with Max-Ram Target on that," Phil concurred. "Wha...? Holy crap, I'm *literally* with Max-Ram Target! Hey! Are you that stupid cowboy who found a living dinosaur?"

"Technically?" I clarified. "No."

"Bucky, we're gonna die!" Mort reminded me, in case I had forgotten in the past nine seconds.

We all jumped and screamed as the dividing window was smashed from behind us, following a sharp elbow drive by Sassy.

"What kind of talk is that?" my sister demanded, sliding new shells into her shotgun.

"How did you even hear us?" I had to ask.

"Suck it up and cinch it up, cowpokes!" Sassy ordered. "We don't give up just because the steaming buffalo chips are down! We are Laroos and Van Der Snoots and Max-Ram Target and a guy named Phil!" She paused dramatically to cuff Mort on the back of the head. "You should be leading the charge, tubby. Be the hero you've always pretended to be!"

"I know that you're just trying to rally us into action, Sassy," Mort sighed. "But look around. We're completely surrounded, and we're running out of ammo."

"Believe in yourself, Max-Ram!" Sassy exclaimed.

"Like every single deluded twit on the *American Idol* auditions?" Mort said dryly.

"I know what this is really about, Max-Ram," Sassy pointed out. "I know that you don't think you're ready to take on a pack of bloodthirsty forest monkeys, because all the contracts in the world can't get you out of messes like this. You think you'll die as just another burned out action hunk. And that's what you are, I'm not going to lie to you. You are a talentless, really fat, burned out action hunk. But you're not the first to go down this road. Remember what happened to Sylvester Stallone? He was in a bad movie slump for twenty years after *Rambo* and *Rocky*. But did he give up? No! He pulled himself out of that hole after twenty meaningless, waste-of-skin years, and he made a stunning comeback ... remaking *Rambo* and *Rocky*."

"I guess I hadn't thought of it that way," Mort confessed.

"Now's not the time to think, son!" Sassy assured him. "Just because you're out of shape doesn't mean that you're out for the count. Look at Arnold Schwarzenegger. He had the motivation and the stamina to go on and become the governor of California! He had the backbone to stand up for the issues that weighed heaviest on his heart. And he had the unparalleled wisdom to foresee that setting *Predator 2* in Los Angeles, rather than in the jungle where it belonged, would strip it of all the primal ferocity which made the original such an enduring classic, eclipsing all sequels and subsequent *Alien* crossover franchises! Seriously, did you guys see *Aliens vs Predator: Requiem*? Just when you thought it couldn't get any worse than *Alien 3....*"

The Sascrunch on the hood had finally spotted us through the window, and was now focussing all of his efforts on bashing through the windshield with his head. Bits of glass were showering us with every strike. However, Sassy's invigorating speech had taken effect, and Mort's eyes were now shining with the dawn of joyous revelation.

"You're right, Sassy," he cried out. "Action hunks really can transcend their 80s heyday and make a difference in the real world. And so can I!"

"Darn tootin'!" Sassy proclaimed, snapping her freshly-loaded Bucky-Blaster closed. "And I haven't even started on the musical careers of Bruce Willis, Chuck Norris, and Steven Seagal. Heck, I've even heard that Dolph Lundgren is really, really smart. It hasn't done him a lick of good in regards to making a theatrical comeback, but I did hear that somewhere. I think it was in a documentary about Dolph Lundgren."

"Here they come!" I warned the others, as the mob of more than twenty Sascrunches abandoned their mother and launched a full-out assault on the limo.

"No, Bucky," Mort said darkly, reaching through the back window to snatch the reloaded M4 Carbine and MP5 out of Sealy's grasp, much to her dismay. "Here *I* come! It's time to make Dolph proud."

He kicked open the passenger door, and went out bullets first. Two more Sascrunches were dropped in an instant, and a third was knocked unconscious when Mort lunged forward and clobbered it across the head with the stock of the M4. I have never seen a shirt disintegrate so fast.

The rest of us were so stunned that, for the first few seconds, all we could do was sit in the limo and stare at the whirling-dervish of high-kicks and spitting machine guns that Mort had suddenly transformed into. He didn't even seem to mind that he was on his own. In fact, he was laughing maniacally and mocking the Sascrunches in Dolph Lundgren's Swedish mother tongue, a language which I had been unaware that Mort had any fluency in.

"For Sverige i tiden!" he bellowed, alternately firing his two automatic weapons in every direction, dropping evil monkeys right and left. *"Stor amper schimpans jag skall krossa ni! Dolph Lundgren, leva ty samtliga tidpunkt! Babian jatte tatning nu!"*

I finally shook myself out of my trance and rallied the others with a shout of, "Okay, we're making a run for the truck! Everybody with a gun is on plowing duty!" I threw Gramps' shotgun and a fistful of shells back at Sealy as replacements for the weapons that had been taken from her, and then Betty-Sue and I grabbed Phil and charged out after Mort. Corky and Sealy were hand-in-hand as they ran from the vehicle in a hail of gunfire, with Sting pushing the rest of the scientists out behind them, not an easy task considering that The Sickle was still barely conscious, and Archie Aptrick's left leg was supported by a full-length cast. Sassy and Junior brought up the rearguard, firing as they came.

And that was when it happened. In the midst of a life-or-death firefight against evil monkeys, Mort spoke six words. It may not sound like much, but, with those two simple improvised sentences, Max-Ram Target would officially be reborn to all of us.

"Okay, monkeys...." Mort rasped, his eyes burning as he raised both of his machine guns while chewing on a matchstick. *"Come get some candy!"*

Sting stopped in his tracks, unable to even keep shooting. I couldn't blame him, and neither could anyone else. There was no doubt about what we had all just seen and heard.

It was the coolest action movie one-liner in history.

"I will never be worthy of The McTiernan Contract now," Sting gasped, his face ashen. "Max-Ram Target *is* 80s action!"

We were all jolted out of the sudden reverie when a Sascrunch pounced on The Sickle, and Sassy had to kill it with her Leatherman Super Tool pocketknife in order to save him. It was obvious that we were still outnumbered, and we would never be able to move fast enough to get away while burdened by injured/borderline sugar-comatose scientists.

"Are you okay?" Sassy asked, pulling the heavy man to his feet.

"*Saaap....*" seemed to be the only thing The Sickle was capable of replying.

"Shoot, I'm empty!" Betty-Sue cried as her .22 clicked on an empty chamber.

"Me too," Sting said, throwing down his Desert Eagles and preparing to combat the monkeys barehanded.

"Bucky, there's too many of them still!" Betty-Sue shouted, as we were forced back against the limo again. She was right. I only had about five shots left, but that was not the only thing bothering me. I could smell gasoline.

"What do we do, Bucky?" Corky asked, bumping into me as he and Sealy were forced to fall back as well. Soon after, all of the others were huddled against the side of the limo once more. Only Mort had made it more than twenty feet, and now we couldn't even see him. I didn't even know if he was still alive, but I couldn't hear his automatic gunfire anymore. And the smell of gasoline was growing stronger by the second.

I dropped to my hands and knees to peer under the limo. Sure enough, a steady stream of gasoline was leaking out from the ruptured fuel tank.

"*Bucky!*" everybody yelled at me in unison. "*What do we do?*"

"What do we do?" I repeated, snatching the Zippo lighter from Phil's hand as he frantically tried to light one last cigarette before he died. "We do what every redneck does in a man versus endangered species in a fragile ecosystem situation.... Set the forest on fire."

I sparked the lighter, and dropped it into the pool of gasoline.

"*Run!*"

"Thank you for choosing Gold Bell Limos!" Phil wailed as he sprinted toward the treeline.

We ran.

The sudden burst of flame caused all the Sascrunches to leap back in horror, and we ran right through the midst of them. The dry sticks and leaves that covered the ground were perfect fodder for the blaze, and the flames had soon spread to the mother tree itself. Indeed, the whole Glen of No Return was igniting almost as fast as we could run away from it. Of course, the extreme wildfire danger advisory from that very dry summer probably had something to do with it, but the speed with which the fire was spreading was absolutely ridiculous. And that wasn't even the oddest part. The oddest part was that the seven Sascrunches who had been closest to the limo didn't just get caught in the fireball. Rather, they instantly exploded into flames.

It was the craziest thing I had ever seen. One second they were ripping the siding off the limo, and the next they were going off like fireworks of spitting grease.

Sassy had always maintained that destroying the environment could save your life, and it turned out she was right. You see, no one in Coyote Yelp Pass wanted to relive the fall of '78, when the marshes had gotten so dry that the Sascrunches began freely wandering into

467

town, and even into Gramps' cabin, as I mentioned at the beginning of this book. Therefore, in an effort to keep the marshes perpetually well lubricated, the entire town had been dumping all of their used motor oil into the marshes along with their placation sacrifices for the past thirty-two years. Apparently, this precautionary measure had adversely affected the Sascrunches' preferred diet of pond slime and moss muskeg, resulting in massive overstimulation of their secreting oil glands. It did give them a thick and lustrous coat, but it also made them simian *flambé* in the presence of open flame.

"They're combustible!" Sassy blurted, as the monkeys continued to explode all around us. "Anybody got hair spray?"

Corky and I were the only ones who had any bullets left. We yelled for Sealy and Betty-Sue to lead the others back to the truck, while we held off the last of the evil monkeys. It was precision combat by that time, and neither one of us dared to fire unless we were guaranteed a kill. Even so, we only managed to drop three more of the beasts before both of our rifles ran dry. With no other way to defend ourselves, we went back-to-back, seized our weapons by the barrels and prepared to bash some monkey skulls with them. But there were at least five of them left, and they had us surrounded.

"Ride hard, Corky!" I called out.

"Ride hard, baby bro," he replied through gritted teeth.

Before the situation had a chance to get any more dramatic, there was a pounding of hooves, and a fully shirtless Max-Ram Target came charging over the crest of the hill on Porkchop, with the reins of Homestretch and Jimmy-Boy III in his teeth and a blazing machine gun in each hand. The remaining Sascrunches scattered, and Mort spat out our horses' reins as he rode past. Corky and I both grabbed the falling reins, swung into the saddle, and the three of us wheeled around to race out of the valley, leaving the last of the hostile mountain spirits at the mercy of the flames.

"*Yeeeee-haw!*" Mort yodelled, flopping around in the saddle like a cowboy Slinky toy. "I could get used to this cowboy thing!"

With Phil setting the pace, Sassy and Junior had led Sting and the scientists in the mad dash to safety, but Betty-Sue and Sealy could not bear to leave us behind, and were waiting anxiously at the top of the hill when we rode up through the inferno. Barely slowing, Corky grabbed Sealy's hand and pulled her onto the back of his steed, and I did the same to Betty-Sue.

"No time for smooches, baby!" Corky whooped, spurring Jimmy-Boy III into a flat-out gallop. "If we don't get through that bog before the fire hits it, we're toast, too."

"*What?*" Sealy squawked.

"Science, Sealy," I called out from the rear of the column. "Swamp gases trapped under the pond scum and muskeg accumulate over time, and the whole thing becomes an organic powder-keg ... and the whole town's been dumping used motor oil in there for the past thirty-two years."

Everyone else was on the far side of the bog by the time our horses splashed into it. Junior was busy locking the fully-subdued scientists in the horse trailer, but Sting and Sassy were still on the shore and cheering us onward as we charged straight through the toxic bog, our horses' hooves throwing up bucket-loads of mud with each stride.

We made it to the other side with less than a minute to spare, and we all stood on the shore, watching the marsh ignite like a sea of gasoline. In the distance, we could see the flames quickly engulfing the slopes of Banshee Screech

Peak, turning the mountain into a fiery beacon that could be seen sixty kilometres away.

"This whole situation just keeps getting weirder," I remarked, wiping mud and motor oil from my eyebrows.

"What did you expect?" Sassy said. "I have said it for years, Bucky. Cowboys and scientists and movie stars and living dinosaurs are a bad mix."

"Good point," I admitted. "Actually, this whole situation is not nearly as weird as the fact that you really have been saying that for years."

Sassy just shrugged. "I know how to roll with what the sooths are saying, Bucky."

Sealy looked a bit glum as she held onto Corky's hand, staring into the flames.

"Maybe somebody should say something," she suggested.

"Like what?" Mort asked, admiring the way the firelight reflected off his glistening torso.

"Good riddance, evil monkeys," I called out respectfully, tossing a salute to the raging wildfire. "We will drink banana smoothie to your memory."

"That's it?" Sealy said in disgust. "You can just turn your back on your own Chinese Zodiac animal, just like that?"

"*Bucky's a Monkey Year baby?*" Corky blurted, delighted by this accidental revelation. "Ha! You're a Monkey Year baby, Bucky! *Ha ha ha!* Bucky the monkey!"

"Thirty years," I sighed, rubbing my eyes. "I managed to keep that from him for nearly thirty years...."

"Monkey baby...." Corky giggled.

"If you listen hard enough, you can almost hear the dying howls of those poor creatures, trapped in ravenous flame," Sealy continued morosely. "We never had a chance to study them, let alone understand them. For all we know, they were the last of their species, and now they're gone.

Maybe they weren't even that different from us.... Crap. I'm a doctor, for Pete's sake! What am I even supposed to say? You tell me, Bucky. What's a doctor supposed to say in a situation like this?"

The following mournful silence was eventually interrupted by Sassy, trying desperately to hold back a laugh as she stood beside us in her chocolate-coloured wedding dress.

"Just say it," I sighed.

"*Mama called the doctor, and the doctor said, 'NO MORE MONKEYS JUMPIN' ON THE BED!'*" Sassy roared out the classic children's song with relish. "*Bahaha!*"

Sealy was the first one to join in the subsequent gales of hysterical laughter. I knew right then that she was going to be just fine. Once our laughter died down, we all joined hands along the shore and sang Minnie Marshmallow's hit single, *You Melt Me, Bonfire Baby* together, swaying in time with the imaginary music. As we finished the final chorus, we were further inspired by the sight of a lone grey bunny rabbit charging through the flaming swamp to the safety on the far side.

"Whoa there, little Thumper!" Sassy announced, stooping to grab the furry creature by the nape of the neck as it tried to pass under her feet. "Humans only."

Before we could intervene, she had punted the little guy back into the flames. The shocked silence that followed probably didn't last longer than fifteen minutes.

"Okay, even for me, that was crossing a line," Corky finally stated.

"What is wrong with you?" I demanded of my sister.

"What?" Sassy said, unfazed. "Fifteen minutes ago, we were all laughing and singing and swaying at nature's misfortune."

"Jeepers, Sassy, nature is one thing," Betty-Sue snapped. "That was a bunny!"

We stared into the flames for another long moment, and then Sassy asked, "Anybody hungry?"

"I'm still working off all the sap," Sting said, rubbing his stomach.

"I'm starving," Sealy admitted.

"Come on back to the ranch," Betty-Sue offered. "We've still got that leftover rabbit stew."

I Love Russian Ballet

◇◇

B ACK AT THE RANCH, we left the scientists in
the horse trailer, then let Gramps out of the empty
pickle barrel down in the cellar, and enjoyed a hearty
meal of rabbit stew ... on the front porch, of course, as all
of us were still covered with mud and sap. As we were
relaxing afterward with tall glasses of Old Bessie's milk, six
helicopters loaded with RCMP officers and ERT personnel
descended on the ranch to take custody of the Galapagos
Brethren. Betty-Sue and I walked down to the bale yard to
greet Sergeant Mudford as he led the warrant team in full
riot gear. He greeted us joyfully, thrilled that we were safe
and back together. Then he followed us back to the horse
trailer, where Sassy was in the midst of a deep theological
debate with Dr Gapps.

"So," she mused, "you're one of those heathen evolutionist
preachers who's going to burn in hell, right?"

"Um, I'm not a preacher," Gapps pointed out. "I'm a
scientist who prescribes to the theory of theistic evolution."

"Whatever you say, butane spark," Sassy snorted.

"Sassy, let's leave the prisoner's alone, okay honey?"
Junior advised gently, leading her away.

"I'm afraid my arrest warrants apply to *all* scientists
involved in these various incidents of kidnapping and

attempted murder," Mudford informed us, spotting Sealy standing next to Corky. "And that includes Dr Kent."

"You can't arrest my fianceé!" Corky protested. "Seriously, Sarge, I'm thirty-three years old, and I can't be alone anymore. I've started having dark thoughts at night."

"I'm sorry, my hands are tied," Mudford said reluctantly. "Please come with us, Doctor."

"I can handle this, Corky-poo," Sealy assured my brother, bravely stepping forward. "I can assure you, Sergeant, that I've changed my evil ways for good, and, furthermore..." She paused dramatically to rip off her lab coat and throw it to the wind. "...I'm not a scientist anymore! You're talking to the highly-educated new steel guitarist and backup vocalist for my fianceé's band, *Lost Cause Kin*!"

Mudford stared at her, and then turned to Corky.

"I'm not sure if she's joking or not," the sergeant confessed.

"No joke, Sarge," Corky assured him, putting an arm around Sealy. "Wedding's tomorrow afternoon."

"The wedding's what?" I said.

Sergeant Mudford had tears in his eyes as he gleefully stated, "I've wanted to do this for a lot of years, Ms Kent!" With a smile that echoed the joy of all of us, except perhaps myself, he proceeded to shred her arrest warrant into tiny pieces.

"Are you insane?" Argo was yelling as he was led away in handcuffs once again. "You're letting her go? She was the first one to open fire with an unregistered submachine gun back at the coven, she was going to brand Bucky, and the entire plot to kidnap Betty-Sue was her idea!"

"Silence, Doc," Mudford snapped. "It's out of our hands. True love is bigger than the law."

"It sure is!" Corky gloated, stealing a kiss from his blushing bride-to-be.

"No it's not," I had to point out.

"Silence, Bucky," Sealy muttered, glowering ominously at me.

"Yeah, silence, Bucky," Betty-Sue agreed cheerily. "How could you try to deny your own brother true love?"

"Sorry," I growled. "Shame on me."

"Exactly," Mudford exclaimed. "By the way, Bucky, about our ... arrangement?"

"Yeah, I'll get Corky's Polaroid camera," I said affably.

After every one of the officers had their picture taken with the baby Pogo, and received complimentary autographed copies of my autobiography, they gathered up their prisoners and Phil and flew away into the sunset. I decided right then and there that we really needed to get Coyote Yelp Pass onto some maps. I wondered how far the cops would get before realizing that they were supposed to be flying away from the sunset.

After saying farewell to everyone else, Mort and Sting walked down to the bale yard with me. I had never seen a Concorde jet before, and I must say that it is a credit to Sting's piloting skills that he was able to land it in such a confined space. Of course, his landing gear had ripped down the south fence-line, and about fifty cows had swarmed in and were now rubbing themselves contentedly against the tires, but it was still an impressive aeronautical feat.

The stairway into the plane had been left down, and Sting was already on the bottom step when he turned around and firmly shook my hand.

"You're an impressively resilient tragedy, Bucky Laroo," he said sincerely. "I could use a comedic sidekick like you in my next picture. You give me a call, and I'll make it happen."

"Thanks, Sting," I replied. "But every aspect of Hollywood currently makes me want to vomit and then shoot myself in the head with one of those cow-killer air guns like the guy in *No Country For Old Men* used."

"That was an awesome movie," Sting remarked.

"That really was an awesome movie, wasn't it?" I agreed. "You just can't go wrong with Tommy Lee Jones. Give me a call if you ever need a sidekick in a community stage production. I was Rothbart in *Swan Lake*."

"Really?" Sting said with abrupt giddiness. "I love Russian ballet! It just gets me, deep in my soul. Will do, cowboy. I'll see you on Broadway. Max-Ram, let's roll. We've got a buddy cop film to plan out."

Then he walked up the ramp and into the supersonic jet. Even while walking up a steep staircase, that man still looked insanely cool. Most people can only look cool walking down stairs.

"Hey, why does it smell like manure in here?" Sting's voice called out, sounding a bit nauseated.

"You're making a movie with him?" I asked Mort.

"Heck, no," Mort scoffed. "I just told him that because I needed a ride back to Hollywood. Trust me, I've got my own movies to make, the kind that'll have your heart racing and your toes tapping."

"Do you really think that's going to catch on?" I had to ask.

"I'm an action hunk, Bucky. I have to utilize the things that I know and the skills that I have, and that's a pretty short list. Honestly, I can't even tell white people apart. But what I do know is great action and tear-jerking musicals."

"You can't tell white people apart?"

"Nope. Seriously, we all look exactly the same. Ironically, I can readily differentiate North and South Koreans, and speak all of their regional dialects fluently."

I paused to stare at him, and then ventured, "You know, that actually sounds like a very useful skill-set."

"I know," Mort said with a touch of pride. "The UN's been trying to get me to have a sit-down with Kim Jong Il for years. Apparently, he's my biggest fan, and has publicly stated that he's willing to give up his dictatorship and North Korea's nuclear arms program if I just make an action-nostalgia pic about Korea's rich cultural heritage in the days before the division. But there's no way I'm going down there and getting munched on by some fire-breathing *Imoogi*. It's bad enough that I've got Canadian dragons to worry about now, let alone Korean ones. Wow, Bucky, there really is no limit to what you've screwed up by finding a living dinosaur, is there?"

"Actually," I said slowly, "I'd rethink that UN offer if I were you."

"Forget it, Bucky. I've got enough radical inroads to forge between Broadway and Hollywood in the coming months. I don't have time for personal favours to North Korea."

"Action musicals...." I mused, still wondering if I should encourage or discourage him from that notion. I chose to just shake his hand and say, "Good luck. God bless.... And at least give Kim Jong Il a call, okay?"

"I'll think about it," Mort said without enthusiasm. "Are you sure you're going to be alright?"

"I think so," I replied. "I'm just going to take the Pogo back to Okanagan. If someone as stupid as me can find it, I'm sure somebody smart and respected will find a way to find it again. Unless you want it."

"Really?" Mort said eagerly. "First The McTiernan Contract, and then my own living dinosaur...? I'll be a celebrity beyond compare. But I'd better not. Customs have been watching me pretty close ever since the whole elephant tusk thing. Not to mention the dimples."

"That's not a problem, Max-Ram," I assured him. "Finding the balance between being loved and being loved to hate is a line that every celebrity must walk. A bit of customs notoriety can only help that. You'll be fine."

Mort responded by hugging me for about forty-five seconds, and then turned to go up the stairs.

"Give my regards to Rumor," I called after him.

"Will do," Mort promptly replied, but then stammered, "No! I mean, uh, I would if I had any idea how to contact her, or who you're talking about. What's a rumour? Isn't that a dirty lie? You shouldn't tell dirty lies, Bucky."

"It's okay," I said. "Your secret's not going anywhere. Well, except to Betty-Sue, of course. And she's discreet. *Heh heh!*"

Mort tossed me a grateful salute, and turned to board the plane. The door was closed, and the jet engines fired up in preparation for takeoff.

I felt a warm hand slip into mine as I watched the jet blast out of the bale yard and into the sky, scaring the crap out of my cows.

"Hey, lover," Betty-Sue said softly, putting her head on my shoulder. "Are we okay?"

"We're always okay," I promised her. "There's a possibility that people may still be trying to kill us, but we're used to that. And we've got the biggest star in Hollywood watching our back now. Hopefully that counts for something."

"Hopefully," Betty-Sue said wistfully. "I want our boring back."

"Me too," I said with a nod. "Mort's secretly married to Bruce Willis's daughter, Rumor Willis. Bruce Willis doesn't know, and Ashton Kutcher is blackmailing Mort to keep it that way. I think."

"Omigosh, I've got to go tell everybody I know!" Betty-Sue gasped. "How did you find out?"

I shrugged, putting my arms around her.

"Rumor's, Betty-Sue. Nothing more."

The next morning, the story of my Ogopogo discovery was barely mentioned, mainly because the media had an even juicier bit of celebrity scandal to cover. Apparently, Sting Ripblood's Concorde had been forced to make an emergency landing in Affluenceville shortly after lifting off from Cattle Poke Ranch. Comeback king Max-Ram Target was being hailed as a hero for managing to land his fellow action hunk's plane without any form of flight training, but Sting was in the hospital with non-life-threatening injuries, and was also facing charges of attempting to smuggle Canadian livestock into the United States.

I may have figured out a thing or two about the way of the cow in my day, but the really technical science of the cow has never played much of a role in my life. However, one scientific fact that I do know is that the physics and anatomy of the cow allows them to walk up a set of stairs, such as those leading into the Concorde jet, but prevents them from coming back down. Unfortunately for Sting, a certain cantankerous old Hereford-Angus cross black-baldy cow named Evil Sue, who really did not like being cornered, had not figured out that last part, curious little rascal that she is. In any case, I still maintain that I am in no way responsible for Sting's multiple compound fractures, or the utter destruction of the new shirt I had just lent to Mort. People just need to learn about their personal safety zones. Being a cowboy can be hazardous to your health. But being an unprepared Hollywood action hunk in a cowboy setting is borderline suicide. Sting Ripblood may have been able to take on giant monkeys in hand-to-hand combat, but cows are a lot tougher and more ornery than monkeys. Trust me, if I thought that giant evil monkeys were scarier than Evil Sue, or even scarier than Sassy, I would have moved to Hollywood a long time ago.

Anyway, I just realized that I'm bored with trying to be a writer, so I'm just going to wrap this book up and be done with it. Let's skip ahead about a week to the day when we took the Pogo home.

July 20, 2010 will forever be remembered as the day that the Ogopogo gained its freedom just as Lindsay Lohan lost it. (Please don't sue me for that horrible joke, Lilo. I'm actually a big fan of yours. I'm a sucker for *The Parent Trap* and that one other good movie you did.) Leaving early in the morning once again, Betty-Sue and I made yet another drive down to Kelowna in Corky's Hummer, borrowed some horses from old Grits, and rode down the lakeshore with the Pogo in my saddlebag. It was a beautiful day for a ride. Betty-Sue claimed that it was the kind of day that signified new beginnings, and I allowed myself to agree with her. For the first time since the 2009 Harvest Potluck, I was able to truly relax and even believe that maybe my life would be better from then on. At the very least, I hoped that I would get my boring back. After all, I was pretty sure that I had just met Bruce Willis, and it was obvious that he had no intention of trying to kill me, which was a celebrity first in my life. On the other hand, the harsh realist in me refuses to let my guard down just yet. Pop superstar Minnie Marshmallow was madly in love with me for ten months before she gave up on the idea and tried to kill me. Just read the first book.

Sometimes change can be a really good thing, but other times we have to just live with the fact that life isn't always going to pan out the way we had hoped. Perhaps Sassy had said it best that morning, when she was finally forced to come to terms with the fact that she was not going to get to eat an Ogopogo after all.

"Everywhere I look, I see it, Bucky," she had glumly informed me as I was preparing to leave. "I see it, and it makes me sad. Every movie that features a child befriending a kindly monster eventually leads to a showdown with redneck hunters who want nothing more than to kill, stuff, and eat the monster, or capture it in an inhumane manner for profit. And, just for once, I wanted to see us win. Is it too much to ask for a redneck to win? I mean, seriously, we're talking about kind and vulnerable monsters. They're just begging for a bullet and a butcher block."

I had rolled my eyes, but put a consolatory hand on Sassy's shoulder as I reminded her, "It's okay, big sister. I killed one of them. And I did it for you."

"You did do that," Sassy acknowledged with grudging appreciation. "Maybe the world will see and learn. Well, anyway, Godspeed, baby brother. I'm not one for emotional farewells, so I'm just going to go into the woods and kill something."

"Happy hunting," I bid her. "Kill something for me, too."

When Betty-Sue and I finally located the lagoon-like inlet where I had first been abducted by the Ogopogo, we tied our horses to some nearby trees and then carried the Pogo hatchling down to the shore. After a week of swimming in bathtubs and toilets, it seemed delighted by the massive expanse of water, and was soon leaping, splashing, and diving in utter joy.

"Now what?" Betty-Sue asked. "I didn't bring any chum and pig's blood."

"Now I stand here and make a complete idiot out of myself," I said. Without another word of explanation, I opened my mouth and unleashed a series of high-pitched girlish shrieks for the next twenty seconds.

"Bee sting?" Betty-Sue asked empathetically when I was finished.

"Baby harp seal," I replied.

The ploy worked, as the most humiliating of ploys often do. Within a minute, ripple trails of all sizes began cutting through the water, circling the baby Pogo. A few moments later, Betty-Sue and I stared in awe as four adult Ogopogos and six other hatchlings crested the surface, raising their heads slightly above the water level in order to get a better look at the tiny newcomer. They all began letting out their familiar volleys of "*Meh, boof,*" vocalizations, almost as if they were talking to each other. Pogo swam up to one of the other hatchlings and the two tiny sea serpents began sniffing one another curiously.

"To think," Betty-Sue breathed, not wanting to disturb them as she frantically took pictures as fast as her digital camera would allow, "after all these years of searching for the Ogopogo, all we had to do was get someone with screams as shrill and girly as yours. It's amazing."

"It's a baby harp seal," I had to remind her.

Betty-Sue chuckled. "Even more brilliant, lover."

Two of the adult Ogopogos, possibly a male and female swam close to examine baby Pogo, and it swam up to them, curious and unafraid. I figured that would be a good moment to take Betty-Sue's hand and lead her back to the horses.

"What are you doing?" Betty-Sue protested, dragging her heels. "I want to see it get adopted. It was so beautiful!"

"Potential trauma inhibitor," I replied dryly. "For all we know, they were about to eat it. And that would be really anticlimactic for me."

"Crap," Betty-Sue muttered. "I hate open endings."

"Well, believe me, they're way better than

uncompromising *National Geographic* endings. Let's go home and get our boring back."

We began riding back to Grits' ranch, but we soon realized that we weren't the only ones there that day. We ran into a yuppie couple on the way back, neither of whom looked as if they had even seen a horse prior to mounting up.

"Hey, I know you!" the man said in delight. "You're that stupid cowboy who found a living dinosaur!"

"Nope," I assured him. "I didn't."

"Wow, this is so awesome!" the man exclaimed, not fooled by my technicality evasion. "Bucky Laroo! I can't believe this. My wife freakin' hates you, man. That's why she's only glaring daggers at you and not saying anything."

"We're used to it," Betty-Sue stated, taking my hand as we rode past them. "I don't care what any of them say, Bucky. You're going to be a legend. You could write a book."

"I can only imagine what the completed rendering of this fiasco would be like," I remarked. "Hey, how's this for a title: *Cowboy Conquistador: The Uncompromisingly Stalwart Legend of Bucky Laroo.*"

Betty-Sue just smiled kindly, and leaned across the saddle to kiss me on the cheek.

"Yeah, that's never going to happen," she assured me. "Bucky, I'm pregnant."

"Speaking of mistakes, did we bring any jumper cables?" I asked. "I think I left the headlights on in the Hummer."

Oddly, the fact that I turned out to be wrong about the headlights did not make Betty-Sue any less mad. That's the toughest part about marriage, I guess. You always have to know exactly the right thing to say in any situation, and I've never been very good at that.

EPILOGUE

◇◇◇◇◇◇◇◇◇◇◇◇◇

Three days after the birth of Rustina Faith Laroo, (6lbs, 6oz, 21") Sting Ripblood discovered and singlehandedly captured a magical, winged, fire-breathing dragon living in a snow cave on Mt Ararat in the Republic of Turkey. Its skeletal and genetic structure matched nothing previously known from nature or the fossil record.

National Geographic Magazine named Sting "The Man Who Saved the Millennium" less than thirty-six hours later.

Appendix:
Thank You For The Pain™

◇◇

From the screenplay *Powerhouse Grindhouse*,
by Max-Ram Target.
Music and Lyrics by Max-Ram Target.
©2011, *Bojangles Disco Pictures*.
All rights reserved. Reprinted with permission.
Featuring *Max-Ram Target's Nitro-Express Chorale*.
(Release delayed pending artist cooperation.)

Verse One

(piano intro.)

Max-Ram Target:
"Violence is never the answer.
It's a lie we live with every day.
But we open our hearts, and we open fire,
With our Uzis and AKs!"

Bruce Willis:
"We're only doing what you want us to do.
The ratings tell us what to be.
So Shakespeare is stuck in the garden,
But Die Hard's on DVD!"

BRIDGE

Max-Ram Target and Bruce Willis:
"And we smear on our camo,
And we load up with ammo,
And we make the bad guys pay!"

Mel Gibson and Danny Glover:
"And the ladies will kiss us,
And the bullets will miss us,
And we'll always save the day!"

CHORUS

All:
"There's a wolf at the door!"

Max-Ram Target:
"But you're not alone."

All:
"There's a wolf at the door!"

Dolph Lundgren:
"But you know who to phone."

Mark Wahlberg:
"When the tensions get higher,
We'll just cut the red wire."

Mr T:
"We'll never leave you on your own!"

All:
"There's a wolf at the door!"

Steven Seagal:
"But don't be afraid."

All:
"When he lets out a roar,"

Chuck Norris:
"Heroes won't be dismayed."

Sting Ripblood:
"There's no problem so grave,
That the day can't be saved,"

All:
"With just a well-placed hand grenade!"

Max-Ram Target:
"Thank you all for the pain!"

(Bruce Willis' harmonica solo.)

Verse Two

Sylvester Stallone:
*"The golden days of the 80s
Will live forever within our hearts."*

Jean-Claude Van Damme:
*"Though the Oscars ignore us, and the critics abhor us,
Our ticket sales are off the charts!"*

Arnold Schwarzenegger:
*"We survived the curse of the 90s,
When the heartthrob invasion began."*

Carl Weathers:
*"Skinny boys with big eyes, making all the girls sigh,
Made me ashamed to be a man."*

(Song is interrupted by C4 explosion, blowing auditorium doors open and sending heroes flying. Max-Ram Target's shirt is reduced to shreds. He reaches into grand piano, pulls out twin Tommy guns as ninjas swarm into auditorium for first action sequence. Key temp action score, which will likely become final score, as no one will be able to hear it over the gunfire anyway.)

Max-Ram Target: (Chewing Matchstick.) "Okay, Bulgarian ninjas.... Come get some candy!"

About the Author
◇◇◇◇◇◇◇◇◇◇◇◇◇◇◇◇◇◇◇◇◇◇◇◇◇◇◇◇◇◇◇◇◇◇◇◇

L ANE BRISTOW LIVES IN Chetwynd, British Columbia, Canada, where he works as a paramedic for the BC Ambulance Service. He would like to encourage all of you to reduce your household waste by recycling everything, even this book. The Scientific Establishment strongly agrees with him on this matter.

Well, that's a start....